WOMEN AND SOCIETY--
CITATIONS 3601 TO 6000

WOMEN AND SOCIETY-- CITATIONS 3601 TO 6000:

An Annotated Bibliography

Compiled and Edited by

JoANN DELORES EEN
MARIE B. ROSENBERG–DISHMAN

SAGE PUBLICATIONS / Beverly Hills / London

For information address:

SAGE PUBLICATIONS, INC.
275 South Beverly Drive
Beverly Hills, California 90212

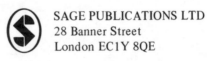

SAGE PUBLICATIONS LTD
28 Banner Street
London EC1Y 8QE

Printed in the United States of America

Library of Congress Cataloging in Publication Data

Een, JoAnn Delores.
    Women and society, citations 3601 to 6000.

    Intended as v. 2. of Women and society, a critical
review of the literature, compiled and edited by
M. B. Rosenberg and L. V. Bergstrom.
    Includes index.
    1. Women—Bibliography.   I.   Rosenberg-Dishman,
Marie Barovic, joint author.   II.   Title.
Z7961.E4   [HQ1399]   016.30141'2   77-18985
ISBN 0-8039-0856-3

CONTENTS

DEDICATION

The first volume of *Women and Society* had its early beginnings in research for a Master's Essay on Pearl Anderson Wanamaker, long an important figure in the elective politics of the State of Washington. That endeavor resulted in a modest bibliography on women in Politics. It resulted as well in a quickening sensitivity to the frequency with which fellow graduate students, professors, and teaching colleagues generally overlooked women as significant members of society.

The first volume was my response to all those educators, predominantly male, who claimed that there was "nothing available [and, therefore, presumably nothing important] to teach about women." The second volume is a continuation of my own resolve to dispel that self-serving delusion.

Marie Barovic Rosenberg-Dishman

This volume is dedicated to my parents, who gave me their unfaltering support; to Marie, who gave me this opportunity to use my abilities; and to all those people who judged me by standards and values for which I refused to settle.

JoAnn Delores Een

PREFACE

WOMEN AND SOCIETY—Citations 3601 to 6000: An Annotated Bibliography was compiled with several objectives in mind, most of which are discussed in the Introduction. However, it is appropriate to elaborate on several aspects of the work here, including the need for continuing effort to provide guidance to the literature available on women.

During the two years since the first volume of WOMEN AND SOCIETY was published, the mass of material available on women has increased at a rate of geometric progression. Much of this is new material, of course, since the "nature of women" has once again come to the foreground as a topic of academic as well as popular interest. Many long out-of-print and obscure materials are being reprinted not only for their historical value, but also to provide yet another perspective on the often overlooked contributions of women—and the interpretations of those contributions—to the foundations of our present society.

The two volumes of WOMEN AND SOCIETY are by no means an exhaustive compilation of all published materials. Due to the very nature of the publishing industry, as well as the authors' limited financial resources, that would have been a monumental task. Furthermore, we were limited in the total number of manuscript pages by the publisher. Therefore, we again have chosen to make this a "selected" bibliography in the pattern of categories developed in the first volume. It is selected in the sense that we have included citations to representative publications from the many materials available to the researcher, and provided "clues" for more intensive bibliographic search. These clues are to be found in the topical organization of the citations within the main body of the manuscript, the four indexes (Author-Organization Index, Index of Journal Issues/Sections Devoted to Women, Index of Persons not Cited as Authors, and Index of Subjects, Topics, and Places), and the variety of forms of publications we have cited. By thorough examination of these, the researcher and student should be able to identify the available resources, and also to become familiar with the sources of materials, i.e., who is doing what on women, what journals, periodicals, and publishers are producing works on women, and what types of studies are being undertaken.

The effort for this second volume of citations literally came out of our hides. We received no "released time," no secretarial assistance. A modest stipend from Sage Publications made it possible to Een to fly to New Hampshire to work directly with Rosenberg-Dishman for the final nine weeks of manuscript preparation. Finally, much of the xeroxing of the final manuscript was provided by

New England College. Because of the character of the work, all but the final typing of the manuscript had to be done by us in our respective homes. The nature of bibliographic work meant that the work-in-progress crept out of the confines of home offices to dining room tables and from there oozed to cabinet tops and chairs. Even floors disappeared beneath the avalanches of paper.

A number of persons have contributed to the preparation of this book. We wish to acknowledge Dr. Len Bergstrom who has left the academic world, but who has cheered us on. Our new colleagues at New England College opened their personal libraries to us and reviewed the manuscript sections concerning their particular disciplines. Our thanks go to Thea Braiterman, Linda Morley, Elizabeth Alexander, Vickie Rachlin, and Peter Sylvester. We wish also to thank Dianne Tibbitts, librarian at the University of New Hampshire, and Joseph Considine, reference librarian at New England College for their indefatigable patience and interest. Dr. Robert B. Dishman deserves special mention. True to the spirit of this endeavor he has demonstrated his flexibility toward role reversal by providing hot meals, moral support, and a fine but critical eye for sustaining quality of product under extraordinary work pressures.

A number of libraries made their facilities and services available to us including New England College Danforth Library, Henniker, New Hampshire; University of New Hampshire Library, Durham, New Hampshire; Lake Forrest College Library, Illinois; University of Wisconsin Library, Eau Claire; University of Wisconsin Library System, Madison; University of Oregon Library, Eugene, Oregon; Eugene Public Library; Stanford University Library, Stanford, California; The University of Copenhagen Library, Denmark; The National Library of Belize, Belize; and the National Library of Mexico.

Finally, the authors wish to acknowledge each other's contributions to the production of this book. Our personal commitments to the project, deep interest in the subject matter, mutual respect and affection enabled us to collaborate successfully in this venture while managing our friendship and senses of humor throughout.

We hope that this new volume will provide additional assistance to those persons seeking to increase their own understanding of women, and of what the women's movement is all about. We hope too, that it will stimulate some to identify and then to embark upon research projects that will help to fill the evident gaps in the resources for the study of women. We welcome the suggestions and criticisms. We wish to state that judgments in selection of citations, classification, and placement within the volume as well as the annotations are solely our responsibility.

J.D.E.
M.B.R.-D.

INTRODUCTION

As every scholar knows, a bibliography can be the most systematic way to determine just what has been published on a given subject. It also can serve to alert the researcher as to what has not yet been done. Both volumes of WOMEN AND SOCIETY are an effort to bring some order to the burgeoning and sometimes confusing volume of materials that have been printed on women and to illustrate the variety of published materials. Most of the works which we cite are still available *somewhere*. We have also included citations to materials that are out of print and/or may be available only through access to special collections.

ORGANIZATION OF THE SECOND VOLUME

We have sought to avoid duplication by including each citation only once even though many works are equally appropriate to more than one category. We recognize the limitations imposed by *any* categorization schemata both in the process of constructing a table of contents and in subsequently trying to fit items into that structure. However, in order to maintain continuity with the first volume and to avoid, as far as possible, its shortcomings, we have retained the categories of the Table of Contents with the following exceptions:

1. We have added a new section (II-H) on "The Political Status of Women." In collecting materials to be considered for inclusion in the second volume, we found a number of citations that did not seem to fit in any of the categories we had previously established, so we felt it necessary to add the additional sub-section.
2. We have added section (XI-F) "Women's Handbooks and Almanacs," again, to accommodate a growing class of publications.
3. We have omitted two sections that were included in the first volume: (XI-D) "Women's Collections and Libraries," and (XI-E) "Women's Periodicals and Newspapers." Although we were concerned with

maximizing use of limited space, more important, we did so because many of these collections can be located in libraries through computerized listings. The outpouring of new periodicals and ephemera has grown to proportions requiring a major bibliographic effort on them alone.

One of the inadequacies of the original section on Political Science was in classifying such related fields as Public Administration. In the second volume citations from that field will be found under (X-H) "Women in the Semiprofessions."

Increasing professionalization in many fields, and the shifting status of many occupations has made it difficult to classify works about them. The traditional standards for distinguishing between a profession and a semiprofession seem to be inadequate in today's changing employment climate for women. Since we do not claim to be experts on that subject, we have relied heavily on THE SEMI-PROFESSIONS AND THEIR ORGANIZATION, edited by Amitai Etzioni (New York: The Free Press, 1969. 328 pp.). We have, however, retained the compiler's privilege of departing from Etzioni's classifications where logic (the level of educational preparation required) seemed to us to demand it.

We have made every effort to provide complete publication data for every citation: the full name of every author, editor, and/or translator; the full title of the work, and its subtitles, if any; the place of publication; the name of the publisher; the date of publication; and the number of pages. Ascertaining the number of pages and verifying them proved to be the most consistently difficult and sometimes impossible task. Publishers are notoriously poor about providing that information either through BOOKS IN PRINT, or through their own catalogs and other advertisements. Though the number of pages provides no guarantee of quality, it does provide perhaps a rough indication of the author's effort.

As compilers, we exercised another privilege. We set an arbitrary page limit on what constitutes a "book" as distinguished from a pamphlet." The kind of cover, and indeed, method of printing we found to be no less arbitrary as distinctions. Thus any publication under one hundred pages we cited in quotation marks; anything over that figure we cited in the traditional all caps. Our purpose was to achieve consistency and a sight clue as to the length of the work. It was not intended to provide any indication of quality.

Wherever possible, we tried to cite to the earliest edition available, particularly when editions were brought out in more than one country. We reasoned that it was preferable to put the reader on notice of the date the work was created and to leave the search for a more recent printing to the reader. Revisions were, of course, the exception to this.

Finally, for purposes of reducing confusion in utilizing the indexes of both volumes, we numbered citations consecutively.

POLICY DECISIONS—MATERIALS EXCLUDED

One of the first editorial policy decisions made, on the basis of sheer volume of works to choose among, was to omit citations to the following types of materials:

1. Journals directed toward women, e.g. SIGNS, AMERICAN ASSOCIATION OF UNIVERSITY WOMEN JOURNAL, QUEST, etc. The growing number of these are generally accessible to the researcher, student, teacher, and interested reader through libraries and/or subscription.
2. Popular press periodicals directed to women, e.g. MS, WOMEN SPORTS, McCALL'S, REDBOOK, etc. These can be excellent resources and should not be overlooked.
3. Unpublished dissertations and theses. All dissertations produced in the United States between 1861 and 1975 are listed in the COMPREHENSIVE DISSERTATION INDEX, available on microfiche. Citations to and abstracts of these materials are indexed in DISSERTATION ABSTRACTS INTERNATIONAL and MASTERS ABSTRACTS. The works themselves are available in Xeroxed form and on microfilm from University Microfilms, Ann Arbor, Michigan. These are among the most current and comprehensive research works available. Our only reason for omitting them is that they are unpublished.
4. Professional papers. Again, these represent the most current on-going research, also unpublished. Collections are generally maintained by the professional associations, and in recent years the microfilm service at Ann Arbor, Michigan has begun collecting them to make them more readily accessible. We are aware of the former custom at, for instance, Columbia University, of considering all dissertations submitted there as publications. Nevertheless, we have opted to maintain consistency in the second volume. It should be noted that a number of publications including dissertations and theses also are available through ERIC Document Reproduction Service, Arlington, Virginia.
5. Newspapers and Newsmagazine articles. Each of us maintains our own clippings files on women, and can attest to the overwhelming volume of

paper involved. We have, with few major exceptions, not cited these, though they could provide a rich source of data for evaluation, analysis, and synthesis.

6. Children's books. They are directed to and written for young people. Although we saw no reason to include them in this bibliography, it should be noted that the volume of production is such that they, too, are deserving of a specialized bibliographic effort.

7. Reprints of materials cited in the first volume either under the original publication date or a subsequent republication date. Our objective was to provide as many additional citations, including new works, as possible, and to avoid duplication wherever possible. Many publishers now specialize in reprints, e.g. Arno Press, AMS Press, Kraus Reprints, Kennikat Press, to name just a few. Some publishers have begun to reprint works in series devoted to particular subject areas on women.

8. Committees on the Status of Women Reports. Section II-D2 in the first volume was devoted to reports by various professional associations and governmental agency status of women committees and commissions. These committees and their reports have developed to such an extent, and in some cases have become so specialized that we could not adequately accommodate the sheer volume within the confines of the second volume. Until a specialized bibliography is compiled, readers may contact the professional associations and/or governmental agencies for their respective reports, generally issued annually.

9. Equal Employment Opportunity/Affirmative Action reports, guidelines, cases, and publications. We have selectively cited only those materials relating specifically to women, and have omitted those dealing generally with discrimination. It should be mentioned here that we are near completion on a substantial EEO/AFF.ACT. bibliography.

10. Films, Slides, Tapes. We have included only compendiums of multi-media resources. Our concern has been with the printed word.

Though many anthologies have been omitted on the ground that much of the material was repetitive and frequently available in other types of publications, we found significant exceptions to those premises. We have, therefore, included anthologies cited under the names of their respective editors. We have not, because of space limitations, acknowledged contributing authors. Because anthologies are not always organized around one theme, the reader is well advised to examine those cited under whichever section to determine the spectrum of topics covered.

OTHER POLICY DECISIONS

As in the first volume, we have included an index of special sections or entire journal issues devoted to topics on women. Within the body of the bibliography these issues are cited in what appeared to be the appropriate topical location. The citations are listed alphabetically under the editor's name if known, and if not, under the title of the journal. We did not list each article from the particular journal separately, but we did acknowledge the contributing authors. It should be noted that the individual articles in special journal issues very often deal with dissimilar major subjects or themes. We have chosen to cite the entire section or issue under the subject which was either most emphasized in the collection, or which seemed to us to be the primary focus. We suggest that these special issues be checked thoroughly as many of the articles fall into several categories, which may not be obvious from the section in which they have been cited.

We omitted annotations entirely where the title and/or subtitles were largely self-explanatory and limited them to a single sentence wherever possible. In this way we were able to include many more titles than would otherwise have been possible.

METHODOLOGY

Though there are no short cuts in an undertaking of this kind, we did have the advantage of previous experience gained in the compilation and publication of the first volume. Because the system developed by Rosenberg and Bergstrom worked well, we followed the same procedural steps for the second volume. Basically the sequence of work consisted of the following steps: collection; classification/categorization; alphabetization; verification; selection/elimination; check against the first volume; elimination of duplicates; selection of substitutions; review by colleagues of sections within their fields of competence; and selection of section introductory quotations. The entire manuscript was typed three times as it was being developed, and each time required proofreading.

Needless to say, none of the above steps developed in totally tidy sequence. Though theoretically we had a cut-off date of December 31, 1976, in fact we continued to add new works right up until the typing of the final copy of the manuscript.

It should be noted, of course, that we did *not* read or even get our hands on all 2,400 articles, pamphlets, and books cited in the second volume anymore than the 3,600 cited in the first volume. Where it was possible we did try to examine the material directly. In the Preface we have acknowledged the librarians who were of great help to us in our searching, and have listed the libraries where we did most of our work collecting and of verifying citations. But, in many cases we had to rely on book reviews (e.g., CHOICE, LIBRARY JOURNAL, PUBLISHER'S WEEKLY, etc.), publishers' catalogs, newspaper reports, communications from authors, and other sources.

In organizing citations we have tried to categorize in order to give a general idea of the subject matter. The annotations are not abstracts, nor an editorial judgment as to quality, but simply a very brief statement on the content.

One of our objectives in compiling the first volume was to illustrate the number and variety of sources and of forms of published materials available to scholars and researchers, whether books, government documents, pamphlets, learned journals, etc. In attempting to be consistent in citing the various types of publications, we found no comprehensive "ready made" style guide. Therefore, in addition to utilizing models from several standard style guides we have developed our own format, adapting to encompass the great variety of published works. Our primary goals were to be as internally consistent as possible, as accurate and complete as possible, and to organize the materials in a logical manner to provide maximum ease of access to the reader.

U.S. Government documents presented major difficulties inasmuch as there is no stable pattern or consistency over time exercised by either the issuing agencies or the Government Printing Office. It seemed to us to make most sense to credit publications to the major department or agency issuing the publication. If one or more authors are acknowledged by the issuing agency, the individuals who actually produced the work are noted in the citation itself, and her/his name(s) appear as such in the Author-Organization Index. This style was devised both to standardize the citation of the U.S. Government publications and to serve the convenience of the reader. An added advantage is that most government publications appear grouped together within each section. This practice does represent an inconsistency with that of the first volume, but in our judgment it is an improvement.

Another problem has been that government agencies tend to change their names from time to time. For example, the former Manpower Administration in the Department of Labor is now known as the Employment and Training Administration. In this case we have retained the agency's original name in the citation, but both the old and the new names are used in the indexes. It was beyond our capacity to check foreign governments' bureaucratic organizations for similar changes.

Biographies provided a special challenge. Where we were familiar with the work or special interests of the subject, we normally placed the biography or autobiography in the appropriate subject matter area. We eliminated many published diaries, memoirs, etc. that seemed to represent what is known as the vanity press. In doing so, we may well have misjudged some of those scanned and eliminated, or, conversely, included. We did include works on or by notable women, but also, at our discretion, included some works that were sensitively written about a particular life style. In short, biographies have been placed throughout the book as well as in the Biography and Autobiography section.

While the primary thrust of the second volume was to include the recent flood of literature since our first volume cut off date of February 1974, a second objective was to reevaluate the 2,600 citations gathered for but excluded from the first volume because of space limitations, and to utilize those which appeared to have merit. With the same 400 page manuscript limiation on the second volume (this time inclusive of indexes, table of contents, etc.) as we had on the first volume, we once again faced the difficult task of making choices. Our selection process was guided by a number of decisions described earlier in this Introduction. We did, however, consciously try to illustrate the "gaps" in the existing literature, for example, in section (II-E) "Women as Voters." Throughout the literature we found relatively little on Black women, Chicanas, American Indian women, Asian American women, and other minority women in the U.S. By looking for such lacunae in the literature researchers can readily identify topic areas in which the printed research is sparse, and in some cases, virtually nonexistent. Such a bibliographic compilation can also assist the researcher in locating other researchers with similar interests, and perhaps even more important, to assist in eliminating or at least reducing duplication of effort.

An interesting sideline "gap"—many of the quotations we have used to introduce each section were taken from THE INTERNATIONAL DICTIONARY OF THOUGHTS: AN ENCYCLOPEDIA OF QUOTATIONS FROM EVERY AGE FOR EVERY OCCASION, compiled by John P. Bradley, Leo F. Daniels, and Thomas C. Jones (Chicago, Il: Ferguson Publishing, 1975 printing. 1,146 pp.). They have included very few quotations by women. This could be viewed as simply an interesting omission in light of the reputed talkativeness of women. However, we believe that while the omissions may not be deliberate, they are but another all too common instance of neglect of the vast body of literature produced *by* women cataloged within both volumes of WOMEN AND SOCIETY. And they do plant the thought that what is needed is an international dictionary of women's thoughts!

SOURCES OF CITATIONS

The citations in both volumes were compiled using the "Rosenberg vacuum cleaner approach," e.g. collecting newspaper clippings noting recently published works, rummaging in book stores and libraries on many campuses and in many cities throughout the United States as well as during travels to Denmark, Sweden, Lithuania, the USSR, Surinam, Belize, and in Mexico (while there as an American Political Science Association delegate to the International Women's Year Tribune). In addition, we systematically utilized the standard reference sources: NEW YORK REVIEW OF BOOKS; NEW YORK TIMES BOOK REVIEW; publishers' catalogs; booksellers' catalogs; BOOKS IN PRINT and FORTHCOMING BOOKS IN PRINT; WOMEN'S STUDIES ABSTRACTS; INDEX TO U.S. GOVERNMENT PUBLICATIONS; publication catalogs of individual governmental agencies; CUMULATIVE BOOK INDEX; Journal indexes such as Public Affairs Information Service Bulletin, Social Sciences Index, Humanities Index (formerly Social Sciences and Humanities Index), Index of Legal Periodicals; industry, volunteer organization, and professional organization publications listings, United Nations publications catalogs; etc.

We have been assisted by friends and colleagues. Some have sent us citations to their own publications as well as specialized or limited unpublished bibliographic lists of their own. Professor Josephine Milburn of the University of Rhode Island, for example, sent us citations collected while she was in New Zealand doing her own research on the status of women. A few have passed along, with due acknowledgement and permission, bibliographic efforts of their students. For the most part, however, we have done the digging ourselves.

We believe, perhaps immodestly, that the 6,000 citations in the combined volumes make available to the most remotely located researcher, student, teacher, and general reader a compact compendium of the vast literature on women throughout the world and across many cultures. We have, however, left much for the serious user to do. As noted previously, many books and articles were equally suited to more than one section/subsection. In seeking to avoid duplication, we have left to the diligent user the tasks of referring to all four indexes as well as the Table of Contents in searching out subject matter of interest. The user will also find a particularly rich resource in the many specialized bibliographies included.

Elsewhere we have indicated our respective professional competencies and our limitations. The specialist in fields other than the compilers' may well recognize works whose contents should have been further cross-indexed.

As we bring this second volume to completion, in the wisdom of hindsight we can already see room for further refinement and improvement. However, weary at present of the task, self-imposed as a contribution to the women's movement, Rosenberg-Dishman after six and a half years, and Een after two and a half years are ready for a respite. We, our colleagues, and, we are certain many others as well, want to commend Sage Publications for its willingness to publish our work.

MBR—D
JDE

I. WOMEN IN SOCIOLOGY

A. Sex Roles, Characteristics and Differences

"We can easily represent things as we wish them to be."
—AESOP'S FABLES

3601. Arthur, Chester Alan, ed. THE CIRCLE OF SEX. New Hyde Park, NY: Univ. Books, 1966. 151 pp. Disputes the classical distinction between the sexes.
3602. Cernea, Mihail. "Makrosocijalne Promjene i Trostruka Uloga Žene u Seljačkoj Porodici [The Macrosocial Changes and Threefold Role of Women in the Peasant Family]," SOCIOLOGIJA SELA, vol. 2-4, no. 40-42 (April-Dec. 1973), pp. 221-228. Examines changes in Rumania's village life from three perspectives: economic position of women, their position as women, and their role as mothers.
3603. Cheris, Kramer. "Stereotypes of Women's Speech: The Word from Cartoons," JOURNAL OF POPULAR CULTURE, vol. 8, no. 3 (Winter 1974), pp. 624-630. Analysis of reader-response to styles of speech in cartoons.
3604. "Current Studies in Sex Stratification," SOCIAL SCIENCE QUARTERLY, vol. 56, no. 4 (March 1976), pp. 547-672. Special Issue. Contributors include Joan Huber, Claudia Koontz, David W. Brady, Kent L. Tedin, Susan B. Hansen, Linda M. Franz, Margaret Metemeyer-Mays, Lee Sigelman, Albert K. Karing, B. Oliver Walter, Shirley S. Angrist, Judith R. Lave, Richard Mickelsen, Judy Corder Tully, Cookie Stephan, Barbara J. Chance, George W. Noblit, Janie M. Burcart, Rita J. Simon, Robert N. Stern, Walter R. Gove, and Omer R. Galle.
3605. Damico, Sandra and Dorothy Nevill. "The Highly Educated Woman: A Study in Role Conflict," COUNCIL ON ANTHROPOLOGY AND

EDUCATION QUARTERLY, vol. 6, no. 3 (Aug. 1975), pp. 16-19. Study of role conflict situations with which women are faced.

3606. Densmore, Dana. "Sex Roles and Female Oppression: A Collection of Articles." Boston, MA: New England Free Press, 1969. 29 pp.

3607. Douglas, Ann. THE FEMINIZATION OF AMERICAN CULTURE. New York: Alfred A. Knopf, 1977. 403 pp. Argues that the Victorian image of genteel womanhood was fostered by ministers and women writers extolling the virtues of motherhood and feminine morality; and further, that these virtues have been carried forward into present-day cultural stereotypes.

3608. Edwards, Carolyn P. and Beatrice B. Whiting. "Women and Dependency," POLITICS AND SOCIETY, vol. 4, no. 3 (1974), pp. 343-355. Suggests that sensitivity has been falsely equated with dependency, a term with negative connotations.

3609. Farrell, Warren. THE LIBERATED MAN, BEYOND MASCULINITY: FREEING MEN AND THEIR RELATIONSHIPS WITH WOMEN. New York: Random House, 1974. 380 pp.

3610. Filene, Peter Gabriel. HIM/HER/SELF: SEX ROLES IN MODERN AMERICA. New York: Harcourt Brace Jovanovich, 1975. 351 pp.

3611. Garskof, Michele Hoffnung, comp. ROLES WOMEN PLAY: READINGS TOWARD WOMEN'S LIBERATION. Belmont, CA: Brooks/Cole, 1971. 210 pp. Anthology of essays and lectures on sex roles.

3612. Gianini Belotti, Elena. LITTLE GIRLS: SOCIAL CONDITIONING AND ITS EFFECTS ON THE STEREOTYPED ROLE OF WOMEN DURING INFANCY. London, England: Writers & Readers Publishing Cooperative, 1975. 158 pp.

3613. Green, Rayna. "The Pocahontas Perplex: The Image of Women in American Culture," MASSACHUSETTS REVIEW, vol. 16, no. 4 (Fall 1975), pp. 698-714. Two images of American Indian women prevail: princess and squaw.

3614. Harris, Linda Hall and Margaret Exner Lucas. "Sex-Role Stereotyping," SOCIAL WORK, vol. 21, no. 5 (Sept. 1976), pp. 390-395. Focuses on the perpetuation of traditional stereotypes as the "norm" by mental health professionals.

3615. Harrison, Lieta. LA DONNA SPOSATA. Milan, Italy: Feltrinelli, 1972. 256 pp. 1,056 interviews with married women in Milan, Rome, and Palermo indicated that the married daughters tended to reject traditional societal roles, especially in attitudes toward sexuality, marital relationships and maternity.

3616. Haskell, Molly. FROM REVERENCE TO RAPE: THE TREATMENT OF WOMEN IN THE MOVIES. New York: Holt, Rinehart & Winston, 1974. 388 pp.

3617. Hollingsworth, L. S. "Social Devices for Compelling Women to Bear Children," AMERICAN JOURNAL OF SOCIOLOGY (July 1916), pp. 19-29.

3618. Holter, Harriet. KÖNSROLLER OCH SAMHÄLLSSTRUKTUR [SEX ROLES AND SOCIAL STRUCTURE]. Stockholm, Sweden: Prisma, 1973. 331 pp.

3619. Iglitzin, Lynne B. "A Case Study in Patriarchal Politics: Women on Welfare," AMERICAN BEHAVIORAL SCIENTIST, vol. 17, no. 4 (March/April 1975), pp. 487-506. Focuses on the ways in which the institution of public welfare reinforces the sex-role stereotype of the dependent, passive woman.

3620. Klein, Viola. THE FEMININE CHARACTER: HISTORY OF AN IDEOLOGY. Urbana, IL: Univ. of Illinois Press, 1971. 202 pp.

3621. Lacy, Dan. "Men's Words: Women's Roles," SATURDAY REVIEW, vol. 2, no. 19 (June 14, 1975), pp. 25-57. The development of women's roles in American society.

3622. Larrick, Nancy and Eve Mirriam, comps. MALE AND FEMALE UNDER 18: FRANK COMMENTS FROM YOUNG PEOPLE ABOUT THEIR SEX ROLES TODAY. New York: Avon Books, 1974. 218 pp. Young people from all over America discuss themselves, each other, their parents, sex, and the changing male/female roles.

3623. Le Masters, Ersel E. "The Battle Between the Sexes," THE WISCONSIN SOCIOLOGIST, vol. 10, nos. 2 & 3 (Spring/Summer 1973), pp. 43-55. Originally a chapter from BLUE COLLAR ARISTOCRATS: LIFE.

3624. Lord, Sharon B. "Sex Roles Today: What's Happened to Women's Role?" JOURNAL OF THE ASSOCIATION FOR THE STUDY OF PERCEPTION, vol. 10, no. 2 (Feb. 1975), pp. 10-14. The history and development of sex roles, and why they are being challenged.

3625. McArthur, Leslie Zebrowitz and Beth Gabrielle Resko. "Portrayal of Men and Women in American Television Commercials," JOURNAL OF SOCIAL PSYCHOLOGY, vol. 97 (Dec. 1975), pp. 209-220. Study finding that ads do not merely respond to existing sex-role attitudes, but can indeed influence them.

3626. Maccoby, Eleanor Emmons and Carol Nagy Jacklin. THE PSYCHOLOGY OF SEX DIFFERENCES. Stanford, CA: Stanford Univ. Press, 1974. 634 pp. Includes a 232-page bibliography summarizing more than 1,400 research studies on sex roles and sex differences.

3627. Mason, Karen Oppenheim, John L. Czajka, and Sara Arber. "Change in U.S. Women's Sex-Role Attitudes, 1964-1974," AMERICAN SOCIOLOGICAL REVIEW, vol. 41 (Aug. 1976), pp. 573-596.

3628. Mason, Karen Oppenheim and Larry L. Bumpass. "U.S. Women's Sex-Role Ideology, 1970," AMERICAN JOURNAL OF SOCIOLOGY, vol. 80, no. 5 (March 1975), pp. 1212-1219. Women's attitudes appear to center on two concerns: the basic division of labor between men and women, and women's labor-market rights.

3629. Mellen, Joan. WOMEN AND THEIR SEXUALITY IN THE NEW FILM. New York: Horizon Press, 1974. 255 pp.

3630. Merrick, Toni. "The American Woman: Her Image and Her Roles." Middleton, CT: Xerox Corp., 1972. 63 pp. Position of women in the 19th century, contemporary images of women, sex roles, and stereotypes.

3631. Navoc, Isabelle. "Como Chicana Mi Madre [How Chicana, My Mother]," ENCUENTRO FEMENIL, vol. 1, no. 2 (1974), pp. 8-12. Mexican American women's role in contemporary society.

3632. Nelson, Cynthia. "Changing Roles of Men and Women: Illustrations from Egypt," ANTHROPOLOGICAL QUARTERLY, vol. 41 (April 1968), pp. 67-76.

3633. Nunes, Maxine and Deanna White. THE LACE GHETTO. Toronto, Ontario: New Press, 1972. 152 pp. A collection (mostly quotations) on sexual stereotyping.

3634. O'Neill, Maureen S. "Women's Sex Role Conflict," COUNSELING AND VALUES, vol. 19, no. 3 (April 1975), pp. 155-161. Report on present findings regarding role conflict in women.

3635. Parelius, Ann P. "Emerging Sex-Role Attitudes, Expectations, and Strains Among College Women," JOURNAL OF MARRIAGE AND THE FAMILY, vol. 37, no. 1 (Feb. 1975), pp. 146-153.

3636. Pastner, Carroll McC. "Accommodations to Purdah: The Female Perspective," JOURNAL OF MARRIAGE AND THE FAMILY, vol. 36, no. 2 (May 1974), pp. 408-414. Female role functioning in purdah societies.

3637. Penn, J. Roger and Mary E. Gabriel. "Role Constraints Influencing the Lives of Women," SCHOOL COUNSELOR, vol. 23, no. 4 (March 1976), pp. 252-256. Interview data indicated that family is a major factor in determining sex roles.

3638. Rapoport, Rhona and Robert N. Rapoport. "Men, Women and Equity," FAMILY COORDINATOR, vol. 24, no. 4 (Oct. 1975), pp. 421-432. Fair allocation of opportunity and equivalent constraints rather than equality.

3639. Richardson, Herbert Warren. NUN, WITCH, PLAYMATE: THE AMERICANIZATION OF SEX. New York: Harper & Row, 1971. 147 pp. Virginity, sex without love, and romantic marriage.

3640. Riencourt, Amaury de. SEX AND POWER IN HISTORY: HOW THE DIFFERENCES BETWEEN THE SEXES HAS SHAPED OUR DESTINIES. New York: McKay, 1974. 469 pp. Puts forth the thesis that the survival of Western civilization depends on the recognition of and allowance for male and female differences.

3641. Rose, Clare. "Women's Sex Role Attitudes: A Historical Perspective," NEW DIRECTIONS FOR HIGHER EDUCATION, vol. 3, no. 3 (Feb. 1975), pp. 1-31.

3642. Rosen, Marjorie. POPCORN VENUS: WOMEN, MOVIES AND THE AMERICAN DREAM. New York: Coward, McCann & Geoghegan, 1974. 416 pp.

3643. Rosenblum, Karen E. "Female Deviance and the Female Sex Role: A Preliminary Investigation," BRITISH JOURNAL OF SOCIOLOGY, vol. 26, no. 2 (June 1975), pp. 169-185. Study of the influence of sex-role characteristics on female prostitutes.

3644. Ruble, Diane N., Irene Hanson Frieze, and Jacquelynne E. Parsons, eds. "Sex Roles: Persistence and Change," THE JOURNAL OF SOCIAL ISSUES, vol. 32, no. 3 (Summer 1976), pp. 1-223. Special Issue. Contributors include Jean E. Hunter, Ruth B. Dixon, Gail L. Zellman, Karen L. Hodges, Ava W. Small, John Condray, Sharon Dyer, Susan Darley, Paula Johnson, Marlaine E. Lockheed, Katherine Peterson Hall,

E. Tory Higgins, Sheila J. Ramsey, Nancy Felipe Russo, Joseph H. Pleck, T. Jeana Wirtenberg, Charles Y. Nakamura, Julia A. Sherman, Meda Rebecca, Robert Hoffner, Barbara Oleshansky, and Jesse Bernard.

3645. Russ, Joanna. "The Image of Women in Science Fiction," in RED CLAY READER 7 (serial), edited by Charleen Whisnant. Charlotte, NC: Southern Review, 1970. Pp. 34-47.

3646. Safilios-Rothschild, Constantina. "Sex Role Socialization Patterns in Selected Societies." Arlington, VA: ERIC Document Reproduction Service, 1975. 17 pp. Examines available research findings on sex role socialization patterns in the United States, Russia, Greece, India, and Eastern Europe.

3647. Shover, Michele J. "Roles and Images of Women in World War I Propaganda," POLITICS AND SOCIETY, vol. 5, no. 4 (1975), pp. 469-486. Survey of WWI poster images.

3648. Skoglund, Elizabeth. WOMAN BEYOND ROLEPLAY. Elgin, IL: David C. Cook, 1975. 112 pp.

3649. Stoll, Clarice Stasz, ed. SEXISM: SCIENTIFIC DEBATES. Reading, MA: Addison-Wesley, 1973. 137 pp. Essays on femininity and masculinity.

3650. Sweden. Advisory Council to the Prime Minister on Equality Between Men and Women. SEX ROLES IN TRANSITION: A REPORT ON A PILOT PROJECT IN SWEDEN: INTERNATIONAL WOMEN'S YEAR 1975. By Rita Liljestrom, Gunilla Furst Mellstrom, and Gillian Liljestrom Svensson. Stockholm, Sweden: The Swedish Institute, 1975. 104 pp.

3651. Tibbetts, Sylvia Lee. "Sex-Role Stereotyping: Why Women Discriminate Against Themselves," JOURNAL OF THE NATIONAL ASSOCIATION FOR WOMEN DEANS AND COUNSELORS, vol. 38, no. 4 (Summer 1975), pp. 177-182. How women prevent women from achieving equal status.

3652. Trebilcot, Joyce. "Sex Roles: The Argument from Nature," ETHICS, vol. 85, no. 3 (April 1975), pp. 249-255. Concludes that the existence of sex roles depends on what kind of society is morally justifiable.

3653. U.S. Dept. of Health, Education, and Welfare. Office of Education. A COMPARATIVE VIEW OF THE ROLES OF WOMEN. By Barbara Miller and Jacquelyn Johnson. Bethesda, MD: ERIC Document Reproduction Service, 1976. 110 pp. Explores the various roles and the effects of political, social, and economic occurrences on those roles.

3654. van der Geest, Sjaak. "Role Relationships Between Husband and Wife in Rural Ghana," JOURNAL OF MARRIAGE AND THE FAMILY, vol. 39, no. 3 (Aug. 1976), pp. 572-578. Interview data indicates that students are in favor of more jointness and companionship in marriage rather than the traditional separateness of marital partners.

3655. Van Dusen, Roxanne A. and Eleanor Bernert Sheldon. "The Changing Status of American Women: A Life Cycle Perspective," AMERICAN PSYCHOLOGIST, vol. 31, no. 2 (Feb. 1976), pp. 106-116. Documentation of the way women of different ages are affected by changes in social structure.

3656. Van Stolk, Mary. MAN AND WOMAN. Toronto, Ontario: McClelland &

Stewart, 1968. 170 pp. Canadian study examining the false premises on which man/woman relationships can be based.

3657. Ward, William. "Process of Sex Role Development," DEVELOPMENTAL PSYCHOLOGY, vol. 1, no. 2 (1969), pp. 163-168. Study of 32 kindergarten, first, and second grade girls and boys, finding that sex-role preferences were established for both sexes by age five.

3658. Whitten, Norman E., Jr. "Ritual Enactment of Sex Roles in the Pacific Lowlands of Ecuador-Colombia," ETHNOLOGY, vol. 13, no. 2 (April 1974), pp. 129-143. The range of sex-role differentiation in relation to community, home, and kinship interaction.

3659. Women on Words and Images. "Dick and Jane as Victims: Sex Stereotyping in Children's Readers: An Analysis." 2nd edition. Princeton, NJ: The Author, 1975. 80 pp. Includes a history of readers.

3660. "Women's Roles, Labels, and Stereotypes," JOURNAL OF THE NATIONAL ASSOCIATION FOR WOMEN DEANS AND COUNSELORS, vol. 34, no. 3 (Spring 1971), pp. 97-144.

3661. Yorburg, Betty. SEXUAL IDENTITY: SEX ROLES AND SOCIAL CHANGE. New York: John Wiley, 1974. 227 pp. Biological bases of sexual identity, variations in sexual identity in nonliterate, agricultural, and industrial societies, and contemporary and historical variation in sexual identity and role conceptions around the world.

B. Family

"The family is a society limited in numbers, but nevertheless a true society, anterior to every state or nation, with rights and duties of its own, wholly independent of the commonwealth."

—*Leo XIII (Gioacchino Vincenzo Pecci)*

3662. Adams, Mrs. Laura Merrihew. MOTHERS. Philadelphia, PA: Union Press, 1924. 113 pp. An inspirational book which glorifies motherhood and attempts to illustrate the joy of motherhood through the lives of some famous 'mothers' in history and in the Bible.

3663. Albrecht, Margaret. A COMPLETE GUIDE FOR THE WORKING MOTHER. Garden City, NY: Doubleday, 1967. 384 pp. Covers every phase of the working mother question including child care, household management, and possible effects on marriage and children.

3664. Alexandersson, Birgitta. "The 1973 Family Law Reform," CURRENT SWEDEN (The Swedish Institute), no. 8 (Sept. 1973), pp. 1-6. Discusses revision of the formalities connected with family law, and retention of practical guidelines to family life.

3665. American Mothers Committee. Bicentennial Project 1974-1976., comp. MOTHERS OF ACHIEVEMENT IN AMERICAN HISTORY: 1776-1976. Rutland, VT: Charles E. Tuttle, 1976. 636 pp.

3666. Ashdown-Sharp, Patricia. A GUIDE TO PREGNANCY AND PARENTHOOD FOR WOMEN ON THEIR OWN. New York: Random

House/Vintage, 1977. 384 pp. Survey of financial and counseling assistance available to unmarried, divorced, or widowed women—pregnant or raising children alone.

3667. Bane, Mary Jo. HERE TO STAY: AMERICAN FAMILIES IN THE TWENTIETH CENTURY. New York: Basic Books, 1976. Concludes that many assumptions made about the quality of family life in the nineteenth century have no basis in fact.

3668. Bassett, Marion P. A NEW SEX ETHICS AND FAMILY STRUCTURE, DISCUSSED BY ADAM AND EVE. New York: Philosophical Library, 1961. 332 pp.

3669. Bernard, Jesse. THE FUTURE OF MOTHERHOOD. New York: Dial Press, 1974. 426 pp. Dissects the many social trends affecting motherhood, noting the coercive social forces which have pressured women to become mothers.

3670. Blumenfeld, Samuel L. THE RETREAT FROM MOTHERHOOD. New Rochelle, NY: Arlington House, 1975. 222 pp. Decline in birth rate and rise in divorce rate have led to indiscriminate sex, crime, suicide, gonorrhea, and abortion.

3671. Brandwein, Ruth A., Carol A. Brown, and Elizabeth Maury Fox. "Women and Children Last: The Social Situation of Divorced Mothers and Their Families," JOURNAL OF MARRIAGE AND THE FAMILY, vol. 36, no. 3 (Aug. 1974), pp. 498-515. Societal supports are not provided for the single parent, because it is assumed that this is a temporary state.

3672. Canadian Council on Social Development. THE ONE-PARENT FAMILY, REPORT OF AN ENQUIRY. Ottowa, Ontario: C.C.S.D., 1971. 167 pp. Study of the widowed and divorced of the late 1960's in Canada.

3673. Cardozo, Arlene Rossen. WOMAN AT HOME. Garden City, NY: Doubleday, 1976. 156 pp. A sugar-coated view of women who have chosen to remain at home with their children. Essentially a sound message, but misleading.

3674. Cook, Gertrude M. Payne. RECOLLECTIONS OF A VICE PRESIDENT OF THE MOTHERS' UNION. Westminster, England: The Mothers' Union, 1958. 128 pp.

3675. Cottrell, Ann Baker. "Outsiders' Inside View: Western Wives' Experiences in Indian Joint Families," JOURNAL OF MARRIAGE AND THE FAMILY, vol. 37, no. 2 (May 1975), pp. 400-407. Illustrates the role restrictions on married women in traditional families in India.

3676. Cuba. Ministry of Justice. "Family Code." Law No. 1289, of Feb. 14, 1975; Official Gazette, Feb. 15, 1975. Havana, Cuba: Cuban Book Institute, ORBE EDITORIAL, 1975. 73 pp. Laws governing marriage, divorce, parent-child relations, and family obligations.

3677. ———. "Ley de la Maternidad de la Trabajadora." Ley No. 1263 de 14 de enero de 1974; Gaceta Oficial de 16 de enero de 1974. La Habana, Cuba: Publicacion Oficial del Ministerio de Justicia, 1975. 15 pp. Laws covering workers' maternity benefits.

3678. De Rham, Edith. THE LOVE FRAUD—WHY THE STRUCTURE OF THE AMERICAN FAMILY IS CHANGING AND WHAT WOMEN MUST DO TO MAKE IT WORK. New York: Clarkson N. Potter, 1965.

319 pp. The situation of the well-educated married woman who is forced by role expectations to stifle her creativity.

3679. Dinnerstein, Dorothy. THE MERMAID AND THE MINOTAUR: SEXUAL ARRANGEMENTS AND HUMAN MALAISE. New York: Harper & Row, 1976. 288 pp. Relationship of men and women to the child-rearing arrangement; men should take a more active role to equalize the power.

3680. Dratch, Howard. "The Politics of Child Care in the 1940's," SCIENCE AND SOCIETY, vol. 38, no. 2 (Summer 1974), pp. 167-204. Discusses the interrelationships of women workers, child welfare officials, industry, organized labor and the Federal government during WW II.

3681. Freedman, Maurice. CHINESE FAMILY AND MARRIAGE IN SINGAPORE. London, England: Her Majesty' Stationery Office, 1957. 249 pp.

3682. Gage, M. Geraldine. "Economic Roles of Wives and Family Economic Development," JOURNAL OF MARRIAGE AND THE FAMILY, vol. 37, no. 1 (Feb. 1975), pp. 121-128. Discusses both paid labor and unpaid housework.

3683. Garber-Talmon, Yonina. FAMILY AND COMMUNITY IN THE KIBBUTZ. Cambridge, MA: Harvard Univ. Press, 1972. 266 pp.

3684. Geiger, H. Kent, comp. COMPARATIVE PERSPECTIVES ON MARRIAGE AND THE FAMILY. Boston, MA: Little, Brown, 1968. 222 pp.

3685. Gough, Donald. "Understanding Unmarried Mothers; Observations by a Psychoanalyst." London, England: National Council for the Unmarried Mother and Her Child, 1966. 16 pp.

3686. Grambs, Jean Dresden. "Good-Bye to Mom," NATIONAL ELEMENTARY PRINCIPAL, vol. 55, no. 5 (May/June 1976), pp. 60-65. Changes in women's perspective on motherhood.

3687. Gutman, Herbert George. THE BLACK FAMILY IN SLAVERY AND FREEDOM, 1750-1925. Westminster, MD: Pantheon Books, 1976. 650 pp.

3688. Hammer, Signe. DAUGHTERS AND MOTHERS: MOTHERS AND DAUGHTERS. New York: Quadrangle, 1975. 175 pp. Interviews with women about their mother/daughter relationships.

3689. Holman, Robert. "Unsupported Mothers and the Care of Their Children." London, England: Mothers in Action, 1972. 60 pp.

3690. Hope, Karol and Nancy Young, eds. MOMMA: THE SOURCEBOOK FOR SINGLE MOTHERS. New York: New American Library, 1976. 416 pp. Collection of reprints from MOMMA, publication of the national organization for single mothers, offering psychological support for those raising children alone.

3691. Howe, Louise Kapp, ed. THE FUTURE OF THE FAMILY: MOTHERS, FATHERS, AND CHILDREN; SEX ROLES AND WORK; REDEFINING MARRIAGE AND PARENTHOOD. New York: Simon & Schuster, 1972. 378 pp. Anthology with emphasis on the impact of "Women's Lib" on the family life style.

3692. Jenkins, Shirley and Elaine Norman. BEYOND PLACEMENT: MOTHERS VIEW FOSTER CARE. New York: Columbia Univ. Press, 1976. 149 pp.

3693. Kobler, Franz, ed. HER CHILDREN CALL HER BLESSED: A PORTRAIT OF THE JEWISH MOTHER. New York: Stephen Daye Press, 1955. 392 pp.

3694. Kramer, Sydelle and Jenny Masur, eds. JEWISH GRANDMOTHERS. Boston, MA: Beacon Press, 1976. 174 pp. The position of the mother in the Jewish community.

3695. Kriesberg, Louis. MOTHERS IN POVERTY: A STUDY OF FATHERLESS FAMILIES. Chicago: Aldine Publishing, 1970. 356 pp. Study of unmarried mothers in Syracuse, New York.

3696. Lazare, Jane. THE MOTHER KNOT. New York: McGraw-Hill, 1976. 188 pp. The ambivalent feelings of mothers for whom children are a definite interruption in life.

3697. Levine, James A. WHO WILL RAISE THE CHILDREN: NEW OPTIONS FOR FATHERS (AND MOTHERS). Philadelphia, PA: J. B. Lippincott, 1976. 192 pp.

3698. McBride, Angela Barron. THE GROWTH AND DEVELOPMENT OF MOTHERS. New York: Harper & Row, 1973. 153 pp.

3699. Marden, Orison Swett. WOMAN AND HOME. New York: Thomas Y. Crowell, 1915. 350 pp.

3700. Margolies, Marjorie and Ruth Gruber. THEY CAME TO STAY. New York: Coward, McCann & Geoghegan, 1976. 352 pp. Unmarried mothers.

3701. Marsden, Dennis. MOTHERS ALONE: POVERTY AND THE FATHERLESS FAMILY. London, England: Allen Lane, 1969. 282 pp. The financial and social problems of unsupported mothers.

3702. Marris, Peter. WIDOWS AND THEIR FAMILIES. London, England: Routledge & Kegan Paul, 1958. 172 pp.

3703. Nimkoff, Meyer Francis, ed. COMPARATIVE FAMILY SYSTEMS. Boston, MA: Houghton Mifflin, 1965. 402 pp. An analysis of family systems in 12 different socio-economic cultures.

3704. Nogina, Olga Pavlovna. "Mother and Child Care in the U.S.S.R." 3rd edition. Moscow: Foreign Language Pub. House, 1952. 83 pp.

3705. Olsen, Nancy J. "The Role of Grandmothers in Taiwanese Family Socialization," JOURNAL OF MARRIAGE AND THE FAMILY, vol. 38, no. 2 (May 1976), pp. 363-372. Study of the familial roles of mothers and grandmothers in three-generation families.

3706. Parsons, Elsie Worthington Clews. THE FAMILY: AN ETHNOGRAPHICAL AND HISTORICAL OUTLINE WITH DESCRIPTIVE NOTES, PLANNED AS A TEXT-BOOK FOR THE USE OF COLLEGE LECTURES AND OF DIRECTORS OF HOME READING CLUBS. New York: G. P. Putnam, 1906. 289 pp. Focus on the woman in her capacity as a member of the family.

3707. Peck, Ellen. THE BABY TRAP. New York: Bernard Geis, 1971. 245 pp. A description of the pressures by the media, manufacturers, and relatives on women to have children.

3708. Phelps, Charlotte D. "Is the Household Obsolete?" AMERICAN
ECONOMIC REVIEW, vol. 62, no. 2 (May 1972), pp. 167-174.
Maintaining a balance of self-satisfaction for each member of the family
within the nuclear family unit.

3709. Pierce, Ruth. SINGLE AND PREGNANT. Boston, MA: Beacon Press,
1970. 222 pp. Advice on alternatives available to the single pregnant
girl and the places where she can seek counseling and medical, legal, and
financial aid.

3710. Pochin, Jean. WITHOUT A WEDDING RING: CASEWORK WITH
UNMARRIED PARENTS. London, England: Constable, 1969. 164 pp.

3711. Pozsony, Judith Baal. "A Longitudinal Study of Unmarried Mothers Who
Kept Their First-Born Children: How Mothers and Children Fare in the
Community." London, Ontario: Family and Children's Services of
London and Middlesex, 1973. 64 pp.

3712. Radl, Shirley L. MOTHER'S DAY IS OVER. New York: Charterhouse,
1973. 256 pp. A review of the myths of the "Mother" image;
examination of the difficulties of being a mother.

3713. Rainwater, Lee. FAMILY DESIGN: MARITAL SEXUALITY, FAMILY
SIZE, AND CONTRACEPTION. Chicago, IL: Aldine, 1965. 349 pp.
An analysis of data from interviews with 257 families concerning their
attitudes toward sex and societal roles, sexual relations, limitation of
family size, and use of contraceptives.

3714. Raphael, Dana. THE TENDER GIFT: BREASTFEEDING. Englewood
Cliffs, NJ: Prentice Hall, 1973. 200 pp. Comprehensive survey of many
cultures concluding that supportive attention to the mother is vital to
successful breastfeeding.

3715. Rich, Adrienne. OF WOMAN BORN: MOTHERHOOD AS
EXPERIENCE AND INSTITUTION. Scranton, PA: W. W. Norton,
1976. 318 pp. Contrasts the myths of motherhood with the actualities
of unwanted pregnancies.

3716. Richmond, Marie LaLiberte. "Beyond Resource Theory: Another Look
at Factors Enabling Women to Affect Family Interaction," JOURNAL
OF MARRIAGE AND THE FAMILY, vol. 38, no. 2 (May 1976), pp.
257-266. Division of labor in families of recent Cuban immigrants.

3717. Rimashevskaia, Natalia. "La Familia Sovietica." Moscú: Editorial de la
Agencia de Prensa Nóvosti, 1975. 17 pp.

3718. Ross, Heather L. and Isabel V. Sawhill. TIME OF TRANSITION: THE
GROWTH OF FAMILIES HEADED BY WOMEN. Washington, D.C.:
The Urban Institute, 1975. 223 pp. Study of divorce rates, remarriage
rates, illegitimacy rates, marital stability, and economic status of
female-headed families.

3719. Ruderman, Florence A. CHILD CARE AND WORKING MOTHERS: A
STUDY OF ARRANGEMENTS MADE FOR DAYTIME CARE OF
CHILDREN. New York: Child Welfare League of America, 1968.
378 pp.

3720. Sebald, Hans. THE SILENT DISEASE OF AMERICA. Chicago, IL:
Nelson-Hall, 1976. 318 pp. Study of insecure mothers who use their

children to project meaning into their lives; advocates mother
employment, child-care centers, and prevention of unwanted
pregnancy.

3721. Sellerberg, Ann-Mari. "The Life of Young Working-Class Mothers in
Sweden," JOURNAL OF MARRIAGE AND THE FAMILY, vol. 37,
no. 2 (May 1975), pp. 416-421. Discusses the mothers' problem of
maintaining personal identity within the family situation.

3722. Spencer, Mrs. Anna Garlin. THE FAMILY AND ITS MEMBERS.
Westport, CT: Hyperion Press, 1976. 322 pp. Reprint of 1923 edition.
Study of the changes in family structure resulting from women's greater
economic opportunities and broader education.

3723. Staples, Robert. THE BLACK WOMAN IN AMERICA: SEX,
MARRIAGE, AND THE FAMILY. Chicago, IL: Nelson-Hall, 1973. 269
pp. Position of the black woman in American society and as head of
household.

3724. Sussman, Marvin B., ed. SOURCEBOOK IN MARRIAGE AND THE
FAMILY. 4th edition. Boston, MA: Houghton Mifflin, 1976. 432 pp.
Compilation of articles by the foremost authorities on marriage and the
family.

3725. Touba, Jacquiline Rudolph. "Sex Role Differentiation in Iranian Families
Living in Urban and Rural Areas of a Region Undergoing Planned
Industrialization in Iran (Arak Shahrestan)," JOURNAL OF
MARRIAGE AND THE FAMILY, vol. 37, no. 2 (May 1975), pp.
437-445. 1972 study of 216 families found that the major role
difference between urban and rural women was in the area of financial
management.

3726. U.S.S.R. "Fundamentals of Legislation of the U.S.S.R. and the Union
Republics on Marriage and the Family." Moscow: Novosti Press Agency
Pub. House, 1975. 31 pp.

3727. U.S. Dept. of Labor. Wage and Labor Standards Administration. Women's
Bureau. CHILD CARE ARRANGEMENTS OF WORKING MOTHERS
IN THE UNITED STATES. By Seth Low and Pearl G. Spindler.
Washington, D.C.: SUDOC, GPO, 1968. 115 pp.

3728. University of Wisconsin-Extension. Center for Women's and Family
Living Education. FEMINISM AND THE FAMILY. Madison, WI:
UWEX, 1973.

3729. Wimperis, Virginia. THE UNMARRIED MOTHER AND HER CHILD.
London, England: G. Allen & Unwin, 1960. 397 pp.

3730. Wolf, Margery. THE HOUSE OF LIM: A STUDY OF A CHINESE FARM
FAMILY. New York: Appleton-Century-Crofts, 1968. 147 pp.
Sociological study of contemporary family life in Nationalist Taiwan.

3731. Yorburg, Betty. THE CHANGING FAMILY. New York: Columbia Univ.
Press, 1973. 230 pp. The historical role of the family and its probable
future in response to the pressure of rapid social change.

3732. Young, Michael Dunlop and Peter Willmott. FAMILY AND KINSHIP IN
EAST LONDON. London, England: Routledge & Kegan Paul/Penguin,
1957. 232 pp.

3733. Youssif, Nadia. "Cultural Ideals, Feminine Behavior, and Family

Control," COMPARATIVE STUDIES IN SOCIETY AND HISTORY, vol. 15, no. 3 (June 1973), pp. 326-347. Inconsistencies between expectations of the female role and actual feminine behavior.

3734. Yudkin, Simon and Anthea Holme. WORKING MOTHERS AND THEIR CHILDREN: A STUDY FOR THE COUNCIL OF CHILDREN'S WELFARE. London, England: Michael Joseph/Sphere, 1963. 199 pp.

C. Marriage and Divorce

"Marriage is that relation between man and woman in which the independence is equal, the dependence mutual, and the obligation reciprocal.
                                                            —*Louis Kaufman Anspacher*

"Oh ye gods, Render me worthy of this noble wife!"
                                                            —*Shakespeare, JULIUS CAESAR, Act II, sc. 1*

3735. Adler, Felix. "Marriage and Divorce." New York: McClure, Phillips, 1905. 58 pp. Two lectures delivered before the Society for Ethical Culture, New York City.

3736. Apstein, Theodore Emanuel. THE PARTING OF THE WAYS: AN EXPOSE OF AMERICA'S DIVORCE TANGLE. New York: Dodge, 1935. 272 pp. Urges uniform divorce laws in the U.S. and advocates a simpler procedure so that those who wish to can obtain a divorce with minimum difficulty.

3737. Bach, George Robert and Peter Wyden. THE INTIMATE ENEMY: HOW TO FIGHT FAIR IN LOVE AND MARRIAGE. New York: Avon, 1970. 384 pp.

3738. Beier, Ernst G. and Daniel P. Sternberg. "Subtle Interactive Cues in Newlyweds." Bethesda, MD: ERIC Document Reproduction Service, 1970. 25 pp. Analysis of extraverbal communication processes, i.e. touching and eye contact.

3739. Bell, Robert R. MARRIAGE AND FAMILY INTERACTION. Homewood, IL: Dorsey Press, 1967. 535 pp. Good basic text.

3740. Berson, Barbara and Ben Bova. SURVIVAL GUIDE FOR THE SUDDENLY SINGLE. New York: St. Martin's Press, 1974. 224 pp. A liberated guide to divorce with chapters on sex, children, money, and lawyers.

3741. Blood, Robert O., Jr. LOVE MATCH AND ARRANGED MARRIAGE: A TOKYO-DETROIT COMPARISON. New York: Free Press, 1967. 264 pp.

3742. Blood, Robert O., Jr. and Donald M. Wolfe. HUSBANDS AND WIVES: THE DYNAMICS OF MARRIED LIFE. Glencoe, IL: Free Press, 1960. 293 pp.

3743. Braudy, Susan. BETWEEN MARRIAGE AND DIVORCE: A WOMAN'S DIARY. New York: W. Morrow, 1975. 252 pp. Focuses on sexual boredom and infidelity between two married roommates who profess to love each other.

3744. Brothers, Joyce. THE BROTHERS SYSTEM FOR LIBERATED LOVE AND MARRIAGE. New York: P. H. Wyden, 1972. 340 pp. How marriage today destroys a woman's potential and cripples her emotionally, while enhancing a man's potential and increasing his happiness.

3745. Brown, Carol A., Rosalyn Feldberg, Elizabeth M. Fox, and Janet Kohen. "Divorce: Chance of a New Lifetime," JOURNAL OF SOCIAL ISSUES, vol. 32, no. 1 (Winter 1976), pp. 119-134. Feminist analysis of the costs and benefits accruing to divorced mothers.

3746. Cantor, Donald J. ESCAPE FROM MARRIAGE: HOW TO SOLVE THE PROBLEMS OF DIVORCE. New York: Morrow, 1971. 160 pp. Proposes divorce by simple notice, with the court handling details. Also discusses archaic divorce laws and Mexican divorces.

3747. Carpenter, Edward. "Marriage in Free Society." Chicago, IL: Stockham, 1906. 47 pp. A progressive pamphlet.

3748. Carson, William English. MARRIAGE REVOLT: A STUDY OF MARRIAGE AND DIVORCE. New York: Hearst's International Library, 1915. 481 pp. Collection of the current opinions on marriage and divorce, including an appendix summarizing U.S. marriage laws.

3749. Clemens, Alphonse Henry. DESIGN FOR A SUCCESSFUL MARRIAGE. 2nd edition. Englewood Cliffs, NJ. Prentice-Hall, 1964. 393 pp.

3750. Comer, Lee. WEDLOCKED WOMEN. London, England: Feminist Book, Ltd., 1974. 285 pp.

3751. Corin, James. MATING, MARRIAGE, AND THE STATUS OF WOMEN. New York: AMS Press, 1976. 181 pp. Reprint of 1910 edition.

3752. Cott, Nancy F. "Eighteenth-Century Family and Social Life Revealed in Massachusetts Divorce Records," JOURNAL OF SOCIAL HISTORY, vol. 10 (Fall 1976), pp. 20-43. Detailed information in divorce petitions and testimony provides much information about the sexual morality of the eighteenth century.

3753. Epstein, Joseph. DIVORCED IN AMERICA: MARRIAGE IN AN AGE OF POSSIBILITY. New York: E. P. Dutton, 1974. 318 pp. Discusses divorce and the aftermath effects, but essentially supports traditional marriage.

3754. Fedder, Raoul Lionel. DIVORCE: THE WAY THINGS ARE NOT THE WAY THINGS SHOULD BE. New York: World Publishing, 1971.

3755. Feminist Divorce Collective. PARTING: A HANDBOOK FOR SELF-HELP DIVORCE IN OREGON. Portland, OR: J. K. Gill, 1976, 106 pp. + appendix. Guidebook for writing own divorce papers, including samples of necessary forms.

3756. Fields, Elizabeth. "Freedom in Marriage." New York: Abbey Press, 1902. 56 pp. Pamphlet advocating that divorce be as free as the marriage license.

3757. Fox, Robin. KINSHIP AND MARRIAGE: AN ANTHROPOLOGICAL PERSPECTIVE. Harmonsworth, England: Penguin, 1967. 271 pp. Traditional marriage and family relationships.

3758. Frohlich, Newton. DIVORCE WITHOUT FEAR: A COMMON SENSE HANDBOOK OF NEGOTIATION. New York: Harper & Row, 1971.

160 pp. Basically how-to book, aimed at $15-30,000/year wage-earning family.

3759. Fulton, Philip N. "Settling of Social Contact and Status Advancement Through Marriage: A Study of Rural Women," RURAL SOCIOLOGY, vol. 40, no. 1 (Spring 1975), pp. 45-54.

3760. Gardiner, Harry W., U. P. Singh, and Donald E. D'Orazio. "Liberated Woman in Three Cultures: Marital Role Preferences in Thailand, India, and the United States," HUMAN ORGANIZATION, vol. 33, no. 4 (Winter 1974), pp. 413-415. Decision-making within the family.

3761. Gelles, Richard J. THE VIOLENT HOME: A STUDY OF PHYSICAL AGGRESSION BETWEEN HUSBANDS AND WIVES. Beverly Hills, CA: Sage, 1974. 230 pp.

3762. Goode, William Josiah. WOMEN IN DIVORCE. New York: Free Press, 1965. 381 pp.

3763. Goodsell, Willystine. A HISTORY OF MARRIAGE AND THE FAMILY. New York: Macmillan, 1934. 590 pp. A textbook on marriage as a social and educational unit.

3764. Hirsch, Barbara B. DIVORCE: WHAT A WOMAN NEEDS TO KNOW. Chicago, IL: H. Regnery, 1973. 256 pp. Handbook of legal information.

3765. Inyamah, Nathaniel G. N. "Polygamy and the Christian Church," CONCORDIA THEOLOGICAL MONTHLY, vol. 43 (March 1972), pp. 138-143.

3766. Jones, Rex and Shirley K. Jones. THE HIMALAYAN WOMAN: A STUDY OF LIMBU WOMEN IN MARRIAGE AND DIVORCE. Palo Alto, CA: Mayfield Publishing, 1976. 155 pp.

3767. Kahn, Robert W. and Lawrence E. Kahn. THE DIVORCE LAWYER'S CASEBOOK. New York: St. Martin's Press, 1972. 207 pp.

3768. Kelley, Robert K. COURTSHIP, MARRIAGE, AND THE FAMILY. New York: Harcourt, Brace & World, 1969. 629 pp.

3769. "Kidnapping and Elopement as Alternative Systems of Marriage," ANTHROPOLOGICAL QUARTERLY, vol. 47, no. 3 (July 1974), pp. 233-346. Special Issue. Contributors include Daniel G. Bates, Francis P. Conant, Ayse Kudat, Barbara Ayres, William G. Lockwood, Jan Brukman, and Brian Stross.

3770. Kodel, John. "Malthus Amiss: Marriage Restrictions in 19th Century Germany," SOCIAL SCIENCE, vol. 47, no. 1 (Winter 1972), pp. 40-45. Included not only minimum age requirements, but demonstration of economic stability and high moral character.

3771. Lantz, Herman R. "Marital Incompatibility and Social Change in Early America." Beverly Hills, CA: Sage, 1976. 48 pp. Comparison of 18th century newspaper ads, some of which indicate female discontent and relative liberation, and the national divorce rates, first appearing in 1870.

3772. Lindenauer, Geoffrey G. and Doris Howard. "A Workbook Approach to Marriage," JOURNAL OF EMOTIONAL EDUCATION, vol. 12 (Winter 1972), pp. 2-19.

3773. Lopata, Helena Znaniecki. "Self-Identity in Marriage and Widowhood,"
SOCIOLOGICAL QUARTERLY, vol. 14, no. 3 (Summer 1973), pp.
407-418. The major factor determining degree of self-identity is the
level of education achieved by women.

3774. LOVE, MARRIAGE, AND DIVORCE, AND THE SOVEREIGNTY OF
THE INDIVIDUAL: A DISCUSSION BETWEEN HENRY JAMES,
HORACE GREELEY, AND STEPHEN PEARL ANDREWS, and
DIVORCE: BEING A CORRESPONDENCE BETWEEN HORACE
GREELEY AND ROBERT DALE OWEN. New York: Source Book
Press, 1972. 192 pp. Reprints of 1853 and 1860 editions respectively.
Both works grew out of correspondence exchanged in New York
newspapers.

3775. McCary, James Leslie. FREEDOM AND GROWTH IN MARRIAGE. New
York: John Wiley & Sons, 1975. 420 pp. Considers marriage from a
personal rather than an academic or moralistic point of view.

3776. Mayer, Michael F. "Divorce and Annulment in the 50 States." New York:
Arno Press, 1967. 89 pp. Description of the various states' laws relating
to divorce.

3777. Mel, Rama. DIVORCED HINDU WOMAN. New York: International
Publications Service, 1976.

3778. Murstein, Barnard I. "Self-Deal-Self-Discrepancy and the Choice of
Marital Partner," JOURNAL OF CONSULTING AND CLINICAL
PSYCHOLOGY, vol. 37 (Aug. 1971), pp. 47-52. Variables such as age,
religion, values, education, and socio-economic standing which affect
choice of marital partners.

3779. Nevill, Dorothy and Sandra Damico. "Decision Making Within the
Family: Role Conflict in Women as a Function of Marital Status,"
HUMAN RELATIONS, vol. 28, no. 5 (July 1975), pp. 487-497. Level
of role conflict is inversely proportionate to financial status.

3780. Newman, F. X., ed. THE MEANING OF COURTLY LOVE. Albany, NY:
SUNY Press, 1969. 102 pp. Appears to be merely a literary concept
when the historical facts of marriage in the medieval period are
considered.

3781. Nilson, Linda Burzotta. "Social Standing of a Married Woman," SOCIAL
PROBLEMS, vol. 23, no. 5 (June 1976), pp. 581-592. Status is
generally determined by both the husband's occupational standing and
an assessment of the wife's contribution.

3782. O'Neil, George and Nena O'Neil. OPEN MARRIAGE: A NEW LIFE
STYLE FOR COUPLES. New York: M. Evans, 1972. 287 pp.

3783. Reed, Angela. THE WOMAN ON THE VERGE OF DIVORCE. London,
England: Nelson, 1970. 164 pp.

3784. Rogers, Carl Ransom. BECOMING PARTNERS: MARRIAGE AND ITS
ALTERNATIVES. New York: Delacorte Press, 1972. 256 pp.
Advocates exploring and experimenting with all possibilities.
Substantial bibliography by Dr. Alice Elliot.

3785. Rosen, Lawrence. "I Divorce Thee," TRANS/ACTION, vol. 7, no. 8
(June 1970), pp. 34-37. Moroccan laws of divorce.

3786. Sanger, Margaret Higgins. HAPPINESS IN MARRIAGE. New York: Blue Ribbon Books, 1926. 231 pp. Advice on the various aspects of married life.

3787. Scanzoni, John Henry. SEX ROLES, LIFE STYLES, AND CHILDBEARING: CHANGING PATTERNS IN MARRIAGE AND THE FAMILY. New York: Free Press, 1975. 259 pp.

3788. ———. SEXUAL BARGAINING: POWER POLITICS IN THE AMERICAN MARRIAGE. Englewood Cliffs, NJ: Prentice-Hall, 1972. 180 pp. Explores alternative futures for marriage including the commune and the kibbutz, finding that they offer little in the way of options.

3789. Schwartz, Mary C. and Judith F. Weintraub. "Prisoners' Wives: A Study in Crisis," FEDERAL PROBATION, vol. 38, no. 4 (Dec. 1974), pp. 20-26. The social and emotional problems of women whose husbands are incarcerated.

3790. Sherman, Charles Edward, ed. "How to do Your Own Divorce in California; and the Forms You will need to do It." Berkeley, CA: Nolo Press, 1971. 63 pp.

3791. Sherwin, Robert Veit. COMPATIBLE DIVORCE. New York: Crown Publishers, 1969. 320 pp. Combination of legal, practical, and psychological advice to the near-divorced.

3792. State Bar of Wisconsin. HANDBOOK OF DIVORCE PROCEDURE. Madison, WI: State Bar of Wisconsin, 1973. 112 pp.

3793. Stegeman, Beatrice. "The Divorce Dilemma: The New Woman in Contemporary African Novels," CRITIQUE, vol. 15, no. 3 (1974), pp. 84-93. The image of women in contemporary literature shows the conflict between traditional tribal values and individual responsibility for one's potential.

3794. United Nations. NATIONALITY OF MARRIED WOMEN. New York: U.N. Publications, 1971. 121 pp. Analysis of conflicting laws regarding nationality of married women, with excerpts from the constitutions, laws, and other legal instruments of 106 countries.

3795. University of Wisconsin-Extension. Women's Education Resources. THE MARRIAGE CONTRACT. Madison, WI: UWEX, 1975, 108 pp. Transcript of class offered in Wisconsin on the Educational Telephone Network (Dec. 2, 9, 16, 1974).

3796. Unterman, Isser Yehuda. "Family Purity—Its Wide Implications," ISRAELI MAGAZINE, vol. 4 (Jan. 1972), pp. 68-74. Copy of an article pertaining to traditional Jewish purity laws, given to every couple who apply for a wedding license in Israel.

3797. Veroff, Joseph and Sheila Field. MARRIAGE AND WORK IN AMERICA: A STUDY OF MOTIVES AND ROLES. New York: Van Nostrand Reinhold, 1970. 404 pp. Motives of affiliation, achievement, and power examined for interaction with role characteristics to affect experience of fulfillment and frustration in these roles. Large national sample.

3798. Vidyasagara, Isvarchandra and Arabinda Podder. MARRIAGE OF HINDU WIDOWS. Columbia, MO: South Asia Books, 1975.

3799. Waller, Willard Walter. THE OLD LOVE AND THE NEW: DIVORCE AND READJUSTMENT. New York: Liveright, 1930. 344 pp. Studies of divorce among 33 men and women.

3800. Wallis, Jack Harold. MARRIAGE OBSERVED. London, England: Routledge & Kegan Paul, 1970. 207 pp. Essays on various aspects of marriage by a marriage counselor.

3801. Ward, Maria. THE MORMON WIFE; A LIFE STORY OF THE SACRIFICES, SORROWS AND SUFFERINGS OF WOMAN. A NARRATIVE OF MANY YEARS PERSONAL EXPERIENCE, BY THE WIFE OF A MORMON ELDER. Hartford, CT: Hartford Pub., 1873. 449 pp.

3802. Warner, Ralph and Toni Ihara. THE PEOPLE'S GUIDE TO CALIFORNIA DIVORCE LAW. Occidental, CA: Nolo Press, 1976.

3803. Washington, Joseph R., Jr. MARRIAGE IN BLACK AND WHITE. Boston, MA: Beacon Press, 1971. 358 pp. Author suggests racial conflict cannot be eliminated until we are willing to confront prejudice on its most personal level—by acceptance of intermarriage.

3804. Wideman, Bernard. "Women's Case for Divorce," FAR EASTERN ECONOMIC REVIEW, vol. 90, no. 47 (Nov. 21, 1975), pp. 30, 33. Proposed legalized divorce in the Philippines.

3805. Wilkinson, Doris Y., comp. BLACK MALE/WHITE FEMALE: PERSPECTIVES ON INTERRACIAL MARRIAGE AND COURTSHIP. Cambridge, MA: Schenkman, 1975. 182 pp. Collection of essays.

3806. Willans, Angela. INSIDE INFORMATION ON CONFLICT IN MARRIAGE. London, England: Dickens Press, 1969. Pages not numbered.

D. Life Styles

"We need courage to throw away old garments which have had their day and no longer fit the requirements of the new generations . . ."
—Fridtjof Nansen

3807. Adams, Margaret. SINGLE BLESSEDNESS: OBSERVATIONS ON THE SINGLE STATUS IN MARRIED SOCIETY. New York: Basic Books, 1976. 264 pp. 27 interviews with women, including widows and divorcees who have chosen to live without the constant presence of a man.

3808. Bach, George R. and Ronald M. Deutsch. PAIRING: HOW TO ACHIEVE GENUINE INTIMACY. New York: P. H. Wyden, 1970. 256 pp. Advocates "leveling" with strangers to achieve intimacy and authenticity.

3809. Baxter, Anne. INTERMISSION, A TRUE STORY. New York: G. P. Putnam's Sons, 1976. 384 pp. The former film star's four-year marriage to Randolph Galt, and their life at Giro, Australia on 37,000 acres in the bush country.

3810. Bernard, Jessie Shirley. WOMEN, WIVES, MOTHERS: VALUES AND OPTIONS. Chicago, IL: Aldine Pub., 1975. 286 pp. Collection of lectures and articles on such topics as the stages of motherhood and their significance, sex roles, socialization, etc.

3811. Black, Alexander. MODERN DAUGHTERS: CONVERSATIONS WITH VARIOUS AMERICAN GIRLS AND ONE MAN. New York: Charles Scribner's Sons, 1899. 212 pp. Conversations with a debutante, a clubwoman, a cynic, a chaperone, and a bride, among others.

3812. Brody, Stanley J. "Public Policy Issues of 'Women in Transition'," GERONTOLOGIST, vol. 16, no. 2 (April 1976), pp. 181-183. How the elderly view the preparations contemporary women are making for old age.

3813. Caine, Lynn. WIDOW. New York: William Morrow, 1974. 222 pp. Especially for women who must live their grief in a society that taboos death and shuns strong emotion.

3814. Christensen, Filli, Charlotte Goubb, Ugge Grøne, Kirsten Hofstätter, and Åse Teken. "Kvinder I Hjemmet [Women in the Home]." København, Denmark: Forlag, Hans Reitzel, 1972. 94 pp. Interviews with housewives on attitudes on lifestyles.

3815. Coble, Betty J. WOMAN: AWARE AND CHOOSING. Nashville, TN: Broadman Press, 1975. 155 pp.

3816. Coleman, Richard P., Gerald Handel, and Lee Rainwater. WORKINGMAN'S WIFE, HER PERSONALITY, WORLD, AND LIFESTYLE. New York: Oceana, 1959. 238 pp. A market research study of the values and habits of workingclass women.

3817. Davison, Jaquie. I AM A HOUSEWIFE!—A HOUSEWIFE IS THE MOST IMPORTANT PERSON IN THE WORLD. New York: Guild Books, 1972. 107 pp.

3818. Dias, Eduardo . . . . HARÉM, CONTOS E DITOS MUÇULMANOS. Lisboa, Portugal: Livraria Clássica Editora, A. M. Teixeira & Co. (filue), 1942. 318 pp.

3819. "Dropout Wife," LIFE, vol. 72 (March 17, 1972), pp. 34B-41. Story of a woman who left her family to move into a commune, leaving her husband with the household duties.

3820. Epstein, Cynthia Fuchs. "Law Partners and Marital Partners: Strains and Solutions in the Dual-Career Family Enterprise," HUMAN RELATIONS, vol. 24, no. 6 (June 1972), pp. 549-564. Study of 12 cases in the New York City area, examining the professional and domestic roles of each partner.

3821. Girson, Rochelle. MAIDEN VOYAGES: A LIVELY GUIDE FOR THE WOMAN TRAVELER. New York: Harcourt, Brace & World, 1967. 264 pp. *Tour de force* of women travelers and what they should do.

3822. Gruenberg, Mrs. Sidonie Matsner and Hilda Sidney Krach. THE MANY LIVES OF MODERN WOMAN: A GUIDE TO HAPPINESS IN HER COMPLEX ROLE. Garden City, NY: Doubleday, 1952. 255 pp. Analysis of the American woman's life pattern; choices and problems.

3823. Harris, Janet. THE PRIME OF MS. AMERICA: THE AMERICAN WOMAN AT FORTY. New York: G. P. Putnam's Sons, 1975. 250 pp.

Debunks the myths about widows' financial status and urges women to "do their own thing."

3824. Janeway, Elizabeth. BETWEEN MYTH AND MORNING: WOMAN AWAKENING. New York: William Morrow, 1974. 279 pp. Includes such essays as "Realizing Human Potential," "Women's Place in a Changing World," and "Breaking the Age Barrier."

3825. Le Shan, Eda J. THE WONDERFUL CRISIS OF MIDDLE AGE: SOME PERSONAL REFLECTIONS. New York: McKay, 1973. 352 pp. Middle years should become the time to insist on freedom of self.

3826. ———. "Mates and Room-mates: New Styles in Young Marriages." PUBLIC AFFAIRS PAMPHLET no. 468, Sept. 1971. 28 pp. Early marriage, alternate life styles, and communal living.

3827. Lewis, Alfred Allen and Barrie Berns. THREE OUT OF FOUR WIVES: WIDOWHOOD IN AMERICA. New York: Macmillan, 1975. 216 pp. 325 widows contributed opinions to this "exposé" of the actual position of widowed women.

3828. Konopka, Gisela. YOUNG GIRLS: A PORTRAIT OF ADOLESCENCE. Englewood Cliffs, NJ: Prentice-Hall, 1976. 176 pp.

3829. Lindsay, Kathryn D. "Success and Femininity—Must They be Mutually Exclusive?" COUNSELING AND VALUES, vol. 17, no. 4 (Summer 1973), pp. 252-255.

3830. Little, Kenneth. AFRICAN WOMEN IN TOWNS: AN ASPECT OF AFRICA'S SOCIAL REVOLUTION. New Rochelle, NY: Cambridge Univ. Press, 1974. 242 pp. Synthesis of available literature augmented by original survey data, on the position of women, sexuality, and economic status.

3831. Loeffler, Marcia. "Counseling Women for Their Complex Life Role," COLLEGE STUDENT JOURNAL, vol. 9, no. 2 (April 1975), pp. 129-132. Focuses on counseling women about their various options.

3832. Lopata, Helena Znaniecki. WIDOWHOOD IN AN AMERICAN CITY. Cambridge, MA: Schenkman, 1973. 369 pp. Concludes that American society fails to prepare women for social communication after the death of the husband.

3833. Lorenzana, Moemi. "La Chicana: Transcending the Old and Carving Out a New Life and Self-Image," DE COLORES, vol. 2, no. 3 (1975), pp. 6-14.

3834. McHugh, Mary. THE WOMAN THING. New York: Praeger, 1973. 127 pp. Condenses and highlights advancing opportunities for women today.

3835. Massey, Carmen and Ralph Warner. SEX, LIVING TOGETHER, AND THE LAW: A LEGAL GUIDE FOR UNMARRIED COUPLES (AND GROUPS). Berkeley, CA: Nolo Press, 1974. 187 pp.

3836. Mazur, Ronald M. THE NEW INTIMACY: OPEN-ENDED MARRIAGE AND ALTERNATIVE LIFE STYLES. Boston, MA: Beacon Press, 1973. 134 pp. Discusses extramarital sex; foresees a new sexual climate without restricting societal judgments.

3837. Mead, Margaret. "What Women Want," FORTUNE, vol. 34, no. 6 (June 1976), pp. 172-175, 218, 220, 223-224. Advocates women being able to act by choice rather than by necessity.

3838. Mernissi, Fatima. BEYOND THE VEIL: MALE-FEMALE DYNAMICS IN A MODERN MUSLIM STATE. Cambridge, MA: Schenkman, 1975. 132 pp.

3839. Movius, Margaret. "Voluntary Childlessness—The Ultimate Liberation," FAMILY COORDINATOR, vol. 25, no. 1 (Jan. 1976), pp. 57-62. Professional women are increasingly considering not bearing children.

3840. Myerson, Abraham. THE NERVOUS HOUSEWIFE. New York: Arno Press, 1972. 273 pp. Reprint of 1927 edition. Examines the various causes and forms of nervousness in housewives.

3841. Papanek, Hanna. "Woman Field Worker in a Purdah Society," HUMAN ORGANIZATION, vol. 23, no. 2 (Summer 1964), pp. 160-162.

3842. Reichardt, Annie. GIRL-LIFE IN THE HAREM: A TRUE ACCOUNT OF GIRL-LIFE IN ORIENTAL CLIMES. London, England: John Ouseley, Ltd., 1908. 253 pp.

3843. Rivers, Caryl. APHRODITE AT MID-CENTURY: GROWING UP FEMALE AND CATHOLIC IN POST WAR AMERICA. Garden City, NY: Doubleday, 1973. 283 pp.

3844. Rogers, Donald I. "Teach Your Wife to be a Widow." New York: Holt Rinehardt, 1953. 93 pp. Program for the management of household finances.

3845. Rosner, Menahem. "Women in the Kibbutz, Changing Status and Concepts," ASIAN AND AFRICAN STUDIES, vol. 3 (Annual 1967), pp. 35-68.

3846. Stark, F. "In a Syrian Harem," CORNHILL (London), vol. 72 (April 1932), pp. 433-450.

3847. Stein, Leon and Annette K. Baxter, eds. LIBERATING THE HOME. New York: Arno Press, 1974. 240 pp. Reprint of 1851 edition of WOMAN AND HER NEEDS by Elizabeth Oakes Smith; and reprint of 1875 edition of A DOMESTIC PROBLEM: WORK AND CULTURE IN THE HOUSEHOLD by Abby M. Diaz.

3848. Stein, Martha L. LOVERS, FRIENDS, SLAVES: NINE MALE SEXUAL TYPES; THEIR PSYCHO-SEXUAL TRANSACTIONS WITH CALL GIRLS. New York: G. P. Putnam's Sons, 1974. 347 pp. Despite its title, a study of call girls.

3849. Tax, Meredith. "Woman and Her Mind: The Story of Daily Life." Cambridge, MA: Bread and Roses Press, 1970. 20 pp.

3850. Tiger, Lionel and Joseph Shepher. WOMEN IN THE KIBBUTZ. New York: Harcourt Brace Jovanovich, 1975. 334 pp. Study of several different types of kibbutzim, and the changes in such concepts as communal child rearing. Authors hold that women have reverted to many of the traditional sex-roles.

3851. Torrie, Margaret. BEGIN AGAIN: A BOOK FOR WOMEN ALONE. New York: International Publications Service, 1975. 196 pp. Widows in Great Britain.

3852. Troll, Lilian E., Joan Israel, and Kenneth Israel, eds. LOOKING AHEAD: A WOMAN'S GUIDE TO THE PROBLEMS AND JOYS OF GROWING OLDER. Englewood Cliffs, NJ: Prentice-Hall, 1977.

E. Sexuality

*"The omnipresent process of sex, as it is woven into the whole texture of our man's
or woman's body, is the pattern of all the process of our life."*
                                                    —(Henry) Havelock Ellis

"The evidence indicates that woman is, on the whole, biologically superior to man."
                                                    —Ashley Montagu

3853. Abbott, Sidney and Barbara Love. SAPPHO WAS A RIGHT ON WOMAN:
A LIBERATED VIEW OF LESBIANISM. New York: Stein & Day,
1972. 251 pp.

3854. Allen, Gina and Clement G. Martin. INTIMACY: SENSITIVITY, SEX
AND THE ART OF LOVE. Chicago, IL: Cowles, 1971. 251 pp.
Focuses on communication as the key to coping with jealousy and
hostility.

3855. Barbach, Lonnie Garfield. FOR YOURSELF—THE FULFILLMENT OF
HUMAN SEXUALITY. Garden City, NY: Doubleday, 1975. 218 pp. A
guide to orgasmic response.

3856. Barker-Benfield, G. J. THE HORRORS OF THE HALF-KNOWN LIFE:
MALE ATTITUDES TOWARD WOMEN AND SEXUALITY IN
NINETEENTH CENTURY AMERICA. Scranton, PA: Harper & Row,
1976. 352 pp. Victorian sexual ideology.

3857. Belliveau, Fred and Lin Richter. UNDERSTANDING HUMAN SEXUAL
INADEQUACY. Boston, MA: Little, Brown, 1970. 242 pp.
Interpretation of the famous study by Masters and Johnson.

3858. Birchall, Ellen F. and Noel B. Gerson. SEX AND THE ADULT WOMAN.
New York: Pocket Books, 1974. 237 pp. Reprint of 1965 edition.

3859. Brecher, Ruth and Edward Brecher. AN ANALYSIS OF HUMAN
SEXUAL RESPONSE. Boston, MA: Little, Brown, 1966. 318 pp.
Restatement of Masters and Johnson study with more of a
psychological emphasis.

3860. Briffault, Robert. SIN AND SEX. London, England: Allen & Unwin,
1932. 253 pp. Study of moral taboos and blue laws; morality and
sexuality.

3861. Bullough, Vern L. SEXUAL VARIANCE IN SOCIETY AND HISTORY.
Somerset, NJ: John Wiley & Sons, 1976. 720 pp. The first study in
English of the history of stigmatized sexual behavior.

3862. Caprio, Frank Samuel. FEMALE HOMOSEXUALITY: A
PSYCHODYNAMIC STUDY OF LESBIANISM. London, England: P.
Owen, 1960. 334 pp. Includes 19-page bibliography.

3863. –––. SEXUALLY ADEQUATE FEMALE. 16th edition. New York:
Citadel Press, 1967. 223 pp.

3864. Chafetz, Janet S., Patricia Sampson, Paula Beck, and Joyce West. "A
Study of Homosexual Women," SOCIAL WORK, vol. 19, no. 6 (Nov.
1974), pp. 714-723. Explores how lesbians live; their relationships,

problems, and perceptions of society's reactions to them.
3865. Cohn, Frederick. UNDERSTANDING HUMAN SEXUALITY. Englewood Cliffs, NJ: Prentice-Hall, 1974. 283 pp.
3866. Comfort, Alexander, ed. THE JOY OF SEX: A CORDON BLEU GUIDE TO LOVEMAKING. New York: Crown Publishers, 1972. 199 pp.
3867. –––. MORE JOY: A BEAUTIFUL LOVEMAKING COMPANION TO "THE JOY OF SEX." New York: Crown Publishers, 1974. 150 pp.
3868. Degler, Carl N. "What Ought To Be and What Was: Women's Sexuality in the Nineteenth Century," AMERICAN HISTORICAL REVIEW, vol. 79 (Dec. 1974), pp. 1467-1490.
3869. De Martino, Manfred F. SEX AND THE INTELLIGENT WOMAN. New York: Springer Pub., 1974. 308 pp. Epilogue by Albert Ellis. Study of 327 members of MENSA (an organization whose members have extremely high IQ's) and their sexual attitudes.
3870. Dingwall, Eric John. GIRDLE OF CHASTITY: A FASCINATING HISTORY OF CHASTITY BELTS. New York: Clarion Press, 1959. 171 pp. Reprint of 1951 edition.
3871. Dreitzel, Hans Peter, ed. SEXUAL REVOLUTION AND FAMILY CRISIS. New York: Macmillan, 1972. 350 pp.
3872. Fisher, Seymour. UNDERSTANDING THE FEMALE ORGASM. Harmondsworth, England: Penguin, 1973. 218 pp. Condensed version of THE FEMALE ORGASM.
3873. Friday, Nancy, comp. MY SECRET GARDEN: WOMEN'S SEXUAL FANTASIES. New York: Trident Press, 1973. 361 pp. Rather unscientific collection and study of several hundred sexual fantasies.
3874. Fulton, Gere B. SEXUAL AWARENESS. Boston, MA: Holbrook Press, 1974. 354 pp.
3875. Hägg, Maud and Barbro Werkmäster. KVINNOR OCH SEX [WOMEN AND SEX]. Göteborg: Författarforl, 1973. 149 pp.
3876. Haller, William and Malleville Haller. "The Puritan Art of Love," HUNTINGTON LIBRARY QUARTERLY, vol. 5 (1942), pp. 235-272.
3877. Hammer, Signe, ed. WOMEN: BODY AND CULTURE: ESSAYS ON THE SEXUALITY OF WOMEN IN A CHANGING SOCIETY. New York: Harper & Row, 1975. 342 pp.
3878. Heiman, Julia, Leslie LoPiccolo, and Joseph LoPiccolo. BECOMING ORGASMIC: A SEXUAL GROWTH PROGRAM FOR WOMEN. Englewood Cliffs, NJ: Prentice-Hall, 1976. 219 pp.
3879. Heinzen, Karl Peter. RIGHTS OF WOMEN, AND THE SEXUAL RELATIONS. New York: Burt Franklin, 1973. Reprint of 1898 edition.
3880. Hill, Justine. WOMEN TALKING. Seacacus, NJ: Lyle Stuart, Inc., 1977. Dialogues of a group of women, ranging in age from early 20's to late 50's, attempting to describe and re-define women's sexuality.
3881. Hirschfeld, Magnus. MEN AND WOMEN: THE WORLD JOURNEY OF A SEXOLOGIST. New York: AMS Press, 1974. 325 pp. Reprint of 1935 edition. Social and sexual customs of Egypt and the Far East.
3882. Hite, Shere, ed. SEXUAL HONESTY, BY WOMEN FOR WOMEN: WRITTEN ANONYMOUSLY BY WOMEN 14-64 IN RESPONSE TO A

NATIONAL QUESTIONNAIRE. New York: Warner Paperback Library, 1974. 294 pp. The unsigned, uncensored responses on how women think, feel, and live with sex.

3883. ———. THE HITE REPORT: A NATIONWIDE STUDY ON FEMALE SEXUALITY. New York: Macmillan, 1976. 496 pp. Data on female masturbation, orgasm, and coitus from the responses of 1,844 women to three questionnaires.

3884. Jones, Kenneth L., Louis W. Shainberg, and Curtis O. Byer. SEX AND PEOPLE. New York: Harper & Row, 1977. 365 pp. Basic text for college level human sexuality course; cultural, emotional, and physical sexuality.

3885. Katchadourian, Herant A. and Donald T. Lunde. FUNDAMENTALS OF HUMAN SEXUALITY. 2nd edition. New York: Holt, Rinehart & Winston, 1972. 514 pp. Excellent reference book summarizing existing knowledge.

3886. Kline-Graber, Georgia and Benjamin Graber. WOMAN'S ORGASM: A GUIDE TO SEXUAL SATISFACTION. Indianapolis, IN: Bobbs-Merrill, 1975. 184 pp.

3887. Kollontai, Alexandra. "Sexual Relations and the Class Struggle," and "Love and the New Morality." Bristol, England: Falling Wall Press, 1972. 15 pp. Reprint of 1937 editions. By a major figure in U.S.S.R. history.

3888. Lauritsen, John and David Thorstad. "The Early Homosexual Rights Movement (1864-1935)." New York: Times Change Press, 1974. 91 pp.

3889. "Lesbian Culture," WIN, vol. 11, no. 22 (June 26, 1975), pp. 5-26. Contributors include Andrea Dworkin, Julia P. Stanley, Lynne D. Shapiro, Karla Jay, and June Rook.

3890. Lewinsohn, Richard. A HISTORY OF SEXUAL CUSTOMS. New York: Harper & Row, 1958. 424 pp.

3891. Loraine, John Alexander, ed. UNDERSTANDING HOMOSEXUALITY: ITS BIOLOGICAL AND PSYCHOLOGICAL BASES. New York: American Elsevier Publishing, 1974. 217 pp. Interdisciplinary approach, dealing with both female and male homosexuality.

3892. Ludovici, Lawrence James. THE FINAL INEQUALITY: A CRITICAL ASSESSMENT OF WOMAN'S SEXUAL ROLE IN SOCIETY. New York: W. W. Norton, 1965. 271 pp.

3893. McCary, James Leslie. SEXUAL MYTHS AND FALLACIES. New York: Van Nostrand Reinholt, 1971. 206 pp. Discussion of factors involved in the development of a homosexual personality; presents fallacies and refutes them with facts.

3894. McDermott, Sandra. FEMALE HOMOSEXUALITY: ITS NATURE AND CONFLICT. New York: Simon & Schuster, 1971. 224 pp. British study based on interviews with 250 women, describing how women are adapting their behavior to a changing sexual environment.

3895. McDonald, John Marshall. FEMALE SEXUALITY. Springfield, IL: C. C. Thomas, 1971.

3896. Mafud, Julio. LA REVOLUCIÓN SEXUAL ARGENTINA [THE ARGENTINIAN SEXUAL REVOLUTION]. Buenos Aires, Argentina:

Editorial Américalee, 1966. 133 pp.

3897. Money, John and Patricia Tucker. SEXUAL SIGNATURES: ON BEING A MAN OR A WOMAN. Boston, MA: Little, Brown, 1975. 250 pp.

3898. Nadol, Joanne. "He had Become What He Always Knew He Was—A Woman," JOHNS HOPKINS MAGAZINE, vol. 22 (Summer 1971), pp. 28-32. A history of transsexuality, discussing Freud's ideas on the origin of female neurosis.

3899. Nagero, Humberto. FEMALE SEXUALITY AND THE OEDIPUS COMPLEX. New York: Jason Aronson, 1975. 143 pp.

3900. Pauly, Ira B. "Female Transsexualism Parts I and II," ARCHIVES OF SEXUAL BEHAVIOR, vol. 3, no. 6 (Nov. 1974), pp. 487-526. Part I summarizes world literature on women who show a fixed preference for the masculine role; Part II deals with psychological evaluation and treatment of women who wish to become men.

3901. Pengelley, Eric T. SEX AND HUMAN LIFE. Reading, MA: Addison-Wesley, 1974. 267 pp.

3902. Pierson, Elaine Catherine and William V. D'Antonio. FEMALE AND MALE: DIMENSIONS OF HUMAN SEXUALITY. Philadelphia, PA: J. B. Lippincott, 1974. 349 pp.

3903. Radicalesbians. "Woman-Identified Woman," RADICAL THERAPIST, vol. 2 (April-May 1972), p. 11. Defines the concept of lesbianism and its place in the women's movement.

3904. Reed, Evelyn. "Is Biology Woman's Destiny?" New York: Pathfinder Press, 1972. 23 pp.

3905. Reuben, David R. ANY WOMAN CAN: LOVE AND SEXUAL FULFILLMENT FOR THE SINGLE, WIDOWED, DIVORCED . . . AND MARRIED. New York: McCay, 1971. 364 pp.

3906. Rosenberg, Charles E. "Sexuality, Class and Role in Nineteenth Century America," AMERICAN QUARTERLY, vol. 25, no. 2 (May 1973), pp. 131-153. Discussion of nineteenth century medical writings on the physical and emotional effects of sex.

3907. Rule, Jane. LESBIAN IMAGES. Garden City, NY: Doubleday, 1975. 246 pp.

3908. Saghir, Marcel T. and Eli Robins. MALE AND FEMALE HOMOSEXUALITY: A COMPREHENSIVE INVESTIGATION. Baltimore, MD: Williams & Wilkins, 1973. 341 pp. Comparisons of the sexual, occupational, political, and social life of homosexuals and heterosexuals.

3909. Saponaro, Aldo. LA VIDA SEXUAL DE LA MUJER. Barcelona, España: Editorial De Vechi, S. A., 1969. 188 pp. Women's sexuality. Originally published in Italian.

3910. Schaefer, Leah Cahan. WOMEN AND SEX: SEXUAL EXPERIENCES AND REACTIONS OF A GROUP OF THIRTY WOMEN AS TOLD TO A FEMALE PSYCHOTHERAPIST. New York: Pantheon Books, 1973. 288 pp. Study of sexual histories and feelings about sex.

3911. "Sexual Rights and Responsibilities: Expanding the Boundaries of Human Sexuality," CURRENT, no. 182 (April 1976), pp. 18-22. Nine

statements which add the dimension of social and societal responsibility
to the consideration of sexuality.

3912. Shope, David F. INTERPERSONAL SEXUALITY. Philadelphia, PA:
Saunders, 1975. 344 pp.

3913. Silva, Jorge Garcia. "Two Cases of Female Homosexuality: A Critical
Study of Sigmund Freud and Helene Deutsch," CONTEMPORARY
PSYCHOANALYSIS, vol. 11, no. 3 (July 1975), pp. 357-376.

3914. Singer, Irving. THE GOALS OF HUMAN SEXUALITY. New York:
W. W. Norton, 1973. 219 pp. Argues that emphasis on "sensuous"
lovemaking overlooks passionate sexuality, a more intense experience
that involves emotions as well as physical response.

3915. Stockham, Alice B. THE LOVER'S WORLD: A WHEEL OF LIFE. New
York: Fenno, 1903. 376 pp. Enlightening sex manual which takes into
account the emancipation and equality of women.

3916. Stopes, Marie Carmichael. MARRIED LOVE: A NEW CONTRIBUTION
TO THE SOLUTION OF SEX DIFFICULTIES. New York: Putnam,
1931. 165 pp.

3917. Taylor, Kathryn. "Generations of Denial: 75 Short Biographies of
Women in History." New York: Times Change Press, 1971. 64 pp.
Biographies of women who were lesbians.

3918. Thomas, William I. SEX AND SOCIETY: STUDIES IN THE SOCIAL
PSYCHOLOGY OF SEX. New York: Arno Press, 1974. 325 pp.
Reprint of 1907 edition.

3919. "Transsexuals in Limbo: The Search for a Legal Definition of Sex,"
MARYLAND LAW REVIEW, vol. 31, no. 3 (1971), pp. 236-254.
Sexual categories not as discrete and distinct as once thought to be.

3920. Wells, John Warren. BEYOND GROUP SEX: THE NEW SEXUAL
LIFE-STYLES. New York: Dell Books, 1972. 236 pp.

3921. Whittaker, Peter. THE AMERICAN WAY OF SEX. New York: G. P.
Putnam's Sons, 1974. 256 pp. Interviews with women in the
massage-parlor trade.

3922. Wilson, Samuel T., Richard L. Row, and Lucy E. Autrey. READINGS IN
HUMAN SEXUALITY. St. Paul, MN: West Publishing, 1975. 249 pp.

3923. Wolfe, Charlotte. LOVE BETWEEN WOMEN. New York: Harper & Row,
1972. 303 pp. Case Studies.

3924. Wolfe, Linda. PLAYING AROUND: WOMEN AND EXTRAMARITAL
SEX. New York: William Morrow, 1975. 248 pp.

3925. Wysor, Bettie. THE LESBIAN MYTH: INSIGHTS AND
CONVERSATION. New York: Random House, 1974. 438 pp.

F. Class and Status

"Women are ever in extremes; they are either better or worse than men."
                                        —Jean de La Bruyère

*"In all societies women have played a much more important role than their menfolk
are generally ready to admit."*
                                        —Ashley Montagu

3926. Aitken, Judith. WOMAN'S PLACE: A STUDY OF THE CHANGING
       ROLE OF WOMEN IN NEW ZEALAND. New York: International
       Publication Services, 1976.
3927. Almquist, Elizabeth M. "Untangling the Effects of Race and Sex: The
       Disadvantaged Status of Black Women," SOCIAL SCIENCE
       QUARTERLY, vol. 56, no. 1 (June 1975), pp. 129-142.
3928. Āmūzgār, Habīb-Allāh. MAQĀM-I E ZAN DAR ĀFARĪNĪSH [THE
       PLACE OF WOMAN IN CREATION]. Tehran, Iran: Eghbal, 1966.
       528 pp.
3929. Appadorai, Angadipuram, ed. STATUS OF WOMEN IN SOUTH ASIA.
       Washington, D.C.: Zenger Publications, 1976. Reprint of 1954 edition.
3930. Arafat, Ibtihaj Said and Betty Yorburg. THE NEW WOMEN:
       ATTITUDES, BEHAVIOR, AND SELF-IMAGE. Columbus, OH:
       Charles E. Merrill, 1976. 160 pp. Examines the changing status of
       women historically and in contemporary United States; focuses on
       today's educated, middle-class young woman and discusses the
       evolution of new personality and behavior patterns.
3931. "Asian Women," BULLETIN OF CONCERNED ASIAN SCHOLARS,
       vol. 7, no. 1 (Jan.-March 1975), pp. 3-70. Special Issue. Contributors
       include Vera Schwartz, Jan MacKinnon, Steve MacKinnon, Agnes
       Smedley, Jan Price, Norma Diamond, Phyllis Andors, Gail Omvedt,
       Susan Moody, Sharayu Mhatre, Maria Mies, Bhaskar Jadhav, Dongar
       Javre, and Betsey Cobb. See also "Supplement: Women in Asia Part II."
3932. Atkinson, Dorothy. "Soviet Women Today," NATION, vol. 221, no. 6
       (Sept. 6, 1975), pp. 166-169. Summarizes the political, economic, and
       social status of women in the Soviet Union.
3933. Bay, Edna, Nancy Hafkin, and African Studies Association Committee on
       Women, eds. "Women in Africa," THE AFRICAN STUDIES REVIEW,
       vol. 18, no. 3 (Dec. 1975), pp. 1-120. Special Issue. Contributors
       include Diane Barthel, Jean O'Barr, Stephanie Urdang, Margaret
       Strobel, United Nations Economic Commission for Africa—Women's
       Research and Training Centre, Christine Oppong, Christine Okali,
       Beverly Houghton, Judith Olmstead, and Audrey Wipper.
3934. "The Black Woman 1975," THE BLACK SCHOLAR, vol. 6, no. 6 (March
       1975), pp. 1-36. Symposium. Contributors include Frances M. Beal,
       Charmeynne D. Nelson, Maulana Ron Karenga, Julian Bond, and Sékou
       Touré.

3935. Braxton, Bernard. WOMEN, SEX, AND RACE: A REALISTIC VIEW OF SEXISM AND RACISM. Washington, D.C.: Verta Press, 1973. 227 pp. Compares the similarities in social definition, historical perspective, and myth-making between blacks and women.

3936. "The Changing Role of Women in Society," HIGH SCHOOL JOURNAL, vol. 59, no. 1 (Oct. 1975), pp. 1-45. Special Issue. Contributors include Mary Turner Lane, Anne Flowers, Amanda J. Smith, Elizabeth Duncan Koontz, and Betsy Levin.

3937. Ciobanu, Lina. "Women in Public Life," WORLD MARXIST REVIEW, vol. 18, no. 3 (March 1975), pp. 132-139. Status of women in Rumanian society.

3938. Committee of Bulgarian Women. "The Status of Women in the People's Republic of Bulgaria." Sofia, Bulgaria: Committee of Bulgarian Women, 1972. 33 pp.

3939. Cressy, Earl Herbert. DAUGHTERS OF CHANGING JAPAN. Westport, CT: Greenwood Press, 1975. 305 pp. Reprint of 1955 edition. Thoughts, feelings, and experiences of young post-World War II Japanese women.

3940. Dalla Costa, Mariarosa and Selma James. "The Power of Women and the Subversion of the Community." Bristol, England: Falling Wall Press, 1973. 78 pp. Reprint of 1972 edition of "Women and the Subversion of the Community," by Mariarosa Dalla Costa; and 1952 edition of "A Woman's Place," by Selma James.

3941. Davies, C. Shane and Gary L. Fowler. "The Disadvantaged Black Female Household Head: Migrants to Indianapolis," SOUTHEASTERN GEOGRAPHER, vol. 11 (Nov. 1971), pp. 113-120.

3942. De Leeuw, Hendrik. WOMAN: THE DOMINANT SEX. New York: T. Yoseloff, 1957. 240 pp.

3943. de Souza, Alfred. WOMEN IN CONTEMPORARY INDIA: TRADITIONAL IMAGES AND CHANGING ROLES. Delhi, India: Manohar Book Service, 1975. 264 pp.

3944. Epstein, Louis M. THE JEWISH MARRIAGE CONTRACT: A STUDY IN THE STATUS OF THE WOMAN IN JEWISH LAW. New York: Arno Press, 1973. 316 pp. Reprint of 1927 edition.

3945. Falk, William W. and Arthur G. Cosbey. "Women and the Status Attainment Process," SOCIAL SCIENCE QUARTERLY, vol. 56, no. 2 (Sept. 1975), pp. 307-314.

3946. Felson, Marcus and David Knoke. "Social Status and the Married Woman," JOURNAL OF MARRIAGE AND THE FAMILY, vol. 36, no. 3 (Aug. 1974), pp. 516-521. Study concluding that status is generally derived from male characteristics—whether spouse or father—and does not generally consider female attainment.

3947. Ferriss, Abbott L. INDICATORS OF TRENDS IN THE STATUS OF AMERICAN WOMEN. Scranton, PA: Basic Books, 1971. 451 pp.

3948. Garnett, Lucy Mary Jane. "Women under Islam: Their Social Status and Legal Rights," 19TH CENTURY (London), vol. 37 (Jan. 1895), pp. 57-70.

3949. Gedge, Evelyn Clara and Mithan Chokski, eds. WOMEN IN MODERN

INDIA. Westport, CT: Hyperion Press, 1976. 161 pp. Reprint of 1929 edition. Collection of 15 papers by Indian women, each renowned in her chosen field, regarding the status of women.

3950. Giele, Janet Z. and Audrey C. Smock. WOMAN: ROLES AND STATUS IN EIGHT COUNTRIES. New York: Wiley Interscience, 1976.

3951. Hate, Chandrakala Anandrao. CHANGING STATUS OF WOMEN IN POST-INDEPENDENCE INDIA. Bombay, India: Allied Pubs., 1969. 284 pp.

3952. Henry, Frances and Pamela Wilson. "Status of Women in Caribbean Societies: An Overview of Their Social, Economic, and Sexual Roles," SOCIAL AND ECONOMIC STUDIES, vol. 24, no. 2 (June 1975), pp. 165-198. Survey of available literature on women in Caribbean culture.

3953. Hong, Lawrence K. "The Role of Women in the People's Republic of China: Legacy and Change," SOCIAL PROBLEMS, vol. 23, no. 5 (June 1976), pp. 545-557.

3954. James, Selma. "Sex, Race and Class." Bristol, England: Falling Wall Press, 1975.

3955. Jimenez, Maria de Refugio Llamas, Dolores Castro de Peñaloza, and Lilia Flores Porras. "Mujer: La Mitad Oscura de la Vida [Woman: The Uncertain Half of Life]," Mexico: Talleres Rotograficos Zaragoza, 1975. 60 pp. Pictorial essay on women's roles in society.

3956. Lagadinova, Yelena. "Status of Women—A Criterion of Social Progress," WORLD MARXIST REVIEW, vol. 18, no. 7 (July 1975), pp. 108-114.

3957. Lahar, Pnina. "The Status of Women in Israel—Myth and Reality," AMERICAN JOURNAL OF COMPARATIVE LAW, vol. 22, no. 1 (Winter 1974), pp. 107-129. Expresses hope that the myth of total equality between the sexes in Israel can be achieved.

3958. Lebra, Joyce, Joy Paulson, and Elizabeth Powers, eds. WOMEN IN CHANGING JAPAN. Boulder, CO: Westview Press, 1976. 322 pp. Collection of essays; includes a 17-page bibliography.

3959. LITERACY DISCUSSION, vol. 6, no. 4 (Winter 1975/1976), pp. 1-162. Special Issue. Contributors include Helvi Sipila, Helen Calloway, Hilda Kokuhirwa, K. D. Sharma, Carla Clason, Paula Campos de Rozsavolgyi, Omar Mustaffa-Kedah, Ester Boserup, and Christina Liljencrantz.

3960. May, Stella B. MEN, MAIDENS, AND MANTILLAS: THE CHANGING ROLE OF WOMEN IN LATIN AMERICA. New York: Gordon Press, 1976.

3961. Ntantala, Phyllis. AN AFRICAN TRAGEDY: THE BLACK WOMAN UNDER APARTHEID. Detroit, MI: Agascha Productions, 1976.

3962. Nyirasafari, Gaudentia. "L'évolution de statut de la femme au Rwanda [Evolution of Women's Status in Rwanda]," LES CARNETS DE L'ENFACE, vol. 27 (July-Sept. 1974), pp. 84-106.

3963. Okamura, Masu. "Women's Status." Tokyo, Japan: International Society for Educational Information, 1973. 87 pp.

3964. Pescatello, Ann, ed. "The Changing Role of Women in Latin America," JOURNAL OF INTERAMERICAN STUDIES AND WORLD AFFAIRS, vol. 17, no. 4 (Nov. 1975), pp. 379-516. Special Issue. Contributors include Cynthia Jeffress Little, Virginia Olesen, Cornelia

B. Flora, Evelyn G. Schipske, Shirley Harkness, Patricia Piron de Lwein, Steffin W. Schmidt, Felicia R. Madiera, and Paul Singer.

3965. Ramabai Sarasvati, Pundita. THE HIGH CASTE HINDU WOMAN. Westport, CT: Hyperion Press, 1976. 142 pp. Reprint of 1901 edition.

3966. Rubenstein, Roberta. "The Third World's Second Citizens," THE PROGRESSIVE (March 1975), pp. 33-35. The status of women in Africa.

3967. Sanday, Peggy R. "Toward a Theory of the Status of Women," AMERICAN ANTHROPOLOGIST, vol. 75, no. 5 (Oct. 1973), pp. 1682-1700. Status is defined in terms of political and economic rights accruing to women.

3968. Schlegel, Alice Hess. MALE DOMINANCE AND FEMALE AUTONOMY: DOMESTIC AUTHORITY IN MATRILINEAL SOCIETIES. New Haven, CT: HRAF Press, 1972. 206 pp. Women tend to have greater autonomy in matrilineal societies than in patrilineal.

3969. Seller, Maxine S. "Beyond the Stereotype: A New Look at the Immigrant Woman," JOURNAL OF ETHNIC STUDIES, vol. 3, no. 1 (Spring 1975), pp. 59-71. Explores how three women from patriarchal cultures overcame the stereotypes to successfully find careers in the United States.

3970. Shaffer, Helen B. "Status of Women," EDITORIAL RESEARCH REPORTS, no. 5 (1973), pp. 565-585.

3971. Sontag, Susan. "The Third World of Women," PARTISAN REVIEW, vol. 40, no. 2 (1973), pp. 180-206. Observations on the power and position of women, based on responses to a questionnaire by LIBRE, a new Spanish language political and literary quarterly.

3972. "Special Section on Women's Sociology," ACTA SOCIOLOGICA, vol. 18, no. 2-3 (1975), pp. 142-244. Contributors include Berit As, Rolv Mikkel Blakar, Irja Eskola, Elina Haavio-Manilla, Erik Gronseth, and Jo Freeman.

3973. Streatfield, Guy, ed. "Women and the Future," FUTURES, vol. 7, no. 5 (Oct. 1975), pp. 362-441. Special Issue. Contributors include Magda Cordell, John McHale, Alexander Szalai, Marjorie Mbilinyi, Marie Jahoda, George Keller, and Pamela Sargeant.

3974. "Supplement: Women in Asia Part II," BULLETIN OF CONCERNED ASIAN SCHOLARS, vol. 7, no. 4 (Oct.-Dec. 1975), pp. 41-65. Contributors include Phyllis Andors, Miyamoto Yuriko, and Yamazaki Tomoko. See also "Asian Women."

3975. U.S. Center for International Women's Year. THE YEAR THAT BECAME A DECADE: THE LIFE AND TIMES OF THE U.S. CENTER FOR INTERNATIONAL WOMEN'S YEAR, 1975. Washington, D.C.: U.S. Center for I.W.Y., 1976. 149 pp. Background and activities of the Center; brief overview of the Conference in Mexico City.

3976. U.S. Citizens Advisory Council on the Status of Women. WOMEN IN 1975. Washington, D.C.: SUDOC, GPO, 1976. 142 pp. Excellent reference book on the status of women.

3977. ———. "Women in 1974." Washington, D.C.: SUDOC, GPO, 1975. 65 pp.

3978. ———. "Women in 1973." Washington, D.C.: SUDOC, GPO, 1974. 85 pp.
3979. ———. "Women in 1972." Washington, D.C.: SUDOC, GPO, 1973. 78 pp.
3980. ———. "Women in 1971." Washington, D.C.: SUDOC, GPO, 1972. 61 pp.
3981. Wakefield, Priscilla Bell. REFLECTIONS ON THE PRESENT
   CONDITION OF THE FEMALE SEX: WITH SUGGESTIONS FOR
   ITS IMPROVEMENT. New York: Garland Publishing, 1974. 195 pp.
   Reprint of 1798 edition.
3982. Wipper, Audrey. "The Politics of Sex," AFRICAN STUDIES REVIEW,
   vol. 41 (1971), pp. 463-482.
3983. "Woman's Estate: A Review Symposium," SUMMATION, vol. 4, no. 1-2
   (Spring-Fall 1974), pp. 62-90. Discussions of economic, political, and
   social status of women based on Juliet Mitchell's WOMAN'S ESTATE.
   Contributors include Quess Barclay, Mary Anne Hering, Peter Lyman,
   Dorothy Remy, and Karen Sachs.
3984. Women for Women. Research and Study Group. WOMEN FOR WOMEN,
   BANGLADESH, 1975. Dacca, Bangladesh: Univ. Press, 1975. 248 pp.
3985. Wrochno, Krystyna. WOMAN IN POLAND. Warsaw, Poland: Interpress
   Publishers, 1969. 107 pp.

G. Education and Socialization

*"When you educate a man you educate an individual; when you educate a woman
you educate a whole family."*
                                                    —Robert Morrison MacIver

3986. Ahlum, Carol and Jacqueline M. Fralley, comps. HIGH SCHOOL
   FEMINIST STUDIES. Old Westbury, NY: Feminist Press, 1976. 192
   pp. 25 English and social studies course syllabi.
3987. Ambassade de France. Service de Presse et d'Information. FRENCH
   WOMEN AND EDUCATION. New York: Service de Presse et
   d'Information, 1974.
3988. Beecher, Catherine Esther. "Suggestions Respecting Improvements in
   Education, Presented to the Trustees of the Hartford Female Seminary
   and Published at Their Request." Hartford, CT: Packard & Butler,
   1829. 84 pp.
3989. Borris, Maria. DIE BENACHTEILIGUNG DER MÄDCHEN IN
   SCHULEN DER BUNDESREPUBLIK UND WESTBERLIN [THE
   DISADVANTAGE OF GIRLS IN SCHOOLS IN THE FEDERAL
   REPUBLIC AND WEST BERLIN]. Frankfurt-am-Main, Germany:
   Europäischer Verlagsanstalt, 1972. 159 pp.
3990. Boslooper, Thomas and Marcia Hayes. THE FEMININITY GAME. New
   York: Stein & Day, 1974. 256 pp. Sexism in sports, and how early
   conditioning of girls causes them to abjure competitive sports in the
   fear that competition is not ladylike.
3991. Cassirer, Sidonie, ed. FEMALE STUDIES IX: TEACHING ABOUT
   WOMEN IN THE FOREIGN LANGUAGES. Old Westbury, NY:

Feminist Press, 1976. 256 pp. Contains bibliographies of suggested reading; impact of women's studies on foreign language curriculum; focuses on Spanish, French, and German. 90 course outlines.

3992. Chmaj, Betty, ed. IMAGE, MYTH AND BEYOND: AMERICAN WOMEN AND AMERICAN STUDIES, PARTS 2 AND 3. Pittsburgh, PA: KNOW, Inc., 1974. 404 pp. Section 1 discusses the status of women; section 2 consists of course outlines and programs; and section 3 contains 13 essays on women's studies.

3993. Cohen, Audrey C. "Women and Higher Education: Recommendations for Change," PHI DELTA KAPPAN, vol. 53, no. 3 (Nov. 1971), pp. 164-167. Discusses some of the roadblocks facing women, with recommendations for reforms.

3994. Crase, Darrell. "A New Dimension in Education: Girls' and Women's Sports," NASSP BULLETIN, vol. 59, no. 394 (Nov. 1975), pp. 104-109. Status report on movement toward equal opportunity for male and female high school athletes.

3995. Douvan, Elizabeth. "Higher Education and Feminine Socialization," NEW DIRECTIONS FOR HIGHER EDUCATION, vol. 3, no. 1 (Spring 1975), pp. 37-50. Postulates that gender differences, whether physiological or learned, affect the way people learn and how they apply that education.

3996. Dunkle, Margaret C. and Bernice Sandler. "Sex Discrimination Against Students: Implications of TITLE IX of the Education Amendments of 1972." Washington, D.C.: Association of American Colleges, Project on the Status and Education of Women, 1975. 28 pp. Includes footnotes documenting several relevant court cases.

3997. Edgeworth, Maria and Richard Lovell Edgeworth. PRACTICAL EDUCATION. New York: Garland Publishing, 1974. 775 pp. Reprint of 1798 edition.

3998. "Elements for a Dossier: Education and Womankind," PROSPECTS, vol. 5, no. 3 (1975), pp. 341-397. Special Section. Contributors include Margaret Mead, Sirimavo Bandaranaike, Jeanne Martin Cissé, Marie Eliou, Fay E. Saunders, Marie-Angélique Savane, Claudia Fonseca, Zoila Franco, and Galina Sergeeva.

3999. Fraser, Stewart E., ed. SEX, SCHOOLS, AND SOCIETY: INTERNATIONAL PERSPECTIVES. New York: John Wiley, 1972. 507 pp. Reference book on sex education in schools around the world.

4000. Frazier, Nancy and Myra Sadker. SEXISM IN SCHOOL AND SOCIETY. New York: Harper & Row, 1973. 215 pp. Focuses on sex role stereotyping at various educational levels.

4001. Gander, Mary. "Feminine and Masculine Role Stereotyping in Physical Education and Competitive Sports." Madison, WI: Univ. of Wisconsin-Extension, Center for Extension Programs in Education, 1975. 29 pp.

4002. Gordon, Sarah H. "Smith College Students: The First Ten Classes, 1879-1888," HISTORY OF EDUCATION QUARTERLY, vol. 15, no. 2 (Summer 1975), pp. 147-167. The family background, college life, and careers of Smith College students.

4003. Henderson, Jean Glidden and Algo D. Henderson. MS. GOES TO COLLEGE. Carbondale, IL: Southern Illinois Univ. Press, 1975. 224 pp. General guide book for women in college, covers both personal and academic areas.

4004. India. Ministry of Education and Social Welfare. "Educational Advancement and Socio-Economic Participation of Women in India." Prepared by Smt. C. Doraiswami. Arlington, VA: ERIC Document Reproduction Service, 1974. 38 pp.

4005. ———. "Misconceptions Influencing Nonformal Education for Women." Prepared by the Directorate of Nonformal (Adult) Education. Arlington, VA: ERIC Document Reproduction Service, 1975. 14 pp. Education does not equate with schooling and teachers; emphasis should focus on survival and decision making.

4006. Kashdin, Gladys S. "Lifelong Education for Women: General and Liberal Studies for Women Fulfilling Traditional Social Roles," PERSPECTIVES: A JOURNAL OF GENERAL & LIBERAL STUDIES, vol. 6, no. 3 (Winter 1974-1975), pp. 195-202.

4007. Kelman, Eugenie and Bonnie Staley. "The Returning Woman Student: Needs of an Important Minority Group on College Campuses." Arlington, VA: ERIC Document Reproduction Service, 1974. 21 pp. The special problems of women in college beyond traditional student age.

4008. Kilpatrick, James J. "And Some Are More Equal Than Others," THE AMERICAN SOCIOLOGIST, vol. 11, no. 2 (May 1976), pp. 85-93. Reprint of critique on "Guidelines for Creating Positive Sexual and Racial Images in Educational Materials" (New York: Macmillan, 1975), with commentaries. Contributors include Jeanne Baldigo, Mary Jo Deegan, Susan Fernandez, Joan Huber, Marion Kilson, Norma J. Shepelak, and Charles V. Willie.

4009. King, Joe, Jr. "Woman/Society/Technology," MAN/SOCIETY/ TECHNOLOGY, vol. 35, no. 8 (May/June 1976), pp. 238-240. Advocates beginning industrial arts education for both sexes in elementary school, to discourage occupational stereotyping.

4010. Ladan, C. J. and Maxine M. Croaks. "Some Factors Influencing the Decision of Mature Women to Enroll for Continuing Education," CANADIAN COUNSELLOR, vol. 10, no. 1 (Oct. 1975), pp. 29-35. Study of the characteristics of mature women who enroll in continuing education, including goals, motives, and obstacles perceived.

4011. Lamel, Linda. "Career Expressions of Women." Arlington, VA: ERIC Document Reproduction Service, 1974. 9 pp. Stereotyped role models in textbooks and in the schools tends to limit students' perceptions of career choices.

4012. Lewis, Ida Belle. "The Education of Girls in China." New York: Columbia Univ. Teachers College, 1919. 92 pp. A contemporary's account of changes in female education toward the end of the Imperial era.

4013. Long, Huey B. "Women's Education in Colonial America," ADULT EDUCATION, vol. 25, no. 2 (Winter 1975), pp. 90-106. Suggests that though women's education was not as formal as men's, through night school, apprenticeship, and home, it was richer than previously supposed.

4014. McGraw-Hill Book Company. "Guidelines for Equal Treatment of the Sexes in McGraw-Hill Book Company Publications." New York: McGraw-Hill, 1974. 16 pp. Elimination of sexist phrases in educational and reference materials.

4015. Macleod, Jennifer S. and Sandra T. Silverman. YOU WON'T DO: WHAT TEXTBOOKS ON U.S. GOVERNMENT TEACH HIGH SCHOOL GIRLS, with —SEXISM IN TEXTBOOKS: AN ANNOTATED SOURCE LIST OF 150+ STUDIES AND REMEDIES. Pittsburgh, PA: KNOW Inc., 1973. 118 pp.

4016. Mitchell, Joyce Slayton. OTHER CHOICES FOR BECOMING A WOMAN. Pittsburgh, PA: KNOW, Inc., 1974. 227 pp. Encourages the view that nothing relevant to a high school woman's choices can be "taboo."

4017. National Association of Women Deans and Counselors. PROBLEMS AND OPPORTUNITIES CHALLENGING WOMEN TODAY. Washington, D.C.: National Association of Women Deans and Counselors, 1970.

4018. Nieto-Gomez, Anna, ed. "New Directions in Education: Estudios Femeniles de la Chicana." Los Angeles, CA: Univ. of California-Extension, Daytime Programs & Special Projects, 1974. 65 pp. Course outlines on "la mujer chicana" in history, literature, sociology, and higher education, including a 219-item bibliography to supplement outlines.

4019. Nowak, Marion. " 'How to Be a Woman': Theories on Female Education in the 1950's," JOURNAL OF POPULAR CULTURE, vol. 9, no. 1 (Summer 1975), pp. 77-83. Emphasis on femininity and women's proscribed role—wife and mother.

4020. Park, Roberta. "Concern for the Physical Education of the Female Sex from 1675 to 1800 in France, England, and Spain," RESEARCH QUARTERLY, vol. 45, no. 2 (May 1974), pp. 104-119.

4021. Peiser, Andrew. "The Education of Women: A Historical View," SOCIAL STUDIES, vol. 67, no. 2 (March-April 1976), pp. 69-72. History of the development of women's educational opportunities.

4022. Project on Equal Education Rights. "Summary of the Regulations for TITLE IX Education Amendments of 1972." Washington, D.C.: PEER, 1975. 4 pp.

4023. "The Proper Study of Womankind," TEACHERS COLLEGE RECORD, vol. 76, no. 3 (Feb. 1975), pp. 385-459. Special Issue. Contributors include Margaret C. Dunkle, Bernice Sandler, Patricia Albjerg Graham, Joan N. Burstyn, Ruth R. Corrigan, JoAnn Boydston, and Winona B. Ackerman.

4024. Renner, Richard R. "Feminine Education Abroad," INDEPENDENT SCHOOL BULLETIN, vol. 35, no. 3 (Feb. 1976), pp. 60-62. Focuses on sex-role differentiation in schools outside the United States.

4025. Rosenfelt, Deborah S., ed. FEMALE STUDIES X: STUDENT WORK—LEARNING TO SPEAK. Old Westbury, NY: Feminist Press,

1976. 256 pp. Some of the topics included are ballads, ideology of the Mormon Church, athletics and journalism, rural women in China.

4026. Ruth, Sheila and Rosanda Richards. "Intellect vs. Femininity or Men Seldom Make Passes at Girls Who Wear Glasses," GIFTED CHILD QUARTERLY, vol. 18, no. 3 (Autumn 1974), pp. 182-187.

4027. Scholtz, Nelle Tumlin, Judith Sosebee Prince, and Gordon Porter Miller. HOW TO DECIDE: A GUIDE FOR WOMEN. New York: College Entrance Examination Board, 1976. 128 pp. How-to workbook for building decision-making skills in both personal decisions and professional choices.

4028. Schramm, Sarah Slavin, ed. FEMALE STUDIES EIGHT. Pittsburgh, PA: KNOW, Inc., 1975.

4029. Shafer, Wilma C., ed. "Realizing Human Potential: Focus on Women," EDUCATIONAL HORIZONS, vol. 52, no. 2 (Winter 1973-1974), pp. 51-101. Contributors include Elizabeth Janeway, Ronald L. Podeschi, Phyllis J. Podeschi, Helen W. Diamond, Norma D. Feshbach, K. Patricia Cross, Elizabeth A. Greenleaf, Ann D. Knutson, Cecelia Zissis, Ruth Hochstetler, Vardine Moore, and Floyd G. Delon.

4030. ———. "Realizing Human Potential: Focus on Women II," EDUCATIONAL HORIZONS, vol. 52, no. 3 (Spring 1974), pp. 107-142. Contributors include Cynthia Fuchs Epstein, Carson M. Bennett, E. Paul Torrance, Nancy Knaak, Frances A. Plotsky, Alvenia L. Scriven, and Michael Y. Nunnery.

4031. Smith, Amanda J. "Combatting the Cinderella Syndrome: How To Educate Women for Today's World," COMMUNITY COLLEGE REVIEW, vol. 3, no. 1 (June 1975), pp. 6-13. Recommends more realistic life-planning for women.

4032. Sprung, Barbara. NON-SEXIST EDUCATION FOR YOUNG CHILDREN: A PRACTICAL GUIDE. Englewood Cliffs, NJ: Citation Press, 1975. 128 pp. Focuses on the pre-school, kindergarten, and primary age children.

4033. "TITLE IX of the Education Amendments of 1972—A Summary of the Implementing Regulation." Washington, D.C.: National Foundation for the Improvement of Education, 1976. 21 pp.

4034. Wasi, Muriel. EDUCATED WOMAN IN INDIA TODAY. New York: McGraw-Hill, 1973.

4035. Watson, Barbara Bellow, ed. WOMEN'S STUDIES: THE SOCIAL REALITIES. New York: Harper & Row, 1976. 225 pp. Collection of readings covering the fields of psychology, anthropology, history of ideas, and the history of two distinct periods in the women's movement: women's suffrage and current women's liberation.

4036. Wisconsin. Dept. of Public Instruction. State Superintendent's Advisory Task Force on Freedom for Individual Development. "Final Report of the Sex Role Stereotyping Sub-Task Force." Madison, WI: Dept. of Public Instruction, 1976. 96 pp. Discusses the problems caused by sex-role stereotyping in the schools and suggests plan for eliminating the practices. Includes a 66-citation annotated bibliography and list of additional teaching materials, by Barbara Roberts.

4037. Wolley, Hannah. THE GENTLEWOMAN'S COMPANION, OR A GUIDE TO THE FEMALE SEX: CONTAINING DIRECTIONS OF BEHAVIOR IN ALL PLACES . . . FROM THEIR CHILDHOOD DOWN TO OLD AGE. . . . WITH LETTERS AND DISCOURSES UPON ALL OCCASIONS . . . WHEREUNTO IS ADDED, A GUIDE FOR COOKMAIDS, DAIRYMAIDS, ETC. London, England, 1675. unpaged.

4038. Wollstonecraft, Mary. THOUGHTS ON THE EDUCATION OF DAUGHTERS: WITH REFLECTIONS ON FEMALE CONDUCT, IN THE MORE IMPORTANT DUTIES OF LIFE. New York: Garland Publishing, 1974. 160 pp. Reprint of 1787 edition.

H. Women in Education

"Women were surely intended to be beautiful, and it is a low trick on the part of Creation to make some of them ravishing and to give Phi Beta keys to the rest of us as a sop."

—*Marjorie Rawlings*

"Teaching is not a lost art, but the regard for it is a lost tradition."
—*Jacques Martin Barzun*

4039. Aggarwal, J. C. INDIAN WOMEN: EDUCATION AND STATUS (INCLUDING MAJOR RECOMMENDATIONS OF THE REPORT OF THE NATIONAL COMMITTEE ON THE STATUS OF WOMEN IN INDIA, 1917-1974). New Delhi, India: Arya Book Depot, 1976. 106 pp.

4040. Anderson, Ellen, ed. "Graduate and Professional Education of Women." Washington, D.C.: American Association of University Women, 1974. 94 pp. Proceedings of AAUW Conference, May 9-10, 1974.

4041. Anderson, Kitty. "Women and the Universities: A Changing Pattern." London, England: Bedford College, 1963. 19 pp.

4042. Angrist, Shirley S. and Elizabeth M. Almquist. CAREERS AND CONTINGENCIES: HOW COLLEGE WOMEN JUGGLE WITH GENDER. Port Washington, NY: Kennikat Press, 1975. 269 pp. Study of career choices of 87 women during their college years.

4043. Baylor, Ruth M. ELIZABETH PALMER PEABODY: KINDERGARTEN PIONEER. Philadelphia, PA: Univ. of Philadelphia Press, 1965. 228 pp. Educator devoted to establishing kindergarten as an American educational institution.

4044. Beecher, Catherine Esther. "The Evils Suffered by American Women and American Children." New York: Harper & Bros., 1846. 36 pp. The causes and the remedy (i.e. education) presented in an address to meetings of ladies in New York and other cities.

4045. Bunkle, P., N. Chick, A. D. M. Glass, M. E. Gordon, E. D. Penny, P. E. Penny, D. R. Perley, J. E. Perley, and J. E. Wells. "Women in Higher

Education." Palmerston North, New Zealand: Inter-University Committee for Sex Equality in Education, 1974. 60 pp. Report to Women's Rights Committee, New Zealand House of Representatives, on behalf of SEE.

4046. Burstyn, Joan N. "Catherine Beecher and the Education of American Women," NEW ENGLAND QUARTERLY, vol. 67, no. 3 (Sept. 1974), pp. 386-403. Excellent article on Beecher's contributions to women's education.

4047. ———. "Education and Sex: The Medical Case Against Higher Education for Women, 1870-1900," PROCEEDINGS OF THE AMERICAN PHILOSOPHICAL SOCIETY, vol. 117, no. 2 (1973), pp. 76-89. The physiological arguments put forth by anthropologists and doctors on the harm education would do to women's reproductive capacities.

4048. Carnegie Commission on Higher Education. OPPORTUNITIES FOR WOMEN IN HIGHER EDUCATION: THEIR CURRENT PARTICIPATION. New York: Carnegie Foundation, 1973. 282 pp. Description of the continuing trends of increased participation of women in graduate studies and teaching.

4049. Cary, Meredith. "Literature and Liberation," COLLEGE ENGLISH, vol. 38, no. 1 (Sept. 1976), pp. 62-67. Describes a course on literature for women's studies.

4050. Centra, John A. and Nancy M. Kuykendall. WOMEN, MEN, AND THE DOCTORATE. Princeton, NJ: Educational Testing Service, 1974. 218 pp. Compares status and professional development of women to that of men.

4051. Change Magazine, eds. WOMEN ON CAMPUS: THE UNFINISHED REVOLUTION. New Rochelle, NY: Change Magazine, 1975. 256 pp. Collection of essays on women as professionals in the field of higher education.

4052. Coppin, Fanny Jackson. REMINISCENCES OF SCHOOL LIFE, AND HINTS ON TEACHING. Philadelphia, PA: African Methodist Book Concern, 1913. 191 pp. Autobiographical.

4053. Cross, Barbara M., ed. EDUCATED WOMAN IN AMERICA: SELECTED WRITINGS OF CATHARINE (sic) BEECHER, MARGARET FULLER, AND M. CAREY THOMAS. New York: Teachers College Press, 1965. 175 pp.

4054. Davies, Emily. THOUGHTS ON SOME QUESTIONS RELATING TO WOMEN, 1860-1908. New York: Kraus Reprint, 1971. 227 pp. Reprint of 1910 edition. Collection of papers on women's higher education.

4055. Donovan, Frances R. THE SCHOOLMA'AM. New York: Arno Press, 1974. 355 pp. Reprint of 1938 edition.

4056. EDUCATIONAL RESEARCHER, vol. 4, no. 9 (Oct. 1975), pp. 3-32. Special issue on women, their roles and status in educational research and development. Contributors include Jean Lipman-Blumen, Patricia E. Stivers, Ann R. Tickamyer, Suzanne Brainard, Carol Kehr Tittle, Terry N. Saario, Elenor R. Denker, Noele Krenkel, and Elizabeth Steiner Maccia.

4057. Faithfull, Theodore. THE FUTURE OF WOMEN AND OTHER ESSAYS. La Cañada, CA: New Age Press, 1968. 183 pp.

4058. Farnsworth, Marjorie Whyte. THE YOUNG WOMAN'S GUIDE TO AN ACADEMIC CAREER. New York: Richards Rosen Press, 1974. 112 pp. Outlines the qualifications of, preparation for, and opportunities in academic careers for women.

4059. Feldman, Saul D. ESCAPE FROM THE DOLL'S HOUSE: WOMEN IN GRADUATE AND PROFESSIONAL SCHOOL EDUCATION. New York: McGraw-Hill, 1974. 208 pp. Excellent study of the professional education of women.

4060. Fénelon, François de Salignac de La Mothe-, abp. TREATISE ON THE EDUCATION OF DAUGHTERS. Boston, MA: Perkins & Marvin, 1831. 182 pp. Translated from the French.

4061. Fitzpatrick, Blanche. WOMEN'S INFERIOR EDUCATION. New York: Praeger Books, 1976. 208 pp. Analyzes options available to women in education, documents the use of tax revenues to support educational institutions discriminating against women, and recommends action to insure equal educational opportunity for women.

4062. Flewellen, W. C., Jr. and Frank A. DeZoort. "Prospects for Additions of Women and Members of Minority Groups to Faculties of Schools of Business," AMERICAN ASSEMBLY OF COLLEGIATE SCHOOLS OF BUSINESS BULLETIN (April 1974), pp. 1-5. Pessimistic outlook for significant change.

4063. Fulton, Margaret E. "Women in Education—Changing Roles and New Challenges," ENGLISH QUARTERLY, vol. 8, no. 4 (Winter 1975-1976), pp. 21-32.

4064. Furniss, W. Todd and Patricia Albjerg Graham, eds. WOMEN IN HIGHER EDUCATION. Washington, D.C.: American Council on Education, 1974. 336 pp. Analyses and suggestions of 38 leaders in government, education, law, etc., regarding decisions facing colleges and universities concerning women students, faculty members, and administrators.

4065. George Washington University. Institute for Educational Leadership. "Hierarchy, Power, and Women in Educational Policy Making." Prepared by the National Conference on Women in Educational Policy Making. Arlington, VA: ERIC Document Reproduction Service, 1975. 28 pp. Suggests that women must learn about the power structure in order to bring about changes within the schools.

4066. ———. "Women in Educational Leadership, An Open Letter to State Legislators." Prepared by the National Conference on Women in Educational Policy Making. Arlington, VA: ERIC Document Reproduction Service, 1975. 27 pp. Suggests changes that state legislators can effect in the educational structure to increase the percentage of women in educational policy making.

4067. Graham, Patricia Albjerg. "Women in Higher Education: A Biographical Enquiry." Arlington, VA: ERIC Document Reproduction Service, 1974. 12 pp. The history of women in education and other influences on current women students, faculty, and administration.

4068. Gross, Neal. THE SEX FACTOR AND THE MANAGEMENT OF SCHOOLS. Somerset, NJ: John Wiley & Sons, 1976. 304 pp. Focus on sex roles rather than the obstacles confronting women whose goals include high managerial positions.

4069. Harris, Seymour E. A STATISTICAL PORTRAIT OF HIGHER EDUCATION. New York: McGraw-Hill, 1972. 978 pp. Report from the Carnegie Commission.

4070. "The Higher Education of Women," IMPROVING COLLEGE AND UNIVERSITY TEACHING, vol. 20, no. 1 (Winter 1972), pp. 2-75. Special Issue. Contributors include Richard K. Morton, R. W. Fleming, Norah Willis Michener, Elbert Hubbard, Alexis de Toqueville, Lady Ogilvie, Frank H. Tucker, Charles Warnath, Jo Anne J. Trow, Roger Garrison, Eleanor F. Dolan, Virginia Senders, Dorothy H. Gambel, C. Warren Horland, Ronald Beasley, Bernice Brown Cronkhite, Constance Smith, Robert L. Loeffelbein, Phillip W. Semas, Ava Milam Clark, Audrey C. Cohen, Marion Royce, Madge Dawson, S. Shridevi, Maj-Britt Sandlund, Yoko Nuita, and Ruth M. Oltman.

4071. Hoffman, Leonore and Gloria De Sole, eds. "Careers and Couples: An Academic Question." New York: Modern Language Association Commission on the Status of Women in the Profession, 1976. 59 pp. Collection of 19 essays on efforts of academic couples to resolve personal and professional conflicts.

4072. Hoffman, Nancy, Cynthia Secor, and Adrian Tinsley, eds. FEMALE STUDIES 6: CLOSER TO THE GROUND, WOMEN'S CLASSES, CRITICISM, PROGRAMS 1972. Old Westbury, NY: Feminist Press, 1972. 256 pp. 22 essays on women's studies; emphasizes teaching of literature.

4073. Hopkins, Mary Alden. HANNAH MORE AND HER CIRCLE. New York: Longmans, 1947. 274 pp. In teaching the wild children of the Cheddar Hills of England, Hannah More and her sisters opened a new field for women.

4074. Hunter, Thelma. "Married Women in Academia: A Personal View," VESTES: AUSTRALIAN UNIVERSITIES REVIEW, vol. 18, no. 1 (June 1975), pp. 51-60. Case study of a woman professor.

4075. Hutchinson, Edward M. "International Women's Year Special Issue," CONVERGENCE: AN INTERNATIONAL JOURNAL OF EDUCATION, vol. 8, no. 1 (1975), pp. 1-109. Contributors include Ana Krajne, Sister Mary Ann Smith, Pumla Kisonkole, Raymond Smyke, Tatiana Nikolaeva, Mario Zolezzi Chocano, Rosalind Loring, Edris Bird, Runa Haukaa, Paul Lengrand, and Michael W. Murphy.

4076. Jex-Blake, Sophia. A VISIT TO SOME AMERICAN SCHOOLS AND COLLEGES. Westport, CT: Hyperion Press, 1976. 250 pp. Reprint of 1867 edition. The British feminist and physician records her impressions and conclusions from an intensive tour of leading coeducational institutions, including Oberlin and Antioch.

4077. Kelsall, Roger Keith. "Women and Teaching." London, England: Her Majesty's Stationery Office, 1963. 59 pp. Report of an independent Nuffield Survey following up on a large national survey of women who entered teaching in England and Wales at various dates pre-war and post-war.

4078. Kitch, Joanne, comp. "AFT Negotiates Change for College Women." Washington, D.C.: AFL-CIO, American Federation of Teachers, 1974. 14 pp.

4079. Koontz, Elizabeth Duncan. "The Best Kept Secret of the Past 5,000 Years: Women are Ready for Leadership in Education." Bloomington, IN: Phi Delta Kappa Educational Foundation, 1972. 47 pp.

4080. Lanier, Ruby J. BLANFORD BARNARD DOUGHERTY: MOUNTAIN EDUCATOR. Durham, NC: Duke Univ. Press, 1974. 282 pp.

4081. Lutes, Mrs. Della Thompson. COUNTRY SCHOOL-MA'AM. Boston, MA: Little, Brown, 1941. 328 pp. Autobiographical account of the author's 16th year when she taught in two rural Michigan schools during the 1880's.

4082. McAllester, Susan, comp. "A Case for Equity: Women in English Departments." Urbana, IL: National Council of Teachers of English, 1971. 94 pp. Articles originally appearing in COLLEGE ENGLISH.

4083. McGuigan, Dorothy Gies, ed. NEW RESEARCH ON WOMEN AND SEX ROLES. Ann Arbor, MI: Univ. of Michigan, Center for Continuing Education of Women, 1976. 404 pp. Includes 24 papers, 19 abstracts, reports on research in progress, and bibliographies.

4084. ———. NEW RESEARCH ON WOMEN: AT THE UNIVERSITY OF MICHIGAN. Ann Arbor, MI: Univ. of Michigan, Center for Continuing Education of Women, 1974. 289 pp. Proceedings of the Conference "New Research on Women." Publication cooperation by the National Coalition for Research on Women's Education and Development.

4085. ———. A SAMPLER OF WOMEN'S STUDIES; PAPERS BY SELMA JEAN COHEN (AND OTHERS). Ann Arbor, MI: Univ. of Michigan, Center for Continuing Education of Women, 1973. 116 pp.

4086. Mackinnon, Annette and Frances Gardner, eds. "The Molding of the Nonsexist Teacher," JOURNAL OF TEACHER EDUCATION, vol. 26, no. 4 (Winter 1975), pp. 293-359. Special Issue. Contributors include Ruth Alexander, Patricia Brown, Kathryn Cirinciones-Coles, F. C. Ellenburg, Mario D. Fantini, Asa G. Hilliard III, Suzanne Howard, Kathryn Garton, Leonard Kaplan, Shirley D. McCune, Marthea Matthews, Ruth H. Osborne, Sandford W. Reitman, Myra Sadker, David Sadker, and Barbara Schramm. The role of educators in eliminating sexism in schools.

4087. Maccia, Elizabeth Steiner, Martha Ann Coleman, Myrna Estep, and Trudy Miller Schiel, eds. WOMEN AND EDUCATION. Springfield, IL: C. C. Thomas, 1975. 381 pp.

4088. Marks, Jeannette. LIFE AND LETTERS OF MARY EMMA WOOLEY. Washington, D.C.: Public Affairs Press, 1955. 300 pp. President of Mount Holyoke for 37 years.

4089. Marting, Leeda and K. Sue Foley. "Women in Broadcast Education," JOURNAL OF BROADCASTING, vol. 19, no. 1 (Winter 1975), pp. 31-42. Study of the status of women in broadcast education.

4090. Matthews, Mildred. "The Life and Times of a Woman Administrator,"

AMERICAN VOCATIONAL JOURNAL, vol. 50, no. 6 (Sept. 1975), pp. 36-37, 39. Author's experiences as acting director of vocational education in Alaska.

4091. Morton, Lena Beatrice. MY FIRST SIXTY YEARS: PASSION AND WISDOM. New York: Philosophical Library, 1965. 175 pp. Autobiography of a Black woman who is head of the Division of Humanities and professor of English at Texas College.

4092. National Association of Women Deans and Counselors. FEMININITY, FEMINISM, AND EDUCATIONAL CHANGE. Washington, D.C.: NAWDC, 1971.

4093. National School Boards Association. "Women on School Boards: Report of Research Conducted for the National School Boards Association Commission on the Role of Women in Educational Governance." Evanston, IL: NSBA, 1974. 62 pp.

4094. Nixon, Mary and L. R. Rue. "Women Administrators and Women Teachers: A Comparative Study," ALBERTA JOURNAL OF EDUCATIONAL RESEARCH, vol. 21, no. 3 (Sept. 1975), pp. 196-206.

4095. O'Donoghue, Sister Mary Xaverius. MOTHER VINCENT WHITTY: WOMAN AND EDUCATOR IN A MASCULINE SOCIETY. Melbourne, Australia: Melbourne Univ. Press, 1972. 189 pp.

4096. "Opportunities for Professional Women in Vocational Education: How Equal?" AMERICAN VOCATIONAL JOURNAL, vol. 49, no. 8 (Nov. 1974), pp. 34-49, 93. Special Section. Contributors include Angelo C. Gillie, Sr., Elizabeth J. Simpson, Elizabeth Camp King, Mary Bach Kievit, Donne Grisham, and Carol Karasik.

4097. Partington, Geoffrey. WOMEN TEACHERS IN THE TWENTIETH CENTURY IN ENGLAND AND WALES. Berkshire, England: N.F.E.R. Publishing, 1976. 107 pp.

4098. Peters, David Wilbur. "The Status of the Married Woman Teacher." New York: AMS Press, 1972. 97 pp. Reprint of 1934 edition.

4099. Peters, Dianne S. "And Pleasantly Ignore My Sex." Ann Arbor, MI: Univ. of Michigan, Center for the Study of Higher Education, 1975. 43 pp. Academic women are "systematically excluded from society at large, from undergraduate, graduate, and doctoral study, from the academic marketplace, and finally from retirement benefits."

4100. Piper, David Warren. "Women in Higher Education." London, England: Univ. Teaching Methods Unit for Staff Development in Universities Programme, 1975. 80 pp.

4101. Rice, Joy K. "Continuing Education for Women, 1960-1975: A Critical Appraisal," EDUCATIONAL RECORD, vol. 56, no. 4 (Feb. 1975), pp. 240-249. Assesses patterns of education, as well as focuses of continuing education for women.

4102. Roberts, Joan I. "Informal Mechanisms Used to Impede the Changing Status of Women in Academe." Madison, WI: Wisconsin Coordinating Council of Women in Higher Education, 1975. 16 pp.

4103. Roberts, Joan I., ed. WOMEN SCHOLARS ON WOMEN: CHANGING PERCEPTION OF REALITY. New York: McKay, 1975.

4104. Robinson, Lora H. "Women's Studies: Courses and Programs for Higher Education." Washington, D.C.: American Association for Higher Education, 1973. 54 pp.
4105. Roby, Pamela Ann. "Vocational Education for Women." Arlington, VA: ERIC Document Reproduction Service, 1975. 63 pp. Analysis of the barriers confronting women seeking vocational education.
4106. Schuck, Victoria, ed. "A Symposium: Masculine Blinders in the Social Sciences," SOCIAL SCIENCE QUARTERLY, vol. 55, no. 3 (Dec. 1974), pp. 563-656. Contributors include Barbara Tovey, George Tovey, Patricia S. Kruppa, Carolyn Shaw Bell, Mary L. Shanley, and Cynthia Fuchs Epstein.
4107. Sexton, Patricia Cayo. WOMEN IN EDUCATION: PERSPECTIVES IN AMERICAN EDUCATION. Bloomington, IN: Phi Delta Kappa, 1976. 183 pp. Discusses the function and history of education of women, work roles, and manpower training.
4108. Smith, Margaret Ruth. "The Voyage of Esther Lloyd-Jones: Travels with a Pioneer," PERSONNEL AND GUIDANCE JOURNAL, vol. 54, no. 9 (May 1976), pp. 473-480. Interview with Esther Lloyd-Jones, pioneer in student personnel work.
4109. Steele, Marilyn. WOMEN IN VOCATIONAL EDUCATION. Arlington, VA: ERIC Document Reproduction Service, 1974. 154 pp. Review and analysis of data on vocational education programs for women, indicating that they tend to be concentrated in traditional female fields.
4110. Stephen, Barbara (Nightingale). EMILY DAVIES AND GIRTON COLLEGE. Westport, CT: Hyperion Press, 1976. 387 pp. Reprint of 1927 edition. The English educator and feminist whose campaign for women's educational rights laid the foundation for Britain's modern secondary and university system, and led to the founding of the first women's college of university rank, Girton College, Cambridge.
4111. Stiehm, Judith, ed. THE FRONTIERS OF KNOWLEDGE. Los Angeles, CA: Univ. of Southern California Press, 1976. Essays by six women in various professions, including their educational backgrounds and the status of women in each profession.
4112. Sullivan, John Cavanaugh. A STUDY OF THE SOCIAL ATTITUDES AND INFORMATION ON PUBLIC PROBLEMS OF WOMEN TEACHERS IN SECONDARY SCHOOLS. New York: AMS Press, 1972. 140 pp. Reprint of 1940 edition.
4113. Tevis, Julia A. SIXTY YEARS IN A SCHOOL ROOM: AN AUTOBIOGRAPHY OF MRS. JULIA A. TEVIS, PRINCIPAL OF SCIENCE HILL FEMALE ACADEMY. TO WHICH IS PREFIXED AN AUTOBIOGRAPHICAL SKETCH OF REV. JOHN TEVIS. Cincinnati, OH: Western Methodist Book Concern, 1878. 489 pp. Mrs. Tevis ran boarding schools for girls in the early nineteenth century.
4114. Thompson, Eleanor Wolf. EDUCATION FOR LADIES, 1830-1860: IDEAS ON EDUCATION IN MAGAZINES FOR WOMEN. London, England: King's Crown Press, 1947. 170 pp. Study of periodical literature on education for women.

4115. Tittle, Carol Kchr, Karen McCarthy, and Jane Faggen Steckler. WOMEN
AND EDUCATIONAL TESTING: A SELECTIVE REVIEW OF THE
RESEARCH LITERATURE AND TESTING PROCEDURES.
Princeton, NJ: Educational Testing Service, 1974. 154 pp. Examines
the two major forms of discrimination in testing: reinforcement of
sex-role stereotypes and restriction of individual choice.

4116. Tuke, Dame Margaret Janson. HISTORY OF BEDFORD COLLEGE FOR
WOMEN, 1849-1937. London, England: Oxford Univ. Press, 1939.
364 pp.

4117. United Nations. Educational, Scientific, and Cultural Organization.
WOMEN, EDUCATION, EQUALITY: A DECADE OF EXPERIMENT.
Paris, France: The UNESCO Press, 1975. 107 pp. Report on
experimental projects in Upper Volta, Nepal, and Chile designed to
promote equal educational opportunities for women.

4118. U.S. Dept. of Health, Education, and Welfare. Office of Education.
National Center for Educational Statistics. BARRIERS TO WOMEN'S
PARTICIPATION IN POSTSECONDARY EDUCATION, REVIEW OF
RESEARCH AND COMMENTARY AS OF 1973-1974. Washington,
D.C.: SUDOC, GPO, 1975.

4119. U.S. Dept. of Health, Education, and Welfare. Office of the Secretary.
Office for Civil Rights. "Elimination of Sex Discrimination in Athletic
Programs." Washington, D.C.: U.S. DHEW, 1975. 11 pp. Memo from
Peter E. Holmes, Director, Office for Civil Rights, to school
administrators, detailing first-year responsibilities under TITLE IX of
the Education Amendments of 1972.

4120. U.S. Dept. of Labor. Employment Standards Administration. Women's
Bureau. CONTINUING EDUCATION FOR WOMEN: CURRENT
DEVELOPMENTS. Washington, D.C.: SUDOC, GPO, 1974.

4121. Vancouver Women's Caucus. "Women Teachers and the Educational
Process or 'It's Something You Can Always Fall Back On'." Vancouver,
B.C.: Vancouver Women's Caucus, 1970. 5 pp.

4122. Wasserman, Elga, Arie Y. Lewin, and Linda H. Bleiweis, eds. WOMEN IN
ACADEMIA: EVOLVING POLICIES TOWARD EQUAL
OPPORTUNITIES. New York: Praeger Publishers, 1975. 169 pp.
Focuses on power balance where departments often have more power
than administration in hiring, promotion, and tenure practices.

4123. WELLESLEY COLLEGE, 1875-1975, A CENTURY OF WOMEN.
Wellesley, MA: Wellesley College, Centennial Office, 1975.

4124. West, Jane. THE ADVANTAGE OF EDUCATION; OR THE HISTORY
OF MARIA WILLIAMS. New York: Garland Publishing, 1974. 2 vols.
Reprint of 1793 edition.

4125. "Why Women Need Their Own MBA Programs," BUSINESS WEEK, no.
2319 (Feb. 23, 1974), pp. 102, 107. New Program at Simmons College,
Boston, emphasizing counseling to help women managers understand
how male-dominated business situations work.

4126. Wilson, Joan H. and Women's Studies Committee, eds. REPORT ON THE
WEST COAST WOMEN'S STUDIES CONFERENCE. Pittsburgh, PA:
KNOW, Inc., 1974.

4127. "Women's Place: A Special Issue," ATLANTIC MONTHLY (March 1970), pp. 81-126. Contributors include Anne Bernays, Benjamin Demott, Elizabeth Janeway, Catherine D. Bowen, Paula Stern, Diana Gerrity, Jane Harriman, Alice S. Rossi, Diane Schulder, and Sandy North.

I. Birth Control, Abortion, and Demography

"Regulations in my state of Connecticut permit an administrative board of three, upon a majority vote, to sterilize a person. Under the statute no notice need be given. The prospective victim cannot appeal the order or even demand an opportunity to be heard."

—Vance Oakley Packard

"There is an old saying here that a man must do three things during life: plant trees, write books, and have sons. I wish they would plant more trees and write more books."

—Luis Muñoz Marín

4128. Adler, Nancy E. "Emotional Responses of Women Following Therapeutic Abortion," SOCIAL PSYCHIATRY, vol. 10, no. 4 (Oct. 1, 1975), pp. 155-160. Responses are affected by social environment, and woman's personal concerns about the pregnancy and its termination.

4129. Alpern, David M. "Abortion and the Law," NEWSWEEK (March 3, 1975), pp. 18-19, 23-26, 29-30. Background on the trial of Dr. Kenneth C. Edelin for manslaughter in an abortion.

4130. Angell, Myra L., Sandra Kadylak, and Roger O. Ginn. "Feminine Stereotypes and the Use of Contraceptives," JOURNAL OF COLLEGE STUDENT PERSONNEL, vol. 16, no. 4 (July 1975), pp. 270-272. Use of contraceptives seemed to have no influence on women's perception of sex-role stereotypes.

4131. Arafat, Ibtihaj S. and Ruby M. Chireau. "The Psychological and Emotional Effects of Abortion." Arlington, VA: ERIC Document Reproduction Service, 1973. 54 pp. Demographic characteristics found to influence general attitudes toward abortion.

4132. Banks, Joseph A. and Olive Banks. PROSPERITY AND PARENTHOOD: A STUDY OF FAMILY PLANNING AMONG THE VICTORIAN MIDDLE CLASSES. London, England: Routledge & Kegan Paul, 1954. 240 pp.

4133. Beeson, Diane. "Women in Aging Studies: A Critique and Suggestions," SOCIAL PROBLEMS, vol. 23 (Oct. 1975), pp. 52-59. Review of the literature, finding that women are often ignored by gerontologists' studies.

4134. BIRTH CONTROL AND MORALITY IN NINETEENTH CENTURY AMERICA: TWO DISCUSSIONS. New York: Arno Press, 1972. 106

pp. Reprint of 1878 edition of "Fruits of Philosophy," by Charles Knowlton; and 1859 edition of "Moral Physiology," by Robert Dale Owen.

4135. Bloom, Philip M. "Modern Contraception: A Practical Guide to Scientific Birth Control." London, England: Delisle, 1961. 48 pp.

4136. Boulding, Elise, Shirley A. Nuss, Dorothy Lee Carson, and Michael A. Greenstein, eds. HANDBOOK OF INTERNATIONAL DATA ON WOMEN. Beverly Hills, CA: Sage, 1976. 468 pp.

4137. Chandrasekhar, Sripati. ABORTION IN A CROWDED WORLD: THE PROBLEM OF ABORTION WITH SPECIAL REFERENCE TO INDIA. London, England: Allen & Unwin, 1974. 184 pp.

4138. Chaney, Elsa M. "Women and Population," in POPULATION AND POLITICS: NEW DIRECTIONS IN POLITICAL SCIENCE, edited by Richard L. Clinton. Lexington, MA: Lexington Books, 1973. 320 pp. Probes the normative and methodological dimensions of population research and policy, population problems in less-advantaged and industrialized countries.

4139. Chernisk, Donna and Alan Foigold. "Birth Control Handbook." Montreal, Quebec: McGill Univ. Students' Society, 1970. 46 pp.

4140. Cohen, Marshall, Thomas Nagel, and Thomas Scanlon, eds. THE RIGHTS AND WRONGS OF ABORTION. Princeton, NJ: Princeton Univ. Press, 1974. 142 pp. Reprint of essays from PHILOSOPHY AND PUBLIC AFFAIRS by John Finnis, Judith Jarvis Thomson, Michael Tooley, and Roger Wertheimer.

4141. Dennett, Mary Ware. BIRTH CONTROL LAWS: SHALL WE KEEP THEM, CHANGE THEM, OR ABOLISH THEM? New York: De Capo Press, 1970. 309 pp. Reprint of 1926 edition. Intended to clarify public thought on the legislation of the time.

4142. Deyak, Timothy A. and V. Kerry Smith. "The Economic Value of Statute Reform: The Case of Liberalized Abortion," JOURNAL OF POLITICAL ECONOMY, vol. 84, no. 1 (Feb. 1976), pp. 83-99. Analysis of data from New York State Dept. of Health statistics on state of origin of women obtaining abortion in New York, indicates savings with liberalized laws of $12-30 million in travel costs.

4143. Dienes, C. Thomas. LAW, POLITICS, AND BIRTH CONTROL. New York: American Univ. Press Services, 1972. 374 pp. Tracing the historical development of American birth control policy, Dienes examines the dynamics through which the legal system responds to the demands of changing society.

4144. Dixon, Ruth B. "Women's Rights and Fertility," REPORTS ON POPULATION/FAMILY PLANNING, no. 17 (Jan. 1975), pp. 1-20. Argues the existence of a strong relationship between the exercise of women's rights and their reproductive behavior.

4145. Drysdale, Charles Vickery. THE SMALL FAMILY SYSTEM: IS IT INJURIOUS OR IMMORAL: WITH THIRTEEN DIAGRAMS OF POPULATION MOVEMENTS, ETC., AT HOME AND ABROAD. New York: B. W. Heubsch, 1914. 119 pp.

4146. Duncan, Gordon W., Richard D. Falb, and J. Joseph Speidel, eds. FEMALE STERILIZATION: PROGNOSIS FOR SIMPLIFIED OUTPATIENT PROCEDURES. New York: Academy Press, 1972. 199 pp. Workshop on Female Sterilization, Airlie House, 1971.

4147. Erickson, Nancy S. "Women and the Supreme Court: Anatomy is Destiny," BROOKLYN LAW REVIEW, vol. 41, no. 2 (Fall 1974), pp. 209-282. Discusses "sex plus theory;" if an employer can avoid liability by showing that he only discriminates against young women, old women, crippled women, blind women, and so on, but not *all* women, no woman is safe from discrimination.

4148. Falik, Marilyn. "The Impact of the Supreme Court Decision on Abortion: Political and Legislative Resistance vs. Court Reactions." Washington, D.C.: The Brookings Institute, 1974. 28 pp.

4149. Feldman, David Michael. MARITAL RELATIONS, BIRTH CONTROL, AND ABORTION IN JEWISH LAW. New York: Schocken Books, 1974. 322 pp. Reprint of 1968 edition.

4150. FEMALE STERILIZATION: GUIDELINES FOR THE DEVELOPMENT OF SERVICES. Albany, NY: World Health Organization, 1976.

4151. Fong, Monica S. "The Early Rhetoric of Women's Liberation: Implications for Zero Population Growth," JOURNAL OF MARRIAGE AND THE FAMILY, vol. 38, no. 1 (Feb. 1976), pp. 127-140. Concludes there is a strong relationship.

4152. Forman, Howard Martin. "*Doe* v. *Doe* [(Mass) 314 N E 2d 128]: The Wife's Right to an Abortion over her Husband's Objections," NEW ENGLAND LAW REVIEW, vol. 11, no. 1 (Fall 1975), pp. 205-224. Determined to be the wife's legal right.

4153. Freedman, Ronald and John Y. Takeshita. FAMILY PLANNING IN TAIWAN: AN EXPERIMENT IN SOCIAL CHANGE. Princeton, NJ: Princeton Univ. Press, 1969. 528 pp.

4154. Gardiner, Reginald Frank Robert. ABORTION: THE PERSONAL DILEMMA: A CHRISTIAN GYNAECOLOGIST EXAMINES THE MEDICAL, SOCIAL, AND SPIRITUAL ISSUES. Exeter, England: Paternoster Press, 1972. 288 pp.

4155. Germain, Adrienne and Audrey Smock. "The Status and Roles of Ghanaian and Kenyan Women: Implications for Fertility Behavior." Arlington, VA: ERIC Document Reproduction Service, 1974. 48 pp. Theorizes that women who have access to roles other than mother will have fewer children.

4156. Gordon, Linda. "Race Suicide and the Feminist Response: Part I," HECATE, vol. 1 (July 1975), pp. 40-53. Concludes that feminists were forced to advocate birth control and reject the motherhood ideology in spite of the concept of "race suicide," i.e. the fear that the declining birth rate of white educated couples and increasing birth rate of others would cause a relative decline in "Yankee Stock."

4157. Grabill, Wilson H., Clyde V. Kiser, and Pascal K. Whelpton. THE FERTILITY OF AMERICAN WOMEN. New York: John Wiley, 1958. 448 pp. Statistical study.

4158. Gray, Virginia. "Women: Victims or Beneficiaries of U.S. Population
Policy," in POLITICAL ISSUES IN U.S. POPULATION POLICY,
edited by Elihu Bergman. Lexington, MA: Lexington Books, 1974.

4159. Hardin, Garrett James. MANDATORY MOTHERHOOD: THE TRUE
MEANING OF "RIGHT TO LIFE." Boston, MA: Beacon Press, 1974.
136 pp. Biologist questions the implications of giving a fetus full rights
of a human being, and when life really begins.

4160. ———. STALKING THE WILD TABOO. Los Altos, CA: William
Kaufman, 1973. 216 pp. Collection of essays on abortion.

4161. Hare, R. M. "Abortion and the Golden Rule," PHILOSOPHY AND
PUBLIC AFFAIRS, vol. 4, no. 3 (Spring 1975), pp. 210-222.
Discussion of the morality of abortion.

4162. Harting, Donald. "Abortion Techniques and Services: A Review and
Critique," AMERICAN JOURNAL OF PUBLIC HEALTH, vol. 61, no.
10 (Oct. 1971), pp. 2085-2105. The legal framework of abortion, the
role of official health agencies, procedures, counseling and referral, and
the social and economic effects of abortion.

4163. Himes, Norman Edward. MEDICAL HISTORY OF CONTRACEPTION.
New York: Schocken Books, 1970. 521 pp. First published in 1936,
study details pre-pill attempt to control fertility from prehistoric times.

4164. Horobin, Gordon, ed. EXPERIENCE WITH ABORTION: A CASE
STUDY OF NORTH-EAST SCOTLAND. London, England: Cambridge
Univ. Press, 1973. 379 pp.

4165. Hudgins, John. "Is Birth Control Genocide?" THE BLACK SCHOLAR,
(Nov.-Dec. 1972), pp. 34-37. Expresses concern for the "Quality of
life" rather than the number of children.

4166. International Conference on Family Planning Programs. FAMILY
PLANNING AND POPULATION PROGRAMS. Chicago, IL: Univ. of
Chicago Press, 1966. 848 pp. Good introductory text and
bibliographical source for background to demographic studies.

4167. International Planned Parenthood Federation (London). "Family
Planning: Improving Opportunities for Women." Arlington, VA: ERIC
Document Reproduction Service, 1974. 28 pp.

4168. ———. "Situation Report—Algeria, Bangladesh, Gilbert and Ellice Islands,
Iran, Jordan, New Zealand, Rwanda, and Sierra Leone." Arlington, VA:
ERIC Document Reproduction Service, 1974. 48 pp.

4169. ———. "Situation Report—Dahomey, Ethiopia, Mali, and Mauritius."
Arlington, VA: ERIC Document Reproduction Service, 1973. 25 pp.

4170. ———. "Situation Report—Ghana, Guyana, India, Japan, Kenya, Khmer
Republic, Nepal, Niger, Republic of Vietnam, Senegal, Thailand, and
Trinidad and Tobago." Arlington, VA: ERIC Document Reproduction
Service, 1974. 90 pp.

4171. Jacobsson, L. and F. Solheim. "Women's Experience of Abortion
Procedure," SOCIAL PSYCHIATRY, vol. 10, no. 4 (Oct. 1, 1975), pp.
155-160. Study of 132 Swedish women's contacts with gynecologists
and social workers in abortion; review of new Swedish laws.

4172. Kantner, John F. and Melvin Zelnik. "Contraception and Pregnancy:
Experiences of Young Unmarried Women in the United States,"

FAMILY PLANNING PERSPECTIVES, vol. 5 (Winter 1973), pp. 21-35.

4173. Keller, Christa and Pamela Copeland. "Counseling the Abortion Patient is More than Talk," AMERICAN JOURNAL OF NURSING, vol. 71, no. 1 (Jan. 1972), pp. 102-106.

4174. Khalifa, Atef M. "The Influence of Wife's Education on Fertility in Rural Egypt," JOURNAL OF BIOSOCIAL SCIENCE, vol. 8, no. 1 (Jan. 1976), pp. 53-60.

4175. Koblinsky, Marjorie A. and Frederick S. Jaffe. REPRODUCTION AND HUMAN WELFARE: A CHALLENGE TO RESEARCH. New York: The Ford Foundation, 1976. 622 pp. Report of a study conducted over the past two years on the reproductive sciences, citing more than 200 promising research developments that could lead to more effective fertility control.

4176. Korpi, Sture. "Swedish Government Proposes New Abortions Act," CURRENT SWEDEN (The Swedish Institute), no. 27 (April 1974), pp. 1-5. Details major provisions of the new bill.

4177. Kupinsky, Stanley, ed. THE FERTILITY OF WORKING WOMEN: A SYNTHESIS OF INTERNATIONAL RESEARCH. New York: Praeger Books, 1977. 400 pp. Original articles on the effect of work-related factors on fertility levels.

4178. Lacey, Louise. LUNACEPTION: A FEMININE ODYSSEY INTO FERTILITY AND CONTRACEPTION. New York: Coward, McCann & Geoghegan, 1975. 166 pp.

4179. Lader, Lawrence, ed. FOOLPROOF BIRTH CONTROL. Boston, MA: Beacon Press, 1972. 269 pp. Practical guide to inexpensive and permanent methods of voluntary sterilization for both men and women.

4180. Langer, William L. "Checks on Population Growth: 1750-1850," SCIENTIFIC AMERICAN, vol. 226, no. 3 (Feb. 1972), pp. 92-99. Concludes that two of the major checks on population growth during this period were the widespread practice of celibacy and infanticide.

4181. Laurel. "Radical Reproduction: Women Without Men," AMAZON QUARTERLY, vol. 2, no. 3 (1974), pp. 4-19. Methods of reproduction allowing women to have children without men.

4182. Lee, Nancy Howell. THE SEARCH FOR AN ABORTIONIST. Chicago, IL: Univ. of Chicago Press, 1969. 207 pp. Study of the women seeking abortions.

4183. Lieberman, E. James and Ellen Peck. SEX AND BIRTH CONTROL: A GUIDE FOR THE YOUNG. New York: Thomas Y. Crowell, 1973. 299 pp.

4184. Llewellyn-Jones, Derek. HUMAN REPRODUCTION AND SOCIETY. London, England: Faber, 1974. 547 pp.

4185. Luker, Kristin. TAKING CHANCES: ABORTION AND THE DECISION NOT TO CONTRACEPT. Berkeley, CA: Univ. of California Press, 1975. 200 pp. Relates "risk-taking sexual behavior to other common risks like smoking."

4186. Luscutoff, Sidney A. and Alan C. Elms. "Advice in the Abortion

Decision," JOURNAL OF COUNSELING PSYCHOLOGY, vol. 22, no. 2 (1975), pp. 140-146. Survey documenting the number of women's contacts-for-advice when forming abortion or pregnancy decisions.

4187. Mark, David J. "Liability for Failure of Birth Control Methods," COLUMBIA LAW REVIEW, vol. 76, no. 7 (Nov. 1976), pp. 1187-1204.

4188. Moore, Edward Robert. THE CASE AGAINST BIRTH CONTROL. New York: The Century, 1931. 311 pp. Discusses the official Roman Catholic attitude toward the subject of birth control.

4189. Muller, Charlotte F. "Feminism, Society, and Fertility Control," FAMILY PLANNING PERSPECTIVES, vol. 6, no. 2 (March-April 1974), pp. 68-72.

4190. Nazer, Isam R., ed. INDUCED ABORTION: A HAZARD TO PUBLIC HEALTH? Beirut, Lebanon: International Planned Parenthood Federation, Middle Eastern and North African Region, 1972. 432 pp.

4191. Neubardt, Selig. A CONCEPT OF CONTRACEPTION. New York: Trident Press, 1967. 118 pp.

4192. Neubardt, Selig and Harold Schulman. TECHNIQUES OF ABORTION. Boston, MA: Little, Brown, 1972. 172 pp.

4193. Nuttal, Ronald L. and Ena Vasquez Nuttal. FAMILY SIZE AND SPACING IN THE UNITED STATES AND PUERTO RICO: FINAL REPORT. Arlington, VA: ERIC Document Reproduction Service, 1975. 497 pp.

4194. Oldershaw, K. Leslie. CONTRACEPTION, ABORTION, AND STERILIZATION IN GENERAL PRACTICE. London, England: Henry Kimpton, 1975. 288 pp.

4195. Osofsky, Howard J. and Joy D. Osofsky, eds. THE ABORTION EXPERIENCE: PSYCHOLOGICAL AND MEDICAL IMPACT. New York: Harper & Row, 1973. 668 pp. Review of the data and literature on the major medical, psychosocial, and legal aspects.

4196. Patton, Dorothy E. "*Roe* v. *Wade* (93 Sup. Ct. 705): Its Impact on Rights of Choice in Human Reproduction," COLUMBIA HUMAN RIGHTS LAW REVIEW, vol. 5, no. 2 (Fall 1973), pp. 497-521. Relied on 14th Amendment to find Constitutional protection for woman's right to terminate pregnancy.

4197. Phelan, Lana Clarke and Patricia Therese Maginnis. THE ABORTION HANDBOOK FOR RESPONSIBLE WOMEN. Los Angeles, CA: Contact Books, 1969. 192 pp. Discusses the existing situation and how to survive in it.

4198. Preston, Samuel H. and Alan Thomas Richards. "Influence of Women's Work Opportunities on Marriage Rates," DEMOGRAPHY, vol. 12, no. 2 (May 1975), pp. 209-222. Regression study of marriage rates between 1960-1970.

4199. Ransil, Bernard J. ABORTION. New York: Paulist Press Deus Books, 1969. 121 pp. Examines religious doctrine regarding abortion; finds that the position of the Catholic Church on abortion is relatively recent, especially the restrictions on therapeutic abortions.

4200. "Rights of Choice in Matters Relating to Human Reproduction: Part I of a Symposium on Law and Population," COLUMBIA HUMAN RIGHTS LAW REVIEW, vol. 6, no. 2 (Fall-Winter 1974-1975), pp. 273-534. Contributors include Harriet F. Pilpel, Dorothy E. Patton, Luke T. Lee, John M. Paxman, Eve W. Paul, Joseph W. Dellpenna, John V. Farley, Steven S. Tokarski, Gloria S. Neuwirth, Phyllis A. Heisler, Kenneth S. Goldrich, Theodore H. Lackland, Sanda M. Kayden, and Ilene P. Karpf. See also "Symposium on Law and Population, Part II: Tunis Symposium."

4201. The Roper Organization, Inc. THE VIRGINIA SLIMS AMERICAN WOMEN'S OPINION POLL: A SURVEY OF THE ATTITUDES OF WOMEN ON MARRIAGE, DIVORCE, THE FAMILY, AND AMERICA'S CHANGING MORALITY. Volume III. New York: Phillip Morris, 1974. 123 pp.

4202. Ryan, William Burke. INFANTICIDE: ITS LAWS, PREVALENCE, PREVENTION, AND HISTORY. London, England: Churchill, 1862. Unpaged.

4203. Sanger, Margaret. MY FIGHT FOR BIRTH CONTROL. New York: Maxwell Reprint, 1969. 360 pp. Reprint of 1931 edition.

4204. Sanger, Margaret, ed. BIRTH CONTROL REVIEW. New York: Da Capo Press, 1970. 9 vols. Reprint of periodical published in New York (Feb. 1917-Jan. 1940) by the American Birth Control League, later by the Planned Parenthood Federation of America under its earlier name, Birth Control Federation of America.

4205. Sarvis, Betty and Hyman Rodman. THE ABORTION CONTROVERSY. New York: Columbia Univ. Press, 1975. 207 pp. Second edition. Account of the moral, legal, and medical issues involved in the ongoing debate.

4206. Schulder, Diane and Florynce Kennedy. ABORTION RAP. New York: McGraw-Hill, 1971. 238 pp.

4207. Stephan, Jan and Edmund H. Kellogg. "The World's Laws on Contraceptives," AMERICAN JOURNAL OF COMPARATIVE LAW, vol. 22, no. 4 (Fall 1974), pp. 615-651. Examination of the laws of almost 60 countries. See also Edward Veitch and R. R. S. Tracey.

4208. Stopes–Roe, Harry Verdon with Ian Scott. "Marie Stopes and Birth Control." London, England: Priory Press, 1974. 96 pp.

4209. "Symposium on Law and Population, Part II: Tunis Symposium," COLUMBIA HUMAN RIGHTS LAW REVIEW, vol. 7, no. 1 (Spring-Summer 1975), pp. 1-309. Contributors include Mezri Chekir, Rafael M. Salas, Jean de Moerloose, Riad B. Tabbarah, Mohamed Mzali, Vida Tomsic, V. I. Chacko, Alexandre Paraiso, Anne-Marie Dourlen-Rollier, Mohieddine Mabrouk, F. M. Shattock, N. R. E. Fendall, Elizabeth Odio, Reuben B. Canoy, David G. Parton, Julia Henderson, and Slaheddine Baly. See also "Rights of Choice in Matters Relating to Human Reproduction: Part I of a Symposium on Law and Population."

4210. Szabody, Egon. "The Legalizing of Contraceptives and Abortions," IMPACT OF SCIENCE ON SOCIETY, vol. 21 (July-Sept. 1971), pp.

265-270. Legalizing contraceptives seen as a way to stop abortions.

4211. Tak, Jean Vander. ABORTION, FERTILITY, AND CHANGING LEGISLATION: AN INTERNATIONAL REVIEW. Lexington, MA: Lexington Books, 1974. 175 pp. Abortion research.

4212. United Nations. Dept. of Economic and Social Affairs. STATUS OF WOMEN AND FAMILY PLANNING: REPORT OF THE SPECIAL RAPPORTEUR APPOINTED BY THE ECONOMIC AND SOCIAL COUNCIL UNDER RESOLUTION 1326 (XLIV). New York: United Nations, 1975. 148 pp. Explores the relationship between women's rights in the family and in society and reproductive behavior.

4213. U.S. Commission on Civil Rights. CONSTITUTIONAL ASPECTS OF THE RIGHT TO LIMIT CHILDBEARING. Washington, D.C.: CCR, Office of Information and Publications, 1975. 223 pp. Report analyzes effects of proposed constitutional amendment on the 1st, 9th, and 14th Amendments to the Constitution; relates the treatment of abortion under common law; and analyzes the effect on private law and the issues of prospective father consent.

4214. U.S. Dept. of Commerce. Bureau of the Census. CHILDSPACING: SPACING OF SUCCESSIVE BIRTHS TO WOMEN, BY AGE, DURATION OF MARRIAGE, AND OTHER CHARACTERISTICS. Washington, D.C.: SUDOC, GPO, 1968. 185 pp.

4215. –––. "Marriage, Fertility, and Childspacing, June 1965." Washington, D.C.: SUDOC, GPO, 1969. 76 pp.

4216. –––. "A Statistical Portrait of Women in the United States." Washington, D.C.: SUDOC, GPO, 1976. 90 pp. Report analyzes trends in population growth, marital and family status, education, labor force participation, crime and victimization, etc.

4217. –––. WOMEN BY NUMBER OF CHILDREN EVER BORN. Washington, D.C.: Bureau of the Census, 1973. 405 pp. 1970 Census of Population, Subject Report.

4218. U.S. Dept. of Labor. Employment Standards Administration. Women's Bureau. "Facts about Women Heads of Households and Heads of Families." Washington, D.C.: U.S. Dept. of Labor, 1973. 10 pp.

4219. –––. "Negro Women . . . In the Population and in the Labor Force." Washington, D.C.: SUDOC, GPO, 1967. 41 pp.

4220. Vaughn, Gladys Gary, comp. "Women's Roles and Education: Changing Traditions in Population Planning." Washington, D.C.: American Home Economics Association, 1975. Collection of readings on the economic status of women and family planning.

4221. Veitch, Edward and R. R. S. Tracey. "Abortion in the Common Law World," AMERICAN JOURNAL OF COMPARATIVE LAW, vol. 22, no. 4 (Fall 1974), pp. 652-696. Examines laws in the United States, England, Canada, and Australia. See also Jan Stephan and Edmund H. Kellogg.

4222. William, Jean Morton and Keith Hindall. "Abortion and Contraception: A Study of Patients' Attitudes." London, England: Political & Economic Broadsheets, 1972. 62 pp.

4223. Williams, Steven J., Nirmala Murphy, and Gretchen Berggren. "Conjugal Unions Among Rural Haitian Women," JOURNAL OF MARRIAGE AND THE FAMILY, vol. 37, no. 4 (Nov. 1975), pp. 1022-1031. Fertility rates.

4224. "Women in the Soviet Union: Statistical Returns." Moscow, U.S.S.R.: Progress Publishers, 1970. 54 pp.

II. WOMEN IN POLITICAL SCIENCE

A. Women as Socializers

"No improvement that takes place in either of the sexes, can be confined to itself; each is a universal mirror to each; and the respective refinement of the one will be in reciprocal proportion to the polish of the other."

—Charles Caleb Colton

4225. Boulding, Elise. "Alternative Capabilities for World Problem-Solving: A Comparison of Religious and Secular Non-Governmental Organizations (NGOs) in the Women's Sector," INTERNATIONAL STUDIES NOTES, vol. 2, no. 3 (Spring 1976), pp. 1-14. Evaluation of the roles of NGOs in the international social and political sectors.

4226. Lavin, Mildred H. and Clara H. Oleson, eds. WOMEN AND PUBLIC POLICY: A HUMANISTIC PERSPECTIVE. Iowa City, IA: Univ. of Iowa, Institute of Public Affairs, 1974. 147 pp.

4227. Milburn, Josephine F. "Women as Citizens: A Comparative Review." Beverly Hills, CA: Sage, 1976. Survey data from 12 nations is assessed in terms of involvement in the economy and political decision making, use of the right to vote, acceptance of responsibility outside the home, and access to political office.

4228. Sheldon, Wilmon H. "Woman's Mission to Humanity." Boston, MA: Christopher Publishing House, 1968. 93 pp.

4229. "Women, Agents of Change," INTERNATIONAL WOMEN'S YEAR, vol. 2, no. 5 (June-July 1975), pp. 1-10. Conference sponsored by International Women's Year Secretariat and the Quebec Status of Women Council, synopsis of proceedings.

B. Victorian Attitudes

"Only the Almighty can make a New Woman. Put broadly, up to the age of puberty, the girl, all other things being equal, beats the boy; with puberty the damsel throws away every month a vast amount of fluid power in the order of Nature. Let us call this pelvic power. Assuming the girl to be the superior of the boy up to the pelvic power stage—which, indeed, any one can observe for himself, in his own sphere,—but once arrived at the stage of pelvic power, and the damsel is left behind in her lessons by her brother in the natural order of things, or.else the girl's brain saps the pelvis of its power, when she will also lose in the race with the boy, because he will be physically well, while she, with disordered pelvic life, must necessarily be in ill health more or less. The whole thing is a mere question of quantity of energy. If it were otherwise, the girl would be able to buy lollipops with her penny and yet keep her penny; while the boy, having spent his penny, would be penniless. You cannot spend your penny and have it."

—J. Compton Burnett (DELICATE, BACKWARD, PUNY, AND STUNTED CHILDREN, 1895)

4230. Aylmer, John. "An Harborowe for Faithfull and Trewe Subiects Agaynst the Late Blowne Blaste, Concerninge the Government of Women, Wherein be Confuted all such Reasons as a Straunger of Late made in that Behalf, with a Brief Exhortation to Obedience." New York: Da Capo Press, 1972. Reprint of 1559 edition. See also John Knox.

4231. Galante, Cosmo. THE DEGENERATION OF THE FEMALE OF THE SPECIES AND THE DECAY OF THE HUMAN SOCIETY. Albuquerque, NM: American Classical College Press, 1973.

4232. Gilder, George F. SEXUAL SUICIDE. New York: Quadrangle Press, 1973. 308 pp. Gilder has decided that women are morally and sexually superior to men by virtue of their "true" biological function through which they find profound fulfillment.

4233. Walters, Ronald G., ed. PRIMERS FOR PRUDERY: SEXUAL ADVICE TO VICTORIAN AMERICA. Englewood Cliffs, NJ: Prentice-Hall, 1974. 175 pp. Selections in this volume mark an important beginning in the study of the historical and cultural aspects of sexuality in American society.

C. Social Reformers

1. General

"Nothing so needs reforming as other people's habits."
—Samuel Langhorn Clemens (Mark Twain)

4234. Bloomer, Dexter C. LIFE AND WRITINGS OF AMELIA BLOOMER. New York: Schocken Books, 1975. 387 pp. Reprint of 1895 edition.

4235. Dabney, Wendell Phillips. MAGGIE L. WALKER AND THE INDEPENDENT ORDER OF ST. LUKE; THE WOMAN AND HER WORK. Cincinnati, OH: Dabney Publishing, 1927. 137 pp. Pioneer of insurance for blacks.

4236. Daniels, Arlene Kaplan. "A Survey of Research Concerns on Women's Issues." Washington, D.C.: Association of American Colleges, Project on the Status and Education of Women, 1975. 48 pp.

4237. Davis, Allen F. AMERICAN HEROINE: THE LIFE AND LEGEND OF JANE ADDAMS. New York: Oxford Univ. Press, 1973. 339 pp.

4238. Jameson, Mrs. Anna Brownell (Murphy). SISTERS OF CHARITY AND THE COMMUNION OF LABOR. Westport, CT: Hyperion Press, 1976. 148 pp. Reprint of 1857 edition. Two lectures on the social employment of women.

4239. Lemons, J. Stanley. THE WOMAN CITIZEN: SOCIAL FEMINISM IN THE 1920's. Urbana, IL: Univ. of Illinois Press, 1973. 260 pp.

4240. Pierce, John B. "A Woman Banker: Mrs. Maggie L. Walker," in IN THE VANGUARD OF A RACE, edited by Lily Hammond. New York: Council of Women for Home Missions and Missionary Education Movement of the United States and Canada, 1922. 176 pp.

4241. Prochaska, F. K. "Women in English Philanthropy, 1790-1830,"
       INTERNATIONAL REVIEW OF SOCIAL HISTORY, vol. 19, no. 3
       (1974), pp. 426-445.
4242. Rauch, Julia B. "Women in Social Work: Friendly Visitors in
       Philadelphia, 1880," SOCIAL SERVICE REVIEW, vol. 49, no. 2 (June
       1975), pp. 241-259. Examines the characteristics of the women
       affiliated with the Philadelphia Society for Organizing Charitable Relief
       and Repressing Mendicancy (S.O.C.), an organization which marked the
       expansion of women's participation in Philadelphia's formally
       organized charitable system.
4243. Rosen, Ruth and Sue Davidson, eds. THE MAIMIE PAPERS. Old
       Westbury, NY: Feminist Press, 1977. Correspondence between Fanny
       Quincy Howe and Maimie Pinzer, a Jewish prostitute, beginning in
       1910. Chronicles Maimie's autobiography of drug addiction and career
       as a social reformer.
4244. Schupf, Harriet Warm. "Single Women and Social Reform in
       Mid-Nineteenth Century England: The Case of Mary Carpenter,"
       VICTORIAN STUDIES, vol. 17, no. 3 (March 1974), pp. 301-317.
       Strong Unitarian who worked behind the scenes for social reform in
       Great Britain, i.e. vocational schools, juvenile reform.
4245. Scribner, Grace. "An American Pilgrimage, Portions of the Letters of
       Grace Scribner." New York: Vanguard, 1927. 89 pp. The record of the
       life of a self-denying social worker through her letters.
4246. Snyder, Charles M., ed. THE LADY AND THE PRESIDENT: THE
       LETTERS OF DOROTHEA DIX AND MILLARD FILMORE. New
       York: Funk & Wagnalls, 1975. 400 pp. Story of the famous reformer
       and President Filmore.
4247. Timpson, Thomas. MEMOIRS OF MRS. ELIZABETH FRY:
       INCLUDING A HISTORY OF HER LABORS IN PROMOTING THE
       REFORMATION OF FEMALE PRISONERS, AND THE
       IMPROVEMENT OF BRITISH SEAMEN. New York: Stanford &
       Swords, 1847. 330 pp.
4248. Truman, Margaret. WOMEN OF COURAGE FROM REVOLUTIONARY
       TIMES TO THE PRESENT. New York: William Morrow, 1976. Profiles
       of 12 women such as Dolley Madison, Marian Anderson, Prudence
       Crandall (educator of black women and children in Conn.), Kate
       Bernard (fought for the rights of Indian children in Okla.), and
       Elizabeth Blackwell (America's first woman doctor).
4249. Vance, Catharine. "Not by Gods, But By People: The Story of Bella Hall
       Gauld." Toronto, Ontario: Progress Books, 1968. 65 pp. Mrs. Gauld, a
       humanitarian and social reformer, helped found the Communist Party
       of Canada and the Montreal Labor College.
4250. Whitney, Janet. ELIZABETH FRY: QUAKER HEROINE. New York:
       Benjamin Blom, 1972. 328 pp. Reprint of 1937 edition. Biography of
       Elizabeth Fry, reformer of the English prison system.

C. 2. Social Reformers—Abolitionists

"On this subject, I do not wish to think, or speak, or write with moderation. . . . I will not equivocate—I will not excuse—I will not retreat a single inch—AND I WILL BE HEARD."

—William Lloyd Garrison

4251. Breault, Judith Colucci. THE WORLD OF EMILY HOWLAND: ODYSSEY OF A HUMANITARIAN. Millbrae, CA: Les Femmes, 1976. 173 pp. Abolitionist, whose primary interest was Negro education, she contributed to over 30 schools, e.g. Tuskegee.

4252. Gilbertson, Catherine. HARRIET BEECHER STOWE. Port Washington, CT: Kennikat Press, 1968. 330 pp. Reprint of 1937 edition. Abolitionist, author of UNCLE TOM'S CABIN.

4253. Haviland, Laura Smith. A WOMAN'S LIFE WORK: LABORS AND EXPERIENCES. Freeport, NY: Books for Libraries, 1969. 554 pp. Reprint of 1887 edition. Her 30 years on the underground railroad.

4254. Kearney, Belle. SLAVEHOLDER'S DAUGHTER. New York: Negro Univ. Press, 1969. 269 pp. Reprint of 1900 edition.

4255. Sterling, Dorothy. FREEDOM TRAIN: THE STORY OF HARRIET TUBMAN. Garden City, NY: Doubleday, 1954. 191 pp.

C. 3. Social Reformers—Peace

"I am not very keen for doves or hawks. I think we need more owls."
—George Aiken

4256. Camp, Kay, ed. "Listen to the Women for a Change." Geneva, Switzerland: Women's International League for Peace and Freedom, 1975. 50 pp. Collection of statements representing different ideologies, regions, and perspectives, from such women as Bella Abzug, Hortensia Bussi de Allende, Elise Boulding, on women's role in the development of peace.

4257. Davis, Allen F. JANE ADDAMS ON PEACE, WAR, AND INTERNATIONAL UNDERSTANDING. New York: Garland Publishing, 1976. 227 pp.

4258. Key, Ellen Karolina Sofia. WAR, PEACE, AND THE FUTURE: A CONSIDERATION OF NATIONALISM AND INTERNATIONALISM, AND OF THE RELATIONSHIP OF WOMEN TO WAR. New York: Garland Publishing, 1972. 211 pp. Reprint of 1916 edition.

4259. Lester, Muriel. IT OCCURRED TO ME. New York: Harper, 1937. 268 pp. Autobiography of a famous English pacifist.

4260. ———. IT SO HAPPENED. New York: Harper, 1947. 240 pp. Continuation of autobiography.

4261. Swanwick, Helena Maria. "The War in its Effect on Women," and
"Women and War." New York: Garland Publishing 1971. 54 pp.
Reprints of 1916 and 1915 editions respectively.

C. 4. Social Reformers—Prohibition

"Every inordinate cup is unblessed, and the ingredient is a devil."
—Shakespeare, OTHELLO, Act I, Sc. 1

4262. Carroll, L. "Temperance Movement in India: Politics and Social Reform,"
MODERN ASIAN STUDIES, vol. 10 (July 1975), pp. 417-447.
4263. Coleman, Emmet G., ed. "The Temperance Songbook: A Peerless
Collection of Temperance Songs and Hymns for the Women's Christian
Temperance Union, Loyal Temperance Legion, Prohibitionists,
Temperance Praise Meetings, Medal Contests, etc." New York:
McGraw-Hill, 1971. 79 pp. Reprint of 1907 edition.
4264. Kellogg, Marion P. "Is Prohibition Being Enforced?" CURRENT
HISTORY, vol. 27, no. 1 (Oct. 1927), pp. 49-54.
4265. Stebbins, Jane E. FIFTY YEARS HISTORY OF THE TEMPERANCE
CAUSE. INTEMPERANCE THE GREAT NATIONAL CURSE. WITH
A FULL DESCRIPTION OF THE ORIGIN AND PROGRESS OF THE
NEW PLANS BY THE WOMEN UP TO THE PRESENT TIME. Printed
by T. A. H. Brown, 1874. 500 pp.
4266. U.S. Bureau of Education. "Laws Relating to Temperance Instruction,"
Chapter VI from REPORT OF THE COMMISSIONER OF
EDUCATION OF 1902. Washington, D.C.: Government Printing
Office, 1903. Pp. 315-338.

C. 5. Social Reformers—Prostitution

"The whore and gambler, by the state
Licensed, build that nation's fate.
The harlot's cry from street to street
Shall weave Old London's winding sheet."

—William Blake

4267. Bennani, Mesdali. "Quelques Considérations sur la Prostitution au Maroc
[Some Considerations on Moroccan Prostitution]," REVUE
TUNISIENNE DE SCIENCES SOCIALES, vol. 4, no. 11 (Oct. 1967),
pp. 79-84. Study of imprisoned prostitutes.
4268. Goldman, Marion. "Prostitution and Virtue in Nevada," SOCIETY, vol.
10, no. 1 (Nov.-Dec. 1972), pp. 32-38. Prostitution in the early mining
towns.
4269. James, Jennifer. THE POLITICS OF PROSTITUTION: RESOURCES

FOR LEGAL CHANGE. Seattle, WA: Social Research Associates, 1975. 118 pp.

4270. Millett, Kate. THE PROSTITUTION PAPERS. New York: Avon Books, 1971. 128 pp. Dialogue with former prostitutes about how they got into and out of prostitution.

4271. Parent-Duchatelet, Alexandre J. PROSTITUTION IN PARIS, CONSIDERED MORALLY, POLITICALLY, AND MEDICALLY: PREPARED FOR PHILANTHROPISTS AND LEGISLATORS FROM STATISTICAL DOCUMENTS. New York: AMS Press, n.d. Reprint of 1845 edition.

4272. Pivar, David Jay. PURITY CRUSADE: SEXUAL MORALITY AND SOCIAL CONTROL, 1868-1900. Westport, CT: Greenwood Press, 1973. 308 pp.

4273. THE PROSTITUTE AND THE SOCIAL REFORMER: COMMERCIAL VICE IN THE PROGRESSIVE ERA. New York: Arno Press, 1974. 298 pp. Reprint of 1911 REPORT OF VICE COMMISSION OF MINNEAPOLIS, and 1913 REPORT ON EXISTING CONDITIONS IN PHILADELPHIA.

4274. PROSTITUTION IN AMERICA: THREE INVESTIGATIONS, 1902-1914. New York: Arno Press, 1976. 533 pp. Reprint of 1912 edition of THE SOCIAL EVIL, WITH SPECIAL REFERENCE TO CONDITION EXISTING IN THE CITY OF NEW YORK; 1913 edition of THE SOCIAL EVIL IN SYRACUSE; and 1914 REPORT OF THE COMMISSION FOR THE INVESTIGATION OF THE WHITE SLAVE TRADE.

4275. PROSTITUTION IN THE VICTORIAN AGE: DEBATES ON THE ISSUE FROM 19TH CENTURY JOURNALS. Farmborough, England: Gregg, 1973. 274 pp. Reprints from the WESTMINSTER REVIEW.

D. Feminism, Equal Rights

1. General

"Those who might themselves be subject to equalization have rarely been enthusiastic about equality as a subject of social comment."

—John Kenneth Galbraith

"At the baths, all are equal."

— Yiddish Proverb

4276. Adelstein, Michael E. and Jean G. Pival, eds. WOMEN'S LIBERATION. New York: St. Martin's Press, 1972. 150 pp.

4277. Afetinan, A. "The Emancipation of the Turkish Woman." Paris, France: UNESCO, 1962. 63 pp.

4278. Allen, Pamela. "Free Space: A Perspective on the Small Group in Women's Liberation." Washington, NJ: Times Change Press, 1970. 64 pp. Handbook for consciousness-raising groups.

4279. Anticaglia, Elizabeth. A HOUSEWIFE'S GUIDE TO WOMEN'S LIBERATION. Chicago, IL: Nelson-Hall, 1972. 232 pp.

4280. Asthana, Pratima. WOMEN'S MOVEMENT IN INDIA. Delhi, India: Vikas Publishing House, 1974. 175 pp.

4281. Atkinson, Ti-Grace. AMAZON ODYSSEY: COLLECTION OF WRITINGS. New York: Link Books, 1974. 288 pp. Works of the political pioneer of the women's movement from 1967-1972.

4282. Babcox, Deborah and Madeline Belkin, comps. LIBERATION NOW: WRITINGS FROM THE WOMEN'S LIBERATION MOVEMENT. New York: Dell Publishing, 1971. 382 pp.

4283. Barber, Benjamin R. LIBERATING FEMINISM. New York: Seabury Press, 1975. 153 pp.

4284. Blackstone, William T. "Freedom and Women," ETHICS, vol. 85 (April 1975), pp. 243-248. Briefly examines some of the differing stances within or on the women's movement, e.g. the traditional view of women's place, the liberal view insisting on other options.

4285. Bluh, Bonnie Charles. WOMAN TO WOMAN: EUROPEAN FEMINISTS. Brooklyn, NY: Starogubski Press, 1974. 317 pp.

4286. Bouten, Jacob. MARY WOLLSTONECRAFT AND THE BEGINNINGS OF FEMALE EMANCIPATION IN FRANCE AND ENGLAND. Philadelphia, PA: Porcupine Press, 1975. 184 pp. Reprint of 1922 edition.

4287. Broyelle, Claudie. LA MOITIÉ DE CIEL: LE MOUVEMENT DE LIBÉRATION DES FEMMES AUJORD'HUI EN CHINE [THE WOMEN'S LIBERATION MOVEMENT IN CHINA TODAY]. Paris, France: Donoel: Gonther, 1975. 277 pp.

4288. Carden, Maren Lockwood. THE NEW FEMINIST MOVEMENT. Scranton, PA: Basic Books, 1973. 226 pp. A detailed study of the movement—structure, membership, and history of organizations that form a major part of present-day feminism.

4289. Carroll, Berenice A., ed. LIBERATING WOMEN'S HISTORY: ESSAYS ON WOMEN'S HISTORY AND WOMEN'S LIBERATION. Urbana, IL: Univ. of Illinois Press, 1976. 434 pp.

4290. Clarke, Mary Stetson, comp. "Women's Rights in the United States." New York: Grossman, 1974. 24 pp. Reproductions of documents and prints, with five explanatory broadsheets.

4291. Colon, Clara. "Enter Fighting: Today's Woman—A Marxist-Leninist View." New York: New Outlook Publishers, 1970. 95 pp.

4292. Cowl, Margaret. "Women and Equality." New York: Workers Library, 1935. 15 pp.

4293. Crafton, Allen and Robert E. Gard. A WOMAN OF NO IMPORTANCE. Madison, WI: Wisconsin House, 1974. 204 pp. The life story of May McDonald, a small town Wisconsin woman (1878-1950) and her confrontations with women's unequal treatment.

4294. Crowell, Suzanne, ed. "Sexism and Racism: Feminist Perspective," CIVIL RIGHTS DIGEST, vol. 6, no. 3 (Spring 1974), pp. 2-81. Symposium. Contributors include Lucy Komisar, William A. Blakely, Lourdes

Miranda King, Shirley Hill Witt, Consuelo Nieto, Robert B. Yoshioka, Betty Jung, Emma Gee, Geraldine Rickman, and Robert Terry.

4295. Dane, Clemence (pseud. for Winifred Ashton). WOMEN'S SIDE. Freeport, NY: Books for Libraries, 1970. 144 pp. Reprint of 1927 edition.

4296. Deckard, Barbara Sinclair. THE WOMEN'S MOVEMENT: POLITICAL, SOCIOECONOMIC, AND PSYCHOLOGICAL ISSUES. New York: Harper & Row, 1975. 519 pp.

4297. Denning, Lord Alfred Thompson. "The Equality of Women." Liverpool, England: Liverpool Univ. Press, 1960. 16 pp. By one of Britain's foremost journalists.

4298. Desanti, Dominique. A WOMAN IN REVOLT: A BIOGRAPHY OF FLORA TRISTAN. New York: Crown Publishing, 1976. 281 pp. Reputed to be France's first feminist.

4299. Dreifus, Claudia. WOMAN'S FATE. New York: Bantam Books, 1973. 288 pp. The record of her own consciousness-raising group in which eight women explore their feelings on childhood, adolescence, sexuality, marriage, work, and old age.

4300. EDITORIAL RESEARCH REPORTS ON THE WOMEN'S MOVEMENT. Washington, D.C.: Congressional Quarterly, 1973. 180 pp. Reports on the status of women, marriage, child care, adoption, rape, prostitution, coeducation, women voters, and women's consciousness-raising.

4301. Epstein, Cynthia Fuchs. "Reflections on the Women's Movement: An Assessment of Change and Its Limits." Arlington, VA: ERIC Document Reproduction Service, 1975. 40 pp. Emphasizes need for economic change because that defines woman's identity.

4302. ———. "Ten Years Later: Perspectives on the Woman's Movement," DISSENT, vol. 22, no. 2 (Spring 1975), pp. 169-176. General overview of the achievements of the current women's movement.

4303. Evans, Richard Thomas. THE FEMINIST MOVEMENT IN GERMANY, 1894-1933. Beverly Hills, CA: Sage, 1976.

4304. Freeman, Jo. "The New Feminism," NATION, vol. 218, no. 10 (March 9, 1974), pp. 297-302. Survey of the movement's achievements and shortcomings.

4305. ———. "Political Organization in the Feminist Movement," ACTA SOCIOLOGICA, vol. 18, nos. 2-3 (1975), pp. 222-244.

4306. Freeman, Jo., ed. WOMEN: A FEMINIST PERSPECTIVE. Palo Alto, CA: Mayfield Pub., 1974. Collection of papers on the effects of sexism, the status of women, and the institutions and values that keep women in their place.

4307. Friedan, Betty. IT CHANGED MY LIFE: WRITINGS ON THE WOMEN'S MOVEMENT. New York: Random House, 1976. Includes speeches and articles, as well as some of her personal memoirs.

4308. Gamble, Eliza Burt. THE SEXES IN SCIENCE AND HISTORY: AN ENQUIRY INTO THE DOGMA OF WOMAN'S INFERIORITY TO MAN. Westport, CT: Hyperion Press, 1976. 407 pp. Reprint of 1916 edition. Scientifically disproves the Darwinian contention of innate male superiority. Pathbreaking work in feminist history.

4309. Goldman, Emma. "The Traffic in Women and Other Essays on Feminism, with a Biography by Alix Kates Shulman." New York: Times Change Press, 1970. 64 pp. Reprint of 1917 edition.

4310. Great Britain. Home Office. "Equality for Women." London, England: Her Majesty's Stationery Office, 1974. 27 pp.

4311. Hägg, Maud and Barbro Werkmäster. FRIHET, JÄMLIKHET SYSTERSKAP: EN HANDBOOK FÖR KVINNOR [FREEDOM, EQUALITY, AND SISTERHOOD: A HANDBOOK FOR WOMEN]. Göteborg: Författarförl, 1972. 136 pp.

4312. Hahn, Emily. ONCE UPON A PEDESTAL: AN INFORMAL HISTORY OF WOMEN'S LIB. New York: Thomas Y. Crowell, 1974. 279 pp. Begins with colonial times and moves into the nineteenth century with portraits of Mrs. Trollope, Harriet Martineau, and Fanny Kemble; but weak on twentieth century women and the rebirth of feminism.

4313. Hall, Gus. "Working-Class Approach to Women's Liberation." New York: New Outlook Publishers, 1970. 12 pp.

4314. Hochschild, Arlie, ed. "The American Woman," TRANS-ACTION, vol. 8, no. 1/2 (Nov./Dec. 1970), pp. 1-112. Special Combined Issue. Contributors include Joan Jordan, Unna Stannard, Jo Freeman, Ruth B. Dixon, Marijean Suelzle, Linda J. M. La Rue, Nathan Hare, Julia Hare, Pauline Bart, Inge Powell Bell, and Anita Lynn Micossi.

4315. Hope, Diane Schaich. "Redefinition of Self: A Comparison of the Rhetoric of the Women's Liberation and Black Liberation Movements," TODAY'S SPEECH, vol. 23, no. 1 (Winter 1975), pp. 17-25.

4316. Horn, Miriam. WHAT YOU SHOULD KNOW ABOUT WOMEN'S LIB. New Canaan, CT: Keats Publishing, 1974.

4317. Howard, Jane. A DIFFERENT WOMAN. New York: E. P. Dutton, 1973. 413 pp.

4318. Jaggar, Alison. "On Sexual Equality," ETHICS, vol. 84, no. 4 (July 1974), pp. 275-291. Philosophical discussion of the ways in which institutional sexism can be eliminated.

4319. Jenness, Linda. "Socialism and the Fight for Women's Rights." New York: Pathfinder Press, 1976.

4320. Kaplan, Marion A. "German-Jewish Feminism in the Twentieth Century," JEWISH SOCIAL STUDIES, vol. 38 (Winter 1976), pp. 39-53. History of the Judischer Frauenbund (League of Jewish Women) founded by Bertha Pappenheim in 1904.

4321. Katz, Naomi and Nancy Milton, eds. FRAGMENT FROM A LOST DIARY AND OTHER STORIES. New York: Pantheon Books, 1973. 317 pp. Unique collection of writings from Asia, Africa, and Latin America which adds a vital literary dimension to our understanding of the liberation of women.

4322. Kennedy, Florynce. COLOR ME FLO: MY HARD LIFE AND GOOD TIMES. Englewood Cliffs, NJ: Prentice-Hall, 1976. 168 pp. Autobiography of the black feminist leader.

4323. Klagsburn, Francine, ed. THE FIRST MS. READER. New York: MS.

Magazine, 1973. 282 pp. Collection of articles from the first 12 issues of MS. Magazine.

4324. Knox, John. "The First Blast of the Trumpet Against the Monstruous Regiment of Women." New York: AMS Press, 1972. 62 pp. Reprint of 1558 version. Appendix includes John Knox's apologetic defense of his first blast and contents of his second blast to Queen Elizabeth. See also John Aylmer.

4325. Kronemann, Michaela. "Ideology and Liberation: Women in the Soviet Union," MELBOURNE JOURNAL OF POLITICS, vol. 8 (1975/1976), pp. 44-50.

4326. Landau, Elaine. WOMAN, WOMEN! FEMINISM IN AMERICA. New York: J. Messner, 1974. 189 pp. Discusses the role of women in American history, stereotypes and discrimination that have kept them from realizing their potential, and the move for equality in the 1960s and 1970s.

4327. Lenin, Vladimir Ilyich (Ulyanov). THE EMANCIPATION OF WOMEN. New York: International Publications, 1969. 135 pp. Reprint of 1934 edition.

4328. Lynn, Mary C., ed. WOMEN'S LIBERATION IN THE TWENTIETH CENTURY. New York: John Wiley, 1975. 139 pp.

4329. McBride, Angela Barron. A MARRIED FEMINIST. New York: Harper & Row, 1976. 244 pp. Men and women are psychologically bisexual; the real goal of both sexes ought to be a synthesis of the best "so-called" masculine and feminine qualities.

4330. McCracken, Robert D. THE FALLACIES OF WOMEN'S LIBERATION. Boulder, CO: Shields Publishing, 1972. 162 pp.

4331. Marlow, H. Carleton and Harrison M. Davis. THE AMERICAN SEARCH FOR WOMAN. Santa Barbara, CA: ABC Clio Press, 1976. 539 pp. Historical perspective on the women's movement. Excellent 50-page bibliography.

4332. Martin, Wendy, comp. THE AMERICAN SISTERHOOD; WRITINGS OF THE FEMINIST MOVEMENT FROM THE COLONIAL TIMES TO THE PRESENT. New York: Harper & Row, 1972. 373 pp.

4333. Mencken, Henry Louis. IN DEFENSE OF WOMEN. New York: Octagon Books, 1976. 210 pp. Reprint of 1918 edition. By the celebrated American cynic on the "Feminine Mind," "The War Between the Sexes," "Marriage," "Woman Suffrage," and "The New Age."

4334. Millett, Kate. FLYING. New York: Alfred A. Knopf, 1974. 545 pp. An autobiography that explores her feelings, attitudes, way of life, and her sexual attitudes.

4335. Millman, Marcia and Rosabeth Moss Kanter, eds. ANOTHER VOICE: FEMINIST PERSPECTIVES ON SOCIAL LIFE AND SOCIAL SERVICES. Garden City, NY: Doubleday, 1975. 382 pp. Reprint of SOCIOLOGICAL ENQUIRY, vol. 95, nos. 2-3 (1975).

4336. Mondo, Duarto. FRONTE ITALIANO DE LIBERAZIONE FEMMINILE. Rome, 1971.

4337. Mothersill, Mary, ed. "Women's Liberation: Ethical, Social, and Political Issues," THE MONIST, vol. 57, no. 1 (Jan. 1973), pp. 1-114.

Contributors include Christine Pierce, Virginia Held, Abigail L.
Rosenthal, Mary Anne Warren, Jan Narveson, and Thomas E. Hill, Jr.

4338. Myrdal, Alva. TOWARDS EQUALITY. Stockholm, Sweden: Prisma,
1971.

4339. Negrin, Su. BEGIN AT START: SOME THOUGHTS ON PERSONAL
LIBERATION AND WORLD CHANGE. New York: Times Change
Press, 1972. 176 pp. Describes how oppressive personal relationships
(sex, family, friendship) connect to oppressive social structure.

4340. News and Letters. "Notes on Women's Liberation: We Speak in Many
Voices." Detroit, MI: The Author, 1970. 86 pp.

4341. Papachristou, Judith, ed. WOMEN TOGETHER: A HISTORY IN
DOCUMENTS OF THE WOMEN'S MOVEMENT IN THE UNITED
STATES. New York: Alfred A. Knopf, 1976. 273 pp. 325 documents.

4342. Parturier, Francoise. LETTRE OUVERTE AUX HOMMES [AN OPEN
LETTER TO MEN]. Paris, France: A. Michel, 1968. 172 pp.

4343. Pollitt, Harry, ed. WOMEN AND COMMUNISM: SELECTIONS FROM
THE WRITINGS OF MARX, ENGELS, LENIN, AND STALIN.
Westport, CT: Greenwood Press, 1973. 104 pp. Reprint of 1950
edition.

4344. Reid, Marion Kirkland. A PLEA FOR WOMEN: BEING A
VINDICATION OF THE IMPORTANCE AND EXTENT OF HER
NATURAL SPHERE OF ACTION. WITH REMARKS ON RECENT
WORKS ON THE SUBJECT. New York: Farmer & Dagger, 1845.
156 pp.

4345. Rendel, Margherita, et al. "Equality for Women." London, England:
Fabian Society, 1968. 43 pp.

4346. Riegal, Robert Edgar. "A High Point of American Feminism." El Paso,
TX: Univ. of Texas, Texas Western Press, 1965. 17 pp.

4347. Robert, Anne. "Politics in Women's Liberation: Is It Necessary?"
Vancouver, B.C.: Vancouver Women's Caucus, 1970.

4348. Robins, Joan. HANDBOOK OF WOMEN'S LIBERATION. North
Hollywood, CA: Now Library Press, 1970. 279 pp.

4349. Rossi, Alice S. "Women: The Terms of Liberation," in THE CONFUSED
EAGLE: DIVISION AND DILEMMA IN AMERICAN POLITICS,
edited by Lewis Lipsitz. Boston, MA: Allyn & Bacon, 1973. 688 pp.

4350. Rossi, Alice S., ed. THE FEMINIST PAPERS: FROM ADAMS TO DE
BEAUVOIR. New York: Columbia Univ. Press, 1973. 716 pp.

4351. Rowbotham, Sheila. HIDDEN FROM HISTORY: REDISCOVERING
WOMEN IN HISTORY FROM THE 17th CENTURY TO THE
PRESENT. New York: Pantheon Books, 1975. 183 pp. Historical
origins of the problems facing the women's movement.

4352. ———. WOMEN, RESISTANCE, AND REVOLUTION: A HISTORY OF
WOMEN AND REVOLUTION IN THE MODERN WORLD. London,
England: Allen Lane, 1972. 288 pp. Relationship between feminism
and social revolution in capitalist and socialist countries; chapters on
Chinese and Vietnamese women's liberation through revolutionary
struggle.

4353. Rubin, Lilian B., ed. "Feminist Perspectives: The Sociological Challenge," SOCIAL PROBLEMS, vol. 23, no. 4 (April 1976), pp. 350-495. Special Issue. Contributors include Joan Huber, Barbara Easton, Jane Cassels Record, Wilson Record, Rosabeth Moss Kanter, Myra Marx Ferre, Jill Quadagno, Nancy Chodorow, Jack W. Sattel, Janet Lever, Barbara Payne, Frank Whittington, Carol B. Stack, and Thomas J. Cottle.

4354. Ruether, Rosemary. "Crisis in Sex and Race: Black Theology vs. Feminist Theology," CHRISTIANITY AND CRISIS, vol. 34, no. 6 (April 15, 1974), pp. 67-73. Black women and white women should not be afraid to compare experience in developing an encompassing theory of feminine liberation.

4355. Sachs, Karen. "Class Roots of Feminism," MONTHLY REVIEW, vol. 27, no. 9 (Feb. 1976), pp. 28-48. Analysis of three factions of the women's movement (1820-1920): the industrial working-class women, the working- and middle-class black women, and the middle-class white women.

4356. Schirmacher, Kathe. THE MODERN WOMAN'S RIGHTS MOVEMENT: A HISTORICAL SURVEY. Westport, CT: Hyperion Press, 1976. 280 pp. Reprint of 1912 edition. First international study of the feminist movement in North, South, and Central America, Western Europe, Asia and the Middle East.

4357. Schreiner, Olive. THE LETTERS OF OLIVE SCHREINER, 1876-1920. Westport, CT: Hyperion Press, 1976. 410 pp. Reprint of 1924 edition. Diary of the most productive years of the South African feminist, agnostic, and pacifist.

4358. Shaffer, Gail S. "Women's Fight for Liberation." Charlotteville, NY: SamHar Press, 1973. 32 pp. Traces the history of the women's movement for equal rights and social status.

4359. Sochen, June. MOVERS AND SHAKERS: AMERICAN WOMEN THINKERS AND ACTIVISTS, 1900-1970. New York: Quadrangle Books, 1973. 320 pp. Survey of feminism with emphasis on women intellectuals who thought, wrote, and acted to elevate the status of women, with a discussion of 30 selected feminists and their organizations.

4360. Streijffert, Helena. "Women's Movement–A Theoretical Discussion," ACTA SOCIOLOGICA, vol. 17, no. 4 (1974), pp. 344-366.

4361. United Nations. Office of Public Information. "Equal Rights for Women–A Call for Action: The United Nations Declaration on the Elimination of Discrimination Against Women." New York: United Nations, 1975. 30 pp.

4362. U.S. Congress. Senate. "National Center for Women Act (S. 2913)," CONGRESSIONAL RECORD, vol. 122, no. 11 (Feb. 2, 1976), pp. 955-960. Bill to reorganize and consolidate various Federal programs concerned with women.

4363. Urdang, Stephanie. "Towards a Successful Revolution: The Women's Struggle in Guinea-Bassau," OBJECTIVE: JUSTICE, vol. 7, no. 1 (Jan./March 1975), pp. 11-17.

4364. Varda One. "Women's Liberation: Who, What, When, Where, Why, and Some How: An Introductory Pamphlet." Los Angeles, CA: Everywoman Publishing, 1970. 9 pp.

4365. Walsh, Correa Moylan. FEMINISM. New York: Sturgis & Walton, 1917. 393 pp.

4366. Wandor, Michelene, ed. THE BODY POLITIC: WRITINGS FROM THE WOMEN'S LIBERATION MOVEMENT IN BRITAIN, 1969-1972. London, England: Stage I, 1972. 262 pp. Appendix contains a list of 25 names and addresses of women's liberation groups in Great Britain.

4367. Ware, Cellestine. WOMAN POWER: THE MOVEMENT FOR WOMEN'S LIBERATION. New York: Tower Publications, 1970. 176 pp. Overview of the women's rights movement.

4368. Warren, Tully E. WOMEN'S STRUGGLE FOR EQUALITY: THE VOTE, POLITICAL OFFICE, AND THE "EQUAL RIGHTS AMENDMENT." Washington, CT: Center for Information on America, 1975. 296 pp.

4369. Welsh, Erwin Kurt. FEMINISM IN DENMARK, 1850-1875. Bloomington, IN: Indiana Univ. Press, 1974. 323 pp.

D. 2. Feminism, Equal Rights—Committees on the Status of Women

When the first volume of WOMEN AND SOCIETY was conceived, Commissions on the Status of Women were neither as prevalent, nor as vital a contributing force to the political scene. Today, nearly every professional organization, every state, and many agencies of the U.S. federal government, the United Nations, and member states thereof, have established them as an integral part of the decision-making process. With due consideration to the importance and impact of these various commissions, the authors have limited this section to general works about commissions, rather than including the contributions and reports of each individual commission.

"When it comes to facing up to serious problems, each candidate will pledge to appoint a committee. And what is a committee? A group of the unwilling, picked from the unfit, to do the unnecessary. But it all sounds great in a campaign speech."
—Richard Long Harkness

4370. U.S. Dept. of Labor. Employment Standards Administration. Women's Bureau. "Commissions on the Status of Women: A Progress Report." Washington, D.C.: SUDOC, GPO, 1975. 21 pp. Report on the officially established state and local commissions.

4371. ———. "Handbook for State and City Commissions on the Status of Women." Madison, WI: Univ. of Wisconsin-Extension, 1968. 26 pp. Brief guidelines for the use of the resources available to commissions.

4372. ———. "Women's Bureaus and Commissions on the Status of Women: A Guide to the Functions and Services." Washington, D.C.: SUDOC, GPO, 1975. 15 pp. Methods of establishing commissions on the status of women and women's bureaus; provides samples of the functions and services of these types of organizations at the national level.

D. 3. Feminism, Equal Rights—Marriage and Divorce

"[Equality in marriage] is a practical impossibility. There must be inequality, and the superiority of the man is the lesser of two evils."
—Dr. Sigmund Freud

4373. Brogger, Suzanne. DELIVER US FROM LOVE: A RADICAL FEMINIST SPEAKS OUT. New York: Delacorte Press, 1976. 298 pp. Attacks monogamy, the nuclear family, and traditional sex roles.

4374. De Benedictis, Daniel J. LEGAL RIGHTS OF MARRIED WOMEN. New York: Cornerstone Library, 1969. 127 pp.

4375. Perrucci, Carolyn C. and Dena B. Targ. MARRIAGE AND THE FAMILY: A CRITICAL ANALYSIS AND PROPOSALS FOR CHANGE. New York: David McKay, 1974. 480 pp. Combines feminist values with a sociological perspective of family and marriage in present-day U.S.

4376. "Reforme de Divorce en France [Divorce Reform in France]," FRANCE—AMERIQUE, series D, no. 147 (March 19-25, 1975), p. 5. Government has approved project law which would institute divorce by mutual consent.

4377. Wheeler, Michael. NO-FAULT DIVORCE. Boston, MA: Beacon Press, 1974. 194 pp.

4378. Women in Transition, Inc. WOMEN IN TRANSITION: A FEMINIST HANDBOOK ON SEPARATION AND DIVORCE. New York: Charles Scribners Sons, 1975. 538 pp.

D. 4. Feminism, Equal Rights—Property

"The accumulation of property is no guarantee of the development of character, but the development of character, or of any other good whatever, is impossible without property."
—William Graham Sumner

4379. McCreery, J. L. "Women's Property Rights and Dowry in China and South Asia," ETHNOLOGY, vol. 15, no. 2 (April 1976), pp. 163-174.

4380. Maher, Vanessa. WOMEN AND PROPERTY IN MOROCCO: THEIR CHANGING RELATIONSHIP TO THE PROCESS OF SOCIAL STRATIFICATION IN THE MIDDLE EAST. London, England: Cambridge Univ. Press, 1974. 238 pp.

4381. Sivaramayya, B. WOMEN'S RIGHTS OF INHERITANCE IN INDIA: A COMPARATIVE STUDY OF EQUALITY AND PROTECTION. Madras, India: Madras Law Journal Office, 1973. 215 pp.

D. 5. Feminism, Equal Rights–Legal Status

"Please remember that law and sense are not always the same."
–Jawaharlal Nehru

4382. Alexander, Shana. SHANA ALEXANDER'S STATE-BY-STATE GUIDE
TO WOMEN'S LEGAL RIGHTS. Los Angeles, CA: Wollstonecraft,
1975. 224 pp.

4383. Baker, Brook and Elliot Taubman. "Equal Credit Opportunity Act: The
Effect of the Regulations on the Poor," CLEARINGHOUSE REVIEW,
vol. 9, no. 8 (Dec. 1975), pp. 543-547. Discusses income factors such as
alimony and child support which can be included in consideration of
financial status, if the woman desires.

4384. Beasley, Jean Karen. "Constitutional Law–Women's Rights–Mandatory
Pregnancy Leave Unconstitutional," WEST VIRGINIA LAW REVIEW,
vol. 77, no. 4 (June 1975), pp. 796-807.

4385. Bissett-Johnson, Alastair. "Mistress's Right to a Share in the 'Matrimonial
Home'," NEW LAW JOURNAL, vol. 125 (June 26, 1975), pp.
614-616.

4386. Box, Muriel, ed. THE TRIAL OF MARIE STOPES. London, England:
Femina Books, 1967. 392 pp. Transcript from the libel case of *Stopes*
v. *H. G. Sutherland* and *Harding & More, Ltd.,* in the High Court of
Justice, King's Bench Division.

4387. Bunnell, Rhoda. "Impact of *Geduldig* v. *Aiello* (94 Sup Ct 2485) on the
EEOC Guidelines on Sex Discrimination," INDIANA LAW JOURNAL,
vol. 50, no. 3 (Spring 1975), pp. 592-606. Urges that the decision,
which refused to invalidate state income maintenance program that
excluded pregnancy from its coverage under the Fourteenth
Amendment, should be read narrowly as to what the Amendment
allows.

4388. California. Commission on the Status of Women. Equal Rights
Amendment Project. IMPACT ERA: LIMITATIONS AND
POSSIBILITIES: THE DEFINITIVE WORK ON THE SUBJECT OF
THE EQUAL RIGHTS AMENDMENT. Los Angeles, CA: Les Femmes,
1976. 287 pp.

4389. Casey, Robert P. "Tax Benefits for Widows, the Supreme Court's
Attitude Toward Remedial Sex Legislation–*Kahn* v. *Shevin*," DE
PAUL LAW REVIEW, vol. 24, no. 3 (Spring 1975), pp. 797-812.
Questions standard of review to be applied to future claims under the
equal protection clause of the Fourteenth Amendment.

4390. Chapman, Jane Roberts, ed. ECONOMIC INDEPENDENCE FOR
WOMEN: THE FOUNDATION FOR EQUAL RIGHTS. Beverly Hills,
CA: Sage, 1976. 285 pp.

4391. Conlin, Roxanne Barton. "Equal Protection Versus Equal Rights
Amendment–Where are We Now?" DRAKE LAW REVIEW, vol. 24,
no. 2 (Winter 1975), pp. 259-335.

4392. Conrad-Rice, Joy Belle. "Women's Names and Women's Places," FRIENDS JOURNAL, vol. 17 (Sept. 15, 1971), pp. 458-459. Discusses the author's proposed bill which would allow use of the name one wanted even after marriage.

4393. Crable, Elizabeth C. "Pros and Cons of the Equal Rights Amendment," WOMEN LAWYERS JOURNAL, vol. 30, no. 3 (Summer 1949).

4394. Cruz Jiménez de Nigaglioni, Olga. "Como Discriminan las Leyes Contra la Mujer Puertorriqueña," REVISTA DEL COLEGIO DE ABOGADOS DE PUERTO RICO, vol. 37 (Aug. 1976), pp. 469-479. Legal discrimination.

4395. Daum, Rosalyn Goodman. "Right of Married Women to Assert Their Own Surnames," UNIV. OF MICHIGAN JOURNAL OF LAW, vol. 8 (Fall 1974), pp. 63-102.

4396. Davidson, Kenneth M., Ruth Bader Ginsburg, and Herma Hill Kay. 1975 SUPPLEMENT TO SEX-BASED DISCRIMINATION. St. Paul, MN: West Publishing, 1975. 167 pp. Updates 1974 text and cases.

4397. DeCrow, Karen. SEXIST JUSTICE: HOW LEGAL SEXISM AFFECTS YOU. New York: Random House, 1974. 329 pp. Interesting and valuable materials for U.S. women on their legal status in such areas as crime, education, marriage, credit, and employment.

4398. Feeley, Dianne. "Why Women Need the Equal Rights Amendment." New York: Pathfinder Press, 1973. 15 pp. Discusses the rationale of the opposition to the ERA, e.g. the John Birch Society's position, protective labor legislation.

4399. Geck, Donna Dunkleberger. "Equal Credit: You Can Get There From Here—the Equal Credit Opportunity Act," NORTH DAKOTA LAW REVIEW, vol. 32, no. 2 (Winter 1975), pp. 381-409. Problem of credit discrimination and remedies under the Equal Credit Opportunity Act, PL 93-495.

4400. Gilsinan, James F., Lynn Obernyer, and Christine A. Gilsinan. "Women Attorneys and the Judiciary," DENVER LAW JOURNAL, vol. 52, no. 4 (1975), pp. 881-909. Interactions of women attorneys with judges during the course of trial, and treatment of women by other functionaries of the system.

4401. Ginsburg, Ruth Bader. TEXT, CASES, AND MATERIALS ON CONSTITUTIONAL ASPECTS OF SEX-BASED DISCRIMINATION. St. Paul, MN: West Publishing, 1974. 129 pp. Reprint of Chapter I from TEXT, CASES, AND MATERIALS ON SEX-BASED DISCRIMINATION by Davidson, Ginsburg, and Kay.

4402. Ginsburgs, George. "Role of Law in the Emancipation of Women in the Democratic Republic of Vietnam," AMERICAN JOURNAL OF COMPARATIVE LAW, vol. 23, no. 4 (Fall 1975), pp. 613-652.

4403. Gorence, Patricia J. "Women's Name Rights," MARQUETTE LAW REVIEW, vol. 59 (1976), pp. 876-899. Excellent review of key cases throughout the U.S. on women's rights to use of a name.

4404. Guggenheim, Malvina H. and Elizabeth F. Defeis. "United States Participation in International Agreements Providing Rights for Women," LOYOLA OF LOS ANGELES LAW REVIEW, vol. 10, no. 1

(Dec. 1976), pp. 1-71. Urges U.S. ratification of the Convention on the Elimination of all Forms of Discrimination Against Women, prepared by the U.N. Commission on the Status of Women.

4405. Hochfelder, Carol G. "Equal Rights—Where Are We Now?" ILLINOIS BAR JOURNAL, vol. 64 (June 1976), pp. 558-567.

4406. Hosta de Guzmán, Magalie. "La Situacion Juridica de la Mujer Puertorriqueña Dentro del Regimen de la Sociedad Legal de Gananciales," REVISTA DEL COLEGIO DE ABOGADOS DE PUERTO RICO, vol. 36 (Aug. 1975), pp. 743-753.

4407. Hunter, Nan D. and Nancy D. Polikoff. "Custody Rights of Lesbian Mothers: Legal Theory and Litigation Strategy," BUFFALO LAW REVIEW, vol. 25, no. 3 (Spring 1976), pp. 691-733.

4408. "Impact of Michigan's Common-Law Disabilities of Coverture on Married Women's Access to Credit," MICHIGAN LAW REVIEW, vol. 74, no. 1 (Nov. 1975), pp. 76-105. Contractual equality must be clearly established by Michigan statute to insure the legislative intent of equality of credit opportunity.

4409. Jacobson, Richard S., ed. "Women and the Law," TRIAL, vol. 9, no. 6 (Nov./Dec. 1973), pp. 10-28. Special Issue. Contributors include U.S. Rep. Martha W. Griffiths, Silvia Roberts, Dorothy Haener, Phyllis Schlafly, U.S. Sen Marlow W. Cook, Carol Burris, Allen R. Derr, Shirley R. Bysiewicz, Dan O'Leary, Lawrence J. Smith, Joe A. Moore, G. Lawrence Roberts, D. Grant Mickel, and Mary Velasco Mercer.

4410. Kanowitz, Leo, comp. SEX ROLES IN LAW AND SOCIETY: 1974 SUPPLEMENT. Albuquerque, NM: Univ. of New Mexico Press, 1974.

4411. Kay, Herma H. SEX-BASED DISCRIMINATION IN FAMILY LAW. St. Paul, MN: West Publishing, 1974. 306 pp.

4412. Kulzer, Barbara Ann. "Law and the Housewife: Property, Divorce, and Death," UNIV. OF FLORIDA LAW REVIEW, vol. 28, no. 1 (Fall 1975), pp. 1-55. Property distribution between husband and wife.

4413. THE LAWS RESPECTING WOMEN. Dobbs Ferry, NY: Oceana Publications, 1974. 449 pp. Reprint of 1777 edition.

4414. Layish, Aharon. WOMEN AND ISLAMIC LAW IN A NON-MUSLIM STATE: A STUDY BASED ON DECISIONS OF THE SHARĪ'A COURTS IN ISRAEL. Jerusalem, Israel: Keter Publishing House, 1975. 369 pp.

4415. LOS DERECHOS DE LA MUJER: MEXICO 1975. Mexico, D.F.: Consejo Nacional de Poblacion, 1975. 126 pp. Discussion of the legal status of women in Mexico, including citations to Mexican law.

4416. McDougal, Myles S., Harold D. Lasswell, and Lung-Chu Chen. "Human Rights for Women and World Public Order: The Outlawing of Sex-Based Discrimination," AMERICAN JOURNAL OF INTERNATIONAL LAW, vol. 69, no. 3 (July 1975), pp. 497-533.

4417. Matthews, William C., Jr. "Married Women and the Name Game," UNIV. OF RICHMOND LAW REVIEW, vol. 11, no. 1 (Fall 1976), pp. 121-161. Focuses on the English common law history of surnames and the legal issues.

4418. Morgenstern, Felice. "Women Workers and the Courts," INTERNATIONAL LABOUR REVIEW, vol. 112, no. 1 (July 1975), pp. 15-27. Analyzes court decisions relating to women's problems of equality of opportunity and treatment, and those relating to the functions of women in the family.

4419. Mulvey, Kenneth J., Jr. "Constitutional Law—Sixth Amendment—Systematic Exclusion of Women from Jury Service Violates the Sixth and Fourteenth Amendments, *Taylor* v. *Louisiana* (95 Sup Ct 692 (1975))," FORDHAM URBAN LAW JOURNAL, vol. 3, no. 3 (Spring 1975), pp. 733-748.

4420. Oakley, Mary Ann B. "Equal Rights Amendment and the Right to Privacy," EMORY LAW JOURNAL, vol. 23 (Winter 1974), pp. 197-209. Reaffirms that the right to privacy precludes unisex bathrooms and required unisex dormitories.

4421. Polson, Terry Ellen. "Rights of Working Women: An International Perspective," VIRGINIA JOURNAL OF INTERNATIONAL LAW, vol. 14, no. 4 (Summer 1974), pp. 729-746. Notes the slowly improving climate.

4422. Rabkin, Peggy A. "Origins of Law Reforms: The Social Significance of the Nineteenth Century Codification Movement and Its Contribution to the Passage of the Early Married Women's Property Acts," BUFFALO LAW REVIEW, vol. 24, no. 3 (Spring, 1975), pp. 683-760. Excellent history of women's legal rights.

4423. Ramstad, Sheryl A. "Female Offenders: A Challenge to Courts and the Legislature," NORTH DAKOTA LAW REVIEW, vol. 51, no. 4 (Summer 1975), pp. 827-853. Surveys the history and treatment of incarcerated women, with suggestions for reform.

4424. Rivers, Theodore John. "Widows' Rights in Anglo-Saxon Law," AMERICAN JOURNAL OF LEGAL HISTORY, vol. 19 (July 1975), pp. 208-215.

4425. Ross, Susan D. THE RIGHTS OF WOMEN: THE BASIC ACLU GUIDE TO A WOMAN'S RIGHTS. New York: Sunrise Books, 1973. 384 pp.

4426. Sadr, Hassan. HUGHUGH É ZAN DAR ISLAM VA URUPA [THE WAGES OF WOMEN IN ISLAM AND IN EUROPE]. Tehran, Iran: Parastu, 1970.

4427. Santiago, William Fred. "Liberación Femenina—¿por que?" REVISTA DEL COLEGIO DE ABOGADO DE PUERTO RICO, vol. 36 (Aug. 1975), pp. 639-647.

4428. Sassower, Doris L. "Women, Power, and the Law," AMERICAN BAR ASSOCIATION JOURNAL, vol. 62 (May 1976), pp. 613-616. Discusses the limitation on women's rights by sex-linked roles defined by men.

4429. Sedwick, Cathy and Reba Williams. "Black Women and the Equal Rights Amendment," BLACK SCHOLAR, vol. 7, no. 10 (July/Aug. 1976), pp. 24-29. Urges mobilization of people for grass roots movement.

4430. Sokolov, V. V. THE RIGHTS OF WOMEN UNDER SOVIET LAW. Moscow, Russia: Yuridicheskoe izdatel'stov NKYU RSFSR, 1928.

4431. Stimpson, Catharine, ed. DISCRIMINATION AGAINST WOMEN: CONGRESSIONAL HEARINGS ON EQUAL RIGHTS AMENDMENT IN EDUCATION AND EMPLOYMENT. New York: Bowker, 1973. 553 pp. Rearranged and edited transcripts of hearings of the 91st Congress (House and Senate) on discrimination. Part I, 23 oral testimonies; Part II, 53 position papers, surveys, charts and tables.

4432. ———. WOMEN AND THE "EQUAL RIGHTS" AMENDMENT: SENATE SUBCOMMITTEE HEARINGS ON THE CONSTITUTIONAL AMENDMENT, 91ST CONGRESS. New York: Bowker, 1972. 538 pp. Edited transcripts of the key hearings in the passage of the ERA.

4433. Switzer, Ellen Eichenwald with Wendy W. Susco. THE LAW FOR A WOMAN: REAL CASES AND WHAT HAPPENED. New York: Charles Scribners Sons, 1975. 246 pp.

4434. Tate, Kathryn Willcox. "TITLE VII: A Remedy for Discrimination Against Women Prisoners," ARIZONA LAW REVIEW, vol. 16, no. 4 (1974), pp. 974-1000. Proposes use of this section of the Civil Rights Act of 1964 as a statutory remedy for disparate vocational rehabilitation programs in prison.

4435. Taubenfeld, Rita Falk and Howard J. Taubenfeld. "Achieving the Human Rights of Women: The Base Line, the Challenge, the Search for a Strategy," HUMAN RIGHTS, vol. 4 (Spring 1975), pp. 125-129.

4436. A TREATISE OF FEME COVERTS: OR, THE LADY'S LAW. South Hackensack, NJ: Rothman Reprints, 1974. 264 pp. Reprint of 1732 edition. The argument of Judge Hyde in the case of *Manky* v. *Scott:* whether and in what cases is the husband bound by the contract of the wife.

4437. Treece, Claude. "The ERA and Texas Marital Law," TEXAS LAW REVIEW, vol. 54, no. 3 (March 1976), pp. 590-615. Discusses the discriminatory aspects of marital law interpretation and suggests the ERA as a major part of solution.

4438. Turner, Kaye and Pauline Vaver, eds. "Women and the Law in New Zealand." Wellington, NZ: Hicks Smith, 1975. 87 pp.

4439. U.S. Dept. of Health, Education, and Welfare. Social Security Administration. "Women and Social Security: Law and Policy in Five Countries." By Dalmer Hoskins and Lenore E. Bixby. Washington, D.C.: SUDOC, GPO, 1973. 95 pp.

4440. U.S. Dept. of Housing and Urban Development. Office of the Asst. Secretary for Fair Housing and Equal Opportunity. WOMEN AND HOUSING: A REPORT ON SEX DISCRIMINATION IN FIVE AMERICAN CITIES. Washington, D.C.: SUDOC, GPO, 1976. 196 pp. Atlanta, GA, St. Louis, MO, San Antonio, TX, San Francisco, CA, and New York City.

4441. White, Collis H. WIN OR LOSE: WHAT YOU SHOULD KNOW ABOUT THE ERA. Hicksville, NY: Exposition Press, 1976. 160 pp.

4442. Whittenberg, George H. "The E.R.A. and You." New York: Vantage, 1975. 81 pp.

4443. Whyte, John D. "The Lavell Case and Equality in Canada," QUEEN'S QUARTERLY, vol. 81, no. 1 (Spring 1974), pp. 28-42. Sex discrimination case involving a conflict between Indian Act and the Canadian Bill of Rights.

4444. Wisconsin. Governor's Commission on the Status of Women. "Wisconsin Women and the Law." Madison, WI: Univ. of Wisconsin-Extension, 1975. 81 pp. Resource handbook on the legal status of women.

4445. "Women and the Law: Special Issue [La Femme et la Droit: Édition Spéciale]," McGILL LAW JOURNAL, vol. 21, no. 4 (Winter 1975), pp. 476-707. Contributors include Susan Altschul, Christine Carron, E. Groffier, Frances Schanfield Freedman, Peter M. Jacobson, H. R. Hahlo, Roy L. Heeman, Edythe I. MacDonald, S. June Menzies, Jack Bernstein, Douglas Sanders, H. Patrick Glenn, and Marguerite E. Ritchie.

D. 6. Feminism, Equal Rights–Employment

"Our business needs massive transfusions of talent. And talent, I believe is most likely to be found among nonconformists, dissenters, and rebels "
—David MacKenzie Ogilvy

"Did you ever expect a Corporation to have a conscience, when it has no soul to be damned, and no body to be kicked?"
—Harry S. Truman

4446. Amsden, Alice H. and Collette Moser. "Supply and Mobility of Women Economists: Job Search and Affirmative Action," AMERICAN ECONOMIC REVIEW, vol. 65, no. 2 (May 1975), pp. 83-107. Amsden's statistical analysis of current employment data found no consistent pattern of differences between men and women; while Moser's survey of affirmative action implementation indicates that improvements in conditions of employment seem to be marginal.

4447. Carr, Shirley, ed. CANADIAN LABOUR, vol. 21, no. 3 (Sept. 1976), pp. 1-46. Special Issue on equal opportunity in employment. Contributors include Laura Sabia, Joy Langan, Mary Eady, Edward F. Ryan, Vivian Zachon, May Britt Carlsson, Jim MacDonald, Clas-Erik Odhner, John Bank, and John Clark.

4448. "Fair Employment–Is Pregnancy Alone a Sufficient Reason for Dismissal of a Public Employee?" BOSTON UNIVERSITY LAW REVIEW, vol. 52 (Winter 1972), pp. 196-201.

4449. Great Britain. Occupational Pensions Board. EQUAL STATUS FOR MEN AND WOMEN IN OCCUPATIONAL PENSION SCHEMES: A REPORT IN ACCORDANCE WITH SECTION 66 OF THE SOCIAL SECURITY ACT OF 1973. London, England: Her Majesty's Stationery Office, 1976. 232 pp.

4450. Gregory, Chester W. WOMEN IN DEFENSE WORK DURING WORLD WAR II: AN ANALYSIS OF THE LABOR PROBLEMS AND WOMEN'S RIGHTS. New York: Exposition Press, 1974. 243 pp.

4451. Kehoe, Mary, ed. CANADIAN LABOUR, vol. 20, no. 2 (June 1975), pp. 1-38. Special issue on equal pay for women. Contributors include Shirley Carr, Sylvia Gelber, Joy Langan, Janet Smith, Freda L. Paltiel, Patrick Kerwin, Marlene Kempthorne, and J. Larry Wagg.

4452. Pettman, Barrie O. and John Fyfe, eds. EQUAL PAY FOR WOMEN: PROGRESS AND PROBLEMS IN SEVEN COUNTRIES. West Yorkshire, England: MCB Books, 1975. 173 pp. Discusses the role of women in the labor forces and other factors in the implementation of equal pay for women in Germany, Japan, Australia, United Kingdom, America, Canada, and New Zealand.

4453. Rosenberg-Dishman, Marie B. "Affirmative Action—Contexts and Compliance for Local Governments," THE MUNICIPALITY, vol. 69, no. 12 (Dec. 1974), pp. 237-246.

4454. U.S. Dept. of Health, Education, and Welfare. Office of Planning, Budget, and Evaluation. "Evaluation of the Availability and Effectiveness of Manpower Development and Training Act (MDTA) Institutional Training and Employment Services for Women: Final Report." Washington, D.C.: SUDOC, GPO, 1974. 79 pp. Analysis of data to determine the impact of institutional training on women.

4455. ———. EVALUATION OF THE AVAILABILITY AND EFFECTIVENESS OF MDTA INSTITUTIONAL TRAINING AND EMPLOYMENT SERVICES FOR WOMEN: REANALYSIS OF THE MDTA OUTCOME STUDY. Washington, D.C.: SUDOC, GPO, 1974. 123 pp.

4456. ———. EVALUATION OF THE AVAILABILITY AND EFFECTIVENESS OF MDTA INSTITUTIONAL TRAINING AND EMPLOYMENT SERVICES FOR WOMEN: A REVIEW OF THE LITERATURE. Washington, D.C.: SUDOC, GPO, 1974. 112 pp.

4457. U.S. Dept. of Labor. Employment Standards Administration. Women's Bureau. "Maternity Standards." Prepared by Jane M. Newman. Washington, D.C.: SUDOC, GPO, 1975. pp. 339-357. Reprint of chapter from 1975 HANDBOOK ON WOMEN WORKERS. Maternity guidelines issued by the Federal government and developments affecting the status of pregnant women in the work force.

4458. ———. "State Labor Laws in Transition: From Protection to Equal Status for Women." Washington, D.C.: SUDOC, GPO, 1976. 21 pp. Documents state laws of special interest to working women.

4459. ———. "A Working Woman's Guide to her Job Rights." Prepared by Rose Terlin. Washington, D.C.: SUDOC, GPO, Rev. 1975. 34 pp. General information which affects women when they are seeking a job, while they are on the job, and when they retire.

4460. U.S. Dept. of Labor. Manpower Administration. Office of Research and Development. "WAGES (Women and Girls Employment Enabling Service): Final Report." Washington, D.C.: SUDOC, GPO, 1974. 69 pp. Documents efforts to open non-traditional fields of employment to women in Memphis, Tennessee.

4461. Wetzel, Janice Wood. "Interaction of Feminism and Social Work in America," SOCIAL CASEWORK, vol. 57, no. 4 (April 1976), pp.

227-236. Reviews feminist social achievements and urges equality of opportunity for women to advance in the field of social work.

D. 7. Feminism, Equal Rights—Education

"During the Middle Ages Europe was far too much influenced by celibate men. Today much too big a part in public life is played by celibate women, and too little by mothers. I find no new ideas more genuinely disgusting than that held by many educated authorities that a woman ceases to be suitable as a teacher when she becomes a mother."
—John Burdon Sanderson Haldane

"Our progress as a nation can be no swifter than our progress in education."
—John Fitzgerald Kennedy

4462. Abramson, Joan. THE INVISIBLE WOMAN: DISCRIMINATION IN THE ACADEMIC PROFESSION. San Francisco, CA: Jossey-Bass, 1975. 248 pp. Sex discrimination in the higher education employment.

4463. Academic Collective Bargaining Information Service. "The Application of Non-Discrimination Law and Regulations to Collective Bargaining in Higher Education." Arlington, VA: ERIC Document Reproduction Service, 1975. 13 pp. Discusses the major equal employment labor legislation, and attempts to shape the principle of the law to fit faculty and nonfaculty collective bargaining issues.

4464. American Association of School Administrators. "Sex Equality in Educational Administration." Arlington, VA: Amer. Assoc. of School Administrators, 1975. 29 pp. AASA Exec. Handbook Series, vol. 7, no. 3. Affirmative Action in education administration.

4465. ———. "Sex Equality in Educational Materials." Arlington, VA: Amer. Assoc. of School Administrators, 1975. 24 pp. AASA Exec. Handbook Series, vol. 4, no. 1. Guidelines for counteracting sex stereotyping in educational materials.

4466. ———. "Sex Equality in Schools." Arlington, VA: Amer. Assoc. of School Administrators, 1975. 31 pp. AASA Exec. Handbook Series, vol. 5, no. 2. Organizational procedures that tend to channel girls and boys into different programs.

4467. American Federation of Teachers. "Women in Education: Changing Sexist Practices in the Classroom." Washington, D.C.: AFL-CIO, A.F.T., 1974. 75 pp. Includes suggested materials for classroom use.

4468. Bolmeier, Edward Claude. SEX LITIGATION AND THE PUBLIC SCHOOLS. Charlottesville, VA: Mitchie, 1975. 215 pp.

4469. Buek, Alexandra and Jeffrey H. Orleans. "Sex Discrimination—A Bar to a Democratic Education: Overview of TITLE IX of the Education Amendments of 1972," CONNECTICUT LAW REVIEW, vol. 6, no. 1 (Fall 1973), pp. 1-27.

4470. Cohen, Audrey C. "Women and Higher Education." New York: College for Human Services, 1971. 16 pp. Discusses some of the professional

education roadblocks for women, as well as the negative policies of
many universities, concludes with a series of recommendations for
reform.

4471. Divine, Thomas M. "Women in the Academy: Sex Discrimination in
University Faculty Hiring and Promotion," JOURNAL OF LAW AND
EDUCATION, vol. 5, no. 4 (Oct. 1976), pp. 429-451.

4472. Education Commission of the States. Equal Rights for Women in
Education Project. "Digest of Federal Laws: Equal Rights for Women
in Education." Denver, CO: Education Comm. of the States, 1975.
44 pp.

4473. French, Larry L. "Nondiscrimination on the Basis of Sex. . . . (TITLE
IX)," Chapter 10 in the SECOND ADMINISTRATORS LEGAL
HANDBOOK. Norman, OK: Univ. of Oklahoma College of Law,
Continuing Legal Education, 1975. 161 pp. Brief overview and history
of TITLE IX of the Education Amendments of 1972 and the impact of
the regulations on recipients of federal financial assistance.

4474. Gough, Pauline. SEXISM: NEW ISSUE IN AMERICAN EDUCATION.
Bloomington, IN: Phi Delta Kappa, 1976.

4475. Hahn, Carol L., ed. "Eliminating Sexism from the Schools: Implementing
Change," SOCIAL EDUCATION, vol. 39, no. 3 (March 1975), pp.
133-147. Special Section. Contributors include Margaret Carter, Mary
Ann Phillips, Betty Pullin, Dorothy Riggs Holman, Myrtle A. Fentress,
and Lois Wilhelm.

4476. Howe, Florence, ed. WOMEN AND THE POWER TO CHANGE. New
York: McGraw-Hill, 1975. 182 pp. Sponsored by the Carnegie
Commission on Higher Education. Discusses institutional reforms,
feminists in education.

4477. Lester, Richard A. ANTI-BIAS REGULATIONS OF UNIVERSITIES:
FACULTY PROBLEMS AND THEIR SOLUTIONS. New York:
McGraw-Hill, 1974. 168 pp. A limited survey of effects of
anti-sex-discriminatory legislation on American universities, prepared
for the Carnegie Comm. on Higher Education.

4478. Lieberman, Myron, ed. "Education and the Feminist Movement," PHI
DELTA KAPPAN, vol. 55, no. 2 (Oct. 1973), pp. 98-159. Special Issue.
Contributors include Florence Howe, Betty Levy, Judith Stacey, Janice
Law Trecker, Celeste Ulrich, Carol Kehr Tittle, Catherine B. Hallman,
Sheila M. Torhman, Guin Hall, Joseph M. Cronin, Florence C. Lewis,
Sharlene Pearlman Hirsch, W. Michael Morrissey, June Marr, Gene A.
Budig, Richard Decker, and Betty Wetzel.

4479. Lupini, Dante. "Women in Administration–Where are They?"
EDUCATION CANADA, vol. 15, no. 4 (Winter 1975), pp. 17-22.
Inequalities in school systems.

4480. McGrath, Patricia L. "The Unfinished Assignment: Equal Education for
Women." Washington, D.C.: Worldwatch Institute, 1976. 47 pp. Traces
development of educational opportunity for women around the world.

4481. National Association for Women Deans, Administrators, and Counselors.
SEXISM AND BIAS. Washington, D.C.: NAWDAC, 1974.

4482. National Organization for Women. New York Chapter. "Report on Sex Bias in the Public Schools." New York: N.O.W., 1971. 50 pp.
4483. North Carolina. State Dept. of Public Instruction. Research and Information Center. ELIMINATING SEX DISCRIMINATION IN SCHOOLS: A SOURCE BOOK. Arlington, VA: ERIC Document Reproduction Service, 1975. 154 pp. Summarizes pertinent information related to all types of sex discrimination in elementary and secondary schools. Includes extensive annotated bibliography.
4484. Pearson, Jessica, ed. A HANDBOOK OF STATE LAWS AND POLICIES AFFECTING EQUAL RIGHTS FOR WOMEN IN EDUCATION. Denver, CO: Education Comm. of the States, 1975. 125 pp.
4485. Pearson, William. AN OVERVIEW OF FEDERAL COURT DECISIONS AFFECTING EQUAL RIGHTS FOR WOMEN IN EDUCATION. Denver, CO: Education Comm. of the States, 1975. 193 pp.
4486. Pennsylvania. State Dept. of Education. "Self-Study Guide to Sexism in Schools." Arlington, VA: ERIC Document Reproduction Service, 1974. 60 pp. Guidelines for determining sexist practices in various aspects of school life.
4487. Reuben, Elaine and Leonore Hoffman, eds. UNLADYLIKE AND UNPROFESSIONAL: ACADEMIC WOMEN AND ACADEMIC UNIONS. New York: Modern Language Assoc., Comm. on the Status of Women in the Profession, 1975.
4488. Richardson, Betty. SEXISM IN HIGHER EDUCATION. New York: Seabury Press, 1974.
4489. Roberts, Joan I., ed. BEYOND INTELLECTUAL SEXISM: A NEW WOMAN, A NEW REALITY. New York: David McKay, 1976. 386 pp.
4490. Tinsley, Adrian, Elaine Reuben, and Diane Crothers, eds. ACADEMIC WOMEN, SEX DISCRIMINATION, AND THE LAW. New York: Modern Language Assoc., Comm. on the Status of Women in the Profession, 1974.
4491. United Nations. Economic and Social Council. "Activities of the Specialized Agencies to Promote the Advancement of Women. Study on UNESCO Activities of Special Interest to Women." Paris, France: UNESCO, 1973. 58 pp. Emphasizes involvement of member states in UNESCO activities, and focuses on equality of educational opportunity.
4492. –––. "Study on the Equality of Access of Girls and Women to Education in the Context of Rural Development." Paris, France: UNESCO, 1973. 87 pp. Examines why women in rural areas encounter particular difficulties in gaining access to out-of-school education.
4493. U.S. Congress. House. Committee on Education and Labor. Subcommittee on Equal Opportunities. "Hearing on House Concurrent Resolution 330 (TITLE IX Regulation). 94th Congress, 1st Session on H. Con. Res. 330." Washington, D.C.: SUDOC, GPO, 1975. 75 pp.
4494. U.S. Congress. House. Committee on Education and Labor. Subcommittee on Postsecondary Education. SEX DISCRIMINATION REGULATIONS. HEARINGS BEFORE THE SUBCOMMITTEE ON

POSTSECONDARY EDUCATION OF THE COMMITTEE ON EDUCATION AND LABOR. 94th Congress, 1st Session. Washington, D.C.: SUDOC, GPO, 1975. 672 pp. Hearings on the regulations issued by the Dept. of Health, Education, and Welfare for the implementation of TITLE IX of Public Law 92-318.

4495. ———. SEX DISCRIMINATION REGULATIONS: HEARINGS, JUNE 17-26, 1975, REVIEW OF REGULATIONS TO IMPLEMENT TITLE IX OF PUBLIC LAW 92-318 CONDUCTED PURSUANT TO SEC. 431 OF THE GENERAL EDUCATION PROVISIONS ACT. 94th Congress, 1st Session. Washington, D.C.: SUDOC, GPO, 1975. 664 pp. Emphasis on college athletics.

4496. U.S. Congress. Senate. Committee on Labor and Public Welfare. Subcommittee on Education. WOMEN'S EDUCATIONAL EQUITY ACT OF 1973. 93rd Congress, 1st Session. Washington, D.C.: SUDOC, GPO, 1973. 426 pp.

4497. U.S. Dept. of Health, Education, and Welfare. REPORT OF THE WOMEN'S ACTION PROGRAM. Washington, D.C.: U.S. Dept. of HEW, 1972. The Women's Action Program was created in 1971 on the premise that change was needed in the status of women both within the Dept. of HEW and in the outside world.

4498. Univ. of Michigan. Institute of Continuing Legal Education. WOMEN'S WORK HAS JUST BEGUN: LEGAL PROBLEMS OF EMPLOYING WOMEN IN UNIVERSITIES. Ann Arbor, MI: Univ. of Michigan, 1972. 310 pp.

D. 8. Feminism, Equal Rights—Innovative

"To innovate is not to reform."

—Edmund Burke

4499. Carlson, Dale. GIRLS ARE EQUAL TOO: THE WOMEN'S MOVEMENT FOR TEENAGERS. New York: Atheneum, 1973. 146 pp.

4500. "High School Women's Liberation." Ann Arbor, MI: Youth Liberation, 1976. 81 pp.

D. 9. Feminism, Equal Rights—Radical

"Revolution is not a dinner party, nor an essay, nor a painting, nor a piece of embroidery; it cannot be advanced softly, gradually, carefully, considerately, respectfully, politely, plainly, and modestly."

—Mao Tse-tung

"To-day is not yesterday. We ourselves change. How then, can our works and thoughts, if they are always to be the fittest, continue always the same. Change, indeed, is painful, yet ever needful; and if memory have its force and worth, so also has hope."

—Thomas Carlyle

4501. Ballen, Dorothy. "Feminism and Marxism." New York: World View Publishers, 1971. 69 pp. Reprinted from WORKERS WORLD.

4502. Baritz, Loren, ed. THE AMERICAN LEFT: RADICAL POLITICAL THOUGHT IN THE TWENTIETH CENTURY. New York: Basic Books, 1971. 522 pp. Contributors on women include Emma Goldman, Naomi Jaffe, Bernadine Dohrn, Robin Morgan, Kathy McAffe, Myrna Wood, Pat Mainardi, and Anne P. Koedt.

4503. Birkby, Phyllis, Bertha Harris, Jill Johnston, Esther Newton, and Jane O'Wyatt, eds. "Amazon Expedition: A Lesbian Feminist Anthology." New York: Times Change Press, 1973. 96 pp. A separate cultural/political movement synthesizing gay politics with feminism.

4504. Johnston, Jill. LESBIAN NATION: THE FEMINIST SOLUTION. New York: Simon & Schuster, 1973. 288 pp.

4505. Koedt, Anne, Ellen Levine, and Anita Rapone, eds. RADICAL FEMINISM. New York: Quadrangle Books, 1973. 424 pp. Collection of 45 articles, photos, and cartoons, most of which are reprinted from NOTES, an annual radical feminist journal.

4506. Redstockings. FEMINIST REVOLUTION. New York: Random House, 1976. 200 pp.

4507. Schein, Muriel and Carol Lopate. "On Engles and the Liberation of Women," LIBERATION, vol. 16 (Feb. 1972), pp. 4-9.

4508. Selivanova, Nina Nikolaevna. RUSSIA'S WOMEN. Westport, CT: Hyperion Press, 1976. 226 pp. Reprint of 1923 edition. Discusses the contributions of the first Russian feminists; Catherine Breshkovskaya, Vera Figner, Sophia Peroskaya, Vera Zasulich, Maria Trubnikova, Nadejhda Stasova, Anna Filosofova, and others.

4509. Strachey, Rachel Conn (Costelloe). SHAKEN BY THE WIND: A STORY OF FANATICISM. London, England: Faber & Gwyer, 1927. 319 pp.

4510. Waters, Mary Alice. "Feminism and the Marxist Movement." New York: Pathfinder Press, 1972. 48 pp.

E. Women as Voters

Although we have cited few publications entirely directed to the topic of women as voters, such analyses appear to be included in general works on women's political participation, and can be found cited elsewhere in this volume.

1. General

"Democracy, if it means anything, means equality; not merely the equality of possessing a vote, but economic and social equality."
> —*Jawaharlal Nehru*

"Voting is the least arduous of a citizen's duties. He has the prior and harder duty of making up his mind."
> —*Ralph Barton Perry*

4511. Anderson, K. "Working Women and Political Participation, 1952-1972," AMERICAN JOURNAL OF POLITICS, vol. 19 (Aug. 1975), pp. 439-453.

4512. Coolidge, Mary Elizabeth Burroughs (Roberts) Smith. "What the Women of California have done with the Ballot." San Francisco, CA: California Civic League, 1916. 8 pp.

4513. Feltner, Paula and Leneen Goldie. "Impact of Socialization and Personality on the Female Voter: Speculations Tested with 1964 Presidential Data," THE WESTERN POLITICAL QUARTERLY, vol. 27, no. 4 (Dec. 1975), pp. 680-692.

E. 2. Women as Voters—Extent of Participation

"Real political issues cannot be manufactured by the leaders of parties, and cannot be evaded by them. They declare themselves, and come out of the depths of that deep which we call public opinion."
—James Abraham Garfield

4514. Goot, Murray and Elizabeth Reid. "Women and Voting Studies: Mindless Matrons or Sexist Scientism?" Beverly Hills, CA: Sage, 1975. 44 pp.

4515. Jones, H. J. "Japanese Women in the Politics of the Seventies," ASIAN SURVEY, vol. 15, no. 8 (Aug. 1975), pp. 708-723. Power of the ballot is not being exercised by women.

4516. Levitt, Morris. "The Political Role of American Women," JOURNAL OF HUMAN RELATIONS, vol. 15, no. 1 (Jan. 1967), pp. 23-35. Offers rationale for female "non-voter" behavior.

E. 3. Women as Voters—Stand on Issues

"People vote their resentment, not their appreciation. The average man does not vote for anything, but against something."
—William Bennett Munro

4517. Rivington, Ann. "Women—Vote for Life." New York: Workers Library, 1940. 15 pp. Urges Communist vote.

F. Woman Suffrage

1. General

"The fears of one class of men are not the measure of the rights of another."
—George Bancroft

"Being a woman is a terribly difficult task, since it consists principally in dealing with men."

—Joseph Conrad

4518. Elshtain, Jean Bethke. "Moral Woman and Immoral Man: A Consideration of the Public-Private Split and Its Political Ramifications," POLITICS AND SOCIETY, vol. 4, no. 4 (1974), pp. 453-473.

4519. Gompers, Samuel. "Labor and Woman Suffrage," AMERICAN QUARTERLY, vol. 27 (Oct. 1920), pp. 936-939. By the famous labor leader.

4520. Grimshaw, Patricia. WOMEN'S SUFFRAGE IN NEW ZEALAND. Auckland, New Zealand: Auckland Univ. Press, 1972. 151 pp.

4521. Hays, Mary. AN APPEAL TO THE MEN OF GREAT BRITAIN IN BEHALF OF WOMEN. New York: Garland Publishers, 1974. 300 pp. Reprint of 1798 edition.

4522. Mackenzie, Midge, ed. SHOULDER TO SHOULDER: A DOCUMENTARY. New York: Alfred A. Knopf, 1975. 342 pp. History of the Militant Suffragettes in Great Britain.

4523. Mackmurdo, Arthur Heygate. PRESSING QUESTIONS: PROFIT SHARING, WOMEN'S SUFFRAGE, ELECTORAL REFORM. London, England: John Lane, 1913. 342 pp.

4524. Metcalfe, Agnes Edith. "At Last: Conclusion of WOMEN'S EFFORT." Oxford, England: B. H. Blackwell, 1917. 79 pp.

4525. ———. WOMAN'S EFFORT: A CHRONICLE OF BRITISH WOMAN'S FIFTY YEARS OF STRUGGLE FOR CITIZENSHIP (1865-1914). Oxford, England: B. H. Blackwell, 1917. 381 pp.

4526. Morgan, David. SUFFRAGISTS AND DEMOCRATS: THE POLITICS OF WOMAN SUFFRAGE IN AMERICA. East Lansing, MI: Michigan State Univ. Press, 1972. 225 pp. Includes 18-page bibliography.

4527. ———. SUFFRAGISTS AND LIBERALS: THE POLITICS OF WOMAN SUFFRAGE IN ENGLAND. Totowa, NJ: Rowman and Littlefield, 1975. 184 pp. Study of the complexity of the woman suffrage issue and how it became ensnarled with the rise of Labour and the Liberal-Tory struggle for political power.

4528. Morris, Homer Lawrence. PARLIAMENTARY FRANCHISE REFORM IN ENGLAND FROM 1885-1918. New York: AMS Press, 1969. 208 pp. Reprint of 1921 edition. Woman suffrage in Great Britain.

4529. Raeburn, Antonia. "The Suffragette View." New York: St. Martin Press, 1976. 95 pp. Suffrage in Great Britain.

4530. Rosen, Andrew. RISE UP, WOMEN! THE MILITANT CAMPAIGN OF THE WOMEN'S SOCIAL AND POLITICAL UNION, 1903-1914. London, England: Routledge & Kegan Paul, 1974. 312 pp.

4531. Scott, Anne Firor and Andrew MacKay Scott. ONE HALF THE PEOPLE: THE FIGHT FOR WOMEN'S SUFFRAGE. Philadelphia, PA: J. B. Lippincott, 1975. 173 pp.

4532. Shafroth, John Franklin. "Equal Suffrage: Speech of Hon. John F. Shafroth of Colorado in the Senate of the United States, Tuesday, April

25, 1916, as Amended by Permission of the Senate, January 24, 1917."
Washington, D.C.: U.S. Gov. Printing Office, 1917. 16 pp.

4533. "Significance of the Woman Suffrage Movement. Session of the American Academy of Political and Social Science, Wednesday Evening, Feb. 9, 1910," Supplement to THE ANNALS OF THE AMERICAN ACADEMY OF POLITICAL AND SOCIAL SCIENCE, vol. 35 (May 1910), pp. 1-37. Contributors include L. S. Rowe, Robert L. Owen, Anna G. Spencer, Mrs. Gilbert E. Jones, Alice Paul, Lyman Abbott, Mrs. Frederick Nathan, and Charles H. Pankhurst.

4534. Strachey, Rachel Conn (Costelloe). MARCHING ON. New York: Harcourt Brace, 1923. 385 pp.

4535. Thonnession, Werner and Wieland Schulz-Keil. THE EMANCIPATION OF WOMEN: THE RISE AND DECLINE OF THE WOMEN'S MOVEMENT IN GERMANY 1863-1933. New York: Urizen Books, 1976.

4536. U.S. Congress. Senate. Committee on the District of Columbia. WOMEN'S SUFFRAGE AND THE POLICE: THREE SENATE DOCUMENTS. New York: Arno Press, 1971. Reprint of 1913 edition.

F. 2. Woman Suffrage—Leaders

"Man has converted her into a domestic drudge and an instrument of his pleasure, instead of regarding her as his helpmate and better half. The result is a semi-paralysis of our society. Woman has rightly been called the mother of the race. We owe it to her and to ourselves to undo the great wrong that we have done her."
                                        —Mohandas Karamchand (Mahatma) Gandhi

"Muse not that I thus suddenly proceed;
For what I will, I will, and there an end."
                                        —Shakespeare, TWO GENTLEMEN OF VERONA,
                                        Act I, Sc. 3

4537. Cowley, Joyce. "Pioneers of Women's Liberation." New York: Pathfinder Press, 1971. 15 pp.

4538. Cunliffe, John William. LEADERS OF THE VICTORIAN REVOLUTION. Port Washington, NY: Kennikat Press, 1973. 343 pp. Reprint of 1934 edition. Includes sections on woman suffrage, women's education, and some notable women of the age.

4539. Dohm, Hedwig. WOMEN'S NATURE AND PRIVILEGE. Westport, CT: Hyperion Press, 1976. 151 pp. Translated from 1876 German edition. By the German novelist and playright, who was the first woman to demand the right to vote and one of the driving forces behind the early women's movement in Germany. Postulates that women's claim to freedom of choice is not based on social consideration, but rather on natural right.

4540. Goldsmith, Margaret. SEVEN WOMEN AGAINST THE WORLD. Westport, CT: Hyperion Press, 1976. 236 pp. Reprint of 1935 edition. The contributions of Charlotte Corday, Théroigne de Méricourt, Flora

Tristan, Louise Michel, Vera Figner, Emma Goldman, and Rosa Luxembourg.

4541. Gurko, Miriam. THE LADIES OF SENECA FALLS. New York: Macmillan, 1974. 328 pp. Events of the women's rights movement prior to the 1848 convention and up to the present time.

4542. Hull, Florence Howe, ed. JULIA WARD HOWE AND THE WOMAN SUFFRAGE MOVEMENT. New York: Arno Press, 1969. 248 pp. Reprint of 1913 edition.

4543. Kisner, Arlene, ed. "WOODHULL AND CLAFLIN'S WEEKLY: The Lives and Writings of Victoria Woodhull and Tennessee Claflin." New York: Times Change Press, 1974. 64 pp. Selections from their (in)famous newsmagazine (1870-1876), interspersed with detailed biographical sketches.

4544. Lumpkin, Katherine Du Pre. THE EMANCIPATION OF ANGELINA GRIMKÉ. Chapel Hill, NC: Univ. of North Carolina Press, 1974. 265 pp.

4545. McGovern, James R. "Anna Howard Shaw: New Approaches to Feminism," JOURNAL OF SOCIAL HISTORY, vol. 3, no. 2 (Winter 1969-1970), pp. 135-153. Study of a key figure in the American suffrage and feminist movement between 1890-1915.

4546. Oakley, Mary Ann B. A NEW BIOGRAPHY OF ELIZABETH CADY STANTON. Old Westbury, NY: The Feminist Press, 1972. 160 pp. Recreates the life of the foremother of the current feminist movement.

4547. Pethick-Lawrence, Emmeline. MY PART IN A CHANGING WORLD. Westport, CT: Hyperion Press, 1976. 367 pp. Reprint of 1938 edition. First-hand account of the women's movement from 1906 to 1914, detailing the rise of the militant faction; she played a vital role in the Women's Social and Political Union, organized under the leadership of the Pankhursts.

4548. Rose, Mrs. Ernestine Louise. "An Address on Woman's Rights, on Sunday Afternoon delivered before the People's Sunday Meeting in Cochituate Hall, Oct. 19, 1851." Boston, MA: J. P. Mendum, 1851. 21 pp.

4549. Sanders, Byrne Hope. EMILY MURPHY, CRUSADER ("JANEY CANUCK"). Toronto, Ontario: Macmillan, 1945. 355 pp. Biography of a leader in the suffrage movement in Alberta, who in 1916 was appointed police magistrate for the City of Edmonton, the first woman in the British Empire to hold such a post.

4550. Sklar, Kathryn K. CATHARINE BEECHER: A STUDY IN AMERICAN DOMESTICITY. New Haven, CT: Yale Univ. Press, 1973. 356 pp.

4551. Somerville, Martha. PERSONAL RECOLLECTIONS, FROM HER EARLY LIFE TO OLD AGE, OF MARY SOMERVILLE, WITH SELECTIONS FROM HER CORRESPONDENCE. Boston, MA: Roberts Bros., 1874. 377 pp. One of the forerunners of the woman's movement in England and a pioneer in the education of women.

4552. Smith, Helen K. PRESUMPTUOUS DREAMERS: A SOCIOLOGICAL HISTORY OF THE LIFE AND TIMES OF ABIGAIL SCOTT DUNIWAY. Lake Oswego, OR: Smith, Smith, & Smith, 1976. 2 vols.

4553. Stevenson, Janet. "Women's Rights." New York: Franklin Watts, 1972. 90 pp. Historical sketches of women who worked for the early women's rights movement.

4554. Strom, Sharon Hartman. "Leadership and Tactics in the American Woman Suffrage Movement: A New Perspective from Massachusetts," JOURNAL OF AMERICAN HISTORY, vol. 62, no. 2 (Sept. 1975), pp. 296-315. The success of the woman's suffrage movement in Massachusetts came from broadening the issues, expanding the membership, and using a variety of political techniques to obtain ratification of the state suffrage law.

4555. Tomalin, Claire. THE LIFE AND DEATH OF MARY WOLLSTONECRAFT. New York: Harcourt Brace Jovanovich, 1974. 316 pp. Critical yet sympathetic, well-documented and well-illustrated.

4556. Wheeler, Ethel Rolt. FAMOUS BLUE STOCKINGS. New York: John Lane, 1910. 352 pp. Biographical sketches of the lives of Mrs. Vesey, Mrs. Thrale, Mrs. Delaney, Mrs. Montagu, Fanny Burney, Elizabeth Carter, and many others active in the suffrage movement.

F. 3. Woman Suffrage—Opponents

> "I am asham'd, that women are so simple
> To offer war, where they should kneel for peace;
> Or seek for rule, supremacy and sway,
> When they are bound to serve, love, and obey."
>
> —Shakespeare, TAMING OF THE SHREW,
> Act V, Sc. 2

4557. Barry, Richard. "The Truth Concerning Four Woman-Suffrage States." New York: National League for the Civic Education of Women, 1910. 16 pp.

4558. Fuller, Paul E. LAURA CLAY AND THE WOMAN'S RIGHTS MOVEMENT. Lexington, KY: Univ. Press of Kentucky, 1975. 216 pp. Active member of the National American Woman Suffrage Association, but her commitment to state's rights ultimately caused her to break with NAWSA and oppose the Nineteenth Amendment.

4559. Nott, Clarkes Cooper. "The New Woman and the Late President of Williams." no publisher, 1895. 4 pp.

F. 4. Woman Suffrage—Allies

> "There is an infinity of political errors which, being once adopted, become principles."
>
> —Guillaume Thomas François Raynal

*"The smallest number, with God and truth on their side, are weightier than
thousands."*
                                                    —Charles Simmons

4560. Aptheker, Bettina. "W. E. DuBois and the Struggle for Women's Rights,
       1910-1920," SAN JOSE STUDIES, vol. 1 (May 1975), pp. 7-16. Writer
       who encouraged the black community to support woman suffrage,
       while attempting to eliminate racism in the woman suffrage movement.
4561. Brittain, Vera. PETHICK-LAWRENCE: A PORTRAIT. London,
       England: Allen & Unwin, 1963. 232 pp. Biography of Frederick
       William Pethick-Lawrence, who financially backed the British women's
       suffrage movement.
4562. Clark, David L. "Brockdon Brown and the Rights of Women." Folcroft,
       PA: Folcroft Editions, 1973. 48 pp. Reprint of 1922 edition.
4563. Gilman, Charlotte Perkins. "Suffrage Songs and Verses." New York: The
       Charleton Co., 1911. 24 pp.
4564. Snapp, Meredith A. "Defeat the Democrats: The Congressional Union for
       Woman Suffrage in Arizona, 1914 and 1916," JOURNAL OF THE
       WEST, vol. 14, no. 4 (Oct. 1975), pp. 131-139. Organized by Alice Paul
       and Lucy Burns to be a more radical tool for woman suffrage than the
       National American Woman Suffrage Association.
4565. Villiers, Brougham (pseud. for John Frederick Shaw), ed. THE CASE
       FOR WOMAN SUFFRAGE. New York: Gordon Press, 1976. 220 pp.
       Reprint of 1907 edition. Collection of essays by the leaders of the
       international suffrage movements covering the current status, and many
       different aspects of the fight for women's rights.

F. 5. Woman Suffrage—Effects of the Movement

*"There is no reason why we should not some day have a female chief of staff or even
a commander in chief."*
                                                    —Lyndon Baines Johnson

*"A fuller blast ne'er shook our battlements:
If it hath ruffian'd so upon the sea,
What ribs of oak, when mountains melt on them
Can hold the mortise?"*
                                                    —Shakespeare, OTHELLO, Act. II, Sc. 1

4566. Beecher, Catherine Esther. WOMAN SUFFRAGE AND WOMAN'S
       PROFESSION. Saint Clair Shores, ME: Scholarly Press, 1976. 133 pp.
       Reprint of 1871 edition. Includes several addresses on woman suffrage.
4567. Gluck, Sherna, ed. FROM PARLOR TO PRISON: FIVE AMERICAN
       SUFFRAGISTS TALK ABOUT THEIR LIVES—AN ORAL HISTORY.
       New York: Random House, 1976. 288 pp. Interviews with five
       little-known women who took part in the suffrage movement.

G. Women Politicians

1. General

"A politician is a person who approaches everything with an open mouth."
—Adlai Ewing Stevenson

4568. Bowman, Kathleen. "New Women in Politics." Mankato, MI: Creative Education, 1976. 47 pp.

4569. Brichta, Avraham. "Women in the Knesset: 1949-1969," PARLIAMENTARY AFFAIRS, vol. 28, no. 1 (Winter 1974-1975), pp. 31-50. The activity of women members of Israel's parliament far exceeded numerical strength.

4570. Dunnigan, Alice E. A BLACK WOMAN'S EXPERIENCE—FROM SCHOOLHOUSE TO WHITE HOUSE. Philadelphia, PA: Dorrance & Co., 1974. 673 pp.

4571. Eagle, Mary Kavanaugh Oldham, ed. THE CONGRESS OF WOMEN HELD IN THE WOMAN'S BUILDING, WORLD'S COLUMBIA EXPOSITION, CHICAGO, U.S.A., 1893. Chicago, IL: International Publishing, 1894. 824 pp.

4572. Edmondson, Madeleine and Alden Duer Cohen. THE WOMEN OF WATERGATE. New York: Simon & Schuster, 1976.

4573. Ferree, M. M. "A Woman for President: Changing Responses: 1958-1972," PUBLIC OPINION QUARTERLY, vol. 38, no. 3 (Fall 1974), pp. 390-399. Attitudinal survey.

4574. Hutheesing, Krishna (Nehru). DEAR TO BEHOLD: AN INTIMATE PORTRAIT OF INDIRA GANDHI. New York: Macmillan, 1969. 221 pp.

4575. Kirkpatrick, Jean, et al THE NEW PRESIDENTIAL ELITE: MEN AND WOMEN IN NATIONAL POLITICS. New York: Russell Sage Foundation and The Twentieth Century Fund, 1976. 606 pp. Study of convention delegates based on interviews with 1,300 delegates to the 1972 Democratic and Republican National Conventions and mail questionnaires completed by 55% of the delegates. Part II deals with personal and political characteristics of women delegates.

4576. Lapidus, Gail Warshofsky. "Political Mobilization, Participation, and Leadership: Women in Soviet Politics," COMPARATIVE POLITICS, vol. 8, no. 1 (Oct. 1975), pp. 90-118. Comparison of the political activities of women to those of men.

4577. Lee, Marcia Manning. "Why Few Women Hold Public Office: Democracy and Sexual Roles," POLITICAL SCIENCE QUARTERLY, vol. 91, no. 2 (Summer 1976), pp. 297-314. Presents the results of a survey conducted among men and women participating in local politics in four suburbs of Westchester County, New York.

4578. Radloff, Barbara. "Political Woman: Public Role and Personal Challenges," CARNEGIE QUARTERLY, vol. 22, no. 3 (Summer 1974), pp. 1-5.

4579. Shapiro, Jane P. "The Politicization of Soviet Women: From Passivity to Protest," CANADIAN SLAVONIC PAPERS, vol. 17 (Winter 1975), pp. 596-616.

4580. Shibrock, Sister Ann Regis, C.S.J. and Brother Gerald J. Schnapp, S.M. "Women in Politics," SOCIAL ORDER, vol. 3 (Oct. 1953), pp. 361-366.

4581. Tai, Dwan L. CHIANG CH'ING: THE EMERGENCE OF A REVOLUTIONARY POLITICAL LEADER. Hicksville, NY: Exposition Press, 1974. 222 pp.

4582. Volgy, Thomas J. and Sandra Sue Volgy. "Women and Politics: Political Correlates of Sex-Role Acceptance." Tucson, AZ: Univ. of Arizona, Institute of Government Research, 1974. 37 pp.

4583. Witke, Roxanne. COMRADE CHIANG CH'ING: RECOLLECTIONS OF HER LIFE AND HISTORY. Boston, MA: Little, Brown, 1977. 549 pp. Based on more than 60 hours of interviews with the Chinese revolutionary.

G. 2. *Women Politicians—Elective Office*

"I'm not going to give up. This is my first race (for political office) and now I know how the game is played."

—Shirley Temple Black

"We should free the state from the past. Weed it out. Fumigate it. Put it back on the job of serving the present."

—Raymond Moley

4584. Bernstein, Robert A. and Jayne D. Polly. "Race, Class and Support for Female Candidates," WESTERN POLITICAL QUARTERLY, vol. 28, no. 4 (Dec. 1975), pp. 733-736. Concludes that support for female candidates is from middle and upper class, and readier acceptance is found among black voters than white.

4585. Diamond, Irene. SEX ROLES IN THE STATE HOUSE. New Haven, CT: Yale Univ. Press, 1977. Analysis of the career patterns of male and female members of the state legislatures.

4586. Dubeck, Paula J. "Women and Access to Political Office: A Comparison of Female and Male Legislators," SOCIOLOGICAL QUARTERLY, vol. 17, no. 1 (Winter 1976), pp. 42-52. Status is analyzed in terms of representation in the U.S.

4587. Faber, Doris. BELLA ABZUG. New York: Lothrop, Lee & Sheppard, 1976. 162 pp. Biography of the former Congresswoman from New York, focusing on her political career.

4588. Good, Uvieja Z. BELVA LOCKWOOD: FIRST WOMAN CANDIDATE
FOR PRESIDENT. Brooklyn, NY: Revisionist Press, 1976.
4589. Josephson, Hannah Geffen. JEANNETTE RANKIN. Indianapolis, IN:
Bobbs-Merrill, 1974. 224 pp. Biography of the first woman elected to
Congress in 1917 and later in 1941, who voted against U.S. entry into
both World Wars, who marched with N.O.W. in New York and endorsed
the presidential campaign of Shirley Chisholm.
4590. Lakeman, Enid. "Electoral Systems and Women in Parliament," THE
PARLIAMENTARIAN, vol. 57, no. 3 (July 1976), pp. 159-162.
Representation of women in parliaments.
4591. Leader, Shelah G. "The Policy Impact of Elected Women Officials," in
THE IMPACT OF THE ELECTORAL PROCESS, edited by Louis
Maisel and Joseph Cooper. Beverly Hills, CA: Sage, 1977.
4592. Wilson, Gary B. "Women in Politics: Images and Voter Support."
Arlington, VA: ERIC Document Reproduction Service, 1975. 13 pp.

G. 3. *Women Politicians–Appointive Office*

*"Men care about power because for them power is linked with sexual performance.
Women achieve positions of power out of a need to do something, not because we
need reassurance."*

–Karin Soeder (Sweden's first
woman Foreign Minister)

4593. Giroud, Françoise. I GIVE YOU MY WORD. Boston, MA: Houghton
Mifflin, 1974. 280 pp. Autobiography of France's first State Secretary
on the Condition of Women.
4594. Lawson, Don. FRANCES PERKINS, FIRST LADY OF THE CABINET.
New York: Abelard-Schuman, 1966. 160 pp. Served as Secretary of
Labor.
4595. Martin, George. MADAM SECRETARY: FRANCES PERKINS. Boston,
MA: Houghton Mifflin, 1976. 589 pp. Frances Perkins served the
longest term as Secretary of Labor, from 1933-1945 (abruptly
dismissed by Truman).
4596. Mesta, Perle with Robert Cahn. PERLE: MY STORY. New York:
McGraw-Hill, 1960. 251 pp. Autobiography of the former ambassador
to Luxembourg.

G. 4. *Women Politicians–Party Activists*

*"There is little to be expected from political parties. They are prone to subordinate
everything to party success or to party expediency."*

–William Edgar Borah

"The political parties that I would call great, are those which cling more to principles than to consequences; to general, and not to special cases; to ideas, and not to men. Such parties are usually distinguished by a nobler character, more generous passions, more genuine convictions, and a more bold and open conduct than others."
—*Alexis de Tocqueville*

4597. Abzug, Bella, Phyllis Segal, and Miriam Kelber. "Women in the Democratic Party: A Review of Affirmative Action," COLUMBIA HUMAN RIGHTS LAW REVIEW, vol. 6, no. 1 (Spring 1974), pp. 3-24. The implementation of Affirmative Action procedures in delegate selection, candidate selection, and other political party activity.

4598. Guerin, Daniel. ROSA LUXEMBURG ET LA SPONTANEITE REVOLUTIONAIRE. Paris, France: Flammarion, 1971. 186 pp. One of the activists and theorists of the Communist movement in Europe in the late 19th and early 20th century.

4599. Roosevelt, Eleanor and Lorena A. Hickok. LADIES OF COURAGE. New York: Putnam, 1954. 312 pp. An account of the most politically active women from 1848 to the 1950's; one chapter dealing with the senior author.

4600. Strangewayes-Booth, Joanna. A CRICKET IN THE THORN TREE. Bloomington, IN: Indiana Univ. Press, 1976. 320 pp. Helen Suzman's 13 years of opposition to white supremacy in South Africa.

4601. "What Women do in Politics," U.S. NEWS & WORLD REPORT, vol. 55 (Dec. 12, 1958), pp. 72-79. Interviews with two women leaders of the Republican and Democratic parties, Claire Williams and Katie Louchheim. Both agree that women have made politics more respectable, but have not achieved full equality yet.

4602. "Women in Revolt," NEWSWEEK (March 23, 1970), pp. 71-78.

G. 5. *Women Politicians—Interest Groups and Voluntary Associations*

"Nowhere are prejudices more mistaken for truth, passion for reason, and invection for documentation than in politics. That is a realm, peopled only by villains or heroes, in which everything is black or white and gray is a forbidden color."
—*John Mason Brown*

4603. Allan, Donald. "Syria's Women Volunteers: A Force for Development," UNICEF NEWS, no. 4 (1974), pp. 21-24.

4604. Bennet, Helen Christine. AMERICAN WOMEN IN CIVIC WORK. New York: Dodd, Mead, 1915. 277 pp. Biographical sketches of women who volunteered their time and efforts to public welfare improvement, i.e. Caroline Bartlett Crane, Sophie Wright, Jane Addams, and Kate Bernard.

4605. Demos, Vasilikie. "Female Role Orientation and Participation in a Woman's Voluntary Association," SOCIAL SCIENCE, vol. 50, no. 3 (Summer 1975), pp. 136-140.

4606. Fletty, Valbourg. PUBLIC SERVICE OF WOMEN'S ORGANIZATIONS; PART OF A STUDY MADE AT THE UNIVERSITY OF SYRACUSE. Menasha, WI: G. Banta Publishing, 1951. 144 pp.

4607. Graziani, Bernice. WHERE THERE'S A WOMAN; 75 YEARS OF HISTORY AS LIVED BY THE NATIONAL COUNCIL OF JEWISH WOMEN. New York: McCall Corp., 1967. 128 pp.

4608. Haughery, Sister M. Catharine Joseph, C.I.M. "A Candle Lighted: A Capsule Biography of Margaret Gaffney Haughery (1813-1882)," AMERICAN CATHOLIC HISTORICAL SOCIETY RECORDS (June 1953), pp. 112-130. Successful businesswoman in New Orleans who founded 11 orphanages and several old people's homes.

4609. Lerner, Gerda. "Early Community Work of Black Club Women," JOURNAL OF NEGRO HISTORY, vol. 59, no. 2 (April 1974), pp. 158-167. Chronicles representative examples of black women's achievements in meeting social needs.

4610. Loeser, Herta. WOMEN, WORK, AND VOLUNTEERING. Boston, MA: Beacon Press, 1975. 224 pp. Explores the potential roles of the volunteer, as well as using volunteer experience as useful job experience; includes extensive bibliography.

4611. National Council of Jewish Women. "Guide for Successful Community Forum." New York: Nat. Council of Jewish Women, 1965. 46 pp.

4612. Smith, Leticia M. "Women as Volunteers: The Double Subsidy," JOURNAL OF VOLUNTARY ACTION RESEARCH, vol. 4, nos. 3-4 (Summer-Fall 1975), pp. 119-136. Concludes that few rewarding types of volunteer work have been developed since 1964, the status system of volunteerism reinforces the secondary role of women, and the recruitment process contributes to isolating women from community decision-making.

4613. "The Work of Women's Organizations," SOCIAL FORCES, vol. 1, no. 1 (Nov. 1922), pp. 50-55. Special Section. Contributors include Nellie Roberson and Gertrude Weil.

H. The Political Status of Women

"Woman reduces us all to a common denominator."
—*George Bernard Shaw*

"I hate all bungling as I do sin, but particularly bungling in politics, which leads to the misery and ruin of many thousands and millions of people."
—*Johann Wolfgang von Goethe*

4614. Amundsen, Kirsten. A NEW LOOK AT THE SILENCED MAJORITY: WOMEN AND AMERICAN DEMOCRACY. Englewood Cliffs, NJ: Prentice-Hall, 1977. 172 pp.

4615. Blackman, Morris J. EVE IN AN ADAMOCRACY: WOMEN AND POLITICS IN BRAZIL. New York: New York Univ. Ibero-American Language and Area Center, 1973.

4616. Bremme, Gabriele. DIE POLITISCHE ROLLE DER FRAU IN DEUTSCHLAND [THE POLITICAL ROLE OF WOMEN IN GERMANY]. Göttingen, Germany: Vandenhoeck & Ruprecht, 1956. 288 pp.

4617. Butler, Phyllis and Dorothy Grey. EVERYWOMAN'S GUIDE TO POLITICAL AWARENESS. Millbrae, CA: Les Femmes, 1976. 128 pp.

4618. Croll, Elisabeth J. "Social Production and Female Status: Women in China," RACE AND CLASS, vol. 18, no. 2 (Summer 1976), pp. 39-52. Degree of participating in political activities which gives women access to and control over the strategic resources of society.

4619. Currell, Melville E. POLITICAL WOMAN. London, England: Croom Helm, 1974. 201 pp. Women in politics in Great Britain.

4620. Freeman, Jo. THE POLITICS OF WOMEN'S LIBERATION: A CASE STUDY OF AN EMERGING SOCIAL MOVEMENT AND ITS RELATION TO THE POLICY PROCESS. New York: David McKay, 1975. 284 pp.

4621. Githens, Marianne and Jewel L. Prestage, eds. A PORTRAIT OF MARGINALITY: THE POLITICAL BEHAVIOR OF THE AMERICAN WOMAN. New York: David McKay, 1977. 384 pp.

4622. King, Mae C. "Oppression and Power: The Unique Status of the Black Woman in the American Political Scene," SOCIAL SCIENCE QUARTERLY, vol. 56, no. 1 (June 1975), pp. 116-128.

4623. MacInnis, Grace. "Women and Politics," THE PARLIAMENTARIAN, vol. 53, no. 1 (Jan. 1972), pp. 8-12. Barriers to women's involvement in Canadian politics.

4624. Newland, Kathleen. "Women in Politics: A Global Review." Washington, D.C.: Worldwatch Institute, 1975. 45 pp. Political status and participation.

4625. Staudt, Kathy. "Politics and Philippine Women: An Exploratory Study," PHILIPPINE JOURNAL OF PUBLIC ADMINISTRATION, vol. 17, no. 4 (Oct. 1973), pp. 466-484. Data on participation, political attitudes, and attitudes toward women in politics.

4626. Tolchin, Susan and Martin Tolchin. CLOUT—WOMANPOWER AND POLITICS. New York: Coward, McCann & Geoghegan, 1973. 320 pp. A landmark analysis of where women stand in politics today and where they are headed.

4627. Young, Louise M. "Women's Place in American Politics: The Historical Perspective," JOURNAL OF POLITICS, vol. 38, no. 3 (Aug. 1976), pp. 295-335. Excellent overview and analysis from 17th century forward.

4628. "Women Around the World," THE CENTER MAGAZINE, vol. 7, no. 3 (May/June 1974), pp. 43-80. Report of conference on "Social and Political Change: The Role of Women," sponsored by the Univ. of California—Santa Barbara, and the Center for the Study of Democratic

Institutions. Contributors include Judith Van Allen, Rae Lesser Blumberg, Kay Boals, Judith Stiehm, Lynn B. Iglitzin, Nora Scott Kinzer, Peter Merkl, Sondra Herman, and Alva Myrdal.

4629. Wormser, Ellen, ed. "Women in Government: Public Policy Forum," THE BUREAUCRAT, vol. 1, no. 3 (Fall 1972), pp. 211-288. Special Issue on public policy formulation regarding women. Contributors include Glen G. Cain, Helene S. Markoff, Daisy B. Fields, Linda Moore, Millicent Allewelt, Marjorie M. Silverberg, George S. Maharay, Harry Flickinger, Gladys Rogers, Barbara Franklin, and Art Buchwald.

III. WOMEN IN HISTORY

A. Women in Society

"There wouldn't be half as much fun in the world if it weren't for children and men, and there ain't a mite of difference between them under their skins."
— Ellen Anderson Gholson Glasgow

"I believe that we already have a science of society—a very young and incomplete science, but one that is steadily growing and that is capable of indefinite extension."
— Beatrice Webb

4630. Ambassade de France. Service de Presse et d'Information. WOMEN IN FRANCE. New York: Service de Presse et d'Information, 1974.

4631. American Association of University Women. Janesville Branch. "We Were Here: Contributions of Rock County Women." Prepared by Ann Allen, et al. Janesville, WI: Susan Keeny, 1975.

4632. "The American Woman on the Move—But Where?" U.S. NEWS & WORLD REPORT, vol. 79 (Dec. 8, 1975), pp. 54-64, 67-68, 70-74. Special Section.

4633. "The American Woman Today," TODAY'S HEALTH, vol. 53, no. 5 (May 1975), pp. 14-56. Special Issue. Contributors include Ellen Sullivan, Barbara Villet, James C. G. Coniff, Marjorie Franco, Claire Safran, James Atwater, Carolyn See, and Patricia Skalka.

4634. AMERICAN WOMEN DURING THE NINETEENTH CENTURY. New York: Somerset Publishing, 1972. 2 vols. Reprint of 1897 edition.

4635. Armstrong, Frieda. "To be Free." Philadelphia, PA: Fortress Press, 1974. 88 pp.

4636. Atkinson, Dorothy, Alexander Dallin, and Gail W. Lapidus, eds. WOMEN IN RUSSIA. Stanford, CA: Stanford Univ. Press, 1977.

4637. Ayscough, Florence Wheelock. CHINESE WOMEN; YESTERDAY AND TODAY. New York: Da Capo Press, 1975. 324 pp. Reprint of 1937 edition. Chronicle of Chinese culture.

4638. Baig, Tara Ali. INDIA'S WOMAN POWER. New Delhi, India: S. Chand, 1976. 301 pp. The historical, spiritual, economic, and social position of Indian women, who provide the stability of India's most vital social unit, the joint family.

4639. Banner, Lois W. WOMEN IN MODERN AMERICA: A BRIEF HISTORY. New York: Harcourt Brace Jovanovich, 1974. 276 pp. Covers three periods: 1890-1920, 1921-1960, and 1961 to the present. Comprehensive bibliography.

4640. Baum, Charlotte, Paula Hyman, and Sonya Michel. THE JEWISH WOMAN IN AMERICA. New York: Dial Press, 1976. 290 pp. Criticism of the behavior of Jewish males, preference for the Jewish woman who rejects religious tradition in favor of socialism and who manages to make a life for herself outside of the institutions of marriage and motherhood.

4641. Bell, Margaret Van Horn Dwight. "A Journey to Ohio in 1810 as Recorded in the Journal of Margaret Van Horn Dwight Bell." New Haven, CT: Yale Univ. Press, 1912. 64 pp.

4642. Bier, William C., ed. WOMAN IN MODERN LIFE. New York: Fordham Univ. Press, 1968. 278 pp. Proceedings of the Institute of Pastoral Psychology held at Fordham, June 1965.

4643. Billington, Mary F. WOMAN IN INDIA. Columbia, MO: South Asia Books, 1973.

4644. "The Black Woman in the Black Struggle," THE BLACK SCHOLAR, vol. 1, no. 3-4 (Jan.-Feb. 1970), pp. 1-64. Special Issue. Contributors include Earl Conrad, Robert Staples, Alice Walker, Julia Reed, Sonia Sanchez, Earl Scarborough, Yvonne R. Chappelle, Shirley Chisholm, Lenneal J. Henderson, Jr., and William J. Middleton.

4645. "Black Women's Liberation," THE BLACK SCHOLAR, vol. 4, no. 6-7 (March-April 1973), pp. 1-55. Special Issue. Contributors include Barbara Sizemore, Mae C. King, S. Jay Walker, Sékou Touré, Trellie Jeffers, Edward Mapp, and Queen Mother Moore.

4646. Borer, Mary Irene Cathcart. WOMEN WHO MADE HISTORY. London, England: Frederick Warne, 1963. 192 pp.

4647. Breitenbach, Josef. WOMEN OF ASIA. London, England: Collins, 1968. 131 pp.

4648. Brown, (Mrs.) Demetra Vaka. THE UNVEILED LADIES OF STAMBOUL. Freeport, NY: Books for Libraries, 1971. 260 pp. Reprint of 1923 edition. Women in Turkey.

4649. Brown, Janet Welsh, Julia Graham Lear, and Donna Shavlik. "Effecting Social Change for Women: Relation Research and Action." Washington, D.C.: Federation of Organizations of Professional Women, 1976. 40 pp.

4650. Buck, Pearl Sydenstricker. OF MEN AND WOMEN. New York: John Day, 1941. 212 pp. American men and women, women and war, the education of men and women for each other, and women and freedom.

4651. Bullough, Vern L. and Bonnie Bullough. THE SUBORDINATE SEX: A HISTORY OF ATTITUDES TOWARD WOMEN. Urbana, IL: Univ. of Illinois Press, 1973. 375 pp. Cross-cultural study of attitudes toward women.

4652. Colton, Helen. "What's on Woman's Future Agenda?" Los Angeles, CA: Family Forum, 1971. 52 pp.

4653. Cook, Anna Marie (Green). THE JOURNAL OF A MIDGEVILLE GIRL, 1861-1867. Athens, GA: Univ. of Georgia Press, 1964. 131 pp. Social life, customs, and U.S. history during the Civil War, as told from the viewpoint of the Confederate side.

4654. Cormack, Margaret Lawson. THE HINDU WOMAN. Westport, CT: Greenwood Press, 1974. 207 pp. Reprint of 1953 edition.

4655. Cornelisen, Ann. WOMEN OF THE SHADOWS. New York: Vintage Books, 1977. 256 pp. Study of five contemporary peasant women in southern Italy.

4656. Crane, Louise. MS. AFRICA: PROFILES OF MODERN AFRICAN WOMEN. Philadelphia, PA: J. B. Lippincott, 1973. 159 pp. Brief biographies of thirteen prominent African women emphasizing their achievements in their chosen fields.

4657. Curtin, Katie. "Women in China." New York: Pathfinder Press, 1975. 95 pp.

4658. Donovan, Hedley, ed. "The American Woman, TIME, vol. 99, no. 12 (March 20, 1972), pp. 25-104. Special Issue. Differences between the sexes in the field of entertainment, art, business, education; also deals with women doctors, sexual behavior, law, politics, women's movement, and religion.

4659. Du Bosc, Jacques. THE COMPLEAT WOMAN. New York: Da Capo Press, 1968. 87 pp. Translation of the first part of L'HONNESTE FEMME.

4660. Elyot, Sir Thomas. "Sir Thomas Elyot's The Defence of Good Women." Oxford, England: The Anchor Press, 1940. 85 pp. Reprint of 1540 manuscript.

4661. Encel, Solomon, Normon Ian Mackenzie, and Margaret Tebbutt. WOMEN AND SOCIETY: AN AUSTRALIAN STUDY. London, England: Malaby Press, 1974. 320 pp. Study of women in Australia concluding that women are not advancing, especially in terms of political and professional status.

4662. Fernea, Elizabeth Warnack and Basima Qattan Bezerigan, eds. MIDDLE EASTERN WOMEN SPEAK. Austin, TX: Univ. of Texas Press, 1976. Massive documentary of the feelings and attitudes of Muslim women, including selections from the KORAN and excerpts from writings from the seventeenth century forward.

4663. Finot, Jean. PROBLEMS OF THE SEXES. New York: Putnam, 1913. 408 pp. Translated from the French, focuses on various aspects of women's lives, e.g. sexuality, education, psychology.

4664. Fischer, Clarc Benedicks, Betsy Brenneman, and Anne McGrew Bennett. WOMEN IN A STRANGE LAND: SEARCH FOR A NEW IMAGE. Philadelphia, PA: Fortress Press, 1975. 133 pp.

4665. Glanz, Rudolph. THE JEWISH FEMALE IN AMERICA: TWO FEMALE IMMIGRANT GENERATIONS, 1820-1929. VOLUME I: THE EASTERN EUROPEAN JEWISH WOMAN. New York: Ktav Publishing House, 1976. 209 pp. Excellent resource book based on extensive research in original sources (English, Yiddish, German, and Hebrew).

4666. ———. THE JEWISH FEMALE IN AMERICA: TWO FEMALE IMMIGRANT GENERATIONS, 1820-1929. VOLUME II: GERMAN-JEWISH WOMAN OF THE "OLD" IMMIGRATION. New York: Ktav Publishing House, forthcoming.

4667. Glazer-Malbin, Nona and Helen Youngelson Waehrer, eds. WOMAN IN A MAN-MADE WORLD: A SOCIO-ECONOMIC HANDBOOK. New York: Rand McNally, 1972. 316 pp. Interdisciplinary textbook, forty articles.

4668. Gould, Elsie M. AMERICAN WOMAN TODAY: FREE OR FRUSTRATED? Englewood Cliffs, NJ: Prentice-Hall, 1972. 122 pp.

4669. Great Britain. Central Office of Information. Research Division. "Women in Britain." London, England: British Information Services, 1975. 56 pp.

4670. Hahner, June E., ed. WOMEN IN LATIN AMERICAN HISTORY: THEIR LIVES AND VIEWS. Los Angeles, CA: Univ. of California, UCLA Latin American Center, 1976. 181 pp. Useful introduction to the study of Latin American women; emphasis on twentieth century.

4671. Halsell, Grace. SOUL SISTER. New York: World Publishing, 1969. 211 pp. First-hand account of the treatment of black women, inspired by John Griffin's BLACK LIKE ME.

4672. Hamilton, Kelley. "Goals and Plans of Black Women: A Sociological Study." Hicksville, NY: Exposition Press, 1975. 79 pp.

4673. Hartley, Catherine Gasquoine. THE TRUTH ABOUT WOMEN: BIOLOGICAL, HISTORICAL, ANTHROPOLOGICAL, and SOCIOLOGICAL. Brooklyn, NY: Revisionist Press, 1974. 404 pp. Reprint of 1914 edition.

4674. Hartman, Mary S. and Lois W. Banner, eds. CLIO'S CONSCIOUSNESS RAISED: NEW PERSPECTIVES ON THE HISTORY OF WOMEN. New York: Harper & Row, 1974. 253 pp.

4675. Heale, William. "An Apologie for Women; or, and Opposition to Mr. Dr. G., his Assertion . . . that it was Lawful for Husbands to Beate Their Wives." Norwood, NJ: W. W. Johnson, 1974. 66 pp. Reprint of 1609 manuscript.

4676. Heggoy, Alf Andrew. "On the Evolution of Algerian Women," THE AFRICAN STUDIES REVIEW, vol. 17, no. 2 (Sept. 1974), pp. 449-456.

4677. Heuer, Berys. MAORI WOMEN. Rutland, VT: A.H. & A.W. Reed Books, 1972.

4678. Hogeland, Ronald W., ed. WOMEN AND WOMANHOOD IN AMERICA. Lexington, MA: D. C. Heath, 1973. 183 pp. Anthology of readings on how to study women in American history; historical discussions of the nature of their roles in the American experience.

4679. Huber, Joan, ed. CHANGING WOMEN IN A CHANGING SOCIETY. Chicago, IL: Univ. of Chicago Press, 1973. 295 pp. Reprint of twenty-one essays from AMERICAN JOURNAL OF SOCIOLOGY, vol. 78, no. 4 (Jan. 1973).

4680. Indian Council of Social Science Research. STATUS OF WOMEN IN INDIA: A SYNOPSIS OF THE REPORT OF THE NATIONAL COMMITTEE ON THE STATUS OF WOMEN (1971-1974). New Delhi, India: Indian Council of Social Science Research, 1975. 188 pp.

4681. Ingraham, Claire R. and Leonard W. Ingraham. "An Album of Women in American History." New York: F. Watts, 1972. 88 pp. Contributions of women emphasizing their struggles for equality; includes brief sketches of prominent American women.

4682. Jain, Davaki, ed. INDIAN WOMEN. New Delhi, India: Ministry of Information and Broadcasting, Publications Division, 1975. 312 pp. Produced for International Women's Year 1975.

4683. Judd, Barbara and Daniel Josephs, eds. WOMEN IN THE UNITED

STATES. Glenview, IL: Scott, Foresman, 1975. 192 pp. Readings on women in society.

4684. Kamiat, Arnold Herman. FEMININE SUPERIORITY AND OTHER MYTHS. New Haven, CT: College and Univ. Press, 1960. 143 pp.

4685. Kartini, Raden Adjeng. LETTERS OF A JAVANESE PRINCESS. New York: W. W. Norton, 1964. 246 pp. Women in Java.

4686. King, Beatrice. "Women in Post-War Russia." London, England: British-Soviet Society, 1947. 32 pp.

4687. Kreuter, Gretchen and Rhoda R. Gilman. "Women in Minnesota's History," in THE MINNESOTA LEGISLATIVE MANUAL, 1975-1976, compiled by Joan Anderson Growe. St. Paul, MN: The State of Minnesota, 1975. pp. 2-24. Chronicles major accomplishments by women in education, suffrage, etc.

4688. Kohler, Ruth Miriam De Young. THE STORY OF WISCONSIN WOMEN. Kohler, WI: Kohler Committee on Wisconsin Women for the 1948 Wisconsin Centennial, 1948. 144 pp.

4689. Laine, Pascal. LA FEMME ET SES IMAGES. Paris, France: Stock, 1974. 200 pp.

4690. Lartigue, Jacques Henri. LES FEMMES. New York: E. P. Dutton, 1974. 126 pp. Photographs of women, 1903-1973.

4691. Lebeson, Anita Libman. RECALL TO LIFE—THE JEWISH WOMAN IN AMERICA. South Brunswick, NJ: Thomas Yoseloff, 1970. 351 pp. Major trends and developments in social, religious, intellectual, and cultural life; emphasizing nineteenth and twentieth century contributions of Jewish-American women.

4692. Lee, Vera. THE REIGN OF WOMEN IN EIGHTEENTH-CENTURY FRANCE. Cambridge, MA: Schenkman Publishing, 1976. 146 pp. Limited examination of the liberty, equality, and power of women of the court and the Paris salons.

4693. Lerner, Gerda. THE WOMAN IN AMERICAN HISTORY: AN AMERICAN DOCUMENTARY. Menlo Park, CA: Addison-Wesley, 1971. 207 pp. Women's diversified roles as homemaker, worker, and citizen.

4694. Lerner, Gerda, ed. BLACK WOMEN IN WHITE AMERICA: A DOCUMENTARY. New York: Pantheon Books, 1972. 630 pp. Collection of readings by black women.

4695. ———. THE FEMALE EXPERIENCE: AN AMERICAN DOCUMENTARY. Indianapolis, IN: Bobbs-Merrill, 1976. Primary source documents—diaries, letters, transcripts of hearings and meetings, 1637-1975.

4696. Lifton, Robert Jay, ed. THE WOMAN IN AMERICA. Boston, MA: Beacon Press, 1967. 293 pp. Reprint of DAEDALUS, vol. 93, no. 2 (Spring 1964).

4697. McBee, Mary Louise and Kathryn A. Blake. THE AMERICAN WOMAN, WHO WILL SHE BE? Beverly Hills, CA: Glencoe Press, 1974. 164 pp. The present status of women and future possibilities.

4698. McCabe, Charles R. TALL GIRLS ARE GRATEFUL: WRY

COMMENTARIES ON THE FEMALE OF THE SPECIES. San Francisco, CA: Chronicle Books, 1973. 170 pp. Anecdotes, satire on women's liberation, male chauvinism, motherhood, sex, etc., by the SAN FRANCISCO CHRONICLE columnist.

4699. Mandel, William M. SOVIET WOMEN. Garden City, NY: Doubleday, 1975. 350 pp. Compares the position and status of women in U.S.S.R. with U.S. women; rosy picture of Soviet life for women.

4700. Mankekar, Kamala. WOMEN IN INDIA. New Delhi, India: Central Institute of Research and Training in Public Cooperation, 1975.

4701. Mattelart, Armand and Michel Mattelart. LA MUJER CHILENA EN UNA NUEVA SOCIEDAD: UN ESTUDIO EXPLORATORIO ACERCA DE LA SITUACIÓN E IMAGEN DE LA MUJER IN CHILE [CHILEAN WOMEN IN A NEW SOCIETY: AN EXPLORATORY STUDY OF THE SITUATION AND IMAGE OF WOMEN IN CHILE]. Santiago de Chile: Editorial del Pacífico, 1968, 227 pp.

4702. Mehta, Rama. WESTERN EDUCATED HINDU WOMAN. New York: Asia Publishing House, 1970. 216 pp. Analysis of data from fifty interviews with women educated in England, assessing the impact of the British educational system.

4703. Millstein, Beth and Jeanne Bodin. WE, THE AMERICAN WOMEN: A DOCUMENTARY HISTORY. New York: Jerome S. Ozer, 1977.

4704. "Moving and the Wife," JOURNAL OF MARRIAGE AND THE FAMILY, vol. 35, no. 2 (May 1973), pp. 181-228. Special Section. Contributors include Curtis L. Barrett, Helen Noble, William Michelson, David Belgue, John Stewart, Jerry Lavin McKain, Stella B. Jones, Edgar W. Butler, Ronald J. McAllister, and Edward J. Kaiser.

4705. LA MUJER IN AMÉRICA LATINA. Mexico: Secretariá de Educación Publica, Subsecretariá de Cultura Popular y Educación Extraescolar, 1975. 2 vols. Collection of papers from a conference, "Perspectivas femininas en investigación en América Latina," Buenos Aires, 1974.

4706. Murray, Eunice G. SCOTTISH WOMEN IN BYGONE DAYS. Norwood, PA: Norwood Editions, 1976. 245 pp. Reprint of 1930 edition. Social and domestic life, sports and pastimes, dress, religion, education, and witchcraft.

4707. National Council of Women of Canada. WOMEN OF CANADA: THEIR LIFE AND WORK. Montreal, Ontario: National Council of Women of Canada, 1975. 442 pp. Reprint of 1900 edition. Prepared for distribution at the Paris International Exhibition, 1900.

4708. Nørgaard, Erik. WHEN LADIES ACQUIRED LEGS. London, England: Spearman, 1967. 144 pp.

4709. Percy, Sen. Charles H. "World Conference of the International Women's Year: Report to the Committee on Government Operations, United States Senate." Washington, D.C.: SUDOC, GPO, 1975. 73 pp. By the U.S. Congressional advisor to the World Conference of IWY, 1975.

4710. Pescatello, Ann M. POWER AND PAWN: THE FEMALE IN IBERIAN FAMILIES, SOCIETIES, AND CULTURES. Westport, CT: Greenwood Press, 1976. 281 pp. Comprehensive study of women's roles (in Spain and Portugal) in historical and anthropological perspectives.

4711. Randriamamonjy, Marie. "Les femmes et le développement national à Madagascar [Women in National Development in Madagascar]," LES CARNETS DE L'ENFANCE, vol. 27 (July-Sept. 1974), pp. 70-83. Though women are still encouraged to remain at home, they are making headway in politics, societal roles, and the professions.

4712. Quint, Howard H. and Milton Cantor, eds. MEN, WOMEN AND ISSUES IN AMERICAN HISTORY. Springfield, IL: Dorsey Press, 1975. 2 vols.

4713. Reintoft, Hanne. KVINDEN I KLASSE-SAMFUNDET [WOMAN IN CLASS-SOCIETY (STATUS OF WOMEN)]. Kobenhavn: Stig Vendelkaers Forlag, 1972. 189 pp. Women and sex roles, education, public and political life, and position in Denmark and the European Economic Community.

4714. "Remarkable American Women 1776-1976," LIFE SPECIAL REPORT MAGAZINE (1976), pp. 1-116. Photographic essay with commentary.

4715. Rogers, Agnes. WOMEN ARE HERE TO STAY: THE DURABLE SEX IN ITS INFINITE VARIETY THROUGH HALF A CENTURY OF AMERICAN LIFE. New York: Harper, 1949. 220 pp. Pictorial history of women.

4716. "The Roles of African Women: Past, Present, and Future," CANADIAN JOURNAL OF AFRICAN STUDIES, vol. 6, no. 2 (1972), pp. 143-377. Special Issue. Contributors include Audrey Wipper, Carol P. Hoffer, Judith Van Allen, Alf Schwartz, David R. Evans, Janet E. Pool, Guy Bernard, Kenneth Little, Josef Gugler, Remi Clignet, Jerome H. Barkow, Miranda Greenstreet, R. Mookodi, and Marjorie J. Mbilinyi.

4717. Roosevelt, Eleanor. IT'S UP TO THE WOMEN. New York: Frederick A. Stokes, 1933. 263 pp. Covers such topics as women and peace, budgeting of income taxes, and occupations for women.

4718. Rosaldo, Michelle Zimbalist and Louise Lamphere, eds. WOMAN, CULTURE AND SOCIETY. Stanford, CA: Stanford Univ. Press, 1974. 352 pp. The relationship of women to economics, politics, reproduction, and socialization.

4719. Ross, Ishbel. SONS OF ADAM, DAUGHTERS OF EVE (THE ROLE OF WOMEN IN AMERICAN HISTORY). New York: Harper & Row, 1969. 340 pp. Surveys the role of women and their influence on men in politics, reform and other areas from prerevolutionary times to the present; concluding that despite a broadened range of activities, women remain essentially "Mothers of men."

4720. Roy, Manisha. BENGALI WOMEN. Chicago, IL: Univ. of Chicago Press, 1975. 205 pp. Study of cultural ideals and social realities in the relationships that make up domestic life for women in contemporary upper-class Bengali society.

4721. Ryan, Mary P. WOMAN IN AMERICA FROM COLONIAL TIMES TO THE PRESENT. New York: New Viewpoints, 1975. 496 pp.

4722. Safilios-Rothschild, Constantina. WOMEN AND SOCIAL POLICY. Englewood Cliffs, NJ: Prentice-Hall, 1974. 197 pp. Describes three kinds of remedies for every sexist problem: Pavlovian (rewarding nonsexist/punishing sexist behavior), paternalism (government support of non-sexist projects), and propaganda (non-sexist oriented media).

4723. Sayers, Dorothy Leigh. "Are Women Human?" Grand Rapids, MI: William B. Eerdmans, 1971. 47 pp.

4724. Schaw, Janet. JOURNAL OF A LADY OF QUALITY; BEING THE NARRATIVE OF A JOURNEY FROM SCOTLAND TO THE WEST INDIES, NORTH CAROLINA, AND PORTUGAL, IN THE YEARS 1774-1776. New Haven, CT: Yale Univ. Press, 1939. 351 pp.

4725. Scott, Anne Firor, comp. WOMEN IN AMERICAN LIFE: SELECTED READINGS. Boston, MA: Houghton-Mifflin, 1970. 214 pp.

4726. Sochen, June. HERSTORY: A WOMAN'S VIEW OF AMERICAN HISTORY. Port Washington, NY: Alfred Publishing, 1974. 448 pp. Surveys women's contributions in each major period of American history.

4727. Solomon, Barbara Bryant, ed. "Special Issue on Women," SOCIAL WORK, vol. 21, no. 6 (Nov. 1976), pp. 417-537. Contributors include Maryann Mahaffey, Diane Kravetz, Joel Fischer, Diane Dulaney, Rosemary T. Fazio, Mary T. Hudak, Ethel Zivotofsky, Dorothy Zietz, John L. Erlich, Alfred Kadushin, David Fanshel, Martha N. Ozawa, Joyce O. Beckett, Linda Rosenman, Gail Arbarbanel, Ellen W. Freeman, Marcella Schuyler, Sharon B. Berlin, Barbara Stephens Brockway, Jane K. Thompson, Maureen M. Underwood, Edwin D. Underwood, Celia Medina, Maria R. Reyes, Mildred Fine Kaplan, Esther Lazarus, Barbara H. Saidel, Maureen R. Killeen, Caroline L. Jacobs, Linn Spencer Hayes, Lynne T. Witkin, Margaret Redfern, Shirley B. Klass, Kaye M. Coleman, Janet Rosenberg, Betty S. Johnson, and Rosalyn Benitez.

4728. Staff of the U.S. Center for IWY. THE YEAR THAT BECAME A DECADE: THE LIFE AND TIMES OF THE U.S. CENTER FOR INTERNATIONAL WOMEN'S YEAR 1975. Washington, D.C.: U.S. Center for IWY, 1976. 149 pp.

4729. Thompson, Carol L., ed. "Women in America," CURRENT HISTORY, vol. 70, no. 416 (May 1976), pp. 193-232. Special Issue. Contributors include Gerda Lerner, Virginia C. Knight, Joan B. Antell, Laurel R. Bergold, John J. Stucker, Heidi I. Hartmann, Sarah Elbert, and Diann Holland Painter.

4730. United Nations. Educational, Scientific and Cultural Organization. "1975, International Women's Year," UNESCO FEATURES, no. 676/677/678 (1975), pp. 1-47. Contributors include Toby Burke, Esmeralda Arboleda Cuevas, Lucille Mair, Yvonne Tabbush, Rosemary Ginn, Barbara Good, Izzett Orujeva, Estefania Aldaba-Lim, Han Suyin, Aziza Husain, and Caroline Diop.

4731. U.S. Civil War Centennial Commission. "Our Women of the Sixties." By Sylvia G. L. Dannett and Katharine M. Jones. Washington, D.C.: U.S. Civil War Centennial Commission, 1963. 44 pp.

4732. U.S. National Commission on the Observance of International Women's Year. ". . . TO FORM A MORE PERFECT UNION . . ." JUSTICE FOR AMERICAN WOMEN. Washington, D.C.: SUDOC, GPO, 1976. 382 pp. Excellent summary of women's economic, political, legal, and social status; appendix includes statistical data, federal laws prohibiting sex discrimination, and much other valuable resource information.

4733. University of Wisconsin-Extension. Women's Education Resources. "International Women's Year: Mexico City and After." Madison, WI: Univ. of Wisconsin-Extension, 1976. 90 pp. Transcribed and edited from Wisconsin Educational Telephone Network course. Moderated by Constance Threinen. Participants included Kathryn F. Clarenbach, Lisa Bogden, Bonita Cornute, Jean Foss, Shirley Haas, Marie Rosenberg-Dishman, Jackie Smith, Norene Smith, Elizabeth Starr, Ebele Amali, Joann Elder, Jeanne DuBois, Norma Briggs, Martin Gruberg, Linda Haas, Sara Scherkow, Catherine East, and Mildred Marcy.

4734. Wald, Carol with Judith Papachristou. MYTH AMERICA: PICTURING WOMEN, 1865-1945. New York: Pantheon Books, 1975. 182 pp. Photographic/pictorial essay.

4735. Welter, Barbara. THE AMERICAN WOMAN IN THE NINETEENTH CENTURY. Athens, OH: Ohio Univ. Press, 1976. 275 pp.

4736. West, Uta, ed. WOMEN IN A CHANGING WORLD. New York: McGraw-Hill, 1975. 170 pp. Anthology of articles collected from sources such as VIVA, NEW YORK TIMES, THE VILLAGE VOICE, etc.

4737. Westin, Jeane. MAKING DO: HOW WOMEN SURVIVED THE THIRTIES. Chicago, IL: Follett, 1976. 329 pp. Reminiscences of 100 women on American life during the 1930's.

4738. Wolf, Margery and Roxanne Witke, eds. WOMEN IN CHINESE SOCIETY. Stanford, CA: Stanford Univ. Press, 1975. 340 pp. The roles of Chinese women in the family, the economy, and political and literary movements; emphasis on pre-1949 China.

4739. "Women in America," THE GALLUP OPINION INDEX, Report no. 128 (March 1976), pp. 1-46. Special issue on women and perceptions of their role in society; comprehensive survey of attitudes toward women in politics, legal status of women, lifestyles, and working women.

4740. "Women in India: A Handbook." Bombay, India: Shreemati Nathibai Damodar Thackersey Women's University, Research Unit on Women's Studies, 1975. 84 pp.

4741. Wong, Aline K. WOMEN IN MODERN SINGAPORE. Singapore: Univ. Education Press, 1975. 143 pp.

4742. Young, Bok Koh. "Women." Seoul, Korea: Korean Overseas Information Service, 1975. 56 pp.

4743. Zinserling, Verena. "Die Frau in Hellas und Rom [Woman in Greece and Rome]." New York: A. Schram, 1973. 86 pp.

B. The Position of Women

"The position of women has no fixed relation to the general level of culture. It has been higher in the past than in recent times, and amongst savages it is by no means uniformly low."

—Leonard Trelawney Hobhouse

4744. Amin, F. NAGHSHÉ ZAN DAR FARHANG VA TAMADON É IRAN [THE ROLE OF WOMEN IN THE CULTURE AND CIVILIZATION OF IRAN]. Tehran, Iran: Women's Organization, 1972.

4745. Anderson, Margaret, comp. MOTHER WAS NOT A PERSON. Montreal, Quebec: Content Publishing, 1972. 252 pp. Collection of articles on the position of Canadian women.

4746. Blackburne, Neville. LADIES' CHAIN. London, England: Falcon Press, 1952. 215 pp. Women in the late eighteenth century and early nineteenth century.

4747. Blackwell, Antoinette Louisa Brown. THE SEXES THROUGHOUT NATURE. Westport, CT: Hyperion Press, 1976. 240 pp. Reprint of 1875 edition. Collection of essays on sex and evolution, by the first woman in America to hold a ministry.

4748. Boulding, Elise. THE UNDERSIDE OF HISTORY: A VIEW OF WOMEN THROUGH TIME. Boulder, CO: Westview Press, 1976. The contributions of women to world society over a period of two million years.

4749. ———. WOMEN IN THE TWENTIETH-CENTURY WORLD. New York: Halsted Press, 1977.

4750. Bridenthal, Renate and Claudia Koontz. BECOMING VISIBLE: WOMEN IN EUROPEAN HISTORY. New York: Houghton Mifflin, 1976.

4751. Catt, Carrie Chapman, ed. "A Symposium on the New Woman," CURRENT HISTORY, vol. 27 (Oct. 1927), pp. 1-48. Contributors include Charlotte Perkins Gilman, Martha Bensley Bruere, Hugh L. McMenamin (Rev.), Joseph Collins, and Magdalene Marx.

4752. de Paredes, Querubina H., Izaquirre P. Maritza, and Inés Vargas Delaunoy. PARTICIPACION DE LA MUJER EN EL DESARROLLO DE AMERICA LATINA Y EL CARIBE. Santiago, Chile: UNICEF, 1975. 117 pp. Overview of the position of women in Latin America and the Caribbean; includes a section on demographic data.

4753. Friedman, Jean E. and William G. Shade. OUR AMERICAN SISTERS: WOMEN IN AMERICAN LIFE AND THOUGHT. Boston, MA: Allyn & Bacon, 1973. 354 pp. Collection of readings on the problem of the representation of women in political, social, psychological, and economic history, as well as attitudes toward women and their roles.

4754. Hecht, Marie B., J. D. Berbich, S. A. Healey, and C. M. Cooper. THE WOMEN, YES! New York: Holt, Rinehart & Winston, 1973. 226 pp. Broad view of opinions about women through the ages.

4755. Higgins, Chester with Harold McDougall. BLACK WOMAN. New York: McCall Publishing, 1970. 1 vol. (unpaged)

4756. Iglitzin, Lynn B. and Ruth Ross, eds. WOMEN IN THE WORLD: A COMPARATIVE STUDY. Santa Barbara, CA: American Bibliographical Center—Clio Press, 1976. 480 pp. Collection of readings describing the efforts of women to gain a voice in the political, religious, and social life of their countries, and showing the similarity of the roles and status of women cross-culturally.

4757. Lakoff, Robin. "Language and Woman's Place." New York: Harper & Row, 1975. 85 pp.

4758. Macksey, Joan and Kenneth John Macksey. THE GUINNESS GUIDE TO FEMININE ACHIEVEMENTS. London, England: Guinness Superlatives, 1975. 288 pp.

4759. Marks, Arno F. MALE AND FEMALE AND THE AFRO-CURACAOAN HOUSEHOLD. The Hague, Netherlands: Nijhoff, 1976. 355 pp. Translation and revision of MAN, VROVW EN HUISHOUD GROEP, DE AFRO-AMERIKAANSE FAMILIE IN DE SAMENLEVINA VAN CURACAO (1973).

4760. Negrin, Su. "A Graphic Notebook on Feminism." New York: Times Change Press, 1974. 64 pp. The evolution of feminist consciousness from ancient Amazon societies through the twentieth century.

4761. Raymond, G. Allison. HALF THE WORLD'S PEOPLE. New York: Appleton-Century-Crofts, 1965. 209 pp.

4762. Richards, Caroline Cowles. VILLAGE LIFE IN AMERICA, 1852-1872: THE DIARY OF A SCHOOL GIRL. Williamstown, MA: Corner House, 1972. 225 pp. Reprint of 1913 edition. Introduction by Margaret Sanger. Rich source of information on the life style young people experienced at that time.

4763. Robins, Elizabeth. ANCILLA'S SHARE: AN INDICTMENT OF SEX ANTAGONISM. Westport, CT: Hyperion Press, 1976. 313 pp. Reprint of 1924 edition. Post-World War I attack on man's ignorance of woman's real nature and history.

4764. Schurz, William Lytle. "The Woman," in THIS NEW WORLD: THE CIVILIZATION OF LATIN AMERICA. New York: E.P. Dutton, 1964. Pp. 276-338. Discusses the historical and sociological roles of women in Latin America.

4765. Scott, Anne Firor. "Women's Perspective on the Patriarchy in the 1850's," THE JOURNAL OF AMERICAN HISTORY, vol. 61, no. 1 (June 1974), pp. 52-64. Discusses the discontent of Southern women; their sympathy with the sexually exploited black women, their unhappiness with the "depravity" of Southern men.

4766. Selid, Betty. WOMEN IN NORWAY: THEIR POSITION IN FAMILY LIFE, EMPLOYMENT, AND SOCIETY. Oslo, Norway: Norwegian Joint Committee on International Social Policy, in association with the Department of Cultural Relations, Royal Ministry of Foreign Affairs, 1970. 114 pp.

4767. Sidel, Ruth. WOMEN AND CHILD CARE IN CHINA. New York:

Penguin Books, 1973. 207 pp. Deals with the liberation of women, marriage, pregnancy, and the "Bitter Past."

4768. Tripp, Maggie, ed. WOMAN IN THE YEAR 2000. New York: Arbor House, 1974. 288 pp. 26 perceptive writers predict what may happen to women by the beginning of the twenty-first century.

4769. U.S. Dept. of Labor. Employment Standards Administration. Women's Bureau. AMERICAN WOMEN AT THE CROSSROADS: DIRECTIONS FOR THE FUTURE. Washington, D.C.: SUDOC, GPO, 1970. 126 pp. Report of the Fiftieth Anniversary Conference of the Women's Bureau (June 11-13, 1970).

4770. University of New Zealand. Dept. of Adult Education. "Women and the Australian Community." Armidale, New Zealand: Univ. of New Zealand, 1961. 63 pp.

4771. Van Vuuren, Nancy. THE SUBVERSION OF WOMEN AS PRACTICED BY CHURCHES, WITCH HUNTERS, AND OTHER SEXISTS. Philadelphia, PA: Westminster Press, 1973. 190 pp. Details how Western institutions have worked together to keep women subordinated.

4772. Watkins, Mel and Jay David (pseud. for Bill Adler), comps. TO BE A BLACK WOMAN: PORTRAITS IN FACT AND FICTION. New York: William Morrow, 1971. 285 pp.

4773. Wright, Marcia. "Women in Peril: A Commentary on the Life Stories of Captives in 19th Century East-Central Africa," AFRICAN SOCIAL RESEARCH, no. 20 (Dec. 1975), pp. 800-915.

4774. Wyon, Olive. THE DAWN WIND: A PICTURE OF CHANGING CONDITIONS AMONG WOMEN IN AFRICA AND THE EAST. London, England: Student Christian Movement Press, 1931. 155 pp.

4775. Zweig, Ferdynand. WOMEN'S LIFE AND LABOUR. London, England: Gollancz, 1952. 190 pp.

C. Women–From Ancient Times Through Victorian

"This I hold to be the chief office of history, to rescue virtuous actions from the oblivion to which a want of records would consign them, and that men should feel a dread of being considered infamous in the opinions of posterity, from their depraved expressions and base actions."

—Tacitus

"The test of civilization is the estimate of woman."

—George William Curtis

4776. Anton, Ferdinand. WOMEN IN PRE-COLUMBIAN AMERICA. New York: A. Schram, 1974. 112 pp. Reviews the role of women in the Aztec, Maya, and Inca cultures based on works of art and historical sources.

4777. Ashdown, Dulcie Margaret. LADIES-IN-WAITING. New York: St. Martins Press, 1976. 212 pp.

4778. Basch, Françoise. RELATIVE CREATURES: VICTORIAN WOMEN IN SOCIETY AND THE NOVEL. New York: Schocken Books, 1975. Compares the fictional life style created by the mid-century novelists (George Eliot, the Brontës), with the actual lives of all classes of Victorian women.

4779. Beattie, J. M. "The Criminality of Women in Eighteenth Century England," JOURNAL OF SOCIAL HISTORY, vol. 8, no. 4 (Summer 1975), pp. 80-116. Examination and analysis of the records of Surrey and Sussex Counties; excellent footnotes. See Also Carol Z. Weiner.

4780. Bell, Susan Groag, ed. WOMEN FROM THE GREEKS TO THE FRENCH REVOLUTION. Belmont, CA: Wadsworth Publishing, 1973. 313 pp. Anthology of contemporary literature, works of recent scholars, and past historians, on the lives of women and men's attitudes toward women from 400 B.C. to 1800 A.D.

4781. Bleackley, Horace. LADIES FAIR AND FRAIL: SKETCHES OF THE DEMI-MONDE DURING THE EIGHTEENTH CENTURY. New York: Dodd, Mead, 1925. 328 pp. Sketches of six women courtesans during the latter half of the eighteenth century in England: Fanny Murray, Kitty Fisher, Nancy Parsons, Kitty Kennedy, Grace Dalrymple Eliot, and Gertrude Mahon.

4782. Brooks, Geraldine. DAMES AND DAUGHTERS OF THE FRENCH COURT. Freeport, NY: Books for Libraries, 1968. 290 pp. Reprint of 1904 edition. Ten biographies of female courtiers (1626-1821): Mme. de Sevigné, Mme. de La Fayette, Mme. Geoffrin, Mlle. de Lespinasse, Mme. Roland, Mme. Le Brun, Mme. de Staël, Mme. Récamier, Mme. Valmore, and Mme. de Rémusat.

4783. Caffrey, Kate. THE NINETEEN-HUNDREDS LADY. New York: Gordon Cremonesi, 1976. Portrait of the Edwardian "lady," forever feminine if it killed her, or articulate dissenter.

4784. Calder-Marshall, Arthur. THE GRAND CENTURY OF THE LADY, 1720-1820. New York: Gordon Cremonesi, 1977.

4785. Cohen, Edgar H. MADEMOISELLE LIBERTINE. Boston, MA: Houghton Mifflin, 1971. 329 pp. Biography of Mlle. Ninon de Lanclos, 17th century French courtesan.

4786. Conrad, Susan Phinney. PERISH THE THOUGHT: INTELLECTUAL WOMEN IN ROMANTIC AMERICA, 1830-1860. New York: Oxford Univ. Press, 1976. 292 pp. Discusses the obstacles women faced in nineteenth century life.

4787. Cunningham, Peter, comp. THE STORY OF NELL GWYN AND THE SAYINGS OF CHARLES II. London, England: Bradbury & Evans, 1852. 212 pp. Women in Restoration society.

4788. Davidoff, Leonore. THE BEST CIRCLES: WOMEN AND SOCIETY IN VICTORIAN ENGLAND. Totowa, NJ: Rowman & Littlefield, 1973. 127 pp.

4789. ———. "Mastered for Life: Servant and Wife in Victorian and Edwardian England (with comments by Alice Kessler-Harris and Louise A. Tilly)," JOURNAL OF SOCIAL HISTORY, vol. 7, no. 4 (Summer 1974), pp. 406-408, 446-459. Comparison of the relationship of servant and master with that of husband and wife.

4790. De Maulde, L. and R. LaClaviere. THE WOMEN OF THE RENAISSANCE: A STUDY OF FEMINISM. New York: Gordon Press, 1976.

4791. D'Humy, Fernand Emile. WOMEN WHO INFLUENCED THE WORLD. New York: Library Publishers, 1955. 342 pp.

4792. Furniss, Harry. SOME VICTORIAN WOMEN; GOOD, BAD, AND INDIFFERENT. Norwood, PA: Norwood Editions, 1975. 226 pp. Reprint of 1923 edition. Sketches of authors, actresses and artists.

4793. Goldsmith, Robert Hillis. "My Lady Tongue: The Witty Women of the Renaissance," ILLINOIS QUARTERLY, vol. 34 (Feb. 1972), pp. 52-64.

4794. Hare, Christopher. THE MOST ILLUSTRIOUS LADIES OF THE ITALIAN RENAISSANCE. Williamstown, MA: Corner House, 1972. 367 pp. Reprint of 1907 edition. A sweeping picture of the daily cares, pleasures, and cultural contributions of women in 14th to 16th century Italy.

4795. Hartman, Mary S. VICTORIAN MURDRESSES: A TRUE HISTORY OF THIRTEEN RESPECTABLE FRENCH AND ENGLISH WOMEN ACCUSED OF UNSPEAKABLE CRIMES. New York: Schocken Books, 1977. Shows how these middle-class women were victims of the strains of rising social obligations.

4796. Hogrefe, Pearl. TUDOR WOMEN: COMMONERS AND QUEENS. Ames, IW: Iowa State Univ. Press, 1975. 170 pp. Emphasizes the contributions of upper-class women.

4797. –––. WOMEN OF ACTION IN TUDOR ENGLAND. Ames, IW: Iowa State Univ. Press, 1977.

4798. Kemp-Welch, Alice. OF SIX MEDIEVAL WOMEN. Williamstown, MA: Corner House, 1972. 189 pp. Reprint of 1903 edition. Portraits of six women who played an important role during the 10th to the 16th century: Roswitha, a German nun; Marie de France, at the court of Henry II of England; Mechtild of Magdeburg, a mystic; Mahaut, Countess of Artois; Christine de Pizan, an Italian at the court of Charles V of France; and Agnes Sorel, confidante of Charles VII.

4799. Knox, Cleone. THE DIARY OF A YOUNG LADY OF FASHION IN THE YEAR 1764-1765. Norwood, PA: Norwood Editions, 1975. 249 pp. Reprint of 1926 edition. Embellished view of the society in which she lived.

4800. Lowenberg, Bert J. and Ruth Bogin, eds. BLACK WOMEN IN NINETEENTH CENTURY AMERICAN LIFE: THEIR WORKS, THEIR THOUGHTS, THEIR FEELINGS. University Park, PA: Pennsylvania State Univ. Press, 1976.

4801. May, Gita. MADAME ROLAND AND THE AGE OF REVOLUTION. New York: Columbia Univ. Press, 1970. 370 pp. Writer during the French Revolution.

4802. Morewedge, Rosemarie Thee, ed. THE ROLE OF THE WOMAN IN THE MIDDLE AGES. Albany, NY: State Univ. of New York Press, 1975.

195 pp. Collection of six essays by top medievalists, each focusing on a different area.

4803. Morgan, Lady Sydney Owenson. WOMAN AND HER MASTER. Westport, CT: Hyperion Press, 1976. 429 pp. Reprint of 1840 edition. Revises the stereotyped versions of the famous and infamous women in oriental and classical antiquity, through the period of the Roman Empire.

4804. Noel, C. M. D. LES AVANTAGES DU SEXE: LE TRIOMPHE DES FEMMES, DANS LEQUEL ON FAIT VOIR PAR DE TRES FORTES RAISONS. Anvers, France: Sleghers, 1698. 129 pp.

4805. Parsa, F. H. Ahi, and M. Talaghani. ZAN DAR IRAN É BASTAN [WOMEN IN ANCIENT IRAN]. Tehran, Iran: The Women's Group of the Univ. of Tehran Press, 1968.

4806. Perowne, Stewart Henry. THE CAESARS' WIVES: ABOVE SUSPICION? Totowa, NJ: Rowman & Littlefield, 1974. 192 pp.

4807. Pike, E. Royston. GOLDEN TIMES: HUMAN DOCUMENTS OF THE VICTORIAN AGE. New York: Praeger Books, 1967. 378 pp. Details the condition of women in industry and agriculture, sex mores and conduct, infant mortality, the trade union movement, etc., from 1850 to 1875 in Great Britain.

4808. Pomeroy, Sarah B. GODDESSES, WHORES, WIVES, AND SLAVES: WOMEN IN CLASSICAL ANTIQUITY. New York: Schocken Books, 1975. 265 pp. Examines the lives and roles of Greek, Roman, and Egyptian women using documents on papyrus equivalent to letters and diaries.

4809. Power, Eileen Edna. MEDIEVAL WOMEN. New York: Cambridge Univ. Press, 1975. 112 pp. Covers the period between 500-1500 A.D.

4810. Razani, Abu Torab. ZAN DAR DURAN E SHAHANSHAHI E IRAN [WOMEN IN THE MONARCHIAL PERIODS OF IRAN]. Tehran, Iran: Women's College, 1972.

4811. Sarashina, Lady (authorship attributed to). AS I CROSSED A BRIDGE OF DREAMS: THE RECOLLECTIONS OF A WOMAN IN ELEVENTH CENTURY JAPAN. London, England: Oxford Univ. Press, 1971. 159 pp.

4812. Sichel, Edith Helen. WOMEN AND MEN OF THE FRENCH RENAISSANCE. Port Washington, NY: Kennikat Press, 1970. 395 pp. Reprint of 1901 edition.

4813. Stebbins, Lucy Poate. LONDON LADIES: TRUE TALES OF THE EIGHTEENTH CENTURY. New York: AMS Press, 1966. 208 pp. Reprint of 1952 edition.

4814. Stuart, Susan Mosher, ed. WOMEN IN MEDIEVAL SOCIETY. Philadelphia, PA: Univ. of Pennsylvania Press, 1976. 219 pp.

4815. Vincent, Arthur, ed. LIVES OF TWELVE BAD WOMEN: ILLUSTRATIONS AND REVIEWS OF FEMININE TURPITUDE SET FORTH BY IMPARTIAL HANDS. Plainview, NY: Books for Libraries, 1972. 324 pp. Reprint of 1897 edition. Murderers, thieves, imposters, witches.

4816. Webb, Robert Kiefer. HARRIET MARTINEAU: A RADICAL
VICTORIAN. New York: Columbia Univ. Press, 1960. 385 pp.
Biography emphasizing her influence as an author and journalist.

4817. Weiner, Carol Z. "Sex Roles and Crime in Late Elizabethan
Hertfordshire," JOURNAL OF SOCIAL HISTORY, vol. 8, no. 4
(Summer 1975), pp. 38-60. Excellent footnotes containing much
valuable statistical information. See also J. M. Beattie.

4818. Wilson, Robert McNair. WOMEN OF THE FRENCH REVOLUTION.
Port Washington, NY: Kennikat Press, 1970. 287 pp. Reprint of 1936
edition. Discusses the Amazons, those women fighting for financial
dictatorship; and "the women of France," the wives and mothers of the
majority.

4819. Wilson, Violet A. SOCIETY WOMEN OF SHAKESPEARE'S TIME. Port
Washington, NY: Kennikat Press, 1970. 258 pp. Reprint of 1924
edition. Shows the freedom and influence of women in the time of
Queen Elizabeth I.

4820. Winehold, Karl. DIE DEUTSCHEN FRAUEN IN DEM MITTELALTER
[GERMAN WOMEN IN THE MIDDLE AGES]. Englewood Cliffs, NJ:
Scholastic Book Service, 1968. 2 vols. Reprint of 1882 edition.

D. Women—Manners and Customs

*"If a woman wears gay colors, rouge and a startling hat, a man hesitates to take her
out. If she wears a little turban and a tailored suit, he takes her out and stares all
evening at a woman in gay colors, rouge and a startling hat."*
—BALTIMORE BEACON

*"To get into the best society nowadays, one has either to feed people, amuse people,
or shock people."*
—Oscar Wilde

4821. Atkinson, James. "Customs and Manners of the Women of Persia and
Their Domestic Superstitions." New York: Scholarly Press, 1971. 93
pp. Reprint of 1832 edition. Translated from original Persian
manuscript "Kitábi Kulsúm Naneh."

4822. Barnes, Djuna. "Ladies Almanack, Showing Their Signs and Their Tides;
Their Moons and Their Changes; the Seasons as it is with Them; Their
Eclipses and Equinoxes; as well as a Full Record of Diurnal and
Nocturnal Distempers (Written and Illustrated by a Lady of Fashion)."
New York: Harper & Row, 1972. 85 pp. Reprint of 1928 edition.
Satire.

4823. Burnap, George Washington. THE SPHERE AND DUTIES OF WOMEN:
A COURSE OF LECTURES. Washington, D.C.: Zenger Publications,
1976. 326 pp. Reprint of 1848 edition.

4824. Duff, William. LETTERS ON THE INTELLECTUAL AND MORAL

CHARACTER OF WOMEN. New York: Garland Publishing, 1974. 335 pp. Reprint of 1807 edition.

4825. THE FEMALE AEGIS, OR THE DUTIES OF WOMEN FROM CHILDHOOD TO OLD AGE. New York: Garland Publishing, 1974. 187 pp. Reprint of 1798 edition.

4826. Fisher, Sydney George. MEN, WOMEN, AND MANNERS IN COLONIAL TIMES. Philadelphia, PA: J. B. Lippincott, 1898. 2 vols.

4827. Gisborne, Thomas. AN ENQUIRY INTO THE DUTIES OF THE FEMALE SEX. New York: Garland Publishing, 1974. 426 pp. Reprint of 1797 edition.

4828. Imamu, Ameer Baraka (LeRoi Jones). "The Coronation of the Black Queen," THE BLACK SCHOLAR, vol. 1, no. 8 (June 1970), pp. 46-48. Ceremony modeled after two traditional black coronation ceremonies, the Ancient Egyptian and the Ashanti; suggests that it be used instead of current ceremonies for Home Coming Queen, etc.

4829. James, Henry. "The Speech and Manners of American Women." Lancaster, PA: Lancaster House Press, 1973. 56 pp. Reprint of two series of essays "The Speech of American Women," and "The Manners of American Women," originally published in HARPERS BAZAAR, 1906-1907.

4830. Trollope, Mrs. Frances Milton. DOMESTIC MANNERS OF THE AMERICANS. New York: Dodd, Mead, 1972. 398 pp. Reprint of 1839 edition.

4831. Whitcomb, Helen. TODAY'S WOMAN. New York: McGraw-Hill, 1976. 376 pp. Advice on clothing and dress, as well as etiquette.

4832. Winn, Mary Day. ADAM'S RIB. New York: Harcourt, Brace & World, 1931. 191 pp. Journalistic view of contemporary feminine manners and morals.

E. Women in Folklore and Witchcraft

"Our heritage is composed of all the voices that can answer our questions."
—André Malraux

"It often happens that only from the words of a good story-teller do we realize what we have done and what we have missed, and what we should have done and what we shouldn't have. It is perhaps in these stories, oral and written, that the true history of mankind can be found and that through them one can perhaps sense if not fully know the meaning of that history."

—Ivo Andrić

4833. Abrahams, Roger D., ed. A SINGER AND HER SONGS: ALMEDA RIDDLE'S BOOK OF BALLADS. Baton Rouge, LA: Louisiana State Univ. Press, 1970. 191 pp. Her life story as recorded by Abrahams, including what she feels to be the effect of major influences in her life.

4834. Bauman, Richard, ed. BLACK GIRLS AT PLAY: FOLKLORIC PERSPECTIVES ON CHILD DEVELOPMENT. Austin, TX: Southwest

Educational Development Laboratory, 1975. 101 pp. Delineates developmental trends in children's folklore.

4835. Beck, Janet C. "A Traditional Witch of the Twentieth Century," NEW YORK FOLKLORE QUARTERLY, vol. 30, no. 2 (June 1974), pp. 101-116. Story of Dolorez Amelia Gomez, a woman with "special powers."

4836. Bede, Cuthbert. THE WHITE WIFE; WITH OTHER STORIES, SUPERNATURAL, ROMANTIC, AND LEGENDARY. Norwood, PA: Norwood Editions, 1972. 252 pp. Reprint of 1865 edition. Folklore from Scotland.

4837. Coffin, Tristam Potter. THE FEMALE HERO IN FOLKLORE AND LEGEND. New York: Seabury Press, 1975. 223 pp. Relates the tales of infamous and notorious women in history, i.e. Belle Starr, Cleopatra, Lydia Pinkham.

4838. Farrer, Claire R., ed. "Women and Folklore." Austin, TX: Univ. of Texas Press, 1976. 99 pp. Reprint of Special Issue of the JOURNAL OF AMERICAN FOLKLORE, vol. 88, no. 347 (Jan.-March 1975).

4839. Forbes, Esther. A MIRROR FOR WITCHES IN WHICH IS REFLECTED THE LIFE, MACHINATIONS, AND DEATH OF FAMOUS DOLL BILBY, WHO WITH A MORE THAN FEMININE PERVERSITY, PREFERRED A DEMON TO A MORTAL LOVER. HERE IS ALSO TOLD HOW AND WHY A RIGHTEOUS AND MOST AWFULL JUDGMENT BEFELL HER, DESTROYING BOTH CORPOREAL BODY AND IMMORTAL SOUL. Boston, MA: Houghton-Mifflin, 1928. 213 pp.

4840. Fowke, Edith, ed. TRADITIONAL SINGERS AND SONGS FROM ONTARIO. Hatsboro, PA: Folklore Association, 1965. 210 pp. Includes chapters on Mrs. Arlington Frazier, and Mrs. Gordon Clark, both renowned Canadian folk singers.

4841. Johnson, Robbie Davis. "Folklore and Women: A Social Interactional Analysis of the Folklore of a Texas Madam," JOURNAL OF AMERICAN FOLKLORE, vol. 86, no. 341 (July-Sept. 1973), pp. 211-224. Her use of the proverbial "dirty joke" as a means of maintaining control over both her guests and her employees.

4842. Lewis, Mary Ellen B. "The Feminists Have Done It: Applied Folklore," JOURNAL OF AMERICAN FOLKLORE, vol. 87, no. 343 (Jan.-March 1974), pp. 85-87. The role of slogans taken from literature in the feminist movement.

4843. Michelet, Jules. SATANISM AND WITCHCRAFT: A STUDY IN MEDIEVAL SUPERSTITION. Secaucus, NJ: Citadel Press, 1974. 332 pp. Reprint of 1958 edition. History of the brutal and bloody treatment of women by the Christian Church in Europe from the tenth to the nineteenth century.

4844. Ruether, Rosemary. "The Persecution of Witches: A Case of Sexism and Agism?" CHRISTIANITY AND CRISIS, vol. 34, no. 22 (Dec. 23, 1974), pp. 291-295. Brief history of witch-hunting as related to the position of the older woman in society, neglected by most social reforms.

4845. Thiselton-Dyer, Thomas F. FOLK-LORE OF WOMEN, AS
ILLUSTRATED BY LEGENDARY AND TRADITIONAL TALES,
FOLK-RHYMES, PROVERBIAL SAYINGS, SUPERSTITIONS, ETC.
Williamstown, MA: Corner House Press, 1968. 253 pp. Reprint of 1906
edition. Rare review of African, European, and Asiatic folklore that
demonstrates similarity of folkwisdom in widely disparate societies.
4846. Whitten, Jeanne Patten. FANNIE HARDY ECKSTROM: A
DESCRIPTIVE BIBLIOGRAPHY OF HER WRITINGS PUBLISHED
AND UNPUBLISHED. Orono, ME: The Univ. Press, 1976. 107 pp.
Excellent study of the Maine history and ballad expert, including an
explanatory essay and an annotated bibliography of works by and
about F. H. Eckstrom.

F. Women and Fashion

"Every generation laughs at the old fashions, but follows religiously the new."
—Henry David Thoreau

4847. Cunnington, Cecil Willett. "Perfect Lady." London, England: M. Parrish,
1948. 71 pp.
4848. Dalvimart, Octavian. THE COSTUME OF TURKEY, ILLUSTRATED BY
A SERIES OF ENGRAVINGS: WITH DESCRIPTIONS IN ENGLISH
AND FRENCH. Istanbul: Zaman Kitaphanesi, 1932-33. 262 pp.
Reprint of 1802 edition.
4849. De Villermont, Comtesse Marie. HISTOIRE DE LA COIFFURE
FÉMININE. Paris, France: Renouard, 1892. 822 pp. Exhaustive study
of fashions in hairstyles from Biblical to late Victorian times.
4850. Earle, Alice Morse. TWO CENTURIES OF COSTUME IN AMERICA,
1620-1820. Rutland, VT: Charles Tuttle, 1971. 824 pp. Reprint of
1903 edition. Illustrated study of dress in colonial America,
interspersed with quotations and description.
4851. Ewing, Elizabeth. HISTORY OF TWENTIETH CENTURY FASHION.
New York: Charles Scribners Sons, 1975. 244 pp. The development of
fashion and the clothing industry; focuses on British trends.
4852. Garland, Madge. THE CHANGING FACE OF BEAUTY. London,
England: Weidenfeld, 1957. 225 pp. History of changing fashion in
feminine beauty.
4853. McClellan, Elisabeth. HISTORIC DRESS IN AMERICA: 1607-1870. New
York: Benjamin Blom, 1969. 655 pp. Reprint of 1904 edition of
HISTORIC DRESS IN AMERICA, 1607-1800, and 1910 edition of
HISTORIC DRESS IN AMERICA, 1800-1870.
4854. Moore, Doris Langley-Levy. THE WOMAN IN FASHION. London,
England: Batsford, 1949. 184 pp. Illustrated with costumes from the
author's collection.
4855. Robida, A. MESDAMES NOS AÏEULES. DIX SIÈCLES D'ÉLÉGANCE.
Paris, France: Librarie Illustrée, 1891. 254 pp. Well-illustrated account

of feminine fashions from the Middle Ages to the late nineteenth century.

4856. Sronkova, Olga. GOTHIC WOMAN'S FASHION. Prague, Czechoslovakia: Artia, 1954. 265 pp. History of Bohemian fashion in the Middle Ages.

4857. Woodrow, Ralph. WOMEN'S ADORNMENT: WHAT DOES THE BIBLE REALLY SAY? Riverside, CA: R. Woodrow Evangelical Association, 1976.

4858. Woolson, Abba Gould, ed. DRESS-REFORM: A SERIES OF LECTURES DELIVERED IN BOSTON. DRESS AS IT AFFECTS THE HEALTH OF WOMEN. New York: Arno Press, 1974. 263 pp. Reprint of 1874 edition.

G. Modern Women—Social and Moral Questions

"The errors of women spring, almost always, from their faith in the good, or their confidence in the true."
—Honoré de Balzac

"The spiritual and moral coordination of the world is the real issue of tomorrow."
—Dorothy Thompson

4859. Adler, Freda. SISTERS IN CRIME: THE RISE OF THE NEW FEMALE CRIMINAL. New York: McGraw-Hill, 1975. Explores changing patterns in prostitution, delinquency, and drugs.

4860. Barreno, Maria Isabel, Maria Velho da Costa, and Maria Teresa Horta. THE THREE MARIAS: NEW PORTUGUESE LETTERS. Garden City, NY: Doubleday, 1975. 432 pp. Collection of letters, verse, and essays by and about women; banned in Portugal as an outrage to public morals.

4861. Beckman, Linda J. "Women Alcoholics: A Review of Social and Psychological Studies," JOURNAL OF STUDIES ON ALCOHOL, vol. 36, no. 7 (July 1975), pp. 797-824.

4862. Beecher, Catherine Esther. TRUTH STRANGER THAN FICTION: A NARRATIVE OF RECENT TRANSACTIONS, INVOLVING INQUIRIES IN REGARD TO THE PRINCIPLES OF HONOR, TRUTH, AND JUSTICE, WHICH OBTAIN IN A DISTINGUISHED AMERICAN UNIVERSITY. Boston, MA: Phillips Sampson, 1850. 296 pp. The case of Miss Delia Salter Bacon.

4863. Bronner, Auguste F. "A Comparative Study of the Intelligence of Delinquent Girls." New York: AMS Press, 1972. 95 pp. Reprint of 1914 edition.

4864. Brownmiller, Susan. AGAINST OUR WILL: MEN, WOMEN, AND RAPE. New York: Simon & Schuster, 1975. 541 pp. A four-year documentary study of rape, tracing its history through psychological studies, newspaper files, legal decisions including religious law, and the ramifications of being a victim.

4865. Burkhart, Kathryn W. WOMEN IN PRISON. Garden City, NY: Doubleday, 1973. 465 pp. Interviews with women in prison about the injustices and brutal treatment.

4866. Chicago Vice Commission. THE SOCIAL EVIL IN CHICAGO. Chicago, IL: Vice Commission of Chicago, 1912. 399 pp.

4867. Cohen, J. "Women in Peace and War," in PSYCHOLOGICAL FACTORS OF PEACE AND WAR, edited by Tom Hatherly Pear. Plainview, NY: Books for Libraries, 1969. Pp. 91-111. Deals with war's psychological effects on women.

4868. Cowie, John, Valerie Cowey, and Eliot Slater. DELINQUENCY IN GIRLS. Atlantic Highlands, NJ: Humanities Press, 1968. 220 pp.

4869. Deming, Richard. WOMEN: THE NEW CRIMINALS. Nashville, TN: Thomas Nelson, 1976.

4870. Fernald, Mabel Ruth, Mary Holmes, Steven Hayes, and Almena Dawley. STUDY OF WOMEN DELINQUENTS IN NEW YORK STATE. Montclair, NJ: Patterson & Smith Publishing, 1968. 542 pp. Reprint of 1920 edition.

4871. Fox, Sandra Sutherland and Donald J. Scheil. "Crisis Intervention with Victims of Rape," SOCIAL WORK, vol. 17, no. 1 (Jan. 1972), pp. 37-41.

4872. Giallombardo, Rose. THE SOCIAL WORLD OF IMPRISONED GIRLS: A COMPARATIVE STUDY OF INSTITUTIONS FOR JUVENILE DELINQUENTS. New York: John Wiley, 1974. 416 pp. Well-documented study of girls' prisons, a continuation of her earlier study.

4873. ———. SOCIETY OF WOMEN: A STUDY OF A WOMEN'S PRISON. New York: John Wiley, 1966. 244 pp. Study of an adult female prison, stressing why kinship, marriage, and family groups are the solution to the deprivations of prison life.

4874. Glueck, Sheldon and Eleanor T. Glueck. FIVE HUNDRED DELINQUENT WOMEN. Millwood, NY: Kraus Reprint, 1965. 569 pp. Reprint of 1934 edition. Life stories of 500 inmates at the Women's Reformatory in Framingham, Massachusetts.

4875. Gregory, John. A FATHER'S LEGACY TO HIS DAUGHTERS. Worchester, MA: I. Thomas, 1796. 120 pp. Collection of ideas on moral, civil, and religious subjects focused on improving the minds of both sexes.

4876. Heffernan, Esther. MAKING IT IN PRISON: THE SQUARE, THE COOL, AND THE LIFE. New York: Wiley-Interscience, 1972. 231 pp. Intensive study of a women's prison, using data obtained by interviewing the inmates and from the institutional records.

4877. Jenkins, Elizabeth. SIX CRIMINAL WOMEN. Freeport, NY: Books for Libraries, 1971. 244 pp. Reprint of 1949 edition. Delinquent women in Great Britain.

4878. Jenson, Gary F. and Dorothy Jones. "Perspectives on Inmate Culture: A Study of Women in Prison," SOCIAL FORCES, vol. 54, no. 3 (March 1976), pp. 590-603. Analysis of data from quantitative study of women's prison in Raleigh, North Carolina.

4879. Langley, Roger and Richard C. Levy. WIFE-BEATING: THE SILENT CRISIS. New York: E. P. Dutton, 1977.

4880. Mitchell, Arlene E. "Informal Inmate Social Structure in Prisons for Women: A Comparative Study." San Francisco, CA: R & E Research Associates, 1975. 80 pp.

4881. Norman, Eve. RAPE. Los Angeles, CA: Wollstonecraft, 1973. Seeks answers to questions regarding a crime that deeply concerns all women.

4882. Reich, Wilhelm. SEX-POL: ESSAYS, 1929-1934. New York: Random House, 1972. 416 pp. Writings on sexual and political liberation.

4883. Salter, Kenneth W. THE TRIAL OF INEZ GARCIA. Berkeley, CA: Justa Publications, 1976. Edited transcript of the trial of Inez Garcia, charged with the murder of her rapist, Miguel Jimenez, in Soledad, California.

4884. Showalter, Elaine, ed. THESE MODERN WOMEN: AUTOBIOGRAPHIES OF WOMEN IN THE TWENTIES. Old Westbury, NY: Feminist Press, 1977. Reprint of 17 essays from THE NATION (1926-1927), orginally published anonymously. Introduction identifies the authors and discusses the issues raised—alcoholism, celibacy, politics—by such women as Crystal Eastman, Mary Austin, and Genevieve Taggard.

4885. Simon, Rita James. WOMEN AND CRIME. Lexington, MA: D. C. Heath, 1975. 126 pp. Analysis of official statistics; paternalism is still characteristic of the treatment of offenders.

4886. Smith, Pauline. THE END OF THE LINE. South Brunswick, NJ: A. S. Barnes, 1970. 189 pp. Case studies of delinquent girls in California.

4887. Strickland, Katherine G. and Henrietta Bartleson. LEGAL RIGHTS FOR WOMEN PRISONERS. Lexington, MA: Lexington Books, n.d.

4888. Sullivan, Katharine. GIRLS ON PAROLE. Westport, CT: Greenwood Press, 1973. 243 pp. Reprint of 1956 edition.

4889. Tappan, Paul Wilbur. DELINQUENT GIRLS IN COURT: A STUDY OF THE WAYWARD MINOR COURT OF NEW YORK. Montclair, NJ: Patter Smith Publishing, 1969. 265 pp. Reprint of 1947 edition. Legal and sociological study of the adolescent female sex offender.

4890. U.S. Dept. of Justice. Law Enforcement Assistance Administration. National Institute of Law Enforcement and Criminal Justice. RAPE AND ITS VICTIMS: A REPORT FOR CITIZENS, HEALTH FACILITIES, AND CRIMINAL JUSTICE AGENCIES. Prepared by Lisa Brodyaga, Margaret Gates, Susan Singer, Marna Tucker, and Richardson White. Washington, D.C.: SUDOC, GPO, 1975. 361 pp. Guidelines for police, medical facilities, prosecutors' offices, and citizens' action groups for responding to the victim of a forcible rape.

4891. U.S. Dept. of Justice. Law Enforcement Assistance Administration. Task Force on Women. "Report, Oct. 1, 1975." Washington, D.C.: SUDOC, GPO, 1976. 70 pp. LEAA's programs dealing with the position of women in the United States criminal justice system; as offenders, prisoners, victims, and employees.

4892. Vedder, Clyde Bennett and Dora B. Somerville. THE DELINQUENT GIRL. Springfield, IL: C. C. Thomas, 1975. 1,974 pp.

4893. Winick, Charles and Paul M. Kinsie. THE LIVELY COMMERCE. Chicago, IL: Quadrangle Books, 1971. 322 pp. Well-documented study of prostitution in the United States.

4894. "Women, Crime, and Criminology," ISSUES IN CRIMINOLOGY, vol. 8, no. 2 (Fall 1973), pp. 1-162. Special Issue. Contributors include Dorie Klein, Virginia Engquist Grabiner, Meda Chesney Lind, Kurt Weis, Sandra S. Borges, Dale Hoffman Bustamante, and Women Endorsing Decriminalization.

4895. Zahn, Margaret A. "The Female Homicide Victim," CRIMINOLOGY, vol. 13 (Nov. 1975), pp. 400-415.

H. Women in Revolutionary and Changing Societies

"To swallow and follow, whether old doctrine or new propaganda, is a weakness still dominating the human mind."
—*Charlotte Perkins Gilman*

"It is not social change alone which is the challenge. It is the rate of change. That rate of change has been vastly accelerated by numerous factors. Peril lies not in change but in that tremendous rate of change."
—*William Orville Douglas*

4896. Aikman, Lonnelle. "Patriots in Petticoats," NATIONAL GEOGRAPHIC MAGAZINE, vol. 148 (Oct. 1975), pp. 474-493. Essay on America's Founding Mothers, with reproductions of paintings by Louis S. Glanzman. Includes Elizabeth Hager, blacksmith, Margaret Cochran Corbin, first woman pensioner (1779), Deborah Sampson, Revolutionary War soldier, Mary Katherine Goddard, editor and publisher who printed the first copies of the Declaration of Independence, including a list of 55 of the 56 signers, and others.

4897. Allendorf, Florence. CHINESE WOMEN YESTERDAY AND TODAY. Boston, MA: Houghton Mifflin, 1937. 324 pp. Presentation of the culture of China comparing the roles of women.

4898. Arendt, Hannah. "Rosa Luxemburg: 1871-1919," in MEN IN DARK TIMES. New York: Harcourt, Brace & World, 1968. Pp. 33-56.

4899. ———. "Isak Dinesen: 1885-1963," in MEN IN DARK TIMES. New York: Harcourt, Brace & World, 1968. Pp. 95-110.

4900. Benyoetz, Elazar. ANNETTE KOLB AND ISRAEL. Heidelberg, Germany: Lothar Stiehm Verlag, 1970. 174 pp.

4901. Bergman, Arlene E. WOMEN OF VIETNAM. San Francisco, CA: Peoples Press, 1975. 253 pp. Historical study of the oppression and resistance of Vietnamese women.

4902. Brockett, Linus Pierpont and Mrs. Mary C. Vaughn. WOMEN'S WORK IN THE CIVIL WAR: A RECORD OF HEROISM, PATRIOTISM, AND PATIENCE. Philadelphia, PA: Zeigler, McCurdy, 1867. 799 pp.

4903. Canada. Liberation Support Movement. THE MOZAMBIQUAN WOMAN IN THE REVOLUTION. Richmond, B.C.: Liberation Support Movement, 1974.

4904. Castro, Fidel. "The Revolution has in Cuban Women Today an Impressive Political Force." La Habana, Cuba: Editorial de Ciencias Sociales, 1974. 59 pp. Text of speech at the closing session of the Second Congress of the Federation of Cuban Women, Nov. 29, 1974.

4905. Chan, Anita. "Rural Chinese Women and the Socialist Revolution: An Enquiry into the Economics of Sexism," JOURNAL OF CONTEMPORARY ASIA, vol. 4, no. 2 (1974), pp. 197-208. The status of the Chinese woman is still inferior to that of men, in terms of unequal sharing of housework, wage structure, and the general belief that women are second to men.

4906. "Chinese Women in the Great Leap Forward." New York: AMS Press, 1976. 96 pp. Reprint of 1960 edition.

4907. Clements, Barbara Evans. "Emancipation through Communism: The Ideology of A. M. Kollontai," SLAVIC REVIEW, vol. 32, no. 2 (June 1973), pp. 321-328. A biographical examination of the political, economic, and social principles advocated by Alexandra Mikhailovna (Domontovich) Kollontai.

4908. Colon, Clara. "Enter Fighting: Today's Woman, A Marxist-Leninist View." New York: New Outlook, 1970. 95 pp.

4909. Confino, Michael, ed. DAUGHTER OF A REVOLUTIONARY: NATALIE HERZEN AND THE BAKUNIN-NECHAYEV CIRCLE. LaSalle, IL: Library Press, 1974. 416 pp. Correspondence, diaries, and documents providing a glimpse of life among Russian radicals-in-exile, and depicting the intrigues of a small group of revolutionaries.

4910. Croll, Elisabeth. THE WOMEN'S MOVEMENT IN CHINA. San Francisco, CA: China Books & Periodicals, 1974. 115 pp. A selection of readings, 1949-1973.

4911. Cuba Resource Center. "Women in Transition," CUBA REVIEW, vol. 4, no. 2 (Sept. 1974), pp. 1-38. Special Issue. Contributors include Carolee Benglesdorf, Alice Hageman, Carol Robb, Heidi Steffins, Margaret Randall, Dee Hopkins, Mary Lou Suhor, Barbara Case, Janet Berkenfield, Olga Kahn, and Michael Prokosh.

4912. Daniels, Elizabeth Adams. JESSIE WHITE MARIO: RISORGIMENTO REVOLUTIONARY. Athens, OH: Ohio Univ. Press, 1972. 199 pp. Biography of an Englishwoman in the radical Italian Movement.

4913. Dannett, Sylvia G. L., ed. NOBLE WOMEN OF THE NORTH. New York: Thomas Yoseloff, 1959. 419 pp. The personal narratives of women in the Civil War; activities in hospitals, charities, etc.

4914. Davin, Delia. WOMAN-WORK: WOMEN AND THE PARTY IN REVOLUTIONARY CHINA. New York: Oxford Univ. Press, 1976. 244 pp. Monograph based on previously available data and new information from party and government sources.

4915. Davis, Angela. ANGELA DAVIS: AN AUTOBIOGRAPHY. New York: Random House, 1974. 400 pp. Her own account of her remarkable life as political theorist and activist, teacher and fugitive.

4916. Dawson, Kipp, Evelyn Reed, Eva Chertov, Dianne Feeley, Linda Jenness, and Caroline Lund. "Kate Millett's SEXUAL POLITICS: A Marxist Appreciation." New York: Pathfinder Press, 1972. 31 pp.

4917. Deming, Barbara and Arthur Kinoy. WOMEN AND REVOLUTION: A DIALOGUE. New York: National Interim Committee for a Mass Party of the People, 1975.

4918. Devlin, Bernadette. THE PRICE OF MY SOUL. New York: Random House, 1969. 309 pp. Leader of the Catholic civil rights movement in Northern Ireland and the youngest female electee to Parliament.

4919. Diaz, Carlos Arturo. "Las Mujeres en la Independencia," BOLETÍN DE HISTORIA Y ANTIGÜEDADES, vol. 55 (July-Sept. 1968), pp. 361-371.

4920. Engel, Barbara Alpern and Clifford N. Rosenthal. FIVE SISTERS: WOMEN AGAINST THE TSAR. New York: Alfred A. Knopf, 1975. 249 pp. Memoirs of Vera Zasulich, Vera Figner, Elizaveta Kovalskaia, Olga Liubatovich, and Praskovia Ivanovskaia; all women dedicated to revolution in Russia.

4921. Engle, Paul, WOMEN IN THE AMERICAN REVOLUTION. Chicago, IL: Follett Publishing, 1976.

4922. Foner, Philip Sheldon, ed. HELEN KELLER: HER SOCIALIST YEARS; WRITINGS AND SPEECHES. New York: International Publications, 1967. 128 pp.

4923. Griffin, Frederick C., ed. WOMAN AS REVOLUTIONARY. New York: New American Library, 1973. Biographies of Margaret Sanger, Emma Goldman, Susan B. Anthony, Helen Keller, and excerpts from their work and works by contemporaries about them.

4924. Hunter, Alexander. THE WOMEN OF THE DEBATABLE LAND. Port Washington, NY: Kennikat Press, 1972. 261 pp. Reprint of 1912 edition. Women in the Confederate States of America.

4925. Hurn, Ethel Alice. WISCONSIN WOMEN IN THE WAR BETWEEN THE STATES. Madison, WI: Wisconsin History Commission, 1911. 190 pp.

4926. Key, Ellen Karolina Sofia. RAHEL VARNHAGEN: A PORTRAIT. Westport, CT: Hyperion Press, 1976. 312 pp. Reprint of 1913 edition. Study of Rahel Levin Varnhagen, Berlin's most renowned "Salon Jewess" at the turn of the nineteenth century; originator of the Goethe cult.

4927. King, Beatrice. "Women in Post-War Russia." London, England: British-Soviet Society, 1947. 32 pp.

4928. Looker, Robert, ed. ROSA LUXEMBURG: SELECTED POLITICAL WRITINGS. New York: Grove Press, 1974. 309 pp.

4929. McCallion, Edna. "Women of Belfast," AMERICA, vol. 125 (Nov. 27, 1971), pp. 453-456. Discusses the Women Together Movement in Belfast.

4930. MacLaine, Shirley. YOU CAN GET THERE FROM HERE. New York: W. W. Norton, 1975. 249 pp. Account of Ms. MacLaine's journey to China as the head of a women's delegation.

4931. Massell, Gregory J. THE SURROGATE PROLETARIAT: MOSLEM WOMEN AND REVOLUTIONARY STRATEGIES IN SOVIET

CENTRAL ASIA, 1919-1929. Princeton, NJ: Princeton Univ. Press, 1974. 448 pp. European Bolsheviks selected the Moslem woman as a surrogate object of oppression and as a vehicle for social upheaval and revolutionary change.

4932. Meyer, Edith Patterson. PETTICOAT PATRIOTS OF THE REVOLUTION. New York: Vanguard Press, 1976. 253 pp.

4933. Nettl, John Peter. ROSA LUXEMBURG. Fairlawn, NJ: Oxford Univ. Press, 1969. 557 pp. Pioneer woman economist and German revolutionary communist.

4934. Pierre, Andre. LES FEMMES EN UNION SOVIETIQUE: LEUR ROLE DANS LA VIE NATIONALE. Paris, France: Spes, 1960. 314 pp.

4935. Pruitt, Ida (as told to). A DAUGHTER OF HAN, THE AUTOBIOGRAPHY OF A CHINESE WORKING WOMAN, NING LAO T'AI-T'AI, 1867-1938. Stanford, CA: Stanford Univ. Press, 1967. 254 pp.

4936. Randall, Margaret, ed. CUBAN WOMEN NOW: INTERVIEWS WITH CUBAN WOMEN. Toronto, Ontario: Canadian Women's Educational Press, 1974. 375 pp. Interviews with more than 100 women; members of the Central Committee of the Communist Party, former prostitutes, peasant women, artists, and housewives.

4937. ———. "Cuban Women Now: Afterword 1974." Toronto, Ontario: Canadian Women's Educational Press, 1975. Update.

4938. Rogers, Douglas. "Letters to a Young Woman: An Introduction to Socialism." London, England: Forum Press, 1944. 24 pp.

4939. Scott, Hilda. DOES SOCIALISM LIBERATE WOMEN? Boston, MA: Beacon Press, 1975. 240 pp. History of women's rights in the European socialist movement, based on her experiences in the socialist society of Czechoslovakia; advocates developing a theory of women's role under socialism as well as capitalism.

4940. Senesh, Hannah. HANNAH SENESH—HER LIFE AND DIARY. New York: Schocken Books, 1972. 257 pp. Israel's national hero, a poet and a martyr.

4941. Smedes, Susan Dabney. MEMORIALS OF A SOUTHERN PLANTER. New York: Alfred A. Knopf, 1965. 337 pp. Romanticized portrayal of life on a plantation in Mississippi during the time of the Civil War; life with slavery.

4942. Smedley, Agnes. PORTRAITS OF CHINESE WOMEN IN REVOLUTION. Old Westbury, NY: Feminist Press, 1976. 208 pp. Edited by Jan Mackinnon and Steve Mackinnon. 18 pieces on Chinese women during the war written 1928-1941, collected by the editors.

4943. "I. The Struggle for Woman's Development and Equality, Cuban Experience; II. The Struggle for Peace." La Habana, Cuba: Instituto Cubano del Libro, 1975. 36 pp. Status of Cuban women.

4944. Turner, Frederick C. "Los Efectos de la Participación Feminina en la Revolución de 1910," HISTORIA MEXICANA, vol. 16 (1967), pp. 602-620.

4945. Van Voris, Jacqueline. CONSTANCE MARKIEVICZ: IN THE CAUSE OF IRELAND. Old Westbury, NY: Feminist Press, 1972. 144 pp.

Biography of the Nationalist hero who fought for the rights of women
and Irish liberation during the late 1920's.

4946. Wiley, Bell Irvin. CONFEDERATE WOMEN. Westport, CT: Greenwood
Press, 1974. 204 pp. Examines letters and diaries of Southern women
of the 1860's.

I. Women as Colonists and Pioneers

"A wild dedication of yourselves
To unpath'd waters, undream'd shores."
—*Shakespeare, WINTER'S TALE, Act IV, Sc. 3*

4947. Bacon, Martha. PURITAN PROMENADE. Boston, MA: Houghton
Mifflin, 1964. 160 pp. Biographies of women in New England including
Phillis Wheatley, Lydia Huntley Sigourney, Catherine Esther Beecher,
and Delia Bacon.

4948. Berkin, Carol. WITHIN THE CONJURORS' CIRCLE: WOMEN IN
COLONIAL AMERICA. Morristown, NJ: General Learning Press, 1974.

4949. Bishop, Isabella Lucy Bird. A LADY'S LIFE IN THE ROCKY
MOUNTAINS. Saint Clair Shores, MI: Scholarly Press, 1976. 296 pp.
Reprint of 1879 edition.

4950. Carrington, Evelyn M., ed. WOMEN IN EARLY TEXAS. Austin, TX:
Jenkins Publishing, 1975. 308 pp. 42 short biographical sketches of
pioneer women in Texas, most written by descendants from family
records and oral traditions.

4951. Crawford, Mary C. SOCIAL LIFE IN OLD NEW ENGLAND. Boston,
MA: Little, Brown, 1914. 515 pp. Covers customs of Puritan men and
women, i.e. getting married, setting up housekeeping, choosing a
profession, amusements, and going to college.

4952. De Pauw, Linda Grant and K. Conner Hunt. REMEMBER THE LADIES:
WOMEN IN AMERICA, 1750-1815. New York: Viking Press, 1976.
168 pp. Documents customs and achievements of women of various
social and economic classes; points out that prior to the establishment
of formal government, there were very few legal and social restrictions
on women, i.e. women had the right to vote in New Jersey until 1807.

4953. Douglas, Emily Taft. REMEMBER THE LADIES: THE STORY OF
GREAT WOMEN WHO HELPED SHAPE AMERICA. New York: G. P.
Putnam's Sons, 1966. 254 pp. Profiles of 15 women from Anne
Bradstreet to Eleanor Roosevelt, who worked for civil and political
freedom for women.

4954. Evans, Elizabeth. WEATHERING THE STORM: WOMEN OF THE
AMERICAN REVOLUTION. New York: Charles Scribners Sons, 1975.
372 pp. Portraits drawn from the diaries of 11 women; their daily lives
as well as activities in support of the British and Continental armies.

4955. Frost, John. PIONEER MOTHERS OF THE WEST: OR, DARING AND
HEROIC DEEDS OF AMERICAN WOMEN [COMPRISING

THRILLING EXAMPLES OF COURAGE, FORTITUDE, DEVOTEDNESS AND SELF-SACRIFICE]. New York: Arno Press, 1974. 348 pp. Reprint of 1869 edition. Women in the Ohio Valley.

4956. George, Carol V. R., ed. "REMEMBER THE LADIES:" NEW PERSPECTIVES ON WOMEN IN AMERICAN HISTORY. Syracuse, NY: Syracuse Univ. Press, 1975. 201 pp. Collection of essays ranging in topic from Anne Hutchinson to the founding of the Children's Bureau.

4957. Gray, Dorothy. WOMEN OF THE WEST. Millbrae, CA: Les Femmes, 1976. 179 pp.

4958. Haines, Frank and Elizabeth Haines. AMERICAN COLONIAL BRIDES, 1594-1820. Totowa, NJ: Athena Publishing, 1976.

4959. Harkness, David J. "Southern Heroines of Colonial Days." Knoxville, TN: Univ. of Tennessee, 1963. 20 pp.

4960. Johnston, Jean Wilson. WILDERNESS WOMEN: CANADA'S FORGOTTEN HISTORY. Toronto, Ontario: Peter Martin Associates, 1973. 242 pp.

4961. Kirkland, Caroline Matilda Stanbury. A NEW HOME WHO'LL FOLLOW? OR, GLIMPSES OF WESTERN LIFE. New Haven, CT: New Haven College & Univ. Press, 1965. 298 pp. Reprint of 1839 edition. Provides a woman's personal insight into the realities of life in the frontier settlements, by a pioneering writer in the field of nineteenth century American realism.

4962. Lebeson, Anita Libman. PILGRIM PEOPLE. New York: Harper & Bros., 1950. 624 pp. Much material on Jewish women in America, excellent bibliography.

4963. McGregor, Miriam. PETTICOAT PIONEERS: NORTH ISLAND WOMEN OF THE COLONIAL ERA. Wellington, New Zealand: A. H. & A. W. Reed, 1973. 264 pp.

4964. Mathews, Winifred. DAUNTLESS WOMEN: STORIES OF PIONEER WIVES. Freeport, NY: Books for Libraries, 1970. 164 pp. Reprint of 1947 edition. Biographies of Ann Judson, Mary Moffat, Mary Livingstone, Christina Coillard, Mary Williams, Agnes Watt, and Lillias Underwood.

4965. Merriam, H. G., ed. FRONTIER WOMAN: THE STORY OF MARY RONAN. Missoula, MT: Univ. of Montana, Publications in History, 1975.

4966. O'Meara, Walter. DAUGHTERS OF THE COUNTRY: THE WOMEN OF THE FUR TRADERS AND MOUNTAIN MEN. New York: Harcourt, Brace & World, 1968. 368 pp. General study of Indian women taken as wives by the white traders and frontiersmen; no life histories.

4967. Pownall, Evelyn. MARY OF MARANOA: TALES OF AUSTRALIAN PIONEER WOMEN. Melbourne, Australia: Melbourne Univ. Press, 1964. 267 pp.

4968. Ray, Grace Ernestine. WILY WOMEN OF THE WEST. San Antonio, TX: Naylor, 1972. 158 pp. Nineteenth and early twentieth century.

4969. Rubashow, Mrs. Rachel Katzenelson, ed. THE PLOUGH WOMEN: RECORDS OF THE PIONEER WOMEN OF PALESTINE. Westport, CT: Hyperion Press, 1975. 306 pp. Reprint of 1932 edition.

4970. Rust, Clara with JoAnne Wold. THIS OLD HOUSE: THE STORY OF
CLARA RUST. Anchorage, AL: Alaska Northwest Publishing, 1976.
262 pp.
4971. Ryan, Mary P. WOMANHOOD IN AMERICA FROM COLONIAL TIMES
TO THE PRESENT. New York: New Viewpoints, 1975. 469 pp. Social
habits and perceptions defining women in America.
4972. Sargent, Shirley. "Pioneers in Petticoats: Yosemite's First Women,
1856-1900." Corona del Mar, CA: Trans-Anglo Books, 1966. 80 pp.
4973. Tillson, Mrs. Christiana Holmes. A WOMAN'S STORY OF PIONEER
ILLINOIS. Chicago, IL: R. R. Donnelly & Sons, 1919. 169 pp.
4974. Williams, Selma R. DEMETER'S DAUGHTERS: THE WOMEN WHO
FOUNDED AMERICA, 1587-1787. Totowa, NJ: Atheneum Publishers,
1975. 359 pp.

J. Women as Soldiers and Spies

*"War will disappear, like the dinosaur, when changes in world conditions have
destroyed its survival value."*
—*Robert Andrews Millikan*

4975. Baker, Nina Brown. CYCLONE IN CALICO. Boston, MA: Little, Brown,
1952. Biography of Mother Mary Ann Bikkerdyke, who collected and
distributed food and supplies to the Union Army during the Civil War.
4976. BLACK WOMEN IN THE ARMED FORCES: A PICTORIAL HISTORY.
Hampton, VA: Jesse J. Johnson, 1975.
4977. Carson, Penelope H. "Women's Role in the American Revolution,"
NATIONAL GUARDSMAN, vol. 30 (May 1976), pp. 2-11.
4978. Downey, Lt. Col. Fairfax, Ret. "Women in War: The Spirit of Boadicea,"
ARMY, vol. 25 (July 1975), pp. 20-25.
4979. Ewing, Elizabeth. WOMEN IN UNIFORM THROUGH THE
CENTURIES. Totowa, NJ: Rowman & Littlefield, 1975. 160 pp.
4980. Galloway, Judith M. "The Impact of the Admission of Women to the
Service Academies on the Role of the Woman Line Officer,"
AMERICAN BEHAVIORAL SCIENTIST, vol. 19, no. 5 (May/June
1976), pp. 647-664.
4981. Hake, Janet. "They (Women Camp Followers) Also Served," SOLDIERS,
vol. 31, no. 6 (June 1976), pp. 50-52.
4982. Halloran, Barney. "Women in the Army: Where Have They Been? Where
Are They Going?" SOLDIERS, vol. 28, no. 5 (May 1973), pp. 4-17.
Background on women in the armed forces; interview with Brigadier
General Mildred Bailey, WAC Director; and, the status of women in the
Israeli Women's Corps, the French Spécilistes de Personnel Féminin de
l'Armee de Terre, the British Women's Royal Army Corps, and the
Soviet Army.
4983. Jones, Carolyn R. "Black Women in the Army: Where the Jobs are,"
CRISIS, vol. 82 (May 1975), pp. 175-177.

4984. McDonald, Lawrence Patton (Dem. Rep., Georgia). "Save Our Women from Military Combat," AMERICAN OPINION, vol. 18, no. 8 (Sept. 1975), pp. 19-28, 95-96. Emotional version of the hearings on opening the military academies to women.

4985. McEwen, Darryl D. "Women at West Point," SOLDIERS, vol. 31, no. 6 (June 1976), pp. 28-31.

4986. Mann, Peggy and Ruth Kluger. THE LAST ESCAPE: THE LAUNCHING OF THE LARGEST SECRET RESCUE MOVEMENT OF ALL TIME. Garden City, NY: Doubleday, 1973. 518 pp. Records the activities of Ruth Kluger in the Mossad to smuggle Jews out of Europe and into Palestine just prior to the outbreak of World War II.

4987. Massey, Mary Elizabeth. BONNET BRIGADES. New York: Alfred A. Knopf, 1966. 371 pp. Women's work in the Civil War.

4988. Stroller, Lt. Col. Dora Dougherty. "The W.A.S.P. (Women's Air Force Service Pilots) Training Program," AMERICAN AVIATION HISTORICAL SOCIETY JOURNAL, vol. 19 (Winter 1974), pp. 298-306.

4989. Truby, David J. WOMEN AT WAR. Boulder, CO: Paladin Press, 1976.

4990. U.S. Congress. House. Committee on Armed Services. Subcommittee No. 2. HEARINGS, HELD MAY 29-AUGUST 8, 1974, ON H.R. 9832, TO ELIMINATE DISCRIMINATION BASED ON SEX WITH RESPECT TO THE APPOINTMENT AND ADMISSION OF PERSONS TO THE SERVICE ACADEMIES, AND H.R. 10705 [AND OTHER BILLS], TO INSURE THAT EACH ADMISSION TO THE SERVICE BE MADE WITHOUT REGARD TO A CANDIDATE'S SEX, RACE, COLOR, OR RELIGIOUS BELIEFS. 93d Congress, 2d Session. Washington, D.C.: SUDOC, GPO, 1975. 304 pp.

4991. Wittig, Monique. LES GUÉRILLÈRES. New York: Viking Press, 1971. 144 pp.

4992. Woster, Carol. "The Women's Army Corps: The Past is Their Prologue," ARMY, vol. 24 (May 1974), pp. 21-27.

K. Women in Ethnic Minorities

"At the best, however, belief in race dogma is just the same as national chauvinism, a symptom of immaturity, lack of experience, and in general of an intellectually poor individuality."

—Fredrich Otto Hertz

4993. Ets, Marie Hall. ROSA, LIFE OF AN ITALIAN IMMIGRANT. Minneapolis, MN: Univ. of Minnesota Press, 1970. 254 pp. Biography of Rosa Cavalleri, exemplifying life as an immigrant from Italy.

4994. Gredley, Marion Eleanor. AMERICAN INDIAN WOMEN. New York: Hawthorn, 1974. 178 pp. Biographies of 18 women, from seventeenth century Queen Wetamoo of the Wampahoags who helped the Pilgrims,

to twentieth century Elaine Ramos, vice president of Sheldon Jackson
College in Alaska.
4995. Kahn, Kathy. HILLBILLY WOMEN. New York: Doubleday, 1974. 230
pp. Mountain women in Southern Appalachia.
4996. Kingston, Maxine Hong. THE WOMAN WARRIOR: MEMOIRS OF A
GIRLHOOD AMONG GHOSTS. New York: Alfred A. Knopf, 1976.
209 pp. Growing up in Chinese-American culture.
4997. Lange, Dorothea. "Dorothea Lange Looks at the American Country
Woman: A Photographic Essay." Pasadena, CA: Ward Ritchie Press,
1968. 72 pp.
4998. Manning, Caroline. IMMIGRANT WOMAN AND HER JOB. New York:
Arno Press, 1970. 179 pp. Reprint of 1930 edition.
4999. Neidle, Cecyle S. AMERICA'S IMMIGRANT WOMEN. Boston, MA:
Twayne Publishers, 1975. 300 pp. With the exception of a section on
Phillis Wheatley, devoted to Russo-European women.
5000. Olivares, Elizabeth. "Women's Rights and the Mexican American
Women," YMCA MAGAZINE, vol. 66 (Jan. 1972), pp. 14-16.
5001. Phillips, Leon. THE FIRST LADY OF AMERICA: A ROMANTICIZED
BIOGRAPHY OF POCAHONTAS. Richmond, VA: Westover
Publishing, 1973. 240 pp. Discloses the fascinating aspects of a
personality that rivals the modern woman in will and independence.
5002. Terrell, John U. and Donna M. Terrell. INDIAN WOMEN OF THE
WESTERN MORNING: THEIR LIFE IN EARLY AMERICA. New
York: Dial Press, 1974. 288 pp. Shows their roles in religious and sex
rites, tribal arts, and as marital companion.

L. Women as Rulers

"The higher we rise, the more isolated we become; all elevations are cold."
—Catherine Stanislas Jean de Boufflers

"She had all the royal makings of a queen;
As holy oil, Edward Confessor's crown,
The rod, and bird of peace, and emblems,
Laid nobly on her."
—Shakespeare, HENRY VIII, Act IV, Sc. 1

5003. Backhouse, Edmund Trelawney and John Otway Percy Bland. CHINA
UNDER THE EMPRESS DOWAGER. BEING THE HISTORY OF THE
LIFE AND TIMES OF TZ'U HSI, COMPILED FROM STATE PAPERS
AND THE PRIVATE DIARY OF THE COMPTROLLER OF HER
HOUSEHOLD. New York: Houghton Mifflin, 1949. 525 pp. Reprint of
1910 edition. Ruled from the 1860's to her death in 1908.
5004. Bradford, Ernie Dusgate Selby. CLEOPATRA. New York: Harcourt
Brace Jovanovich, 1972. 279 pp. Queen of Egypt, 30 B.C.
5005. Bruce, Marie Louis. ANNE BOLEYN. New York: Coward, McCann &
Geoghegan, 1972. 380 pp. Explores the personal motivations and

political forces that brought her to share the throne of Henry VIII.

5006. Chun, Jinsie. I AM HEAVEN. Philadelphia, PA: Macrae Smith, 1974. 276 pp. Portrait of the Empress Chao of the T'ang Dynasty in China.

5007. Foreman, Carolyn Thomas. "Indian Women Chiefs." Washington, D.C.: Zenger Publications, 1976. 86 pp. Reprint of 1954 edition.

5008. Haslip, Joan. CATHERINE THE GREAT. New York: G. P. Putnam's Sons, 1977. 382 pp. Catherine II, ruler of Russia for 34 years.

5009. Hussey, Harry. VENERABLE ANCESTOR: THE LIFE AND THE TIMES OF TZ'U HSI, 1835-1908, EMPRESS OF CHINA. New York: Doubleday, 1949. 354 pp.

5010. Johnson, Paul. ELIZABETH I: A BIOGRAPHY. New York: Holt, Rinehart & Winston, 1974. 511 pp. Biography of a controversial queen, by the former editor of THE NEW STATESMAN.

5011. Lewis, Hilda. I AM MARY TUDOR. New York: Warner Books, 1973. 510 pp.

5012. Luke, Mary M. CATHERINE THE QUEEN. New York: Coward, McCann & Geoghegan, 1967. 510 pp. The contributions of Catherine of Aragon to the reign of Henry VIII.

5013. ———. A CROWN FOR ELIZABETH. New York: Coward, McCann & Geoghegan, 1970. 573 pp.

5014. ———. GLORIANA: THE YEARS OF ELIZABETH I. New York: Coward, McCann & Geoghegan, 1973. 734 pp.

5015. Macurdy, Grace Harriet. VASSAL QUEENS AND SOME CONTEMPORARY WOMEN IN THE ROMAN EMPIRE. Baltimore, MD: Johns Hopkins Press, 1937. 148 pp. Account of Zenobia, queen of the East (third century A.D.) and of women in the royal houses subject to Rome in the first century A.D.

5016. Morrah, Dermot, et al. QUEEN'S VISIT: ELIZABETH II IN INDIA AND PAKISTAN. New York: Asia Publishing House, 1974.

5017. Neale, Sir John Ernest. QUEEN ELIZABETH I, A BIOGRAPHY. Garden City, NY: Doubleday, 1957. 424 pp.

5018. Plunkett, Irene Arthur Lifford. ISABEL OF CASTILE AND THE MAKING OF THE SPANISH NATION, 1451-1504. New York: AMS Press, 1974. 432 pp. Reprint of 1919 edition.

5019. Raeff, Marc, ed. CATHERINE THE GREAT: A PROFILE. New York: Hill & Wang, 1972. 331 pp. Catherine II, Empress of Russia.

5020. Roider, Karl A.; Jr., ed. MARIA THERESA. Englewood Cliffs, NJ: Prentice-Hall, 1973. 186 pp. Empress of Austria. Selections from her own writings as well as nineteenth and twentieth century historians, showing her thoughts and actions regarding conflict with Prussia, finance reform, the army, the law codes, etc.

5021. Sergeant, Philip Walsingham. THE GREAT EMPRESS DOWAGER OF CHINA. London, England: Hutchinson, 1910. 344 pp. Tz'u Hsi.

5022. Tarbell, Ida Minerva. A LIFE OF NAPOLEON BONAPARTE; WITH A SKETCH OF JOSEPHINE, EMPRESS OF THE FRENCH. New York: McClure, Philips, 1901. 485 pp.

5023. Warner, Marina. THE DRAGON EMPRESS: THE LIFE OF TZ'U HSI,

DOWAGER EMPRESS OF CHINA, 1835-1908. New York: Macmillan. 1972. 272 pp.

5024. Williams, Neville. ALL THE QUEEN'S MEN: ELIZABETH AND HER COURTIERS. New York: Macmillan, 1972. 272 pp. Portrays the court of Elizabeth and her life and relationships.

5025. Wu Yung. THE FLIGHT OF AN EMPRESS. London, England: Faber & Faber, 1937. 222 pp. Tz'u Hsi's flight from Peking in 1900 during the Boxer Rebellion.

5026. Zweig, Stefan. MARIE ANTOINETTE, THE PORTRAIT OF AN AVERAGE WOMAN. New York: Viking Press, 1933. 476 pp. Queen consort of Louis XVI, King of France.

IV. WOMEN IN PHILOSOPHY AND RELIGION

Publications for this section have been chosen for their scholarship and utility to researchers.

"Our generation is remarkable, or seems remarkable to those who have known no other, for the number of persons who must believe something, but do not know what."

—*Evelyn Underhill*

"God is for men and religion for women."

—*Joseph Conrad*

5027. Aguilar, Grace. WOMEN OF ISRAEL, OR, CHARACTERS AND SKETCHES FROM THE HOLY SCRIPTURES AND JEWISH HISTORY, ILLUSTRATIVE OF THE PAST HISTORY, PRESENT DUTIES, AND FUTURE DESTINY OF HEBREW FEMALES, AS BASED ON THE WORD OF GOD. Plainview, NY: Books for Libraries, 1974. 576 pp. Reprint of 1879 edition.

5028. Bachofen, Johann Jakob. MYTH, RELIGION, AND MOTHER RIGHTS: SELECTED WRITINGS OF J. J. BACHOFEN. Princeton, NJ: Princeton Univ. Press, 1967. 309 pp. Noted nineteenth century philosopher.

5029. Bainton, Roland Herbert. WOMEN OF THE REFORMATION: IN FRANCE AND ENGLAND. Boston, MA: Beacon Press, 1975. 287 pp. Biographical sketches of French and English women prominent in the Catholic and Protestant reformation movements.

5030. Brunner, Peter. "The Ministry and the Ministry of Women." St. Louis, MO: Concordia Publishing House, 1971. 39 pp. Women as ministers and in church work.

5031. Cahill, Susan. EARTH ANGELS: PORTRAITS FROM CHILDHOOD AND YOUTH. New York: Harper & Row, 1976. 213 pp. Discusses parochial school education.

5032. Campion, Nardi Reeder. ANN THE WORD. Boston, MA: Little, Brown, 1977. 195 pp. Biography of Mother Ann Lee, founder of the Shakers, or the United Society of Believers.

5033. Cavendish, Margaret (Duchess of Newcastle). THE PHILOSOPHICAL AND PHYSICAL OPINIONS. London, England: for J. Martin & J. Alleystrye, 1965. 174 pp.

5034. Chapin, Edwin Hubbell. DUTIES OF YOUNG WOMEN. Boston, MA: Briggs, 1848. 218 pp. Nineteenth century Christian philosophical and ethical treatise.

5035. Clark, Elizabeth and Herbert W. Richardson, eds. WOMEN AND RELIGION: READINGS IN THE WESTERN TRADITION FROM AESCHYLUS TO MARY DALY. New York: Harper & Row, 1976.

5036. Code, Joseph B. GREAT AMERICAN FOUNDRESSES. Freeport, NY: Books for Libraries, 1968. 512 pp. Reprint of 1929 edition.

Biographies of 16 women who founded monastic and religious orders for women, i.e. Mother Elizabeth Ann Seton, Mother Mary Rhodes, and Mother Catherine Spaulding.

5037. Curley, Richard T. ELDERS, SHADES, AND WOMEN: CEREMONIAL CHANGE IN LANGO, UGANDA. Berkeley, CA: Univ. of California Press, 1973. 223 pp.

5038. Dakin, Edwin Franden. MRS. EDDY: THE BIOGRAPHY OF A VIRGINAL MIND. New York: Charles Scribners Sons, 1929. 553 pp. Mary Baker Eddy, founder of the Christian Scientists.

5039. Daly, Mary. THE CHURCH AND THE SECOND SEX: WITH A NEW FEMINIST POST-CHRISTIAN INTRODUCTION BY THE AUTHOR. New York: Harper & Row, 1975. 229 pp.

5040. Daughters of St. Paul. SAINT OF THE IMPOSSIBLE: SAINT RITA OF CASCIA. Boston, MA: St. Paul Editions, 1973. 100 pp. The life of the nineteenth century Italian woman who was canonized in 1900.

5041. de Lescure, Mathurin François Adolphe. LES FEMMES PHILOSOPHES AU 18 EME SIECLE. Paris, France: Dentu, 1881. 393 pp. Biographies of women such as La Marquise de Lambert, Madame d'Epinay, and Le Couvent de Rousseau.

5042. Doig, Desmond. MOTHER TERESA: HER WORK AND HER PEOPLE. New York: Harper & Row, 1976. 175 pp. Theresa of Ávila, founder of the reformed order of Carmelites and canonized in 1622.

5043. Donnelly, Sister Dorothy H., E.C.S.J. "Women-Priests: Does Philadelphia have a Message for Rome?" COMMONWEAL, vol. 102, no. 7 (June 20, 1975), pp. 206-210. Highlights of the current movement for the ordination of women as ministers and priests, and urging support.

5044. Durkin, Mary G. THE SUBURBAN WOMAN: HER CHANGING ROLE IN THE CHURCH. New York: Seabury Press, 1976. 112 pp.

5045. Fischer, Clare Benedicks, Betsy Brenneman, and Ann McGrew Bennett, eds. WOMEN IN A STRANGE LAND: A SEARCH FOR A NEW IMAGE. Philadelphia, PA: Fortress Press, 1975. 133 pp. Essays on the image and position of women in religion.

5046. Foot, Philippa. "The Doctrine of the Double Effect," in READINGS FOR AN INTRODUCTION TO PHILOSOPHY, edited by James R. Hamilton, Charles E. Reagan, and B. R. Tilghman. New York: Macmillan, 1976. Pp. 71-80. Addresses itself to the abortion issue.

5047. Fromm, Erich. "Sex and Character," in DOGMA OF CHRIST. Garden City, NY: Doubleday, 1966. Pp. 111-132. Analysis of Christian ideas on sex and motherhood.

5048. Fryer, Judith. "American Eves in American Edens," AMERICAN SCHOLAR, vol. 44 (Winter 1975), pp. 78-99. The status of women in religious communal living or utopian experiment; Ann Lee, founder of the Shaker movement; the Mormon faith and polygamy; Oneida Community and sexual communism; and non-religious communities, e.g. New Harmony and Nashoba Community—both with Frances Wright, and Brook Farm.

5049. Gardiner, Anne Marie, S.S.N.D., ed. WOMEN AND CATHOLIC PRIESTHOOD: AN EXPANDED VISION. Paramus, NJ:

Paulist/Newman Press, 1976. 259 pp. Urges that women be placed in consultative positions within their dioceses.

5050. Gilman, Charlotte Perkins. HIS RELIGION AND HERS: A STUDY OF THE FAITH OF OUR FATHERS AND THE WORK OF OUR MOTHERS. Westport, CT: Hyperion Press, 1976. 300 pp. Reprint of 1923 edition. Discusses religion in its sociological context, showing how male-managed religions led to discrimination against women.

5051. Goldenberg, Judith Plaskow, ed. WOMEN AND RELIGION. Missoula, MT: American Academy of Religion, Working Group on Women and Religion, 1973. 165 pp. See also Joan Arnold Romero.

5052. Gould, Carol D. and Marx W. Wartofsky, eds. WOMEN AND PHILOSOPHY: TOWARD A THEORY OF LIBERATION. New York: G. P. Putnam's Sons, 1976. 364 pp. Reprint of THE PHILOSOPHICAL FORUM, vol. 5, no. 1 & 2 (Fall-Winter 1973).

5053. Hamilton-Merritt, Jane. A MEDITATOR'S DIARY: A WESTERN WOMAN'S EXPERIENCES IN THAILAND TEMPLES. New York: Harper & Row, 1976. 157 pp. Account of the period of time the war correspondent spent as an acolyte in a Buddhist temple.

5054. Hartshorn, Leon R., comp. REMARKABLE STORIES FROM THE LIVES OF LATTER-DAY SAINT WOMEN. Salt Lake City, UT: Deseret Books, 1973. 274 pp.

5055. Hedgeman, Anna Arnold. THE TRUMPET SOUNDS: A MEMOIR OF NEGRO LEADERSHIP. New York: Holt, Rinehart & Winston, 1964. 202 pp. Author's memoir of the Negro church and religion in the South.

5056. Heyward, Carter. A PRIEST FOREVER. New York: Harper & Row, 1976. 146 pp. Ordination of women in the Protestant Episcopal Church in America.

5057. Hollis, Harry N. Jr., ed. CHRISTIAN FREEDOM FOR WOMEN AND OTHER HUMAN BEINGS. Nashville, TN: Broadman Press, 1975. 192 pp.

5058. Jennings, Rev. Ray. "Ms. Evelyn Morgan Jones, I Love You . . . Letters to a Woman in Ministry; Addressed to a Representative of the Emerging Breed of Women in Ministry by a Middle-aged Male Minister." Valley Forge, PA: Judson Press, 1975. 64 pp.

5059. Jeter, Jeremiah Bell. A MEMOIR OF MRS. HENRIETTA SHUCK. Boston, MA: Gould, Kendall & Lincoln, 1846. 251 pp. The first American female missionary to China.

5060. Jorns, Auguste. THE QUAKERS AS PIONEERS IN SOCIAL WORK. Port Washington, NY: Kennikat Press, 1969. 268 pp. Reprint of 1931 edition. Shows a Quaker view of the position of women.

5061. Koltun, Elizabeth, ed. THE JEWISH WOMAN: NEW PERSPECTIVES. New York: Schocken Books, 1976. 294 pp.

5062. Kress, Robert. WHITHER WOMANKIND? THE HUMANITY OF WOMEN. St. Meinrad, IN: Abbey Press, 1975. 336 pp.

5063. Lantero, Erminie Huntress. "Feminine Aspects of Divinity." Wallingford, PA: Pendle Hill Publications, 1973. 32 pp.

5064. Lowenthal, Marvin. HENRIETTA SZOLD: LIFE AND LETTERS. Westport, CT: Greenwood Press, 1975. 350 pp. Reprint of 1942 edition. Biography of the American Jewish Zionist leader.

5065. Luder, Hope Elizabeth. "Women and Quakerism." Wallingford, PA: Pendle Hill Publications, 1974. 36 pp.

5066. MacKay, William Mackintosh. BIBLE TYPES OF MODERN WOMEN: A COURSE OF LECTURES TO YOUNG WOMEN. London, England: Hodder & Stoughton, 1929. 328 pp.

5067. Mernissi, Fatima. BEYOND THE VEIL: MALE-FEMALE DYNAMICS IN A MODERN MUSLIM SOCIETY. Cambridge, MA: Schenkman Publishing, 1976. 148 pp. Examines the changing status of women in Morocco away from the traditional mores and values.

5068. Morris, Joan. THE LADY WAS A BISHOP: THE HIDDEN HISTORY OF WOMEN WITH CLERICAL ORDINATION AND THE JURISDICTION OF BISHOPS. New York: Macmillan, 1973. 192 pp. Women's historical participation in the administrative and jurisdictional sphere; six appendices disclosing biblical, traditional, and church theology of women.

5069. Ockenga, Harold J. WOMEN WHO MADE BIBLE HISTORY. Grand Rapids, MI: Zondervan Publishing, 1971.

5070. O'Connor, Catherine R. WOMAN AND COSMOS: THE FEMININE IN THE THOUGHT OF PIERRE TEILHARD DE CHARDIN. Englewood Cliffs, NJ: Prentice-Hall, 1974. 188 pp. Details Teilhard's thinking on the notion of the feminine; study of his ideas on religious experience, love, women, and the church.

5071. Penn-Lewis, Jessie. THE MAGNA CARTA OF WOMAN. Minneapolis, MN: Bethany Fellowship, 1975. 103 pp. Re-edit of 1948 edition, originally published as THE MAGNA CARTA OF WOMAN ACCORDING TO THE SCRIPTURES.

5072. Pétrement, Simone. SIMONE WEIL: A LIFE. New York: Pantheon Books, 1977. 577 pp. Translated by Raymond Rosenthal. Biography of the eminent French philosopher and mystic.

5073. Powell, Lyman P. MARY BAKER EDDY: A LIFE SIZE PORTRAIT. Boston, MA: Christian Science Publishing Society, 1950. 271 pp.

5074. Priesand, (Rabbi) Sally. JUDAISM AND THE NEW WOMAN. New York: Behrman House, 1975. 144 pp. The position of women within Orthodox, Conservative, and Reform Judaism, and in the Reconstruction Movement.

5075. Proctor, Priscilla and William Proctor. WOMEN IN THE PULPIT: IS GOD AN EQUAL OPPORTUNITY EMPLOYER? Garden City, NY: Doubleday, 1976. 176 pp. Survey of women at different levels of various clerical hierarchies.

5076. Raming, Ida. THE EXCLUSION OF WOMEN FROM THE PRIESTHOOD: DIVINE LAW OR SEX DISCRIMINATION? A HISTORICAL INVESTIGATION OF THE JURIDICAL AND DOCTRINAL FOUNDATIONS OF THE CODE OF CANON LAW, CANON 968, § 1. Metuchen, NJ: Scarecrow Press, 1976. 263 pp.

Investigates the traditional and exegetical arguments in support of preventing women from obtaining the priestly vocation.

5077. Romero, Joan Arnold, comp. WOMEN AND RELIGION: 1973. Tallahassee, FL: American Academy of Religion, Working Group on Women and Religion, 1973. 127 pp. See also Judith Plaskow Goldenberg.

5078. Ruether, Rosemary Radford. NEW WOMAN—NEW EARTH: SEXIST IDEOLOGIES AND HUMAN LIBERATION. New York: Seabury Press, 1975. 221 pp. First part discusses the influence of religious symbols (Virgin Mary, Witch) on the status of women; the rest is an attempt to show that sexism is part of a complex structure of oppression and that many movements toward human freedom perpetuate male dominance.

5079. Ruether, Rosemary Radford, ed. RELIGION AND SEXISM: IMAGES OF WOMEN IN THE JEWISH AND CHRISTIAN TRADITION. New York: Simon & Schuster, 1974. 356 pp. Ten essays, each focused on a specific period or group of thinkers, ranging from the Old Testament to Modern Protestant theory; one essay on the Talmud.

5080. Russell, Letty M. HUMAN LIBERATION IN A FEMINIST PERSPECTIVE: A THEOLOGY. Philadelphia, PA: Westminster Press, 1974. 224 pp. Places the women's movement into the context of other liberation movements in the Church, and outlines the common themes, perspectives, and methodologies for women to construct a viable past and future for themselves.

5081. Russell, Letty M., ed. THE LIBERATING WORD: A GUIDE TO NON-SEXIST INTERPRETATION OF THE BIBLE. Philadelphia, PA: Westminster Press, 1976. 121 pp.

5082. Schepps, David D. REMARKABLE WOMEN OF THE SCRIPTURES. Ardmore, PA: Dorrance, 1976. 210 pp.

5083. Seton, Cynthia Propper. A SPECIAL AND CURIOUS BLESSING. New York: W. W. Norton, 1968. 184 pp. 16 essays on the problems women face today.

5084. Smith, Margaret. RABI'A THE MYSTIC AND HER FELLOW SAINTS IN ISLAM. Berkeley, CA: Rainbow Bridge, 1976.

5085. Spafford, Belle S. A WOMAN'S REACH. Salt Lake City, UT: Deseret Books, 1974. 165 pp. Mormon women in church work.

5086. — — —. WOMEN IN TODAY'S WORLD. Salt Lake City, UT: Deseret Books, 1971. 483 pp.

5087. Stenhouse, Mrs. T. B. H. (Fanny). "TELL IT ALL:" THE STORY OF A LIFE'S EXPERIENCE IN MORMONISM, AN AUTOBIOGRAPHY. Hartford, CT: A. D. Worthington, 1875. 623 pp. Her 25 years in Mormonism, feelings and experience with polygamy—how women feel about polygamy.

5088. STUDY GUIDE TO "THE WOMAN'S BIBLE." Seattle, WA: Coalition Task Force on Women and Religion, 1975. 100 pp. Elizabeth Cady Stanton wrote THE ORIGINAL FEMINIST ATTACK ON THE BIBLE (THE WOMAN'S BIBLE).

5089. Swidler, Arleen. WOMAN IN A MAN'S CHURCH: FROM ROLE TO
PERSON. New York: Paulist/Newman Press, 1972. 111 pp. Examines
the ancient biblical precepts on which the dogma of organized religion
(Jewish, Catholic, Protestant) is based, i.e. woman is unclean part of
each month.
5090. Swidler, Leonard J. WOMEN IN JUDAISM: THE STATUS OF WOMEN
IN FORMATIVE JUDAISM. Metuchen, NJ: Scarecrow Press, 1976.
242 pp. Analysis of the status of women during the period of formative
Judaism (200 B.C.E.–500 C.E.) and the impacts on the present-day
position of women in the Jewish faith.
5091. Tavard, George H. WOMAN IN CHRISTIAN TRADITION. Notre Dame,
IN: Univ. of Notre Dame Press, 1974. 257 pp. Attempts to show the
benevolence of the New Testament and the Church fathers; blames
Judeo-Christians and their attitudes for the status of women in the
Church.
5092. Turner, Rodney. WOMAN AND THE PRIESTHOOD. Salt Lake City,
UT: Deseret Books, 1972. 344 pp.
5093. van der Meer, Haye. WOMEN PRIESTS IN THE CATHOLIC CHURCH?
A THEOLOGICAL-HISTORICAL INVESTIGATION. Philadelphia,
PA: Temple Univ. Press, 1973. 190 pp. Original title PRIESTERTUM
DER FRAU?, translated by Arleen Swidler and Leonard Swidler.
5094. Verdesi, Elizabeth Howell. IN BUT STILL OUT: WOMEN IN THE
CHURCH. Philadelphia, PA: Westminster Press, 1976. 218 pp.
5095. Wallace, Irving. THE TWENTY-SEVENTH WIFE. New York: Simon &
Schuster, 1961. 443 pp. Story of Ann Eliza Young, last wife of
Brigham Young, who divorced her Mormon husband to crusade against
the practice of polygamy.
5096. Washbourne, Penelope. "Authority or Idolatry: Feminine Theology and
the Church," CHRISTIAN CENTURY, vol. 92 (Oct. 29, 1975), pp.
961-964. Feminine theology calls for an end to traditional authoritarian
relationships within the church, i.e. pope/church, priest/laity.
5097. –––. BECOMING WOMAN: THE QUEST FOR SPIRITUAL
WHOLENESS IN FEMALE EXPERIENCE. New York: Harper & Row,
1976. 174 pp.
5098. Wisbey, Herbert A. PIONEER PROPHETESS: JEMIMA WILKINSON,
THE PUBLICK UNIVERSAL FRIEND. Ithaca, NY: Cornell Univ.
Press, 1964. 256 pp. Portrait of a religious fanatic.
5099. WOMEN AND THE WAY: CHRIST AND THE WORLD'S
WOMANHOOD: A SYMPOSIUM. New York: Friendship Press, 1938.
198 pp.
5100. Wold, Margaret. THE SHALOM WOMAN. Minneapolis, MN: Augsburg
Publishing House, 1975. 128 pp. Study guide available.
5101. Wurmbrand, Sabina. PRAESTENS KONE [THE PASTOR'S WIFE].
København: Forlaget Royal, 1970. 328 pp.

V. WOMEN IN MEDICINE AND HEALTH

"Some people think that doctors and nurses can put scrambled eggs back into the shell."

—*Dorothy Canfield Fisher*

"Medicine is the only profession that labors incessantly to destroy the reason for its own existence."

—*James Bryce*

5102. Alcott, William Andrus. THE PHYSIOLOGY OF MARRIAGE. New York: Arno Press, 1972. 259 pp. Reprint of 1866 edition.

5103. Anon. ARE AMERICAN WOMEN DEGENERATING? New York: Exposition Press, 1955. 406 pp.

5104. Boston Women's Health Book Collective. OUR BODIES, OURSELVES: A BOOK BY AND FOR WOMEN. New York: Simon & Schuster, 1976. Revised and enlarged edition.

5105. Bowman, Kathleen. "New Women in Medicine." Mankato, MN: Creative Educational Society, 1976. 47 pp.

5106. Brook, Danaë. NATURE BIRTH: YOU, YOUR BODY, AND YOUR BABY. New York: Pantheon Books, 1976. 304 pp. Covers all aspects of childbirth.

5107. Campbell, Margaret A. (pseud Dr. Mary Howell). WHY WOULD A GIRL GO INTO MEDICINE? MEDICAL EDUCATION IN THE UNITED STATES: A GUIDE FOR WOMEN. Old Westbury, NY: Feminist Press, 1975. 126 pp. Survey of 41 medical schools documenting bias and offering suggestions for counteraction.

5108. Delaney, Janice, Mary Jane Lupton, and Emily Toth. THE CURSE: A CULTURAL HISTORY OF MENSTRUATION. New York: E. P. Dutton, 1976. 276 pp. The menses and its effects on people from ancient times to modern, in a variety of cultures; its treatment in literature, art, and myth.

5109. Ehrenreich, Barbara and Deirdre English. "Complaints and Disorders: The Sexual Politics of Sickness." Old Westbury, NY: Feminist Press, 1974. 96 pp. Sequel to "Witches, Midwives and Nurses," examines women's participation in the health care system and the treatment of women patients. Includes bibliography.

5110. ———. "Witches, Midwives and Nurses: A History of Women Healers." Old Westbury, NY: Feminist Press, 1972. 48 pp. Focuses on the takeover of the medical profession by men in the nineteenth century.

5111. Futoran, Jack M. and May Annexton. YOUR BODY: A REFERENCE BOOK FOR WOMEN. New York: Ballantine Books, 1977. Describes the parts and functions of the female body, and the terms physicians use with patients.

5112. Gordon, Elizabeth Putnam. THE STORY OF THE LIFE AND WORK OF CORDELIA GREENE, M.D. Castile, NY: The Castilian, 1925. 208 pp.

Biography of an early woman physician and founder of a sanitarium for women in Castile, New York.

5113. Grissum, Marlene and Carol Spengler. WOMAN POWER AND HEALTH CARE. Boston, MA: Little, Brown, 1976. 314 pp.

5114. Hamilton, Alice. EXPLORING THE DANGEROUS TRADES: THE AUTOBIOGRAPHY OF ALICE HAMILTON, M.D. Boston, MA: Little, Brown, 1943. 433 pp. Dr. Hamilton wrote on public health hazards in trades and business.

5115. Haseltine, Florence and Yvonne Yaw. WOMAN DOCTOR. Boston, MA: Houghton Mifflin, 1976. 336 pp.

5116. Hay, Ian. ONE HUNDRED YEARS OF ARMY NURSING. London, England: Cassell, 1953. 387 pp. Study of British Army Nursing Services, based on nurses' diaries.

5117. Hendrick, Gladys West. MY FIRST THREE HUNDRED BABIES. South Pasadena, CA: The Author, 1975.

5118. Horos, Carol V. VAGINAL HEALTH: WITH A NATIONWIDE DIRECTORY OF WOMEN'S CENTERS, HEALTH CARE CLINICS, AND REFERRAL SERVICES (COMPILED BY THE WOMEN'S ACTION ALLIANCE). New Canaan, CT: Tobey Publishing, 1975. 174 pp.

5119. Hughes, Muriel Joy. WOMEN HEALERS IN MEDIEVAL LIFE AND LITERATURE. Freeport, NY: Books for Libraries, 1968. 180 pp. Reprint of 1943 edition.

5120. Hunt, Harriott K. GLANCES AND GLIMPSES: OR, FIFTY YEARS SOCIAL, INCLUDING TWENTY YEARS PROFESSIONAL LIFE. Cincinnati, OH: Source Book Press, 1970. 430 pp. Reprint of 1856 edition. Discusses her childhood, medical education and studies, as well as observations of contemporary social movements and their leaders.

5121. Hurd-Mead, Kate Campbell. A HISTORY OF WOMEN IN MEDICINE FROM THE EARLIEST TIMES TO THE BEGINNING OF THE NINETEENTH CENTURY. New York: AMS Press, 1976. 111 pp. Reprint of 1938 edition.

5122. Jameson, Anna Brownell. SISTERS OF CHARITY AND THE COMMUNION OF LABOR. Westport, CT: Hyperion Press, 1976. 302 pp. Reprint of 1857 edition. Compilation of experiences, studies, and conclusions about the training of workers in hospitals and charitable institutions.

5123. Jansen, Michael Elin. "Nursing in the Arab East," ARAMCO WORLD MAGAZINE, vol. 25, no. 2 (March-April 1974), pp. 14-23. Women are at the top of their profession while men tend to be concentrated in practical nursing and nurses' aide positions.

5124. Jennings, Samuel K. THE MARRIED LADY'S COMPANION: OR, POOR MAN'S FRIEND. New York: Arno Press, 1972. 214 pp. Reprint of 1808 edition. Four addresses on various aspects of women's health concerns.

5125. Lanson, Lucienne. FROM WOMAN TO WOMAN: A GYNECOLOGIST ANSWERS QUESTIONS ABOUT YOU AND YOUR BODY. New York: Alfred A. Knopf, 1975. 358 pp.

5126. Llewellyn-Jones, Derek. EVERYWOMAN: A GYNAECOLOGICAL GUIDE FOR LIFE. London, England: Faber & Faber, Ltd., 1971. 317 pp.

5127. Ludovici, Anthony M. THE TRUTH ABOUT CHILDBIRTH: LAY LIGHT ON MATERNAL MORBIDITY AND MORTALITY. New York: E. P. Dutton, 1938. 294 pp. Presents theories and statistics to prove his contention that childbirth should be a pleasure.

5128. Lutzker, Edythe. EDITH PECHEY-PHIPSON, M.D.: THE STORY OF ENGLAND'S FOREMOST PIONEERING WOMAN DOCTOR. Hicksville, NY: Exposition Press, 1973. 259 pp.

5129. –––. WOMEN GAIN A PLACE IN MEDICINE. New York: McGraw-Hill, 1969. 160 pp. Traces the struggles of five women in the nineteenth century–Sophia Jex-Blake, Edith Pechey-Phipson, Isabel Thorne, Matilda Chaplin, and Helen Evans–as they fought to make medical education available to women.

5130. THE MALE MIDWIFE AND THE FEMALE DOCTOR. New York: Arno Press, 1974. 218 pp. Reprint of 1820 "Remarks on the Employment of Females as Practitioners in Midwifery," by a physician; 1850 "Letter to Ladies, in Favor of Female Physicians," by S. Gregory; 1848 "Man-Midwifery Exposed and Corrected," by S. Gregory; 1853 "Medical Morals," by G. Gregory; and 1850 "Report of the Trial: *The People* v. *Dr. Horatio N. Loomis,* for Libel," by F. T. Parsons.

5131. Marks, Geoffrey and William K. Beatty. WOMEN IN WHITE. Totowa, NJ: Charles Scribners Sons, 1972. 239 pp. Women in medicine.

5132. Mauriceau, A. M. THE MARRIED WOMAN'S PRIVATE MEDICAL COMPANION. New York: Arno Press, 1974. 238 pp. Reprint of 1847 edition.

5133. Morini, Simona. SIMONA MORINI'S ENCYCLOPEDIA OF BEAUTY AND HEALTH FOR WOMEN. Indianapolis, IN: Bobbs-Merrill, 1976. 426 pp.

5134. Morton, Rosalie Slaughter. A WOMAN SURGEON: THE LIFE AND WORK OF ROSALIE SLAUGHTER MORTON. New York: Stokes, 1937. 399 pp.

5135. Nightingale, Florence. "Notes on Nursing: What It Is and What It Is Not." London, England: Harrison, 1859. 79 pp.

5136. Noall, Clair Augusta Wilcox. GUARDIANS OF THE HEARTH: UTAH'S PIONEER MIDWIVES AND WOMEN DOCTORS. Bountiful, UT: Horizon Publishers, 1974. 189 pp.

5137. Noble, Iris. FIRST WOMAN AMBULANCE SURGEON: EMILY BARINGER. New York: Julian Messner, 1962. 192 pp.

5138. –––. NURSE AROUND THE WORLD: ALICE FITZGERALD. New York: Julian Messner, 1964. 191 pp.

5139. –––. PHYSICIAN TO THE CHILDREN: DR. BÉLA SCHICK. New York: Julian Messner, 1963. 189 pp.

5140. Parker, Elizabeth Bowen. SEVEN AGES OF WOMAN. Baltimore, MD: Johns Hopkins Press, 1960. 600 pp. Discusses menstruation, pregnancy, menopause, and other aspects of the life cycle; compares attitudes toward and of women in various cultures.

5141. Parr, John Anthony (pseud.) and J. J. Nel. TO BE A WOMAN: YOUR DOCTOR'S ADVICE ON COMMON DISORDERS. North Pomfrey, VT: David & Charles, 1975. 123 pp.

5142. Parrish, Dr. Louis. NO PAUSE AT ALL: LIVING THROUGH THE MIDDLE YEARS–A GUIDE TO THE MALE AND FEMALE CLIMACTERIC. New York: Reader's Digest Press, 1976. 215 pp.

5143. Pollard, Eliza F. FLORENCE NIGHTINGALE: THE WOUNDED SOLDIER'S FRIEND. London, England: Partridge, 1960. 160 pp.

5144. Preston, Frances Isabella. LADY DOCTOR, VINTAGE MODEL. Rutland, VT: Charles E. Tuttle, 1974. 159 pp.

5145. Riddle, Dorothy. "What the Doctors Forget to Tell You (Or How to Survive Vaginal and Urinary Infections)." Pittsburgh, PA: KNOW, Inc., 1971.

5146. Ross, Ishbel. CHILD OF DESTINY: THE LIFE OF ELIZABETH BLACKWELL. New York: Harper & Bros., 1949. 309 pp. Biography of the first woman awarded M.D. degree in the United States.

5147. –––. ANGEL OF THE BATTLEFIELD: THE LIFE OF CLARA BARTON. New York: Harper & Bros., 1956. 305 pp. Founder of the American Red Cross and its head for 33 years.

5148. Rush, Anne Kent. GETTING CLEAR: BODY WORK FOR WOMEN. New York: Random House, 1973. 290 pp.

5149. Sayre, Anne. ROSALIND FRANKLIN AND DNA. New York: W. W. Norton, 1975. 221 pp. Franklin's contributions to the discovery of the structure of the DNA molecule.

5150. Stevens, Barbara J. THE NURSE AS EXECUTIVE. Wakefield, MA: Contemporary Publishing, 1975. 260 pp.

5151. Tabor, Margaret Emma. PIONEER WOMEN: ELIZABETH FRY, ELIZABETH BLACKWELL, FLORENCE NIGHTINGALE, MARY SLESSOR. New York: Macmillan, 1925. 126 pp.

5152. Tanzer, Deborah with Jean Libman Block. WHY NATURAL CHILDBIRTH? A PSYCHOLOGIST'S REPORT OF THE BENEFITS TO MOTHERS, FATHERS, AND BABIES. New York: Schocken Books, 1976. 289 pp.

5153. Trembly, Diane L. PETTICOAT MEDIC IN VIETNAM: ADVENTURES OF A WOMAN DOCTOR. New York: Vantage Press, 1976. 275 pp.

5154. Tunnell, Willis Earl. WHAT EVERY WOMAN SHOULD KNOW ABOUT HER BODY AND THOSE DISEASES EXCLUSIVELY HERS. New York: Vantage Press, 1973. 112 pp.

5155. Walker, Mary Edward. UNMASKED, OR THE SCIENCE OF IMMORALITY. TO GENTLEMEN. BY A WOMAN PHYSICIAN AND SURGEON. Jersey City, NJ: Walker Publishing, 1888. 135 pp. By the Civil War woman doctor who later won the Medal of Honor; traces, rather unscientifically, the spread of unchaste behavior and immorality in late nineteenth century America–believed that syphilis was spread by kissing.

5156. Washburn, Robert Collyer. LIFE AND TIMES OF LYDIA PINKHAM. New York: G. P. Putnam's Sons, 1931. 221 pp. Her famous "vegetable compound" launched her fortune.

5157. Weideger, Paula. MENSTRUATION AND MENOPAUSE: THE
PHYSIOLOGY AND PSYCHOLOGY, THE MYTH AND REALITY.
New York: Alfred A. Knopf, 1975. 257 pp. The taboo represents man's
historic fear and envy of women, and a desire to keep her from gaining
equal status.

5158. Weiss, M. Olga. "Kibbutz Nurse," AMERICAN JOURNAL OF
NURSING, vol. 71 (Sept. 1971), pp. 1762-1765.

5159. Wharton, May Cravath. DOCTOR WOMAN OF THE CUMBERLANDS:
THE AUTOBIOGRAPHY OF MAY CRAVATH WHARTON. Pleasant
Hills, TN: Uplands, 1953. 208 pp.

5160. Whitehouse, Geoffrey T. EVERYWOMAN'S GUIDE TO NATURAL
HEALTH. New York: British Book Center, 1976.

5161. Wilson, Dorothy Clarke. LONE WOMAN: THE STORY OF ELIZABETH
BLACKWELL, THE FIRST WOMAN DOCTOR. Boston, MA: Little,
Brown, 1970. 469 pp.

5162. Wintle, William James and Florence Witts. FLORENCE NIGHTINGALE
AND FRANCES E. WILLARD: THE STORY OF THEIR LIVES.
London, England: Sunday School Union, 1928. 157 pp.

5163. Withington, Alfreda. MINE EYES HAVE SEEN: A WOMAN DOCTOR'S
SAGA. New York: E. P. Dutton, 1941. 311 pp. Autobiography of a
woman doctor who began her career in the 1880's.

5164. Women's Work Project. "Women in Health." Washington, D.C.: Union for
Radical Political Economics, 1975. 21 pp.

5165. Wood, Ann Douglas. "The Fashionable Diseases: Women's Complaints
and Their Treatment in Nineteenth-Century America," JOURNAL OF
INTERDISCIPLINARY HISTORY, vol. 4, no. 1 (Summer 1973), pp.
25-52.

VI. WOMEN IN BIOGRAPHY, AUTOBIOGRAPHY, AND MEMOIRS

"Even in this world they will have their judgment day; and their names, which went down in the dust like a gallant banner trodden in the mire, shall rise again all glorious in the sight of nations."

—Harriet Elizabeth Beecher Stowe

"Most biographies are of little worth. They are panegyrics, not lives. The object is, not to let down the hero; and consequently what is most human, most genuine, most characteristic in his history, is excluded. No department of literature is so false as biography."

—William Ellery Channing

5166. Addison, Daniel Dulaney. LUCY LARCOM: LIFE, LETTERS, DIARY. New York: Houghton Mifflin, 1895. 295 pp. Writer who chronicled the experiences of the Lowell mill women.

5167. Alliluyeva, Svetlana (Stalina) ONLY ONE YEAR. New York: Harper & Row, 1969. 440 pp.

5168. Alta. "Momma: A Start on all the Untold Stories." New York: Times Change Press, 1974. 80 pp. Autobiographical story of her struggle to raise two small daughters and develop her career as a writer.

5169. Armour, Richard. IT ALL STARTED WITH EVE. Boston, MA: G. K. Hall, 1976. 136 pp. Reprint of 1956 edition. Satirical biographies of women in history, from Eve to Mata Hari.

5170. Ayer, Margaret Hubbard and Isabella Taves. THE THREE LIVES OF HARRIET HUBBARD AYER. Philadelphia, PA: J. B. Lippincott, 1957. 284 pp. Nineteenth century health and beauty "expert."

5171. Babbitt, Katharine M. "Janet Montgomery: Hudson River Squire." Monroe, NY: Library Research Associates, 1975. 55 pp. Biography of Janet Livingston Montgomery.

5172. Bax, Clifford. BIANCA CAPELLO. Norwood, PA: Norwood Editions, 1975. Reprint of 1927 edition.

5173. Binion, Rudolph. FRAU LOU: NIETZSCHE'S WAYWARD DISCIPLE. Princeton, NJ: 1968. 587 pp. Biography of Lou Andreas-Salome, close friend of Nietzsche and Freud; discusses her relationships.

5174. Bleeker, Ann E. THE HISTORY OF MARIA KITTLE: IN A LETTER TO MISS TENEYCK. New York: Somerset Publishers, 1972. Reprint of 1797 edition.

5175. Blunt, Hugh Frances. THE GREAT MAGDELENS. Freeport, NY: Books for Libraries, 1969. 335 pp. Reprint of 1928 edition. 18 biographical essays on women's contributions to the history of the Catholic Church, such as Madame Pompadour, Saint Margaret of Cortona, and Beatrice Cenci.

5176. Boccaccio, Giovanni. CONCERNING FAMOUS WOMEN. London, England: Allen & Unwin, 1964. 257 pp. Translation of 14th century manuscript.

5177. Bolton, Sarah K. LIVES OF GIRLS WHO BECAME FAMOUS. Norwood, PA: Norwood Editions, 1976. 347 pp. Reprint of 1886 edition. 19 biographies of such women as Louisa May Alcott, Helen Hunt Jackson, and Jean Ingelow.

5178. ———. SUCCESSFUL WOMEN. Plainview, NY: Books for Libraries, 1974. 233 pp. Reprint of 1888 edition. Ten biographies of such women as Frances E. Willard, Mary Virginia Terhune, and Clara Barton.

5179. Brenneman, Helen Good. RING A DOZEN DOORBELLS: TWELVE WOMEN TELL IT LIKE IT IS. Scottdale, PA: Herald Press, 1973. 199 pp.

5180. Bridgman, Richard. GERTRUDE STEIN IN PIECES. Fair Lawn, NJ: Oxford Univ. Press, 1970. 428 pp. Biography of the American playwright, novelist, and essayist.

5181. Brown, Mrs. Harriet Conner. GRANDMOTHER BROWN'S HUNDRED YEARS, 1827-1927. Boston, MA: Little, Brown, 1929. 369 pp. Biography of Maria Dean Foster Brown.

5182. Brown, Victoria. "Uncommon Lives of Common Women: The Missing Half of Wisconsin History." Madison, WI: Project of Wisconsin Feminists Project Fund, 1974. 40 brief biographies.

5183. Bryant, Dorothy. ELLA PRICE'S JOURNAL. Philadelphia, PA: J. B. Lippincott, 1973. 227 pp.

5184. Burdick, Loraine. THE SHIRLEY TEMPLE SCRAPBOOK. New York: Jonathon David, 1975. 160 pp. Account of the film career, private life, and political achievements of the present diplomat, Shirley Temple Black.

5185. Burns, Edward, ed. STAYING ON ALONE: LETTERS OF ALICE B. TOKLAS. New York: Random House, 1974. 448 pp. Collection of her reminiscences about her life with Gertrude Stein, from letters she wrote to the famous people who had been their friends.

5186. Casey, Jane Barnes. I KRUPSKAYA: MY LIFE WITH LENIN. Boston, MA: Houghton Mifflin, 1974. 327 pp.

5187. Challice, Annie E. ILLUSTRIOUS WOMEN OF FRANCE, 1790-1873. Freeport, NY: Books for Libraries, 1973. 352 pp. Reprint of 1873 edition. Ten biographies of women courtiers, including Empress Josephine and Duchess d'Orleans.

5188. Chappell, Jennie. NOBLE WORKERS: SKETCHES OF THE LIFE-WORK OF FRANCES WILLARD, AGNES WESTON, SISTER DORA, CATHERINE BOOTH, THE BARONESS BURDETT-COUTTS, LADY HENRY SOMERSET, SARAH ROBINSON, MRS. FAWCETT, AND MRS. GLADSTONE. London, England: Partridge, 1910. 320 pp.

5189. Clark, Electa. LEADING LADIES: AN AFFECTIONATE LOOK AT AMERICAN WOMEN OF THE TWENTIETH CENTURY. New York: Stein & Day, 1976. 252 pp.

5190. Clarke, Robert. ELLEN SWALLOW, THE WOMAN WHO FOUNDED ECOLOGY. Chicago, IL: Follett Publishing, 1973. 276 pp. Biography of Ellen Henrietta (Swallow) Richards.

5191. Coburn, Kathleen, ed. THE LETTERS OF SARA HUTCHINSON, 1800-1835. Toronto, Ontario: Univ. of Toronto Press, 1954. 474 pp.

5192. Coleman, Elizabeth Tyler. PRISCILLA COOPER TYLER AND THE AMERICAN SCENE, 1816-1889. Auburn, AL: Univ. of Alabama Press, 1955. 203 pp. Biography of the official White House hostess during John Tyler's term as President.

5193. Courtney, Janet Elizabeth. THE WOMEN OF MY TIME. London, England: Lovat Dickson, 1934. 249 pp. Biographies of women in Great Britain.

5194. Crouch, Marcus. "Beatrix Potter." New York: Henry S. Walsh, 1960. 71 pp. Biography of the writer and illustrator of children's books.

5195. Dark, Sydney. TWELVE MORE LADIES: GOOD, BAD, AND INDIFFERENT. Freeport, NY: Books for Libraries, 1969. 285 pp. Reprint of 1932 edition. Such women as Nell Gwynne, Florence Nightingale, Queen Elizabeth.

5196. ———. TWELVE ROYAL LADIES. Freeport, NY: Books for Libraries, 1970. 339 pp. Reprint of 1929 edition. Biographies of women such as Queen Christina of Sweden, Mary Queen of Scots.

5197. David, Lester. JOAN: THE RELUCTANT KENNEDY. New York: Funk & Wagnalls, 1974. 264 pp.

5198. Delany, Mrs. Mary (Granville) Pendarves. THE AUTOBIOGRAPHY AND CORRESPONDENCE OF MARY GRANVILLE, MRS. DELANY: WITH INTERESTING REMINISCENCES OF KING GEORGE THE THIRD AND QUEEN CHARLOTTE, EDITED BY THE RIGHT HONORABLE LADY LLANOVER. New York: AMS Press, 1974. 6 vols. Reprint of 1861-1862 editions. Considered one of the 18th century's leading women writers, based chiefly on her autobiography.

5199. Desai, Bhadra. INDIRA GANDHI: CALL TO GREATNESS. Bombay, India: Popular Prakashan, 1966. 117 pp. Biography of the former Prime Minister of India.

5200. Dobson, Austin. FOUR FRENCHWOMEN. Freeport, NY: Books for Libraries, 1972. 207 pp. Reprint of 1893 edition. Biographies of Mademoiselle de Corday, Madame Roland, the Princess de Lambelle, and Madame de Genlis.

5201. Dufour, Antoine. LES VIES DES FEMMES CÉLÉBRES. Geneva, Switzerland: Droz, 1970. 214 pp.

5202. Dunbar, Janet. PORTRAIT OF CHARLOTTE SHAW. New York: Harper & Row, 1963. 303 pp. Biography of Charlotte Frances Payne-Townshend Shaw.

5203. Earle, Alice Morse. MARGARET WINTHROP: FIRST LADY OF MASSACHUSETTS BAY COLONY. Williamstown, MA: Corner House, 1975. 341 pp. Reprint of 1895 edition. Includes excerpts from letters, diaries, and pertinent documents, combining the portrayal of a prominent woman with the social history of the colony.

5204. Earle, Alice Morse, ed. DIARY OF ANNA GREEN WINSLOWE, A BOSTON SCHOOLGIRL OF 1771. Williamstown, MA: Corner House, 1974. 121 pp. Reprint of 1874 edition. Child's journal of life in Boston.

5205. Edwards, Matilda Barbara Betham. SIX LIFE STORIES OF FAMOUS WOMEN. Freeport, NY: Books for Libraries, 1972. 303 pp. Reprint of 1880 edition. Biographies of Fernan Caballero (Spanish novelist),

Alexandrine Tinné (African explorer), Caroline Herschel (astronomer and mathematician), Marie Pope-Carpantier (educational reformer), Elizabeth Carter (scholar), and Matilda Betham (littérateur and artist).

5206. Falk, Bernard. RACHEL THE IMMORTAL: STAGE QUEEN, GRANDE AMOUREUSE, STREET URCHIN, FINE LADY, A FRANK BIOGRAPHY. New York: Arno Press, 1972. 334 pp. Reprint of 1935 edition. Biography of Elisa Rachel Félix.

5207. Fawcett, Dame Millicent Garrett. SOME EMINENT WOMEN OF OUR TIMES: SHORT BIOGRAPHICAL SKETCHES. Philadelphia, PA: Richard West, 1975. 231 pp. Reprint of 1889 edition. 21 biographical sketches of women from many different countries.

5208. Ffrench, Yvonne. SIX GREAT ENGLISHWOMEN: QUEEN ELIZABETH I, SARAH SIDDONS, CHARLOTTE BRONTË, FLORENCE NIGHTINGALE, QUEEN VICTORIA, GERTRUDE BELL. London, England: Hamilton, 1953. 246 pp.

5209. Ford, Hugh, ed. NANCY CUNARD: BRAVE POET, INDOMITABLE REBEL. Philadelphia, PA: Chilton Press, 1968. 383 pp. Biography of the famous Negro writer; founder of the Hours Press and the magazine NEGRO; and of her fight for the causes of the American Negro and the Spanish Civil War.

5210. Friedmann, Marion Valerie. "Olive Schreiner: A Study in Latent Meanings." Johannesburg, South Africa: Witwaterstrand Univ. Press, 1954. 68 pp.

5211. Fyvie, John. SOME FAMOUS WOMEN OF WIT AND BEAUTY: A GEORGIAN GALAXY. Norwood, PA: Norwood Editions, 1973. 296 pp. Reprint of 1905 edition. Biographies of Mrs. Fitzherbert (wife of George I), Lady Hamilton, Mrs. Montagu, Lady Blessington, Mrs. Lennox, Mrs. Grote, the Honorable Mrs. Norton, and Lady Eastlake.

5212. Gallagher, Dorothy. HANNAH'S DAUGHTERS: SIX GENERATIONS OF AN AMERICAN FAMILY, 1876-1976. New York: Thomas Y. Crowell, 1976. 343 pp.

5213. Gilfond, Henry. HEROINES OF AMERICA. New York: Fleet Press Corp., 1970. 136 pp. Biographies of famous American women over the past 100 years, from Jane Addams to Coretta King.

5214. Goldsmith, Margaret. SEVEN WOMEN AGAINST THE WORLD. Westport, CT: Hyperion Press, 1976. 236 pp. Reprint of 1935 edition. Biographical studies of Charlotte Corday, Theroigne de Mericourt, Flora Tristan, Louise Michel, Vera Figner, Emma Goldman, and Rosa Luxemburg.

5215. Goncourt, Edmund Louis Antoine. MADEMOISELLE CLAIRON D'APRES: SES CORRESPONDENCES ET LES RAPPORTS DE POLICE DU TEMPS [HER CORRESPONDENCES (LETTERS) AND POLICE REPORTS OF THE TIME]. New York: Somerset Publications, 1972. 524 pp. Reprint of 1890 edition.

5216. Griffith, Helen. DAUNTLESS IN MISSISSIPPI: THE LIFE OF SARAH A. DICKEY, 1838-1904. Washington, D.C.: Zenger Publications, 1976. 173 pp. Reprint of 1966 edition. Promoted education of Negro girls and founded Mount Hermon Female Seminary in 1875 (closed 1924).

5217. Guffy, Ossie. OSSIE: THE AUTOBIOGRAPHY OF A BLACK WOMAN. New York: W. W. Norton, 1971. 224 pp. Offers insight into the lives of average black people, in contrast to the lives of well-known black personalities.

5218. Guizot, François Pierre. LOVE IN MARRIAGE: A HISTORICAL STUDY: LADY RACHEL RUSSELL. New York: Coulton & Porter, 1865. 159 pp.

5219. Hale, Mabel. BEAUTIFUL GIRLHOOD. New York: Christian Alliance, 1922. 224 pp.

5220. Hall, Evelyn Beatrice. WOMEN OF THE SALONS, AND OTHER FRENCH PORTRAITS. Freeport, NY: Books for Libraries, 1969. 235 pp. Reprint of 1926 edition. 11 biographies of such women as Madame de Staël and Madame de Sévigné.

5221. Hemingway, Mary Walsh. HOW IT WAS. New York: Alfred A. Knopf, 1976. 450 pp. Memoirs of the World War II newspaper correspondent and her 17 years of marriage to Ernest Hemingway.

5222. Hitchman, Janet. SUCH A STRANGE LADY: AN INTRODUCTION TO DOROTHY L. SAYERS. London, England. New English Library, 1976. 203 pp. Established her career as a detective novelist, then was converted to religious playwright.

5223. Hopper, Hedda. FROM UNDER MY HAT. New York: Doubleday, 1952. 311 pp. The autobiography of the Hollywood actress and radio and newspaper gossip.

5224. Hsieh, Pingying. GIRL REBEL: THE AUTOBIOGRAPHY OF HSIEH PINGYING WITH EXTRACTS FROM HER "NEW WAR DIARIES." New York: Da Capo Press, 1975. 270 pp. Reprint of 1940 edition.

5225. Infield, Glenn B. EVA AND ADOLF. New York: Grosset & Dunlap, 1974. 330 pp. Biography of Eva Braun, best known as the mistress of Adolf Hitler.

5226. James, Alice. THE DIARY OF ALICE JAMES. New York: Dodd, Mead, 1964. 241 pp. Autobiography of the invalid sister of the psychologist William James and the novelist Henry James.

5227. James, George Payne, ed. MEMOIRS OF CELEBRATED WOMEN. Freeport, NY: Books for Libraries, 1974. 374 pp. Reprint of 1876 edition. Joan of Arc, Margaret of Anjou, Lady Jane Grey, Ann Comnena, Frances d'Aubigne—Marchioness de Maintenon, Queen Elizabeth, and Donna Maria Pacheco.

5228. Jerrold, Walter and Clare Jerrold. FIVE QUEER WOMEN. Norwood, PA: Norwood Editions, 1976. 356 pp. Reprint of 1929 edition. Biographies of Aphra Behn, Mary de la Riviere Manley, Susanna Centlivre, Eliza Haywood, and Letitia Pilkington.

5229. Johnson, George W. and Lucy A. Johnson, eds. JOSEPHINE BUTLER: AN AUTOBIOGRAPHICAL MEMOIR. Bristol, England: Arrowsmith, 1909. 1 vol. Social reformer devoted to supporting "the moral elevation of her sex" through higher education; improvement of working conditions of women and prostitution reform.

5230. Johnston, Johann. WOMEN THEMSELVES. New York: Dodd, Mead, 1973. 126 pp. Stories of such women as Anna Hutchinson, Anne

Bradstreet, Elizabeth Blackwell, Emma Willard, Elizabeth Stanton, etc.

5231. Kamm, Josephine. HOW DIFFERENT FROM US: A BIOGRAPHY OF MISS BUSS AND MISS BEALE. London, England: Bodley Head, 1958. 272 pp. Dorothea Beale, principal of Cheltenham Ladies' College, and her colleague.

5232. Kelly, Joseph J., Jr. and Sol Feinstone. COURAGE AND CANDLELIGHT: THE FEMININE SPIRIT OF '76. Harrisburg, PA: Stackpole Books, 1974. 240 pp. Portraits of Deborah Franklin, Abigail Adams, Peggy Shippen Arnold, Annis Boudinot Stockton, Phillis Wheatley, Betsey Hamilton, and Sally Hemings.

5233. Klock, Frank. THE PREDATERS: TALES OF LEGENDARY LIBERATED WOMEN. New York: Drake Publishers, 1974. 304 pp. Relates tales of women such as Zsa Zsa Gabor, Eva Peron, Lizzie Bordon, and Lucrezia Borgia.

5234. Kostman, Samuel. TWENTIETH CENTURY WOMEN OF ACHIEVEMENT. New York: Richards Rosen Press, 1976. 178 pp.

5235. Kramer, Rita. MARIA MONTESSORI: A BIOGRAPHY. New York: G. P. Putnam's Sons, 1976. 410 pp. First woman physician to graduate from the University of Rome, social reformer and educational pioneer.

5236. Levenson, Samuel. MAUDE GONNE. New York: Reader's Digest Press, 1977. 436 pp. Victorian beauty, Irish nationalist, street orator, actress, and inamorata of W. B. Yeats.

5237. Lindbergh, Anne Morrow. LOCKED ROOMS AND OPEN DOORS: DIARIES AND LETTERS OF ANNE MORROW LINDBERGH, 1933-1935. New York: Harcourt Brace Jovanovich, 1974. 352 pp.

5238. Linder, Leslie. A HISTORY OF THE WRITINGS OF BEATRIX POTTER: INCLUDING UNPUBLISHED WORKS. New York: Frederick Warne, 1971. 446 pp. The author of PETER RABBIT and COCK ROBIN. Part I is devoted to pictures and miniature letters to children; Part II is Potter's books, published and unpublished; while Part III is miscellaneous writings.

5239. McCarthy, Mary Therese. MEMOIRS OF A CATHOLIC GIRLHOOD. New York: Harcourt Brace & World, 1957. 245 pp. Childhood of the American novelist, author of THE GROUP.

5240. McClung, Nelli L. THE STREAM RUNS FAST: MY OWN STORY. Toronto, Ontario: Thones Allen, 1946. 316 pp. Canadian woman suffrage leader.

5241. McGovern, Eleanor with Mary Finch Hoyt. UPHILL: A PERSONAL STORY. Boston, MA: Houghton Mifflin, 1974. 234 pp. Campaign life of a wife.

5242. MacLaine, Shirley. DON'T FALL OFF THE MOUNTAIN. New York: W. W. Norton, 1970. 292 pp. Autobiography of the famous actress, including her travels to remote parts of the world.

5243. Madden, Bill. MISTRESSES OF MAYHEM. Cranbury, NJ: A. S. Barnes, 1973. 137 pp.

5244. Madison, Dolley. MEMOIRS AND LETTERS OF DOLLY MADISON: WIFE OF JAMES MADISON, PRESIDENT OF THE UNITED

STATES. Port Washington, NY: Kennikat Press, 1971. 210 pp. Reprint of 1886 edition.

5245. Maitland, Edward. ANNA KINGSFORD: HER LIFE, LETTERS, DIARY, AND WORK. New York: Gordon Press, 1972. 2 vols. Reprint of 1896 edition.

5246. Masson, Flora. "The Brontës." Port Washington, NY: Kennikat Press, 1970. 92 pp. Reprint of 1912 edition.

5247. Masterman, Lucy, ed. MARY GLADSTONE: HER DIARIES AND LETTERS. Norwood, PA: Norwood Editions, 1976. Reprint of 1930 edition.

5248. Matsui, Haru. RESTLESS WAVE: MY LIFE IN TWO WORLDS. New York: Modern Age Books, 1940. 272 pp. Autobiography of a Japanese woman who spoke for the Japanese in America who were against Japan's invasion of China during the 1930's.

5249. Matsuoka, Yoko. DAUGHTER OF THE PACIFIC. New York: Harper & Bros., 1952. 245 pp. Recalls her life as the daughter of educated, middle-class parents, and the changes she underwent during the years of transition between traditional and modern Japan.

5250. Megroz, Louis Rudolph. THE THREE SITWELLS: A BIOGRAPHICAL AND CRITICAL STUDY. Port Washington, NY: Kennikat Press, 1969. 333 pp. Reprint of 1927 edition. Dame Edith Sitwell and her two brothers.

5251. Miller, Florence Fenwick. HARRIET MARTINEAU. Port Washington, NY: Kennikat Press, 1971. 224 pp. Reprint of 1884 edition.

5252. Mitford, Nancy. ZELDA. New York: Harper & Row, 1970. 424 pp. Novelist and dancer who married F. Scott Fitzgerald.

5253. Montagu, Lady Mary Pierrepont Wortley. LETTERS OF THE RIGHT HONOURABLE LADY MARY WORTLEY MONTAGU. Paris, France: Printed for Barrois, Sr., 1793. 2 vols. Written during her travels in Europe, Asia, and Africa. Among other curious relations, accounts of the policy and manners of the Turks, from sources inaccessible to other travelers.

5254. Montgomery, James W. LIBERATED WOMAN: A LIFE WITH MAY ARKWRIGHT HUTTON. Spokane, WN: Gingko House Publishers, 1974. 134 pp.

5255. Nevill, Ralph Henry. WOMEN OF SOME IMPORTANCE. Norwood, PA: Norwood Editions, 1976. 304 pp. Reprint of 1929 edition.

5256. Northcroft, Dorothea Mary. FAMOUS GIRLS OF THE PAST. Mystic, CT: Lawrence Verry, 1966. 144 pp. Biographies of 11 women such as Hannah More and Caroline Herschel.

5257. Nystrom, Louise Hamilton. ELLEN KEY: HER LIFE AND WORK. Norwood, PA: Norwood Editions, 1973. 187 pp. Reprint of 1913 edition. Biography of Ellen Karolina Sofia Key.

5258. O'Higgins, Patrick. MADAME, AN INTIMATE BIOGRAPHY OF HELENA RUBENSTEIN. New York: Viking Press, 1971. 296 pp.

5259. Oliphant, Mrs. Margaret. JEANNE D'ARC: HER LIFE AND DEATH. New York: AMS Press, 1974. Reprint of 1896 edition.

5260. OUR FAMOUS WOMEN: AN AUTHORIZED RECORD OF THE LIVES AND DEEDS OF DISTINGUISHED AMERICAN WOMEN OF OUR TIMES; AN ENTIRELY NEW WORK, FULL OF ROMANTIC STORY, LIVELY HUMOR, THRILLING EXPERIENCES, TENDER PATHOS, AND BRILLIANT WIT, WITH NUMEROUS ANECDOTES, INCIDENTS, AND PERSONAL REMINISCENCES BY THE FOLLOWING TWENTY EMINENT AUTHORS: ELIZABETH STUART PHELPS, ETC. Freeport, NY: Books for Libraries, 1971. 715 pp. Reprint of 1883 edition.

5261. Parton, James, Horace Greeley, T. W. Higginson, J. S. C. Abbott, James M. Hoppin, William Winter, Theodore Tilton, Fanny Fern, Grace Greenwood, Mrs. Elizabeth Cady Stanton, etc. EMINENT WOMEN OF THE AGE: BEING NARRATIVES OF THE LIVES AND DEEDS OF THE MOST PROMINENT WOMEN OF THE PRESENT GENERATION. New York: Arno Press, 1974. 628 pp. Reprint of 1869 edition.

5262. Peabody, Marian Lawrence. TO BE YOUNG WAS VERY HEAVEN. Boston, MA: Houghton Mifflin, 1967. 366 pp. Autobiography of the Boston philanthropist and socialite.

5263. Peacock, Virginia Tatnall. FAMOUS AMERICAN BELLES OF THE NINETEENTH CENTURY. Freeport, NY: Books for Libraries, 1970. 207 pp. Reprint of 1900 edition. Biographies of 18 women socialites; includes a chapter on "New York as a Social Centre."

5264. Pearce, Charles E. POLLY PEACHUM: THE STORY OF LAVINIA FENTON AND "THE BEGGAR'S OPERA." New York: Benjamin Blom, 1972. 382 pp. Reprint of 1913 edition. Biography of the woman who created the role of Polly in the successful ballad opera, and became the Duchess of Bolton.

5265. Pearson, Hesketh. THE MARRYING AMERICANS. New York: Coward McCann, 1961. 313 pp. Collection of short narrations of American women who married into European families, such as Jenny Jerome who married Winston Churchill, Alice Astor and Prince Obolensky, Wallis Simpson and the Duke of Windsor; emphasizing their roles as political observers and historical figures.

5266. Peters, Heinz Frederick. MY SISTER, MY SPOUSE. New York: Norton Library, 1974. 320 pp. Biography of Lou Andreas-Salomé, who was loved by Nietzsche, a confidante of Wagner, Rilke, Tolstoy, Rodin, Strindberg, Buber, Hauptmann, and Freud.

5267. Ray, Gordon N. H. G. WELLS AND REBECCA WEST. New Haven, CT: Yale Univ. Press, 1974. 215 pp. Frank portrayal of the lives of Dame Rebecca West (Cicely Esabel Fairchild) and the great science fiction writer.

5268. Richards, Laura E. ABIGAIL ADAMS AND HER TIMES. New York: D. Appleton, 1917. 282 pp.

5269. Richey, Elinor. EMINENT WOMEN OF THE WEST. Berkeley, CA: Howell-North Books, 1975. 276 pp. Essays on nine women of the American west: novelist Gertrude Atherton, Congresswoman Jeanette Rankin, Gertrude Stein, Isadora Duncan, photographer Imogen

Cunningham, architect Julia Morgan, Indian princess Sarah
Winnemucca, medical researcher Florence Sabin, and suffragist Abigail
Scott Duniway.

5270. Roberts, Charles Henry. THE RADICAL COUNTESS: THE HISTORY
OF THE LIFE OF ROSALIND, COUNTESS OF CARLISLE. Carlisle,
England: Steel Bros., 1962. 198 pp. Biography of Rosalind Frances
Howard, leader in the fight for women's rights and temperance reform.

5271. Robinson, Marion O. EIGHT WOMEN OF THE YWCA. New York:
National Board of the Y.W.C.A., 1966. 118 pp. Preface by Mary French
Rockefeller. Biographies of Grace A. Dodge, Mabel Cratty, Emma
Bailey Speer, Mary Billings French, Vera Scott Cushman, Martha
Boydon Finley, Florence Simms, and Teresa Wilbur Paist.

5272. Roosevelt, Felicia W. DOERS AND DOWAGERS: IN-DEPTH
INTERVIEWS WITH LIVING AMERICAN WOMEN OVER 70. Garden
City, NY: Doubleday, 1975. 228 pp.

5273. Ross, Ishbel. THE PRESIDENT'S WIFE: MARY TODD LINCOLN. New
York: G. P. Putnam's Sons, 1973. 378 pp.

5274. Rowson, Susannah. CHARLOTTE TEMPLE: A TALE OF TRUTH. New
Haven, CT: College & Univ. Press, 1964. 163 pp.

5275. Russell, Dora B. THE TAMARISK TREE: MY QUEST FOR LIBERTY
AND LOVE. New York: G. P. Putnam's Sons, 1975. 304 pp.
Autobiography of the travels and studies of the founder of an
experimental school, who married Bertrand Russell.

5276. St. John, Adela R. SOME ARE BORN GREAT. Garden City, NY:
Doubleday, 1974. 297 pp. Biographies of such women as Judy Garland,
Amelia Earhart, and Margaret Mitchell, by the newspaper reporter.

5277. Schmidt, Margaret F. PASSION'S CHILD: THE EXTRAORDINARY
LIFE OF JANE DIGBY. New York: Harper & Row, 1976. 268 pp.

5278. Seabury, R. I. DAUGHTER OF AFRICA. Boston, MA: Pilgrim Press,
1945. 144 pp. Biography of Mina Soga, African woman and Christian
leader.

5279. Sengupta, Padmini. PANDITA MAMBAI SARAWATI. New York: Asia
Publishing House, 1971. 364 pp.

5280. Serebriakova, Galina Iosifovna. NINE WOMEN, DRAWN FROM THE
EPOCH OF THE FRENCH REVOLUTION. Freeport, NY: Books for
Libraries, 1969. 287 pp. Reprint of 1932 edition. Biographies of such
women as Charlotte Corday, Manon Roland, and Josephine Bonaparte.

5281. Sergeant, Philip Walsingham. DOMINANT WOMEN. Freeport, NY:
Books for Libraries, 1964. 288 pp. Reprint of 1929 edition.
Biographies of such women as Cleopatra, Zenobia, Theodora of
Byzantium, Tarabai Rani, etc.

5282. Sinclair, May. THE THREE BRONTËS. Port Washington, NY: Kennikat
Press, 1967. 296 pp. Reprint of 1912 edition.

5283. Smith, George Barnett. WOMEN OF RENOWN: NINETEENTH
CENTURY STUDIES. Freeport, NY: Books for Libraries, 1972. 478
pp. Reprint of 1893 edition. Ten biographies of women such as Jenny
Lind, Mary Somerville, and Lady Hester Stanhope.

5284. Smith, Goldwin. LIFE OF JANE AUSTIN. Port Washington, NY:

Kennikat Press, 1971. 191 pp. Reprint of 1890 edition.
5285. Smith, Margaret Chase and H. Paul Jeffers. GALLANT WOMEN. New
York: McGraw-Hill, 1968. 124 pp. Biographies of Anne Hutchinson,
Dolley Madison, Harriet Tubman, Harriet Beecher Stowe, Clara Barton,
Elizabeth Blackwell, Susan B. Anthony, Annie Sullivan, Amelia
Earhart, Althea Gibson, Frances Perkins, and Eleanor Roosevelt.
5286. Smythe, Colin, ed. SEVENTY YEARS: THE AUTOBIOGRAPHY OF
LADY GREGORY. New York: Macmillan, 1976. 583 pp.
5287. Sorell, Walter. THREE WOMEN: LIVES OF SEX AND GENIUS.
Indianapolis, IN: Bobbs-Merrill, 1975. 234 pp. Biographies of Lou
Andreas-Salomé, Alma Schindler Mahler Werfel, and Gertrude Stein.
5288. Stein, Gertrude. EVERYBODY'S AUTOBIOGRAPHY. New York:
Random House, 1973. 352 pp. Reprint of 1937 edition. Stein's analysis
of the major figures of the day and of her own life and work.
5289. Steinberg, Alfred. MRS. R.: THE LIFE OF ELEANOR ROOSEVELT.
New York: G.P. Putnam's Sons, 1958. 384 pp. A biography drawn
from Eleanor Roosevelt's personal papers, books, and voluminous
writings.
5290. Sterne, Emma Gelders. MARY MCLEOD BETHUNE. New York: Alfred
A. Knopf, 1957. 268 pp.
5291. Syrkin, Marie. WAY OF VALOR: A BIOGRAPHY OF GOLDA
MYERSON. New York: Sharon Books, 1955. 309 pp.
5292. Talmadge, John E. REBECCA LATIMER FELTON: NINE STORMY
DECADES. Athens, GA: Univ. of Georgia Press, 1960. 187 pp. Active
in Georgia politics and government.
5293. Thorp, Margaret. FEMALE PERSUASION: SIX STRONG-MINDED
WOMEN. Hamden, CT: Shoe String Press, 1971. 253 pp. Reprint of
1949 edition. Catherine E. Beecher, Jane G. Swisshelm, Amelia
Bloomer, Sara J. C. Lippincott, Louisa S. McCord, and L. Maria Child.
5294. Tomalin, Claire. THE LIFE AND DEATH OF MARY
WOLLSTONECRAFT. New York: Harcourt Brace Jovanovich, 1974.
316 pp.
5295. Tsuzuki, Chushichi. LIFE OF ELEANOR MARX, 1855-1898: A
SOCIALIST TRAGEDY. Fairlawn, NJ: Oxford Univ. Press, 1967. 354
pp. Biography of Eleanor Marx.
5296. Turney, Catherine. BYRON'S DAUGHTER: A BIOGRAPHY OF
ELIZABETH MEDORA LEIGH. New York: Charles Scribner's Sons,
1972. 320 pp. Life story of the child of Lord Byron and his half-sister,
Augusta.
5297. Wales, Nym (Helen Foster Snow). RED DUST. Stanford, CA: Stanford
Univ. Press, 1952. 238 pp. Includes some biographies of women
collected by the author in China in 1952.
5298. Waley, Arthur. YUAN MEI. New York: Macmillan, 1956. 227 pp.
Biography of an eighteenth-century poet who was among other things,
a Confucian feminist.
5299. Walker, Margaret. "For My People." New Haven, CT: Yale Univ. Press,
1942. 58 pp.

5300. Wickes, George. THE AMAZON OF LETTERS: THE LIFE AND LOVES OF NATALIE BARNEY. New York: G.P. Putnam's Sons, 1977.
5301. Winter, Ella. AND NOT TO YIELD; AN AUTOBIOGRAPHY. New York: Harcourt, Brace & World, 1963. 308 pp.
5302. Yonge, Charlotte M. HANNAH MORE. Boston, MA: Roberts, 1890. 227 pp.

VII. WOMEN IN LITERATURE AND THE ARTS

"Women do about all the reading and playgoing that is done in America; at least they are responsible for most of the playgoing, since men mostly 'go along' under their influence. They keep up most of our music; they maintain most of our painting and sculpture, they are the mainstay of our churches, our educational, cultural, and social institutions, they are the arbiters of taste and style for both sexes and in all particulars."

—Henry Augustine Beers

"I'll match my flops with anybody's, but I wouldn't have missed 'em. Flops are a part of life's menu and I've never been a girl to miss out on any of the courses."
—Rosalind Russell

5303. Adams, Hazard. LADY GREGORY. Lewisburg, PA: Bucknell Univ. Press, 1973. 106 pp. Brief but perceptive analysis of the noted Irish author with a good overview of her activities in several spheres and genres.
5304. Addison, Hilda. MARY WEBB: HER LIFE AND WORK. Philadelphia, PA: Richard West, 1975. 189 pp. Reprint of 1931 edition. Biography of the novelist, poet, and essayist who became famous posthumously.
5305. Aird, Eileen. SYLVIA PLATH: HER LIFE AND WORK. New York: Harper & Row, 1975. 114 pp. Biography of the author of THE BELL JAR.
5306. Alloway, Lawrence. "Isabel Bishop, the Grand Manner and the Working Girl," ART IN AMERICA, vol. 63, no. 5 (Sept./Oct. 1975), pp. 61-65. Analysis of the style and subject matter of the 1930's realist painter.
5307. Auchincloss, Louis. EDITH WHARTON: A WOMAN IN HER TIME. New York: Viking Press, 1971. 191 pp. Biography of the turn-of-the-century novelist.
5308. Banning, Evelyn I. HELEN HUNT JACKSON. New York: Vanguard, 1973. 248 pp. Biography placing Jackson's writings in the annals of American literature of the 19th century, and describing her dedication to the rights of the Native American Indian.
5309. Betancourt, Jeanne. WOMEN IN FOCUS. New York: Pflaum/Standard, 1974. 186 pp. Compilation of films with complete production and rental data, each citation including suggested corresponding feminist reading.
5310. Bigland, Eileen. MARIE CORELLI: THE WOMAN AND THE LEGEND: A BIOGRAPHY. Philadelphia, PA: Richard West, 1953. 274 pp.
5311. Black, Helen C. NOTABLE WOMEN AUTHORS OF THE DAY. Freeport, NY: Books for Libraries, 1972. 342 pp. Reprint of 1893 edition. Biographical sketches of 26 English women writers, e.g. Jean Ingelow.
5312. Blackstone, Bernard. "Virginia Woolf: A Commentary." New York: Harcourt Brace Jovanovich, 1972. 39 pp. Reprint of 1962 edition. Short exegetical study of the British novelist.

5313. Bowman, Kathleen. "New Women in Art and Dance." Mankato, MN: Creative Educational Society, 1976. 47 pp.

5314. ———. "New Women in Entertainment." Mankato, MN: Creative Educational Society, 1976. 47 pp.

5315. Brée, Germaine. "Women Writers in France: Variations on a Theme." New Brunswick, NJ: Rutgers Univ. Press, 1973. 90 pp. Survey of French women writers from medieval to modern times, with a witty and acute commentary on Colette and on de Beauvoir.

5316. Bremer, Charlotte, ed. LIFE, LETTERS, AND POSTHUMOUS WORKS OF FREDERICKA BREMER. New York: AMS Press, 1976. 439 pp. Reprint of 1868 edition. Swedish writer.

5317. Brooks, Gwendolyn. REPORT FROM PART ONE: AN AUTOBIOGRAPHY. Detroit, MI: Broadside Press, 1972. 215 pp. Autobiography of her life, and her views on her childhood, the black struggle, and black womanhood.

5318. Browning, Oscar. LIFE OF GEORGE ELIOT. Port Washington, NY: Kennikat Press, 1972. 174 pp. Reprint of 1890 edition. Critical biography of Mary Ann Evans, analyzing the principal characteristics of her art and her development as a writer.

5319. Caro, Elme Marie. GEORGE SAND. Port Washington, NY: Kennikat Press, 1970. 198 pp. Reprint of 1888 edition. Discusses the life, works, and style of Mme. Amandine Aurore Lucie Dupin Dudevant.

5320. Chevigny, Bell Gale. THE WOMAN AND THE MYTH: MARGARET FULLER'S LIFE AND WRITINGS. Old Westbury, NY: Feminist Press, 1976. 512 pp. Critical anthology and biography of one of America's most prominent literary figures.

5321. Chicago, Judy. THROUGH THE FLOWER: MY STRUGGLE AS A WOMAN ARTIST. Garden City, NY: Doubleday, 1975. 226 pp. Introduction by Anais Nin.

5322. Clarke, Isabel Constance. ELIZABETH BARRETT BROWNING: A PORTRAIT. Port Washington, NY: Kennikat Press, 1973. 304 pp. Reprint of 1929 edition.

5323. Coghill, Mrs. Anna Louisa. AUTOBIOGRAPHY AND LETTERS OF MRS. MARGARET OLIPHANT. Atlantic Highlands, NJ: Humanities Press, 1974. 464 pp. Reprint of 1899 edition. Includes a bibliography of her works and contributions to BLACKWOOD'S MAGAZINE.

5324. Colby, Vineta. YESTERDAY'S WOMAN: DOMESTIC REALISM IN THE ENGLISH NOVEL. Princeton, NJ: Princeton Univ. Press, 1974. 269 pp. Discussion of novels by women and the roots of the Victorian novel's hominess, attention to manners, education for women, and domestic virtues.

5325. Crosland, Margaret. COLETTE: THE DIFFICULTY OF LOVING, A BIOGRAPHY. Indianapolis, IN: Bobbs-Merrill, 1973. 200 pp. Biography of the French writer, Sidonie Gabrielle Colette.

5326. ———. WOMEN OF IRON AND VELVET: FRENCH WOMEN WRITERS AFTER GEORGE SAND. New York: Taplinger Publishing, 1976. 255 pp. Biographical and literary commentary on French writers, emphasizing the influences of religion and feminism on their work.

5327. de Beauvoir, Simone. ALL SAID AND DONE. New York: G. P. Putnam's Sons, 1974. 463 pp. Memoirs for the years 1962-1972. Her fifth volume of autobiography.

5328. De Mille, Agnes. SPEAK TO ME, DANCE WITH ME. Boston, MA: Little, Brown, 1974. 404 pp. An account of Agnes de Mille, choreographer, from early dance steps to recent musicals such as CAROUSEL, including techniques and history.

5329. Donovan, Josephine, ed. "Feminist Literary Criticism: Explorations in Theory." Lexington, KY: Univ. Press of Kentucky, 1975. 94 pp.

5330. Doumic, Rene. GEORGE SAND: SOME ASPECTS OF HER LIFE AND WRITINGS. Port Washington, NY: Kennikat Press, 1973. 362 pp. Reprint of 1910 edition.

5331. Elwood, Anne Katharine. MEMOIRS OF THE LITERARY LADIES OF ENGLAND FROM THE COMMENCEMENT OF THE LAST CENTURY. New York: AMS Press, 1973. 2 vols. Reprint of 1843 edition.

5332. Erens, Patricia, ed. SEXUAL STRATAGEMS: THE WORLD OF WOMEN IN FILM. New York: Horizon Press, 1976.

5333. Ewbank, Inga-Stina. THEIR PROPER SPHERE: A STUDY OF THE BRONTË SISTERS AS EARLY VICTORIAN NOVELISTS. Cambridge, MA: Harvard Univ. Press, 1968. 239 pp.

5334. Farrar, Geraldine. SUCH SWEET COMPULSION: THE AUTOBIOGRAPHY OF GERALDINE FARRAR. New York: Da Capo Press, 1970. 303 pp. Reprint of 1938 edition. The opera from 1905 to 1922 as portrayed by the soprano who created the role of Madame Butterfly.

5335. FEMALE ARTISTS: PAST AND PRESENT. Berkeley, CA: Women's History Research Center, 1974. 158 pp. Purpose is to identify female artists and open lines of communication between them.

5336. "Female Artists Past and Present: International Women's Year 1975 Supplement." Berkeley, CA: Women's History Research Center, 1975. 66 pp. Note: This is the last publication of the Women's History Research Center.

5337. Fitzgerald, R. D. "Australian Women Poets," TEXAS QUARTERLY, vol. 15 (Summer 1972), pp. 75-97.

5338. Fowler, Carol. CONTRIBUTIONS OF WOMEN: ART. Minneapolis, MN: Dillon Press, 1976. 151 pp.

5339. Friedman, Myra. BURIED ALIVE: THE BIOGRAPHY OF JANIS JOPLIN. New York: Bantam Books, 1974. 333 pp. Biography of the rock singer who died from an overdose of drugs.

5340. Godbold, E. Stanley, Jr. ELLEN GLASGOW AND THE WOMAN WITHIN. Baton Rouge, LA: Louisiana State Univ. Press, 1972. 322 pp. Biography of Ellen Glasgow, novelist of life in Virginia, drawn from an analysis of her works.

5341. Gould, Jean. THE POET AND HER BOOK: BIOGRAPHY OF EDNA ST. VINCENT MILLAY. New York: Dodd Mead, 1969. 308 pp.

5342. Griswold, Rufus Wilmot. FEMALE POETS OF AMERICA. New York: Mss Information, 1972. 486 pp. Reprint of 1873 edition.

5343. Halsey, Francis W., ed. WOMEN AUTHORS OF OUR DAY IN THEIR HOMES, PERSONAL DESCRIPTIONS AND INTERVIEWS. Philadelphia, PA: Richard West, 1969. 300 pp. Reprint of 1903 edition.

5344. Hamilton, Catherine Jane. WOMEN WRITERS: THE WORKS AND THEIR WAYS. Freeport, NY: Books for Libraries, 1971. 280 pp. Reprint of 1892 edition.

5345. Hardwick, Elizabeth. SEDUCTION AND BETRAYAL: WOMEN AND LITERATURE. New York: Random House, 1975. 224 pp. Psychological and social history of women as seen through literature: analyzes the lives and works of the Brontës, Sylvia Plath, and Virginia Woolf, as well as fictional portrayals of women.

5346. Harris, Ann Sutherland and Linda Nochlin. WOMEN ARTISTS: 1550-1950. New York: Alfred A. Knopf, 1976. 367 pp. 400 years of painting by women.

5347. Hess, Thomas B. and Elizabeth C. Baker, eds. ART AND SEXUAL POLITICS: WOMEN'S LIBERATION, WOMEN AS ARTISTS, AND ART HISTORY. New York: Macmillan, 1973. 150 pp. Revision of essays originally appearing in ART NEWS, vol. 69, no. 9 (Jan, 1971); includes bibliography.

5348. Hinkley, Laura L. LADIES OF LITERATURE. Freeport, NY: Books for Libraries, 1970. 374 pp. Reprint of 1946 edition. Fanny Burney, Jane Austin, Charlotte and Emily Brontë, Elizabeth Barrett Browning, and George Eliot.

5349. Horner, Joyce Mary. THE ENGLISH WOMEN NOVELISTS AND THEIR CONNECTION WITH THE FEMINIST MOVEMENT. Folcroft, PA: Folcroft Library Editions, 1973. 152 pp. Reprint of 1930 edition.

5350. Hu P'in-Ch'ing. LI CH'ING-CHAO. New York: Twain, 1966. 128 pp. Biography of Sung female poet, 1081-1141.

5351. Jacob, Naomi. ME AND THE SWANS. London, England: William Kimber, 1963. 159 pp. Reminiscences of actresses in Great Britain.

5352. Johnson, Reginald Brimley. SOME CONTEMPORARY NOVELISTS (WOMEN). Freeport, NY: Books for Libraries, 1967. 220 pp. Reprint of 1920 edition. Biographies of 14 female novelists, e.g. Virginia Woolf, Eleanor Mordant.

5353. ———. THE WOMEN NOVELISTS. Saint Clair Shores, MI: Scholarly Press, 1971. 229 pp. Reprint of 1918 edition. 18th and 19th century English writers.

5354. Jones, Margaret E. DELORES MEDIO. Boston, MA: Twayne Publishers, 1974. 196 pp.

5355. Kallir, Otto. GRANDMA MOSES. New York: Harry Abrams, 1973. 360 pp. 253 illustrations, with text, of the American artist and her paintings.

5356. Kaplan, Cora. SALT AND BITTER AND GOOD: THREE CENTURIES OF ENGLISH AND AMERICAN WOMEN POETS. St. Lawrence, MA: Two Continents Publishing Group, 1975. 304 pp.

5357. Kavanaugh, Julia. FRENCH WOMEN OF LETTER: BIOGRAPHICAL SKETCHES. Norwood, PA: Norwood Editions, 1974. 2 vols. Reprint of 1862 edition.

5358. Kearns, Martha. KÄTHE KOLLOWITZ: WOMAN AND ARTIST. Old Westbury, NY: Feminist Press, 1976. 256 pp. Biography of the German graphic artist whose career spanned two World Wars.

5359. Kelley, Philip and Ronald Hudson, eds. DIARY BY E. B. B. Athens, OH: Ohio Univ. Press, 1969. 358 pp. Unpublished diary of Elizabeth Barrett Browning.

5360. Kirkland, Winifred M. and Francis Kirkland. GIRLS WHO BECAME WRITERS. Freeport, NY: Books for Libraries, 1971. 121 pp. Reprint of 1933 edition. Fanny Burney, Selma Lagerlof, Edna St. Vincent Millay, Pearl Buck, Mary Roberts Rinehart, Sara Josepha Hale, Anne Shannon Monroe, Louisa May Alcott, and Dorothy Canfield Fisher.

5361. Knies, Earl A. THE ART OF CHARLOTTE BRONTË. Athens, OH: Ohio Univ. Press, 1969. 234 pp. Discusses the implications of "point of view."

5362. Lesser, Allen. ENCHANTING REBEL: THE SECRET OF ADAH ISAACS MENKEN. Port Washington, NY: Kennikat Press, 1973. 224 pp. Reprint of 1947 edition. During Lincoln's day, she was a sex symbol, "actress," and dancer.

5363. Lessing, Doris. A SMALL PERSONAL VOICE: ESSAYS, REVIEWS, INTERVIEWS. New York: Alfred A. Knopf, 1974. 171 pp.

5364. Limmer, Ruth. WHAT THE WOMAN LIVED: SELECTED LETTERS 1920-1970. New York: Harcourt Brace Jovanovich, 1974. 401 pp. Selected letters of Louise Bogan, whose poetry suggested the lack of options that are a part of being a woman, but whose life exemplified the courage it took to write her poetry.

5365. Linder, Leslie. THE JOURNAL OF BEATRIX POTTER FROM 1881 to 1897. New York: Frederick Warne, 1966. 448 pp. Presents an interesting view of Victorian English life, includes discussion of her family lines with geneological tables.

5366. Longsworth, Polly. I, CHARLOTTE FORTEN, BLACK AND FREE. New York: Thomas Y. Crowell, 1970. 248 pp. Her teaching and writing.

5367. Lynn, Loretta with George Vacsley. LORETTA LYNN: COAL MINER'S DAUGHTER. Chicago, IL: Henry Regnery, 1976. 204 pp. Autobiography of the country singer.

5368. McGinley, Phyllis. SIXPENCE IN HER SHOE. New York: Macmillan, 1964. 281 pp. Autobiography of Phyllis McGinley's profession as a writer, and a view of the American housewife.

5369. McLeod, Enid. THE ORDER OF THE ROSE: THE LIFE AND IDEAS OF CHRISTINE DE PIZAN. Totowa, NJ: Rowman & Littlefield, 1976. 185 pp.

5370. Marks, E. COLETTE. New Brunswick, NJ: Rutgers Univ. Press, 1960. 265 pp. Biography of the French writer, Sidonie Gabrielle Colette.

5371. May, Caroline, ed. THE AMERICAN FEMALE POETS. New York: Garrett Press, 1969. 559 pp. Reprint of 1850 edition.

5372. Miner, Dorothy E. "Anastaise and Her Sisters: Women Artists of the Middle Ages." Baltimore, MD: Walters Art Gallery, 1974. 24 pp. The illumination of books and manuscripts.

5373. Moers, Ellen. LITERARY WOMEN: THE GREAT WRITERS. New York: Doubleday, 1975. 264 pp. Discusses female writers' approaches to everything, from the Brontës to Erica Jong.

5374. Moffat, Mary J. and Charlotte Painter. REVELATIONS: DIARIES OF WOMEN. New York: Random House, 1974. 448 pp. Diary selections organized under themes of love, power, and work, by such writers as Louisa May Alcott, George Sand, Anais Nin, and Virginia Woolf.

5375. Moglen, Helene. CHARLOTTE BRONTË: THE SELF CONCEIVED. Scranton, PA: W. W. Norton, 1976. 256 pp. Excellent biography of the author of JANE EYRE.

5376. Møller, Hanne Inger Stauning, Karen Syberg, Lisbeth Dehn Holgersen, and Signe Arnfred. UDSIGTEN FRA DET KVINDELIGE UNIVERS: EN ANALYSE AF EVA [VIEW FROM THE FEMALE UNIVERSE: AN ANALYSIS OF EVA (WOMEN'S MAGAZINE)]. Kobenhavn, Denmark: Forlaget Rode Hane, 1972. 221 pp.

5377. Money, Keith. THE ART OF MARGOT FONTEYN. New York: William Morrow, 1966. 261 pp. Biography, with photographs, of the great British dancer. Commentary contributed by Ninette de Valois, Frederick Ashton, and Margot Fonteyn.

5378. Moore, Doris Langley. E. NESBIT: A BIOGRAPHY. Philadelphia, PA: Chilton Press, 1966. 313 pp. Biography of the children's writer.

5379. Moore, Virginia. DISTINGUISHED WOMEN WRITERS. Port Washington, NY: Kennikat Press, 1968. 253 pp. Reprint of 1934 edition. Biographies of 17 writers from Sappho to George Sand.

5380. Moult, Thomas. MARY WEBB: HER LIFE AND HER WORK. Philadelphia, PA: Richard West, 1973. 287 pp. Reprint of 1932 edition. Biography of Mary Gladys Meredith Webb.

5381. Munsterberg, Hugo. THE HISTORY OF WOMEN ARTISTS. New York: Clarkson N. Potter, 1975. 192 pp. From neolithic times to the present, covers full range of arts.

5382. "Music's Wonder Lady," TIME (Nov. 10, 1975), pp. 52-54, 59, 65. The first lady of american opera, conductor Sarah Caldwell.

5383. Nemser, Cindy. CONVERSATIONS WITH TWELVE WOMEN ARTISTS. Totowa, NJ: Charles Scribners Sons, 1975. 367 pp. Interviews with contemporary artists.

5384. Newman, Charles, ed. THE ART OF SYLVIA PLATH: A SYMPOSIUM, SELECTED CRITICISM, WITH A COMPLETE BIBLIOGRAPHY AND AN APPENDIX OF UNCOLLECTED AND UNPUBLISHED WORK. Bloomington, IN: Indiana Univ. Press, 1970. 320 pp.

5385. Oliver, Paul. "Kings of Jazz: Bessie Smith." Cranbury, NJ: A. S. Barnes, 1971. 82 pp. Jazz singer of the 1920's.

5386. Ortiz Aponte, Sally. LAS MUJERES DE "CLARIN:" ESPERMENTOS Y CAMAFEOS. Rio Piedros, Puerto Rico: Editorial Unversitaria, Universidad de Puerto Rico, 1971. 197 pp.

5387. Paston, George. MRS. DELANEY (MARY GRANVILLE): A MEMOIR

1780-1788. Philadelphia, PA: Richard West, 1968. Reprint of 1900 edition.

5388. Pattee, Fred Lewis. THE FEMININE FIFTIES. New York: D. Appleton-Century, 1940. 339 pp.

5389. Petersen, Karen and J. J. Wilson. WOMEN ARTISTS: RECOGNITION AND REAPPRAISAL FROM THE EARLY MIDDLE AGES TO THE TWENTIETH CENTURY. New York: Harper & Row, 1976. Handbook of painting, sculpture, and drawing by women over the past thousand years.

5390. Rayson, Ann L. "The Novels of Zora Neale Hurston," STUDIES BLACK LITERATURE, vol. 5, no. 4 (Winter 1974), pp. 1-10. Analysis of the style of the author of THEIR EYES WERE WATCHING GOD.

5391. Read, Thomas B., ed. THE FEMALE POETS OF AMERICA, WITH PORTRAITS, BIOGRAPHICAL NOTICES, AND SPECIMENS OF THEIR WRITINGS. New York: Mss Information, 1972. 478 pp. Reprint of 1857 edition.

5392. Robertson, Eric Sutherland. ENGLISH POETESSES: A SERIES OF CRITICAL BIOGRAPHIES. Freeport, NY: Books for Libraries, 1971. 381 pp. Reprint of 1883 edition. Elizabeth Barrett Browning, George Eliot, Christina Rossetti, etc.

5393. Rogat, Ellen Hawkes. "The Virgin in the Bell Biography," TWENTIETH CENTURY LITERATURE, vol. 20, no. 2 (April 1974), pp. 96-113. Criticizes Quentin Bell's biography of Virginia Woolf for its lack of understanding of her sexuality as reflected in her writing.

5394. Sand, George. INTIMATE JOURNAL OF GEORGE SAND. New York: Haskell House, 1974. 198 pp. Reprint of 1929 edition.

5395. Saul, George B. "Quintet: Essays on Five American Women Poets." Atlantic Highlands, NJ: Humanities Press, 1967. 50 pp. Sara Teasdale, Elinor Wylie, Hazel Hall, Abbie Huston Evans, and Winifred Wells.

5396. Secrest, Meryle. BETWEEN ME AND LIFE: A BIOGRAPHY OF ROMAINE BROOKS. Garden City, NY: Doubleday, 1974. 432 pp. Portrait of the female artist, obscure while in America, who became part of the world of Joyce, Pound, Colette, Valéry, D'Annunzio, and Stein.

5397. Seeley, Leonard Benton. MRS. THRALE, AFTERWARDS MRS. PIOZZI: A SKETCH OF HER LIFE AND PASSAGES FROM HER DIARIES, LETTERS, AND OTHER WRITINGS. Louisville, KY: Lost Cause Press, 1956. 336 pp. Reprint of 1891 edition. Hester Lynch Thrale Piozzi.

5398. Sewall, Richard Benson. THE LIFE OF EMILY DICKINSON. New York: Farrar, Strauss, Giroux, 1974. 2 vols. Biography of the 19th century American poet.

5399. Seward, Anna. THE POETICAL WORKS OF ANNA SEWARD: WITH EXTRACTS FROM HER LITERARY CORRESPONDENCE, EDITED BY WALTER SCOTT. New York: AMS Press, 1974. 3 vols. Reprint of 1810 edition.

5400. Showalter, Elaine A. A LITERATURE OF THEIR OWN–BRITISH WOMEN NOVELISTS FROM BRONTË TO LESSING. Princeton, NJ:

Princeton Univ. Press, 1977. 378 pp.

5401. Slice, Anthony. EARLY WOMEN DIRECTORS. Cranbury, NJ: A. S. Barnes, 1976.

5402. Slote, Bernice and Virginia Faulkner, eds. THE ART OF WILLA CATHER. Lincoln, NB: Univ. of Nebraska-Lincoln, 1974. 267 pp. The life of the novelist and her works portrayed in more than 160 illustrations.

5403. Smith, Sharon. WOMEN WHO MAKE MOVIES. New York: Hopkinson & Blake, 1975. 307 pp. Contributions of women filmmakers throughout the 80 years of motion pictures.

5404. Sonstrom, David. ROSSETTI AND THE FAIR LADY. Middletown, CT: Wesleyan Univ. Press, 1970. 252 pp. Women in literature and art.

5405. Springer, John and Jack D. Hamilton. THEY HAD FACES THEN. Secaucus, NJ: Citadel Press, 1974. Over 900 photographs of memorable women in the movies.

5406. Stebbins, Lucy Poate. A VICTORIAN ALBUM: SOME LADY NOVELISTS OF THE PERIOD. New York: AMS Press, 1970. 226 pp. Reprint of 1946 edition. Charlotte Bronte, Elizabeth Gaskell, George Eliot, and Margaret Oliphant.

5407. Steegmuller, Francis. "YOUR ISADORA:" THE LOVE STORY OF ISADORA DUNCAN AND GORDON CRAIG. New York: Random House, 1974. 399 pp. The phenomenal dancer and her relationship with the theatrical designer.

5408. Stein, Gertrude. LECTURES IN AMERICA. New York: Random House, 1975. 256 pp. Collection of essays on writing, poetry, and music.

5409. Stewart-Baxter, Derrick. MA RAINEY AND THE CLASSIC BLUES SINGERS. New York: Stein & Day, 1970. 112 pp. Critical study of Ma Rainey, Bessie Smith, and the women singers of the 1920's.

5410. Taranow, Gerda. SARAH BERNHARDT: THE ART WITHIN THE LEGEND. Princeton, NJ: Princeton Univ. Press, 1972. 287 pp.

5411. Tenisen, Eva Mabel. LOUISE IMOGEN GUINEY: HER LIFE AND WORKS, 1861-1920. Philadelphia, PA: Richard West, 1972. 348 pp. Reprint of 1923 edition.

5412. Thwaite, Ann. WAITING FOR THE PARTY: THE LIFE OF FRANCES HODGSON BURNETT, 1849-1924. New York: Charles Scribners Sons, 1974. 274 pp. Author of LITTLE LORD FAUNTLEROY.

5413. Tufts, Eleanor. OUR HIDDEN HERITAGE: FIVE CENTURIES OF WOMEN ARTISTS. New York: Paddington Press, 1973. 256 pp. Series of biographical portraits of famous women artists, including Levina Teerling (painter to Henry VIII); Elizabeth Vigee-Lebrun (portraitist to Marie Antoinette); Angelica Kauffmann (one of the founders of the Royal Academy in London); and Sofonisba Anguissola, who was admired by Michelangelo.

5414. Ventura, Jeffrey. THE JACQUELINE SUSANN STORY. Hauppage, NY: Universal Publishing and Distribution, 1975.

5415. Weil, Dorothy. IN DEFENSE OF WOMEN: SUSANNA ROWSON 1762-1864. University Park, PA: Pennsylvania State Univ. Press, 1976.

5416. Wetherby, Terry, ed. NEW POETS: WOMEN. Millbrae, CA: Celestial

Arts, 1975.

5417. Williams, Jane. THE LITERARY WOMEN OF ENGLAND, INCLUDING A BIOGRAPHICAL EPITOME OF ALL THE MOST EMINENT TO THE YEAR 1700; AND SKETCHES OF ALL THE POETESSES TO THE YEAR 1850; WITH EXTRACTS FROM THEIR WORKS AND CRITICAL REMARKS. Norwood, PA: Norwood Editions, 1974. 564 pp. Reprint of 1861 edition.

5418. Wilson, Mona. THESE WERE MUSES. Port Washington, NY: Kennikat Press, 1970. 235 pp. Reprint of 1924 edition. Includes biographies of Susannah Centilivre, Sydney Morgan, Frances Trollope, and Sara Coleridge.

5419. "Women: A Historical Survey of Works by Women Artists." Raleigh, NC: North Carolina Museum of Art, 1972. 58 pp.

5420. WOMEN NOVELISTS OF QUEEN VICTORIA'S REIGN: A BOOK OF APPRECIATIONS. Folcroft, PA: Folcroft Editions, 1969. 311 pp. Reprint of 1897 edition. Includes Margaret Oliphant, etc.

5421. Woolcott, Alexander. MRS. FISKE: HER VIEW ON ACTORS, ACTING, AND THE PROBLEMS OF PRODUCTION. New York: Benjamin Blom, 1972. 225 pp. Reprint of 1917 edition. Drama critic's conversations with the actress-director-producer, on women's role in the theater, among other things.

5422. Yurka, Blanche. BOHEMIAN GIRL: BLANCHE YURKA'S THEATRICAL LIFE. Athens, OH: Ohio Univ. Press, 1970. 306 pp.

VIII. WOMEN IN PSYCHOLOGY

"A wonderful discovery—psychoanalysis. Makes quite simple people feel they're complex."

—Samuel Nathaniel Behrman

5423. Angrist, Shirley S., et al. WOMEN AFTER TREATMENT: A STUDY OF FORMER MENTAL PATIENTS AND THEIR NORMAL NEIGHBORS. New York: Appleton-Century-Crofts, 1968. 333 pp.
5424. Arafat, Ibtihaj S. and Betty Yorburg. THE NEW WOMAN: ATTITUDES, BEHAVIOR, AND SELF IMAGE. Columbus, OH: Charles E. Merrill, 1976. 149 pp.
5425. Ardener, Shirley, ed. PERCEIVING WOMEN. New York: Halsted Press, 1975. 167 pp. Deals with the problems of eliciting the images women hold of themselves, rather than the image in male-centered thought.
5426. Association for Counselor Education. Commission for Women. WOMEN AND ACES: PERSPECTIVES AND ISSUES. Muncie, IN: Accelerated Development, 1975. 120 pp. The status of women in counseling and the status of counseling education programs as they relate to women clients.
5427. Baer, Jean L. HOW TO BE AN ASSERTIVE (NOT AGGRESSIVE) WOMAN IN LIFE, IN LOVE, AND ON THE JOB: A TOTAL GUIDE TO SELF-ASSERTIVENESS. New York: New American Library. 1976. 311 pp. Based on the assumption that it is wrong to be aggressive, teaches women how to say "no," express anger, etc.
5428. Bardwick, Judith M., ed. READINGS ON THE PSYCHOLOGY OF WOMEN. New York: Harper & Row, 1972. 335 pp.
5429. Baum, O. Eugene and Christina Herring. "The Pregnant Psychotherapist in Training: Some Preliminary Findings and Impressions," AMERICAN JOURNAL OF PSYCHIATRY, vol. 132, no. 4 (April 1975), pp. 419-422. Study of the reactions of personnel, patients, and the resident herself to the pregnancy; recommends working toward more understanding and support.
5430. Bloom, Lynn Z., Karen Coburn, and Joan Pearlman. THE NEW ASSERTIVE WOMAN. New York: Delacorte Press, 1975. 230 pp. Distinguishes between aggressive (stepping on toes), assertive (standing up for your rights without stepping on toes), and nonassertive (doing nothing or underhanded sabotage).
5431. Boulette, Teresa Ramirez. DETERMINING NEEDS AND APPROPRIATE COUNSELING APPROACHES FOR MEXICAN-AMERICAN WOMEN: A COMPARISON OF THERAPEUTIC LISTENING AND BEHAVIORAL REHEARSAL. San Francisco, CA: R & E Research Associates, 1976. 127 pp.
5432. Bronzaft, Arline L. "College Women want a Career, Marriage and Children," PSYCHOLOGICAL REPORTS, vol. 35, no. 3 (Dec. 1974), pp. 1031-1034. Results of a survey of 210 female graduating seniors;

79% planned to have a career as well as marry and have children.
5433. Butler, Pamela. SELF-ASSERTION FOR WOMEN: A GUIDE TO BECOMING ANDROGYNOUS. Scranton, PA: Canfield Press, 1976.
5434. Chapman, Joseph Dudley. THE FEMININE MIND AND BODY: THE PSYCHOSEXUAL AND PSYCHOSOMATIC REACTIONS OF WOMEN. New York: Citadel Press, 1968. 325 pp.
5435. Cook, Barbara and Beverly Stone. COUNSELING WOMEN. Boston, MA: Houghton Mifflin, 1973. 114 pp.
5436. Cox, Sue. FEMALE PSYCHOLOGY: THE EMERGING SELF. Chicago, IL: Science Research Associates, 1976.
5437. de Castillejo, Irene Claremont. KNOWING WOMAN: A FEMININE PSYCHOLOGY. New York: G. P. Putnam's Sons, 1973. 188 pp. By a noted Jungian psychologist.
5438. Deutsch, Helene. CONFRONTATIONS WITH MYSELF. New York: W. W. Norton, 1973. 217 pp. Autobiographical memoir of one of the first women analysts of the Freudian era.
5439. DuBrin, Andrew J. WOMEN IN TRANSITION. Springfield, IL: C. C. Thomas, 1972. 178 pp.
5440. Franks, Violet and Vasanti Burtle, eds. WOMEN IN THERAPY: NEW PSYCHOTHERAPIES FOR A CHANGING SOCIETY. New York: Brunner/Mazel, 1974. 441 pp.
5441. Friedman, Richard C., Ralph M. Richart, and Raymond L. Vande Wiele, eds. SEX DIFFERENCES IN BEHAVIOR. New York: John Wiley & Sons, 1974. 495 pp.
5442. Fromme, Allan. A WOMAN'S CRITICAL YEARS. New York: Grosset & Dunlap, 1972. 210 pp. Confronts women with the realities of their emotions to enable them to face personal relationships without fear.
5443. Galenson, Eleanor. "Psychology of Women: (1) Infancy and Early Childhood, (2) Latency and Early Adolescence," JOURNAL OF THE AMERICAN PSYCHOANALYTICAL ASSOCIATION, vol. 24, no. 1 (1976), pp. 141-160.
5444. Gault, Una, ed. "Women and Psychology," AUSTRALIAN PSYCHOLOGIST, vol. 10, no. 3 (Nov. 1975), pp. 291-342. Special Issue. Contributors include Jillian Mears, Norma Grieve, Ann D. Murray, Mary Westbrook, Gordon Stanley, Marilyn Boots, Christina Johnson, Margaret Anderson, The Feminist Psychology Group, Elizabeth Wilson, and Lorraine Dalgleish.
5445. Granger, Peggy. EVERYWOMAN'S GUIDE TO A NEW IMAGE. Millbrae, CA: Les Femmes, 1976. 125 pp.
5446. Grinnell, Robert. ALCHEMY IN A MODERN WOMAN: A STUDY IN THE CONTRASEXUAL ARCHETYPE. New York: Spring Publications, 1973. 181 pp.
5447. Hunt, Gladys. MS. MEANS BEING MYSELF: BEING A WOMAN IN AN UNEASY WORLD. Grand Rapids, MI: Zondervan Publishing House, 1972. 145 pp.
5448. Hyde, Janet Shibley and Benjamin George Rosenberg. HALF THE HUMAN EXPERIENCE: THE PSYCHOLOGY OF WOMEN. Lexington, MA: D. C. Heath, 1975. 306 pp.

5449. Jefferson, Lara (Pseud.). THESE ARE MY SISTERS: A JOURNAL FROM THE INSIDE OF INSANITY. Garden City, NY: Doubleday, 1975. 196 pp. Reprint of 1947 edition. Manuscript written in the "violent ward" of a state hospital, by a woman diagnosed as a schizophrenic.

5450. Jongeward, Dorothy and Dru Scott. WOMEN AS WINNERS: TRANSACTIONAL ANALYSIS FOR PERSONAL GROWTH. Reading, MA: Addison-Wesley, 1976. 318 pp.

5451. Jurjevich, Ratibor-Ray M. NO WATER IN MY CUP: EXPERIENCES AND A CONTROLLED STUDY OF PSYCHOTHERAPY OF DELINQUENT GIRLS. New York: Libra Books, 1968. 185 pp.

5452. Lewis, Judith A., ed. "Women and Counselors," THE PERSONNEL AND GUIDANCE JOURNAL, vol. 51, no. 2 (Oct. 1972), pp. 84-156. Special Issue. Contributors include L. Sunny Hansen, Jean Bernstein, Jane B. Berry, Dorothy Haener, Mary A. Julius Guttman, Shirley Chisholm, Jean Eason, Joyce A. Smith, and Nancy K. Schlossberg.

5453. McHugh, Mary. PSYCHOLOGY AND THE NEW WOMAN New York Franklin Watts, 1976. 114 pp.

5454. Mander, Anica Vesel and Anne Kent Rush. FEMINISM AS THERAPY. New York: Random House, 1975. 127 pp. Integrating mind and body in a feminist consciousness.

5455. Manis, Laura G. WOMANPOWER: A MANUAL FOR WORKSHOPS IN PERSONAL EFFECTIVENESS. Cranston, RI: Carroll Press, 1977.

5456. Martin, Del. BATTERED WIVES. San Francisco, CA: Glide Urban Center Publications, 1976. 269 pp. Analyzes British studies on wife battery and interviews with victims; recommendations include list of hostels (few) available.

5457. Mednick, Martha, Tamara Schuch, Sandra Schwartz Tangri, and Lois Wladis Hoffman, eds. WOMEN AND ACHIEVEMENT: SOCIAL AND MOTIVATIONAL ANALYSIS. New York: Halsted Press, 1975. 447 pp.

5458. Miller, Jean Baker. TOWARD A NEW PSYCHOLOGY OF WOMEN. Boston, MA: Beacon Press, 1976. 143 pp. Urges redefinition of sex roles away from traditional (Freudian) concepts.

5459. Mitchell, Juliet. PSYCHOANALYSIS AND FEMINISM. New York: Pantheon Books, 1974. 456 pp. Tries to rehabilitate Freud for feminists by developing a new "interface" between fathers and mothers in the family.

5460. "New Tensions in Women," SIMMONS REVIEW, vol. 58, no. 4 (Late Summer—Early Fall, 1976). Special Issue. Contributors include Alice S. Rossi, Deanne R. Peterson, Susan Aucella, Suzanne Langdon, Jannie John, Cynthia Naturale, J. En-York Wu, Judith Burke, Phyllis Whitman, Leah-Rachel Hoffman, Hilary Sametz, Colleen Winn, Cherylle Young, Nancy Farber, Katherine Morris, Deborah Bemstein, Beverly White, Catherine Wilson, Christine Rand, Ellen Barlow, and Kathryn Furlong.

5461. Phelps, Stanlee and Nancy Austin. THE ASSERTIVE WOMAN. Fredricksburg, VA: IMPACT Publications, 1975. 177 pp. Focuses on assisting women to overcome anxiety in decision-making.

5462. Rawlings, Edna and Dianne K. Carter. PSYCHOTHERAPY FOR WOMEN: TREATMENT TOWARD EQUALITY. Springfield, IL: Charles C. Thomas, 1977.

5463. Schreiber, Flora Rheta. SYBIL. New York: Warner Paperback Library, 1974. 359 pp. The true story of a woman possessed by sixteen separate personalities.

5464. Sherman, Julia Ann. ON THE PSYCHOLOGY OF WOMAN: A SURVEY OF EMPIRICAL STUDIES. Springfield, IL: Charles C. Thomas, 1975. 304 pp. First issued in 1971.

5465. Strouse, Jean, ed. WOMEN AND ANALYSIS: DIALOGUES ON PSYCHOANALYTIC VIEWS OF FEMININITY. New York: Grossman Publishers, 1974. 375 pp. Presents a series of analytic writers, such as Freud, Deutsch, and Jung, and comments assessing the bases for determining femininity, i.e. history, culture, biology, psychology, and personality.

5466. Taubman, Bryna. HOW TO BECOME AN ASSERTIVE WOMAN. New York: Pocket Books, 1976. 214 pp.

5467. Thomas, William Isaac. UNADJUSTED GIRL, WITH CASES AND STANDPOINT FOR BEHAVIOR ANALYSIS. Montclair, NJ: Patterson Smith Publishing, 1969. 261 pp. Reprint of 1923 edition. Case studies of delinquent girls.

5468. Unger, Rhoda and Florence L. Denmark. WOMAN: DEPENDENT OR INDEPENDENT VARIABLE. New York: Psychological Dimensions, 1977.

5469. Weissman, Myrna and Eugene S. Paykel. THE DEPRESSED WOMAN: A STUDY OF SOCIAL RELATIONSHIPS. Chicago, IL: Univ. of Chicago Press, 1974. 289 pp.

5470. Williams, Elizabeth Friar. NOTES OF A FEMINIST THERAPIST. New York: Praeger Books, 1976. 194 pp. How psychotherapy can help women attain feminist objectives; emphasizes that external oppression, in addition to internal factors, contributes to personal depression and mental illness.

5471. Wilson, Pauline P. COLLEGE WOMEN WHO EXPRESS FUTILITY: A STUDY BASED ON FIFTY SELECTED LIFE HISTORIES OF WOMEN COLLEGE GRADUATES. New York: AMS Press, 1972. 166 pp. Reprint of 1950 edition.

5472. Wolkon, Kenneth A., Catherine M. Sobota, Elizabeth Useem, and Nancy P. White. "Counseling Girls and Women: A Guide for Jewish and Other Minority Women." Washington, D.C.: B'nai B'rith Career Counseling, 1973.

5473. Yates, Martha. COPING: A SURVIVAL MANUAL FOR WOMEN ALONE. Englewood Cliffs, NJ: Prentice-Hall, 1976.

IX. WOMEN IN ANTHROPOLOGY

*"That past which is so presumptuously brought forward as a precedent for the
present, was itself founded on some past that went before it."*
— Madame de Staël

5474. Andreski, Iris. OLD WIVES' TALES—LIFE STORIES OF AFRICAN
WOMEN. New York: Schocken Books, 1970. 190 pp. Stories and
biographies of more than 24 elderly women of the Ibibio of
Southeastern Nigeria. Discusses rituals and ceremonies.

5475. Ardener, Shirley G. "Sexual Insult and Female Militancy," MAN, vol. 8,
no. 3 (1973), pp. 422-440. Instances of female militancy in response to
insults are described among the Bakweri, the Balong, and the Kom of
West Cameroon.

5476. Aswad, Barbara C. "Visiting Patterns Among Women of the Elite in a
Small Turkish City," ANTHROPOLOGICAL QUARTERLY, vol. 47,
no. 1 (Jan. 1974), pp. 9-27. Social rituals of women. See also Peter
Benedict.

5477. Benedict, Peter. "Kabal günü: Structured Visiting in an Anatolian
Provincial Town," ANTHROPOLOGICAL QUARTERLY, vol. 47, no.
1 (Jan. 1974), pp. 28-47. See also Barbara C. Aswad.

5478. Borun, Minda, Molly McLaughlin, Gina Oboler, Norma Perchonock, and
Lorraine Sexton. "Women's Liberation: An Anthropological View."
Pittsburgh, KNOW, Inc., 1972. 69 pp.

5479. Fisbie, C. J. A STUDY OF THE NAVAHO GIRLS' PUBERTY
CEREMONY. Middletown, CT: Wesleyan Univ. Press, 1967.

5480. Golde, Peggy, ed. WOMEN IN THE FIELD: ANTHROPOLOGICAL
EXPERIENCES. Chicago, IL: Aldine Publishing, 1970. 343 pp.
Intensive interviews with 12 female anthropologists.

5481. Jones, Bessie and Bess Lomax Hawes. STEP IT DOWN: GAMES, PLAYS,
SONGS, AND STORIES FOR THE AFRO-AMERICAN HERITAGE.
New York: Harper & Row, 1972. 233 pp. The memoirs of a Black
woman through her entertainment; a cultural digest.

5482. Little, Kenneth. "Some Methodological Considerations in the Study of
African Women's Urban Roles," URBAN ANTHROPOLOGY, vol. 4,
no. 2 (1975), pp. 107-121. Urges that women's current roles be
analyzed in terms of the culture from which the women came, rather
than using Western models.

5483. Martin, M. Kay and Barbara Voorhies. FEMALE OF THE SPECIES. New
York: Columbia Univ. Press, 1975. 432 pp. Discusses the treatment of
women in traditional and contemporary evolutionary theory,
emphasizing factors affecting women's control over their own destinies.

5484. Mathieu, Nicole-Claude. "Homme-Culture et Femme-Nature? [Man as
Culture and Woman as Nature?]" L'HOMME, vol. 13, no. 3 (1973), pp.
101-113.

5485. Matthiason, Carolyn J., ed. MANY SISTERS: WOMEN IN
      CROSS-CULTURAL PERSPECTIVE. Riverside, NJ: Free Press, 1974.
      443 pp.
5486. Mead, Margaret. RUTH BENEDICT. New York: Columbia Univ. Press,
      1974. 180 pp. Biography of the noted anthropologist who broke out of
      the restrictions of woman's role, but was continually at the mercy of
      male professionals.
5487. ———. SEX AND TEMPERAMENT IN THREE PRIMITIVE SOCIETIES.
      New York: William Morrow, 1963. 335 pp. Reprint of 1935 edition.
5488. Murphy, Yoland and Robert F. Murphy. WOMEN OF THE FOREST.
      New York: Columbia Univ. Press, 1974. 236 pp. Life among the
      Mundurucu, an Indian tribe of Amazonian Brazil.
5489. Reed, Evelyn. WOMAN'S EVOLUTION: FROM MATRIARCHAL CLAN
      TO PATRIARCHAL FAMILY. New York: Pathfinder Press, 1975. 510
      pp. The importance of the matriarchal system and the reasons for its
      decline.
5490. Reiter, Rayna R. TOWARD AN ANTHROPOLOGY OF WOMEN. New
      York: Monthly Review Press, 1975. 416 pp.
5491. Robles Mendo, Caridad. ANTROPOLOGIA DE LA MUJER MARROQUI
      MUSULMANA. Tetuan, España: Editora Marroqui (Institute General
      Franco de Estudios e Envestigacion Hispano-Arabe), 1953. 142 pp.
5492. Rohrlich-Leavitt, Ruby, ed. WOMEN CROSS-CULTURALLY: CHANGE
      AND CHALLENGE. Chicago, IL: Aldine Publishing, 1975. 669 pp.
5493. Strathern, Marilyn. WOMEN IN BETWEEN: FEMALE ROLES IN A
      MALE WORLD, MOUNT HAGEN, NEW GUINEA. New York:
      Academic Press, 1972. 372 pp.
5494. Van Baal, J. RECIPROCITY AND THE POSITION OF WOMEN:
      ANTHROPOLOGICAL PAPERS. Atlantic Highlands, NJ: Humanities
      Press, 1976.
5495. "Women and Migration," ANTHROPOLOGICAL QUARTERLY, vol. 49,
      no. 1 (Jan. 1976), pp. 1-76. Special Issue. Contributors include
      Judith-Maria Hess Buechler, Harriet Bloch, Bette S. Denich, M. Estelle
      Smith, Nancy Foner, Nancie L. Gonzalez, Jean Gossen, Margaret
      Gulick, John Gulick, and Anthony Leeds.

X. WOMEN IN ECONOMICS

A. The Economic Position of Women—General

"Money is like a sixth sense—and you can't make use of the other five without it."
—(William) Somerset Maugham

"I have heard a lot of opinions about the life of Russian women and the way they are dressed. But the worst work for a woman is prostitution. . . . In Paris you cannot walk down the street without having a woman accost you in order to subsist. Here in Russia, if a woman works like a man, she is at least not in a degrading situation but honestly earns her living."
—Nikita Sergeevich Khrushchev

5496. Ahern, Dee Dee and Betsy Bliss. THE ECONOMICS OF BEING A WOMAN: OR, WHAT YOUR MOTHER NEVER TOLD YOU. Riverside, NJ: Macmillan, 1976. 212 pp.

5497. Ambassade de France. Service de Presse et d'Information. THE FRENCH WORKING WOMEN. New York: Service de Presse et d'Information, 1974.

5498. Angel, Juvenal Londoño. MATCHING COLLEGE WOMEN TO JOBS. New York: World Trade Academy Press, 1973.

5499. Avery, Edwina Austin. IT DID HAPPEN HERE: WOMAN AS MARGINAL LABOR AFTER THE FIRST WORLD WAR. New York: Vantage Press, 1975. 260 pp.

5500. Berent, Jerzy. "Some Demographic Aspects of Female Employment in Eastern Europe and the U.S.S.R.," INTERNATIONAL LABOUR REVIEW, vol. 101, no. 2 (Feb. 1970), pp. 175-192.

5501. Bird, Caroline. ENTERPRISING WOMEN: THEIR CONTRIBUTION TO THE AMERICAN ECONOMY, 1776-1976. New York: New American Library, 1976. 216 pp. 23 chapters illustrate the various roles women have played in the development of America's economy, e.g. Mary Goddard who printed the first signed copies of the Declaration of Independence, Lucy Taylor the first woman dentist, and Tillie Lewis who introduced the Italian tomato industry to California.

5502. ———. EVERYTHING A WOMAN NEEDS TO KNOW TO GET PAID WHAT SHE'S WORTH. New York: David McKay, 1973. 304 pp.

5503. Bobroff, Anne. "The Bolsheviks and Working Women, 1905-1920," SOVIET STUDIES, vol. 26, no. 4 (Oct. 1974), pp. 540-567. Details the conflict between the Bolshevik party philosophy that unity was the tool to end economic oppression of all workers, and the separatist needs of the women workers.

5504. Bodichon, Mrs. Barbara L. "Women and Work." New York: C. S. Francis, 1859. 35 pp. Introduction by Catherine M. Sedgwick.

5505. Brandt, Catherine. A WOMAN'S MONEY: HOW TO PROTECT AND INCREASE IT IN THE STOCK MARKET. New York: Cornerstone Library, 1971. 192 pp.

5506. Brophy, Mrs. Loire. IF WOMEN MUST WORK. New York: D. Appleton-Century, 1936. 153 pp. Written by a vocational guidance counselor; concerned with questions such as "How can I get a job?" and "How can I keep my job?"

5507. Brown, Janet Welsh, Julia Graham Lear, and Donna Lee Shavlik. "Effecting Social Change for Women: Relating Research and Action: Workshops on Achieving Economic Parity for Women." Washington, D.C.: Federation of Organizations for Professional Women, 1976. 40 pp. Appendices are available.

5508. Brownlee, W. Elliot and Mary M. Brownlee. WOMEN IN THE AMERICAN ECONOMY: A DOCUMENTARY HISTORY, 1695-1929. New Haven, CT: Yale Univ. Press, 1976. 360 pp. Selection of source readings exploring the varied experience of women in the marketplace before the impact of the Great Depression and World War II.

5509. Butler, Josephine Elizabeth, ed. WOMEN'S WORK AND WOMEN'S CULTURE. New York: Gordon Press, 1976. 367 pp. Reprint of 1896 edition. Ten essays about education, the professions, marriage, and financial status by such persons as Sophia Jex-Blake.

5510. Chapman, Jane Roberts, ed. ECONOMIC INDEPENDENCE FOR WOMEN: THE FOUNDATION FOR EQUAL RIGHTS. Beverly Hills, CA: Sage, 1976. 285 pp. Collection of ten essays discussing the current economic condition of American women.

5511. Corrective Collective. NEVER DONE: THREE CENTURIES OF WOMEN'S WORK IN CANADA. Toronto, Ontario: Canadian Women's Educational Press, 1974. 150 pp. Covers the period from 1650 through 1915.

5512. Cowley, Susan Cheever, Mary Lord, and Lisa Whitman. "Women at Work," NEWSWEEK (Dec. 6, 1976), pp. 68-81. Overview of women in the labor force, their economic contribution, and fields of endeavor.

5513. Dall, Caroline W. WOMAN'S RIGHT TO LABOR: OR, LOW WAGES AND HARD WORK: IN THREE LECTURES DELIVERED IN BOSTON, NOVEMBER, 1859. Boston, MA: Walker, Wise, 1860. 184 pp. Study of the legal status of employed women. See also Marie E. Zakrzewska.

5514. Darling, Martha, ed. THE ROLE OF WOMEN IN THE ECONOMY: SUMMARY OF TEN NATIONAL REPORTS. Washington, D.C.: Organization for Economic Cooperation and Development, Publications Center, 1975. 128 pp.

5515. Daubie, Julia. LA FEMME PAUVRE AU DIX-NEUVIEME SIECK. CONDITION ECONOMIQUE. CONDITION PROFESSIONNELLE. New York: Clearwater Publishing, 1974. 3 vols. Reprint of 1869 edition.

5516. Davies, Margaret Llewelyn, ed. LIFE AS WE HAVE KNOWN IT: WORKING WOMEN DESCRIBE THEIR JOBS, FAMILIES, AND POLITICAL AWAKENING IN EARLY TWENTIETH CENTURY ENGLAND. New York: W. W. Norton, 1975. 141 pp. Reprint of 1931 edition.

5517. Elizaga, Juan C. "The Participation of Women in the Labour Force of Latin America: Fertility and Other Factors," INTERNATIONAL LABOUR REVIEW, vol. 109, no. 5-6 (May-June 1974), pp. 519-538. Fertility rate appears to be less important than improving levels of education and structural changes in the general economy of the Latin American countries in increasing the labour force participation of women.

5518. Erb, Charlotte. "Do Women Invest Wisely? A Study of Savings for Retirement." Washington, D.C.: Business and Professional Women's Foundation, 1970. 7 pp. Concludes that women need economic counseling to help them assess their current financial status and status after retirement.

5519. Flynn, John T. "Hetty Green: The Miser," in MEN OF WEALTH: THE STORY OF 12 SIGNIFICANT FORTUNES FROM THE RENAISSANCE TO THE PRESENT DAY. New York: Simon & Schuster, 1941. Pp. 215-249.

5520. Fullam, Maryellen. "Half the World: Women and Economic Development," CIVIL RIGHTS DIGEST, vol. 7, no. 4 (Summer 1975), pp. 3-12.

5521. Gadgil, Dhananjaya Ramchandra. "Women in the Working Force in India." New York: Asia Publishing House, 1965. 33 pp.

5522. Galenson, Marjorie. WOMEN AT WORK: AN INTERNATIONAL COMPARISON. Ithaca, NY: New York State School of Industrial and Labor Relations, Cornell Univ., 1973. 120 pp.

5523. Gales, Kathleen E. and P. H. Marks. "Twentieth Century Trends in the Work of Women in England and Wales," JOURNAL OF ROYAL STATISTICAL SOCIETY, series A, vol. 137, part I (1974), pp. 60-74.

5524. Great Britain. Dept. of Employment. "Women and Work: Overseas Practice." London, England: Her Majesty's Stationery Office, 1975. 96 pp.

5525. –––. "Women and Work: A review." London, England: Her Majesty's Stationery Office, 1975. 63 pp.

5526. –––. "Women and Work: Sex Differences and Society." London, England: Her Majesty's Stationery Office, 1974. 36 pp.

5527. –––. "Women and Work: A Statistical Survey." London, England: Her Majesty's Stationery Office, 1974. 71 pp.

5528. Gubbels, Robert. LA CITOYENNETE ECONOMIQUE DE LA FEMME [THE ECONOMIC CITIZENSHIP OF WOMEN]. Brussels, Belgium: Editions de l'Institut de Sociologie, 1966.

5529. Halifax Women's Bureau. WOMEN AT WORK IN NOVA SCOTIA. Toronto, Ontario: Canadian Women's Educational Press, 1973.

5530. Hall, Cynthia Holcomb. "The Working Woman and the Federal Income Tax," AMERICAN BAR ASSOCIATION JOURNAL, vol. 61, no. 6 (June 1975), pp. 716-720. Review of some major features of the Internal Revenue Code by a judge of the U.S. Tax Court.

5531. International Labour Organization. EQUALITY OF OPPORTUNITY AND TREATMENT FOR WOMEN WORKERS. Geneva, Switzerland:

International Labour Office, 1975. 123 pp. Excellent and well-documented study of women's evolving status in the workforce, including recommendations for promoting equality of treatment.

5532. —––. WOMEN WORKERS AND SOCIETY: INTERNATIONAL PERSPECTIVES. Geneva, Switzerland: International Labour Office, 1976.

5533. Jackson, Larry R. "Welfare Mothers and Black Liberation," THE BLACK SCHOLAR, vol. 1, no. 6 (April 1970), pp. 31-37. Women are organizing for provision of the basic necessities of life, food and shelter, rather than political rhetoric.

5534. James, Alice. "Poverty: Canada's Legacy to Women." Vancouver, B.C.: Vancouver Women's Caucus, 1970. 24 pp.

5535. Kahne, Hilda and Andrew I. Kohen. "Economic Perspectives on the Roles of Women in the American Economy," JOURNAL OF ECONOMIC LITERATURE, vol. 13, no. 4 (Dec. 1975), pp. 1249-1292. Review of the literature, discussion of the changing roles of women, and predictions of future trends in labor force activity. Includes 267-citation bibliography.

5536. Kapur, Promilla. THE CHANGING STATUS OF THE WORKING WOMAN IN INDIA. Delhi, India: Vikas Publishing House, 1974. 178 pp.

5537. Keyserling, Mary Dublin. "The Economic Status of Women in the United States," AMERICAN ECONOMIC REVIEW, vol. 66, no. 2 (May 1976), pp. 205-212.

5538. Kievet, Mary Bach. "Review and Synthesis of Research for Women in the World of Work." Columbus, OH: Ohio State Univ., ERIC Clearing House on Vocational and Technical Education, 1972. 91 pp. Includes 229–citation bibliography.

5539. Kreps, Juanita M., ed. WOMEN AND THE AMERICAN ECONOMY: A LOOK TO THE 1980's. Englewood Cliffs, NJ: Prentice-Hall, 1976. 177 pp. By the Secretary of Commerce during the Carter administration.

5540. Kreps, Juanita M. and Robert Clark. "Sex, Age, and Work: The Changing Composition of the Work Force." Baltimore, MD: Johns Hopkins Press, 1976. 95 pp. Discusses the impact of the changing composition of the work force on full employment programs and policies, and concentrating on the labor force supply rather than demand.

5541. Kutner, Luis. THE INTELLIGENT WOMAN'S GUIDE TO FUTURE SECURITY. New York: Dodd, Mead, 1970. 202 pp. Common sense advice about wills, probate, estate and tax planning, insurance, finances, social security, etc.

5542. Laselle, Mary A. THE YOUNG WOMAN WORKER. New York: The Pilgrim Press, 1914. 189 pp.

5543. Lederer, Muriel and the Editors of Consumer Guide. NEW OPPORTUNITIES FOR WOMEN. New York: Simon & Schuster, 1975. 275 pp.

5544. McKensie, Paige. HEAVENS HELP THE WORKING GIRL. Bronxville, NY: Franconia Publishing, 1972. 268 pp.

5545. Mallan, Lucy B. "Women Born in the Early 1900's: Employment, Earnings, and Benefit Levels," SOCIAL SECURITY BULLETIN, vol. 37, no. 3 (March 1974), pp. 3-25. Statistical report on the background for Social Security benefit differences between men and women eligible for retirement in 1970.

5546. Markoff, Helene S. "The Federal Women's Program," PUBLIC ADMINISTRATION REVIEW, vol. 32, no. 2 (March-April 1972), pp. 144-149. The history of women in federal government employment is outlined.

5547. Medsger, Betty. WOMEN AT WORK: A PHOTOGRAPHIC DOCUMENTARY. New York: Sheed & Ward, 1975. 212 pp.

5548. Meyer, Annie Nathan, ed. WOMAN'S WORK IN AMERICA. New York: Arno Press, 1972. 457 pp. Reprint of 1891 edition. Introduction by Julia Ward Howe. 18 articles by authorities in their fields describing the transition period when women were not welcomed in male-dominated areas.

5549. Mickelwait, Donald R., Mary Ann Riegelman, and Charles F. Sweet. WOMEN IN RURAL DEVELOPMENT: A SURVEY OF THE ROLES OF WOMEN IN GHANA, LESOTHO, KENYA, NIGERIA, BOLIVIA, PARAGUAY, AND PERU. Boulder, CO: Westview Press, 1976. 224 pp. Seven-country survey concluding, in part, that integration of women into economic life will take place more rapidly within the context of total rural development, rather than women-only projects.

5550. Miller, Miriam, ed. "Third World Women," UNICEF NEWS, issue 76 (July 1973), pp. 1-31. Special Issue. Contributors include Helvi Sipila, Donald A. Allan, Alastair Matheson, Claudia Dreifus, M. A. Kankalil, and Sumalee Viravaidya.

5551. Milwaukee County Welfare Rights Association. WELFARE MOTHERS SPEAK OUT: WE AIN'T GONNA SHUFFLE NO MORE. New York: W. W. Norton, 1972. 190 pp. Account of the way in which the poor are treated.

5552. Mossell, Mrs. N. F. THE WORK OF THE AFRO-AMERICAN WOMAN. Freeport, NY: Books for Libraries, 1971. 178 pp. Reprint of 1894 edition.

5553. Nash, June and Helen Icken Safa, eds. SEX AND CLASS IN LATIN AMERICA. New York: Praeger Publishing, 1976. 340 pp. Synthesizes results of recent studies on sex differences in industrial, agricultural, and domestic work and their relation to labor force exploitations.

5554. "New Women in New China." New York: China Books & Periodicals, 1973. 80 pp. Current political and economic status of Chinese women.

5555. Oliphant, Mrs. Rosamond D. "Woman's Work." Cincinnati, OH: C. T. Woodrow, 1881. 35 pp.

5556. O'Neill, William L., ed. WOMEN AT WORK. New York: Quadrangle Books, 1972. 303 pp. Reprint of 1905 edition.

5557. Padan-Eisenstark, Dorit D. "Are Israeli Women Really Equal? Trends and Patterns of Israeli Women's Labor Force Participation: A Comparative Analysis," JOURNAL OF MARRIAGE AND THE FAMILY, vol. 35, no. 3 (Aug. 1973), pp. 538-545.

5558. Penny, Virginia. HOW WOMEN CAN MAKE MONEY, MARRIED OR SINGLE, IN ALL BRANCHES OF THE ARTS AND SCIENCES, PROFESSIONS, TRADES, AGRICULTURAL AND MECHANICAL PURSUITS. New York: Arno Press, 1971. 500 pp. Reprint of 1870 edition. Describes working conditions in the U.S. and other countries, pay rates, and extent of participation of women; proves that there are at least 500 jobs that women can do as well as men.

5559. Pinder, Pauline. WOMEN AT WORK. London, England: Political and Economic Planning, 1969. 131 pp.

5560. Rein, Mildred. WORK OR WELFARE: FACTORS IN THE CHOICE FOR AFDC MOTHERS. New York: Praeger Books, 1974. 144 pp. Emphasizes welfare policy, cultural, and situational factors in the decision.

5561. Republica de Panama. Ministerio de Desarrollo Agropecuario. Dirreccion General de Desarrollo Social. "La Mujer Dentro del Desarrollo Rural Panameño." Republica de Panama: Department de Promocion y Comunicacion Social, 1975. 20 pp. The role and status of women in the Republic of Panama.

5562. Sacks, Michael Paul. WOMEN'S WORK IN SOVIET RUSSIA: CONTINUITY IN THE MIDST OF CHANGE. New York: Praeger Books, 1976. 240 pp. Evaluates economic and social status of women in industrialized Soviet economy over the last 20 years.

5563. San Francisco Women's History Group. "What Have Women Done? A Photo Essay on the History of Working Women in the U.S." San Francisco, CA: United Front Press, 1974. 58 pp.

5564. Schwartz, Felice N. "New Work Patterns—for Better Use of Womanpower," MANAGEMENT REVIEW, vol. 63, no. 5 (May 1974), pp. 4-12. Discusses various flexible scheduling options, including consultant positions and paired positions.

5565. Seear, B. N. RE-ENTRY OF WOMEN TO THE LABOUR MARKET AFTER AN INTERRUPTION IN EMPLOYMENT. Paris, France: Organization for Economic Cooperation and Development, 1971. 135 pp.

5566. Seear, Nancy. "The Economic Position of Women in the United Kingdom," AMERICAN ECONOMIC REVIEW, vol. 66, no. 2 (May 1976), pp. 213-221.

5567. Seed, Suzanne. SATURDAY'S CHILD: 36 WOMEN TALK ABOUT THEIR JOBS. New York: Bantam Books, 1974. 184 pp. Interviews and photographs.

5568. Seidenberg, Robert. CORPORATE WIVES—CORPORATE CASUALTIES. Garden City, NY: Doubleday, 1975. 177 pp. The unique problems facing the executive wife of the 1970's.

5569. Seifer, Nancy. "Absent from the Majority: Working Class Women in America." New York: The American Jewish Committee, Institute of Human Relations, 1973.

5570. Sherman, Sally R. "Labor-Force Status of Nonmarried Women on the Threshold of Retirement," SOCIAL SECURITY BULLETIN (Sept.

1974), pp. 3-15. Examines the effects of age, marital status, race, and education on the likelihood of being in the labor force.

5571. Sommers, Dixie. "Occupational Rankings for Men and Women by Earnings," MONTHLY LABOR REVIEW, vol. 97, no. 8 (Aug. 1974), pp. 34-51. Data extrapolated from the 1970 Census of Population.

5572. Sorkin, A. L. "On the Occupational Status of Women, 1870-1970," AMERICAN JOURNAL OF ECONOMICS AND SOCIOLOGY, vol. 32, no. 3 (July 1973), pp. 235-243.

5573. Struyk, R. J. "Explaining Variations in the Hourly Wage Rates of Urban Minority Group Females," JOURNAL OF HUMAN RESOURCES, vol. 8, no. 3 (Summer 1973), pp. 349-364. Women are unable to exercise workchoice because of family income constraints.

5574. Tinker, Irene and Michele Bo Bramson, eds. WOMEN AND WORLD DEVELOPMENT. New York: Praeger Books, 1976. 382 pp. Summarizes the proceedings of the American Association for the Advancement of Science conference in Mexico City (June 1975), including recommendations of the workshops: urban affairs, education and communication, professional organization, nutrition and family planning, and food preparation and small technology.

5575. Tsuchigave, Robert and Norton Dodge. ECONOMIC DISCRIMINATION AGAINST WOMEN IN THE UNITED STATES: MEASURES AND CHANGES. Lexington, MA: Lexington Books, 1974. 152 pp.

5576. United Nations. Development Programme. "Integration of Women in Development: Why, When, How." By Ester Boserup and Christina Liljencrantz. New York: United Nations, 1975. 42 pp. Overview of the role of women in economic development.

5577. United Nations. Division of Human Rights (in Cooperation with the Government of the U.S.S.R.). SEMINAR ON THE PARTICIPATION OF WOMEN IN THE ECONOMIC LIFE OF THEIR COUNTRIES (WITH REFERENCE TO THE IMPLEMENTATION OF ARTICLE 10 OF THE DECLARATION ON THE ELIMINATION OF DISCRIMINATION AGAINST WOMEN). New York: United Nations, 1970. 116 pp.

5578. U.S. Civil Service Commission. Bureau of Intergovernmental Personnel Programs. "Equal Employment Opportunity Court Cases." Washington, D.C.: SUDOC, GPO, 1976. 86 pp.

5579. ———. "Equal Employment Opportunity Court Cases." Washington, D.C.: SUDOC, GPO, 1974. 81 pp.

5580. U.S. Civil Service Commission. Manpower Statistics Division. Bureau of Manpower Information Systems. STUDY OF EMPLOYMENT OF WOMEN IN THE FEDERAL GOVERNMENT: 1975. Washington, D.C.: SUDOC, GPO, 1976. 355 pp.

5581. ———. STUDY OF EMPLOYMENT OF WOMEN IN THE FEDERAL GOVERNMENT: 1974. Washington, D.C.: SUDOC, GPO, 1976. 358 pp.

5582. ———. STUDY OF EMPLOYMENT OF WOMEN IN THE FEDERAL GOVERNMENT: 1973. Washington, D.C.: SUDOC, GPO, 1974. 243 pp.

5583. ———. STUDY OF EMPLOYMENT OF WOMEN IN THE FEDERAL GOVERNMENT: 1972. Washington, D.C.: SUDOC, GPO, 1973. 239 pp.

5584. ———. STUDY OF EMPLOYMENT OF WOMEN IN THE FEDERAL GOVERNMENT: 1971. Washington, D.C.: SUDOC, GPO, 1973. 184 pp.

5585. - ———. STUDY OF EMPLOYMENT OF WOMEN IN THE FEDERAL GOVERNMENT: 1970. Washington, D.C.: SUDOC, GPO, 1972. 236 pp.

5586. U.S. Commission on Civil Rights. MINORITIES AND WOMEN AS GOVERNMENT CONTRACTORS. Washington, D.C.: U.S. Commission on Civil Rights, 1975. 189 pp. Analyzes the extent to which women and minorities share in federal, state, and local government contracts, problems encountered in seeking contracts, and the extent to which non-minority women are entitled to participate.

5587. ———. WOMEN AND POVERTY: STAFF REPORT. Washington, D.C.: SUDOC, GPO, 1974.

5588. U.S. Congress. House. Select Committee on Aging. Subcommittee on Retirement Income and Employment. "Income Security for Older Women: Path to Equality." 94th Congress, 1st Session. Washington, D.C.: SUDOC, GPO, 1975. 34 pp. Analysis of flaws and inequities in the Social Security system.

5589. U.S. Congress. Joint Economic Committee. HEARINGS ON THE ECONOMIC PROBLEMS OF WOMEN. 93rd Congress, 1st Session. Washington, D.C.: SUDOC, GPO, 1973. Part I (July 10-12, 1973), 220 pp.; Part II (July 24-26, 1973), pp. 221-441; Part III "Statements for the Record," pp. 443-579. Congresswoman Martha W. Griffiths presiding.

5590. U.S. Congress. Senate. Special Committee on Aging. WOMEN AND SOCIAL SECURITY, Parts 18 and 19 (Oct. 22-23, 1975) of the HEARINGS ON FUTURE DIRECTIONS IN SOCIAL SECURITY. 94th Congress, 1st Session. Washington, D.C.: SUDOC, GPO, 1976. Pp. 1665-1786.

5591. ———. "Women and Social Security: Adapting to a New Era, A Working Paper." Prepared by the Task Force on Women and Social Security. Washington, D.C.: SUDOC, GPO, 1975. 87 pp.

5592. U.S. Dept. of Health, Education, and Welfare. Social Security Administration. "A Woman's Guide to Social Security." Washington, D.C.: SUDOC, GPO, 1975. 12 pp.

5593. U.S. Dept. of Labor. Bureau of Labor Statistics. "U.S. Working Women: A Chartbook." Washington, D.C.: SUDOC, GPO, 1975. 57 pp. Data on the characteristics of the American female labor force, covering the past 25 years.

5594. U.S. Dept. of Labor. Employment Standards Administration. Women's Bureau. 1975 HANDBOOK ON WOMEN WORKERS. Washington, D.C.: SUDOC, GPO, 1975. 435 pp. Statistical data on female participation in the work force.

5595. U.S. Dept. of Labor. Manpower Administration. DUAL CAREERS: A LONGITUDINAL STUDY OF LABOR MARKET EXPERIENCE OF WOMEN, VOLUME 4. Washington, D.C.: SUDOC, GPO, 1976. 328 pp. (Note: "On November 12, 1975, the Secretary of Labor announced a change in name from the Manpower Administration (MA) to the Employment and Training Administration (ETA).")

5596. – – –. DUAL CAREERS: A LONGITUDINAL STUDY OF LABOR MARKET EXPERIENCE OF WOMEN, VOLUME 3. Washington, D.C.: SUDOC, GPO, 1975. 192 pp.

5597. – – –. DUAL CAREERS: A LONGITUDINAL STUDY OF LABOR MARKET EXPERIENCE OF WOMEN, VOLUME 2. Washington, D.C.: SUDOC, GPO, 1973. 133 pp.

5598. – – –. DUAL CAREERS: A LONGITUDINAL STUDY OF LABOR MARKET EXPERIENCE OF WOMEN, VOLUME 1. Washington, D.C.: SUDOC, GPO, 1970. 285 pp.

5599. – – –. YEARS FOR DECISION: A LONGITUDINAL STUDY OF THE EDUCATIONAL AND LABOR MARKET EXPERIENCES OF YOUNG WOMEN. By Roger D. Roderick and Andrew I. Kohen. Washington, D.C.: SUDOC, GPO, 1973. 3 vols.

5600. U.S. Dept. of Labor. Women's Bureau. "The Woman Wage Earner, Her Situation Today." Prepared by Elisabeth D. Benham. Washington, D.C.: USGPO, 1939. 56 pp.

5601. – – -. WOMEN'S OCCUPATIONS THROUGH SEVEN DECADES. By Janet W. Hooks. Washington, D.C.: Zenger Publications, 1976. Reprint of 1947 edition.

5602. University of Wisconsin-Extension. Women's Education Resources. WOMEN'S WORK–UP FROM .878: REPORT ON THE DOT (DICTIONARY OF OCCUPATIONAL TITLES) RESEARCH PROJECT. Prepared by Mary Witt and Patricia K. Naherny. Madison, Univ. of Wisconsin-Extension, 1975. 143 pp.

5603. Verma, P.C. "Trend-Analysis of Woman Employment in India in the Organized Sector," ECONOMIC AFFAIRS, vol. 20, no. 11 (Nov. 1975), pp. 441-445.

5604. Vogel-Polsky, Elaine. LES CONDITIONS DE TRAVAIL DES FEMMES SALARIÉES DANS SIX PAYS DES COMMUNAUTÉS EUROPÉENNES. Paris, France: Mouton, 1975.

5605. Wallace, Phyllis A. PATHWAYS TO WORK: UNEMPLOYMENT AMONG BLACK FEMALE TEENAGERS. Lexington, MA: Lexington Books, 1974. 116 pp. Study of work force participation rates among young black women in New York City; recommendations for remedy.

5606. Washburn, Charles. COME INTO MY PARLOR: A BIOGRAPHY OF THE ARISTOCRATIC EVERLEIGH SISTERS OF CHICAGO. New York: National Library Press, 1934. 255 pp. Story of Aida and Minna Simms who successfully ran the most luxurious bordello in Chicago.

5607. Waugh, Catherine G. "Women's Wages." Rockford, IL: Daily Gazette Office, 1888. 54 pp.

5608. Wertheimer, Barbara Meyer. WE WERE THERE: THE STORY OF

WORKING WOMEN IN AMERICA. Westminster, MD: Pantheon Books, 1977. 427 pp. Women's involvement in work from Colonial days to the textile mill strikes, shortly before World War I.

5609. Wightwick, M. Irene. VOCATIONAL INTEREST PATTERNS: A DEVELOPMENTAL STUDY OF COLLEGE WOMEN. New York: AMS Press, 1972. 231 pp. Reprint of 1945 edition.

5610. Willard, Frances Elizabeth, Helen M. Winslow, and Sally Joy White. OCCUPATIONS FOR WOMEN: A BOOK OF PRACTICAL SUGGESTIONS FOR THE MATERIAL ADVANCEMENT, THE MENTAL AND PHYSICAL DEVELOPMENT, AND THE MORAL AND SPIRITUAL UPLIFT OF WOMEN. Washington, D.C.: Zenger Publications, 1976. 504 pp. Reprint of 1897 edition.

5611. Williams, Lady. "The Changing Pattern of Women's Employment." London, England: Liverpool Univ. Press, 1965. 16 pp.

5612. Wisconsin. Dept. of Administration. "Women's Network Referral System." Madison, WI: Dept. of Administration, State Bureau of Personnel, 1973. 94 pp.

5613. Wolfe, Allis Rosenberg. "Women, Consumerism, and the National Consumers' League in the Progressive Era, 1900-1923," LABOR HISTORY, vol. 16, no. 3 (Summer 1975), pp. 378-392. Using the power women can exert as consumers to improve working conditions for women and children.

5614. Wolfe, Helen B. "Women in the World of Work." Albany, NY: Univ. of the State of New York, State Educational Dept., Division of Research, 1969. 65 pp.

5615. "Women and the Economy," THE REVIEW OF RADICAL POLITICAL ECONOMICS, vol. 8, no. 1 (Spring 1976), pp. 1-122. Special Issue. Contributors include Terry Fee, Carmen Diana Deere, Lourdes Beneria, Batya Weinbaum, Harold Barnett, Ruth Milkman, Jane Humphries, and Kate Ellis.

5616. "Women at Work," MONTHLY LABOR REVIEW, vol. 93, no. 6 (June 1970), pp. 3-44. Special Section. Contributors include Elizabeth Duncan Koontz, Elizabeth Waldman, Janice Neipert Hedges, Robert D. Moran, H. M. Willacy, H. J. Hilasky, and Edmund Nash.

5617. "Women in the Workplace: A Special Section," MONTHLY LABOR REVIEW, vol. 97, no. 5 (May 1974), pp. 3-89. Contributors include Elizabeth Waldman, Beverly J. McEaddy, Janice Neipert Hedges, Stephen E. Bemis, Edna E. Raphael, Rudolph C. Blitz, John B. Parrish, Martin J. Gannon, Robert Whitmore, and Susan Silver.

5618. "Women Win More Credit," BUSINESS, no. 2313 (Jan. 12, 1974), pp. 76-78. Changing the attitudes of retailers and financial institutions in regard to women as credit risks.

5619. "Women's Labor," RADICAL AMERICA, vol. 7, no. 4 & 5 (July-Oct. 1973), pp. 1-192. Special Double Issue on women in the work force in the United States and Great Britain. Contributors include Lisa Vogel, Selma James, Sheila Rowbotham, Angela Weir, Elizabeth Wilson, and Ira Gerstein.

5620. "Women's Role in Future Development," LITERACY WORK, vol. 4, no. 3 (Jan./March 1975), pp. 1-26. Overview of women's economic and national development role, emphasizing Africa and Asia.

5621. WORKING GIRLS OF CINCINNATI: AN ORIGINAL ANTHOLOGY. New York: Arno Press, 1974. 173 pp. Reprint of 1918 edition of "Women Workers in Factories," by A. Mann; 1927 edition of "Wage-Earning Girls in Cincinnati," by F. I. Rich; and 1930 edition of "What Girls Live On—And How," by F. R. Whitney.

5622. Working Women's Association. WOMEN'S WORK: A SELECTION OF ARTICLES BY WORKING WOMEN. Vancouver, B.C.: Press Gang Distribution, 1975.

5623. Wright, Carroll D. THE WORKING GIRLS OF BOSTON. New York: Arno Press, 1969. Reprint of 1889 edition. Case study outlining the working situations of women in Boston, by the first Commissioner of the Bureau of Labor (1884).

5624. Youssef, Nadia Haggag. WOMAN AND WORK IN DEVELOPING SOCIETIES. Westport, CT: Greenwood Press, 1976. 137 pp. Reprint of 1974 edition.

5625. Zakrzewska, Marie E. A PRACTICAL ILLUSTRATION OF "WOMEN'S RIGHT TO LABOR;" OR, A LETTER FROM MARIE ZAKRZEWSKA. Boston, MA: Walker, Wise, 1860. 167 pp. See also Caroline W. Dall.

B. Women and Job Discrimination

"Despite our demonstrated capacity for cooperative teamwork, some among us seem to accept the shibboleth of an unbridgeable gap between those who hire and those who are employed . . . that for one side to profit, the other must be depressed. Such distorted doctrine is false and foreign to the American scene."

—Dwight David Eisenhower

5626. Alexander, Rodney and Elizabeth Sapery. SHORTCHANGED: MINORITIES AND WOMEN IN BANKING. Port Washington, NY: Kennikat Press, 1973. 186 pp. Revealing study of discrimination in the banking business.

5627. Babcock, Barbara Allen, Ann E. Freedman, Eleanor Holmes Norton, and Susan D. Ross. SEX DISCRIMINATION AND THE LAW: CAUSES AND REMEDIES. Boston, MA: Little, Brown, 1975. 1,092 pp.

5628. Baker, Elizabeth A. PROTECTIVE LABOR LEGISLATION, WITH SPECIAL REFERENCE TO WOMEN IN THE STATE OF NEW YORK. New York: AMS Press, 1969. 467 pp. Reprint of 1925 edition.

5629. Baker, Joan E. "Employment Discrimination Against Women Lawyers," AMERICAN BAR ASSOCIATION JOURNAL, vol. 59 (Sept. 1973), pp. 1029-1032. Discusses recruiting procedure in relation to federal law.

5630. Becker, Robert. SUPREME COURT CASES ON SEX
DISCRIMINATION. Washington, D.C.: Univ. Press of America, 1976.
330 pp.

5631. Blau, Francine D. "Sex Segregation of Workers by Enterprise in Clerical
Occupations," in LABOR MARKET SEGMENTATION edited by
Richard C. Edwards, Michael Reich, and David Gordon. Lexington,
MA: D. C. Heath, 1975. Pp. 257-275. Sex segregation among workers in
the same occupation. See also Alice Kessler-Harris and Mary Stevenson.

5632. Blaxall, Martha and Barbara B. Reagan. WOMEN AND THE
WORKPLACE: THE IMPLICATIONS OF OCCUPATIONAL
SEGREGATION. Chicago, IL: Univ. of Chicago Press, 1976. 312 pp.
Proceedings of conference sponsored by the American Economic
Association-Commission on the Status of Women in the Economic
Profession. Considers not only economic dimensions, but legal,
sociological, and historical perspectives, and recommends courses of
action to counteract occupational segregation of women.

5633. Boulding, Kenneth and Barbara B. Reagan. "Combatting Role Prejudice
and Sex Discrimination," AMERICAN ECONOMIC REVIEW, vol. 63,
no. 5 (Dec. 1973), pp. 1049-1061. Informative discussion of possible
solutions to the problem of sex discrimination.

5634. Buckingham, Graeme L. WHAT TO DO ABOUT EQUAL PAY FOR
WOMEN IN THE UNITED KINGDOM. Epping, England: Gower Press,
1973. 114 pp.

5635. Cook, Alice H. "Equal Pay: Where Is It?" INDUSTRIAL RELATIONS,
vol. 14, no. 2 (May 1975), pp. 158-177.

5636. Deckard, Barbara and Howard Sherman. "Monopoly Power and Sex
Discrimination," POLITICS AND SOCIETY, vol. 4, no. 4 (1974), pp.
475-482. Discusses the economics of job discrimination.

5637. Denmark, Florence, ed. "Who Discriminates Against Women?"
INTERNATIONAL JOURNAL OF GROUP TENSIONS, vol. 4, no. 1
(March 1974), pp. 3-143. Special Issue. Contributors include Ellen
Mintz, Miriam G. Keiffer, Dallas M. Cullen, Thomas W. Miller, Benjamin
B. Wolman, Philip A. Goldberg, Ruana Starer, Rhoda K. Unger, Beth J.
Raymond, Stephen M. Levine, Marie Groszko, Richard Morgenstern,
Rona M. Fields, Helen Mayer Hacker, and Leigh Marlowe.

5638. Dunlap, Mary C., ed. SEX DISCRIMINATION IN EMPLOYMENT:
APPLICATION OF TITLE VII. Santa Cruz, CA: Community Law
Reports, 1976. 1 vol. Bound in looseleaf form for updating.

5639. "Employment Discrimination," THE BUSINESS LAWYER, vol. 29, no.
2 (Jan. 1974), pp. 577-614. Panel discussion with William A. Carey,
Evangeline Swift, David S. Tatel, David Rose, Stephen Feigin, and Bea
Rosenberg.

5640. "Europe's Working Women: EC Commission Finds Pay Bias,"
EUROPEAN COMMUNITY, no. 171 (Dec. 1973), pp. 7-11. The bias
exists not only in legislation, but also persists in stereotyped roles
assigned to women.

5641. Foxley, Cecelia H. LOCATING, RECRUITING, AND EMPLOYING
WOMEN: AN EQUAL OPPORTUNITY APPROACH. Garret Park, MD:

Garret Park Press, 1976. 357 pp. Includes 64-page bibliography.

5642. Gordon, Nancy M., Thomas E. Morton, and Ina C. Braden. "Faculty Salaries: Is There Discrimination by Sex, Race and Discipline?" THE AMERICAN ECONOMIC REVIEW, vol. 64, no. 3 (June 1974), pp. 419-427. The average salary difference between men and women is $1,602 at the university level.

5643. Johnston, John D. "Sex Discrimination and the Law–1975," UCLA LAW REVIEW, vol. 23 (Dec. 1975), pp. 235-265.

5644. Jongeward, Dorothy and Dru Scott, eds. AFFIRMATIVE ACTION FOR WOMEN: A PRACTICAL GUIDE FOR WOMEN AND MANAGEMENT. Reading, MA: Addison-Wesley, 1973. 334 pp.

5645. Kessler-Harris, Alice. "Stratifying by Sex: Understanding the History of Working Women," in LABOR MARKET STRATIFICATION edited by Richard C. Edwards, Michael Reich, and David Gordon. Lexington, MA: D. C. Heath, 1975. Pp. 217-242. How sexual stratification has sustained and obscured discrimination against working women. See also Francine D. Blau and Mary Stevenson.

5646. Kollontai, Alexandra. "Women Workers Struggle for Their Rights." Bristol, England: Falling Wall Press, 1973. 16 pp. By the Communist theoretician and activist in the early 1920's.

5647. Larson, E. Richard. "Employment Discrimination in State and Local Government," CLEARINGHOUSE REVIEW, vol. 7, no. 2 (June 1973), pp. 63-78. Discusses the constitutional, statutory, and regulatory provisions prohibiting discrimination in state and local government employment.

5648. Lloyd, Cynthia B., ed. SEX, DISCRIMINATION, AND THE DIVISION OF LABOR. New York: Columbia Univ. Press, 1975. 432 pp. 16 essays on the economics of women in the labor market.

5649. Lyle, Jerolyn R. "An Empirical Study of the Occupational Standing of Women in Multinational Corporations," LABOR LAW JOURNAL, vol. 24, no. 8 (Aug. 1973), pp. 458-468. Analysis of the level of occupational discrimination against women.

5650. Madden, Janice Fanning. THE ECONOMICS OF SEX DISCRIMINATION. Lexington, MA: D. C. Heath, 1973. 140 pp. Discusses wage, occupational, and cumulative discrimination. Much demographical data, includes bibliography.

5651. Mepham, George James. EQUAL OPPORTUNITY AND EQUAL PAY FOR WOMEN: A REVIEW OF OBJECTIVES, PROBLEMS, AND PROGRESS. London, England: Institute of Personnel Management, 1974. 209 pp.

5652. National Association of Women Deans and Counselors. "Affirmative Action?" Washington, D.C.: National Association for Women Deans, Administrators, and Counselors, 1976.

5653. Pross, Helge. GLEICHBERECHTIGUNG IM BERUF: EINE UNTERSUSCHUNG MIT 7,000 ARBEITNEHMERINNEN IN DER EWG [EQUALITY IN WORK? A STUDY OF 7,000 WOMEN WORKERS IN THE FCC]. Frankfort, Germany: Athenaeum Verlag, 1973.

5654. Reid, Elizabeth. "Women at a Standstill: The Need for Radical Change," INTERNATIONAL LABOUR REVIEW, vol. 111, no. 6 (June 1975), pp. 458-468. Lack of progress in reducing inequality.

5655. ———. WOMEN WORKERS AND SOCIETY: INTERNATIONAL PERSPECTIVES. Geneva, Switzerland: International Labor Office, 1974. 211 pp. Social inequalities facing women, written by the once personal advisor to the Prime Minister of Australia.

5656. Sawhill, Isabel. "The Economics of Discrimination Against Women: Some New Findings," JOURNAL OF HUMAN RESOURCES, vol. 8, no. 3 (Summer 1974), pp. 383-395.

5657. Schwartz, Eleanor Brantley. THE SEX BARRIER IN BUSINESS. Atlanta, GA: Georgia State Univ. School of Business Administration, Publishing Services Division, 1971. 116 pp.

5658. Shaeffer, Ruth G. NONDISCRIMINATION IN EMPLOYMENT, 1973-1975: A BROADENING AND DEEPENING NATIONAL EFFORT. New York: The Conference Board, 1975. 125 pp.

5659. Simpson, Wendell, Mary Lauderdale, and Candy Calaway. AFFIRMATIVE ACTION CATALOGUE. Oklahoma City, OK: Office of Community Affairs and Planning, 1973. 595 pp. Federal and state laws and legislation.

5660. Stevenson, Mary. "Women's Wages and Job Segregation," in LABOR MARKET SEGMENTATION edited by Richard C. Edwards, Michael Reich, and David Gordon. Lexington, MA: D. C. Heath, 1975. Pp. 243-256. Argues that inferior economic position may result from highly segregated occupational structure. See also Francine D. Blau and Alice Kessler-Harris.

5661. Takahashi, Nobuko. "Women's Wages in Japan and the Question of Equal Pay," INTERNATIONAL LABOUR REVIEW, vol. 111, no. 1 (Jan. 1975), pp. 51-68. The problem of implementing equal pay forms part of the broader problem of the position of women in society.

5662. U.S. Commission on Civil Rights. A GUIDE TO FEDERAL LAWS PROHIBITING SEX DISCRIMINATION. Washington, D.C.: SUDOC, GPO, 1974. 113 pp.

5663. U.S. Congress. House. Committee on Education and Labor. Special Subcommittee on Education. DISCRIMINATION AGAINST WOMEN: HEARINGS. 91st Congress. Washington, D.C.: Zenger Publications, 1976. 2 vols. Reprint of 1970 edition.

5664. U.S. Equal Employment Opportunity Commission. Research Division. TOWARD FAIR EMPLOYMENT AND THE EEOC: A FINAL REPORT. Prepared by Arvil V. Adams. Washington, D.C.: U.S. EEOC, 1972.

5665. Vangsnes, Kari. "Equal Pay in Norway," INTERNATIONAL LABOUR REVIEW, vol. 103, no. 4 (April 1971), pp. 379-392.

5666. Vogel, Elaine. "Some Suggestions for the Advancement of Working Women," INTERNATIONAL LABOUR REVIEW, vol. 112, no. 1 (July 1975), pp. 29-43. Discusses revisions necessary in social policy to eliminate discrimination against women in the workplace.

5667. Wallace, Phyllis, ed. EMPLOYMENT OPPORTUNITY AND THE AT&T CASE. Cambridge, MA: MIT Press, 1976. 355 pp. Consent decree: *Equal Employment Opportunity Commission, et al* v. *American Telephone & Telegraph, et al* (Jan. 13, 1973-May 31, 1974).

5668. Walsh, Ethel Bent. "Sex Discrimination and the Impact of TITLE VII," LABOR LAW JOURNAL, vol. 25, no. 3 (March 1974), pp. 150-154.

5669. Women's Action Alliance. THE FORGOTTEN FIVE MILLION: WOMEN IN PUBLIC EMPLOYMENT: PRACTICAL GUIDE FOR ELIMINATING SEX DISCRIMINATION. New York: Women's Action Alliance, 1975.

C. Economic Effects of the Employment of Married Women

"It is not education which makes women less domestic, but wealth."
—Katharine Jeanne Gallagher

"Any woman who has a career and a family automatically develops something in the way of two personalities, like two sides of a dollar bill, each different in design. But one can complement the other to make a valuable whole. Her problem is to keep one from draining the life from the other. She can achieve it only as long as she keeps the two in balance."
—Ivy Baker Priest

5670. Arnow, Harriet. THE DOLLMAKER. New York: Avon Books, 1972. 608 pp. Reprint of 1954 edition. The story of a Kentucky woman's struggles for survival and industrial unionism in wartime Detroit.

5671. Baldridge, Letitia. JUGGLING: THE ART OF BALANCING MARRIAGE, MOTHERHOOD, AND A CAREER. New York: Viking Press, 1976. 270 pp. Directed to the career woman.

5672. Barker, P. L. and Allen, eds. DEPENDENCE AND EXPLOITATION IN WORK AND MARRIAGE. New York: Longmans, 1976.

5673. BERUFSTAETIGE FRAU UND FAMILIE [THE WORKING WOMAN AND THE FAMILY]. East Berlin, Germany: Deitz Verlag, 1972.

5674. Cain, Glen G., Walter Nicholson, Charles D. Mallar, and Judith Wooldridge. "The Labor-Supply Responses of Married Women, Husband Present," THE JOURNAL OF HUMAN RESOURCES, vol. 9, no. 2 (Spring 1974), pp. 201-222. Statistical analysis.

5675. Cook, Alice H. "The Working Mother: A Survey of Problems and Programs in Nine Countries." Ithaca, NY: New York State School of Industrial and Labor Relations, Cornell Univ., 1975. 84 pp. Countries surveyed include Sweden, Israel, East Germany, West Germany, Rumania, Austria, Russia, Japan, and Australia.

5676. Curtis, Jean. WORKING MOTHERS. Garden City, NY: Doubleday, 1976. 214 pp.

5677. Duker, Jacob M. "House-Wife and Working Wife Families: A Housing Comparison," LAND ECONOMICS, vol. 46 (May 1970), pp. 138-145.

5678. Hayghe, Howard. "Families and the Rise of Working Wives—An Overview," MONTHLY LABOR REVIEW, vol. 99, no. 5 (May 1976), pp. 12-19.

5679. ———. "Labor Force Activity of Married Women," MONTHLY LABOR REVIEW, vol. 96, no. 4 (April 1973), pp. 31-36.

5680. ———. "Marital and Family Characteristics of the Labor Force in March 1973," MONTHLY LABOR REVIEW, vol. 95, no. 4 (April 1972), pp. 9-13.

5681. Hoffman, Leonore and Gloria DeSole, eds. "Careers and Couples: An Academic Question." New York: Modern Language Association, Commission on the Status of Women in the Profession, 1976. 59 pp.

5682. Institute of Life Insurance. Research Services. "DataTrack No. 1: Women." New York: Institute of Life Insurance, 1974. 36 pp. Data on changing work roles and family roles of women as related to the purchase of life insurance.

5683. Keiran, Patricia. HOW WORKING MOTHERS MANAGE. London, England: Clifton Books, 1970. 142 pp.

5684. Kherchev, A. G. and S. I. Golod. "Recommendations of the Symposium on 'Women's Employment and the Family,' Minsk, June 21-24, 1969," THE SOVIET REVIEW, vol. 14, no. 4 (Winter 1973), pp. 55-66. Offers solutions to the problem of coordinating women's occupations with their homes and families.

5685. Klein, Viola. "Employing Married Women." London, England: Institute of Personnel Management, 1961. 51 pp.

5686. McEaddy, Beverly Johnson. "Women Who Head Families: A Socio-Economic Analysis," MONTHLY LABOR REVIEW, vol. 99, no. 6 (June 1976), pp. 3-9. Presents data showing that women who head families were younger and more likely to work in 1975 than in 1960.

5687. Michel, Andrée, ed. FAMILY ISSUES OF EMPLOYED WOMEN IN EUROPE AND AMERICA. Atlantic Highlands, NJ: Humanities Press, 1971. 172 pp.

5688. Musgrave, Beatrice and Joan Wheeler-Bennett, eds. WOMEN AT WORK: COMBINING FAMILY AND A CAREER. London, England: Owen, 1972. 152 pp. Directory to the professions.

5689. Pogrebin, Letty Cottin. HOW TO MAKE THE SYSTEM WORK FOR THE WORKING WOMAN. New York: David McKay, 1975. 349 pp. Geared to married women with children who have spent much of their time in the home.

5690. Rapoport, Rhona and Robert Rapoport. DUAL-CAREER FAMILIES. Baltimore, MD: Penguin Books, 1971. 327 pp. Case studies of five families in which husbands and wives pursue independent careers; examines the effects on their families, personal relationships, etc.

5691. Spencer, Byron G. "Determinants of the Labour Force Participation of Married Women: A Micro-Study of Toronto Households," CANADIAN JOURNAL OF ECONOMICS, vol. 6, no. 2 (May 1973), pp. 222-238. Sample of over 1,600 households considering the factors of child status, income, education, age and religion.

5692. Toner, Barbara. DOUBLE SHIFT: A PRACTICAL GUIDE FOR
WORKING MOTHERS. London, England: Arrow Books, 1975.
200 pp.
5693. "Working Wives: How Well is Business Talking Their Language?"
MANAGEMENT REVIEW, vol. 56 (April 1967), pp. 4-21. Special
Section. Contributors include Mary Dublin Keyserling, Alice S. Rossi,
and Michael J. O'Connor.

D. Women's Labor Unions and Organizations

*"With a few notable exceptions, American labor unions generally stick pretty close to
routine business—the representation of their members, encounters with management,
and maintenance of their own internal power structure."*
—Herbert Lewis Marx, Jr.

5694. Berquist, Virginia A. "Women's Participation in Labor Organizations,"
MONTHLY LABOR REVIEW, vol. 97, no. 10 (Oct. 1974), pp. 3-9.
Details the growth of women's membership in unions, and the lack of
growth in women's leadership in unions.
5695. Canada. Dept. of Labour. "Women in Trade Unions," LABOUR
GAZETTE (Oct. 1971), pp. 682-685.
5696. CAROLA WOERISHOFFER: HER LIFE AND WORK. By Bryn Mawr
College, Class of 1907. New York: Arno Press, 1974. 137 pp. Reprint
of 1912 edition. Early woman trade unionist.
5697. Goldman, Harold. EMMA PATERSON: SHE LED WOMEN INTO A
MAN'S WORLD. London, England: Lawrence & Wishart, 1974. 127
pp. Emma Smith Anne Paterson, Women's Trade Union League.
5698. Hamilton, Mary Agnes. MARY MACARTHUR, A BIOGRAPHICAL
SKETCH. Westport, CT: Hyperion Press, 1976. 209 pp. Reprint of
1926 edition. Secretary of the Women's Trade Union in London at the
age of 20, formed the National Federation of Women Workers, stood
for Parliament in 1918 as a Labour candidate.
5699. ———. WOMEN AT WORK: A BRIEF INTRODUCTION TO TRADE
UNIONISM FOR WOMEN. London, England: G. Routledge & Sons,
1941. 188 pp.
5700. James, Selma. WOMEN, THE UNIONS, AND WORK: OR, WHAT IS
NOT TO BE DONE. Pittsburgh, PA: KNOW, Inc., 1972. 16 pp.
Analysis of contemporary feminist ideologies, and the co-optative
strategies against them.
5701. Johnstone, Jenny Elizabeth. "Women in Steel." New York: Workers
Library, 1937. 30 pp.
5702. Kelley, Florence. SOME ETHICAL GAINS THROUGH LEGISLATION.
New York: Arno Press, 1969. 341 pp. Reprint of 1905 edition.
5703. Landorganisationen i Sverige. THE TRADE UNIONS AND THE
FAMILY: A REPORT BY THE LO COUNCIL FOR FAMILY

QUESTIONS. Stockholm, Sweden: Prisma, 1970.

5704. Lewenhak, Sheila. WOMEN IN TRADE UNIONS: A SHORT HISTORY OF WOMEN IN THE BRITISH TRADE UNION MOVEMENT. New York: St. Martins Press, 1977. 320 pp. Surveys women's work and working conditions from the medieval craft guilds to the present.

5705. Maupin, Joyce. "Working Women and Their Organizations: 150 Years of Struggle." Berkeley, CA: Union WAGE Educational Committee, 1974. 33 pp. Women's labor union history from the Lowell mill strikes to the 1974 formation of the Coalition of Labor Union Women (CLUW).

5706. National Women's Trade Union League of America. "Women in Trade Unions in the United States." Chicago, IL: National Women's Trade Union League of America, 1919. 15 pp.

5707. Nestor, Agnes. WOMEN'S LABOR LEADER: AN AUTOBIOGRAPHY OF AGNES NESTOR. Washington, D.C.: Zenger Publications, 1976. 307 pp. Reprint of 1954 edition.

5708. Scharnau, Ralph. "Elizabeth Morgan, Crusader for Labor Reform," LABOR HISTORY, vol. 14, no. 3 (Summer 1973), pp. 340-351. Initiated the organization of the Ladies' Federal Labor Union No. 2703 and the Illinois Women's Alliance in 1888, both organized to protect women and children in Chicago industry.

5709. Sibble, Edward Matson. "Remedies for Labor Union Sex Discrimination," THE GEORGETOWN LAW JOURNAL, vol. 63 (March 1975), pp. 939-954. Analysis of the impact of the National Labor Relations Board and Federal court decisions relating to TITLE VII of the Civil Rights Act of 1964, on women's representation and participation in labor union decision-making.

5710. Tepperman, Jean. NOT SERVANTS, NOT MACHINES: OFFICE WORKERS SPEAK OUT. Boston, MA: Beacon Press, 1976. 188 pp. White-collar women workers and union organization.

5711. U.S. Dept. of Labor. Wage and Labor Standards Administration. Women's Bureau. "To Benefit Women at Work." Washington, D.C.: U.S. Dept. of Labor, 1969. 10 pp. History of the U.S. Women's Bureau, created in 1920.

5712. Wertheimer, Barbara M. and Anne H. Nelson. TRADE UNION WOMEN: A STUDY OF THEIR PARTICIPATION IN NEW YORK CITY LOCALS. New York: Praeger Books, 1975. 202 pp. Studies of 110 New York City unions with 25-90% female members; attributes women's lack of key positions to lack of experience rather than lack of interest.

5713. Wise, Audrey. "Women and the Struggle for Workers' Control." Nottingham, England: The Bertrand Russell Peace Foundation, 1974. 95 pp. Socialist view urging women's participation in unionism.

5714. "Women in the Trade Union Movement." London, England: Trades Union Congress, 1955.

E. Women in Domestic Labor

"The graveyards are full of women whose houses were so spotless you could eat off the floor. Remember the second wife always has a maid."
                                                                  —Heloise Cruse

5715. Bell, Carolyn Shaw. "The Next Revolution," SOCIAL POLICY, vol. 6, no. 3 (Sept.-Oct. 1975), pp. 5-11. Division of labor within the home and economic compensation and responsibility.

5716. The Conference of Socialist Economists. "On the Political Economy of Women." London, England: Stage I, 1975. 37 pp. Two essays, "Women's Domestic Labour," and "Women, The State, and Reproduction Since the 1930's," focus on women's work and role within the household.

5717. Federici, Sylvia. "Wages Against Housework." Bristol, England: Falling Wall Press, 1975. 9 pp. Argues that housework should be viewed not only as an economic commodity, but also as a political perspective that affects the entire working class, male and female.

5718. Gathorne-Hardy, Jonathon. THE UNNATURAL HISTORY OF THE NANNY. New York: Dial Press, 1973. 350 pp. Examines the institution of the British nursemaid.

5719. Gronau, Reuben. "The Intrafamily Allocation of Time: The Value of Housewives' Time," AMERICAN ECONOMIC REVIEW, vol. 63, no. 4 (Sept. 1973), pp. 634-651.

5720. Hawes, Elizabeth. WHY WOMEN CRY: OR, WENCHES WITH WRENCHES. Clifton, NY: Reynal & Hitchcock, 1943. 221 pp. The problem of domestic labor for employed women.

5721. Lopate, Carol. "Pay for Housework?" SOCIAL POLICY, vol. 4, no. 3 (Sept./Oct. 1974), pp. 27-31. Brief discussion raising questions on productivity, economic value, and determination of benefits of housework.

5722. Oakley, Ann. THE SOCIOLOGY OF HOUSEWORK. New York: Pantheon Books, 1975. 242 pp. Challenges demeaning attitudes toward the consideration of housework as a serious topic.

5723. ———. WOMAN'S WORK: THE HOUSEWIFE, PAST AND PRESENT. New York: Pantheon Books, 1974. 275 pp. First sociological and historical study of housework, from pre-industrial to the present time.

5724. Rosen, H. S. "Monetary Value of a Housewife: A Replacement Cost Approach," AMERICAN JOURNAL OF ECONOMICS AND SOCIOLOGY, vol. 33, no. 1 (Jan. 1974), pp. 65-73.

5725. Spring-Rice, Mrs. Margery Garrett. WORKING-CLASS WIVES: THEIR HEALTH AND CONDITIONS, BEING THE SURVEY OF THE CONDITIONS OF 1,250 MARRIED WORKING WOMEN. Hammondsworth, England: Penguin Books, 1939. 214 pp.

5726. U.S. Dept. of Health, Education, and Welfare. Office of Research and Statistics. ECONOMIC VALUE OF A HOUSEWIFE. By Wendyce H.

Brody. Washington, D.C.: SUDOC, GPO, 1975.

5727. Walker, Kathryn and William H. Gauger. THE DOLLAR VALUE OF HOUSEHOLD WORK. Ithaca, NY: New York State College of Human Ecology, Cornell Univ., 1973.

5728. Warrior, Betsey and Lisa Leghorn, eds. HOUSEWORKER'S HANDBOOK. Cambridge, MA: Woman's Center, 1975. 109 pp. 3rd revised edition. The status quo, history, and implications of women's unpaid labor, as expressed in essays, cartoons, quotations, and other literary media.

5729. West, Katherine. CHAPTER OF GOVERNESSES: A STUDY OF THE GOVERNESS IN ENGLISH FICTION, 1800-1949. London, England: Cowan & West, 1949. 263 pp.

F. Women in Business, Industry, and Production

"No business which depends for existence on paying less than living wages to its workers has any right to continue in this country."
— *Franklin Delano Roosevelt*

"It violates right order whenever capital so employs the working or wage-earning classes as to divert business and economic activity entirely to its own arbitrary will and advantage without any regard to the human dignity of the workers, the social character of economic life, social justice, and the common good."
— *Pius XI (Achille Ambrogio Damiano Ra*

5730. Anthony, Susan B., II. OUT OF THE KITCHEN–INTO THE WAR: WOMAN'S WINNING ROLE IN OUR NATION'S DRAMA. New York: Stephen Daye, 1943. 246 pp.

5731. Anthony, Sylvia. WOMEN'S PLACE IN INDUSTRY AND HOME. London, England: G. Routledge & Sons, 1932. 243 pp.

5732. Baetjer, Anna M. WOMEN IN INDUSTRY: THEIR HEALTH AND EFFICIENCY. New York: Arno Press, 1977. 344 pp. Reprint of 1946 edition. The physical effect of wartime work on women; sickness and absenteeism, accidents and injuries, gynecological and obstetrical problems.

5733. Baxandall, Rosalyn, Susan Reverby, and Linda Gordon, eds. AMERICA'S WORKING WOMEN: A DOCUMENTARY HISTORY–1600 TO THE PRESENT. New York: Random House, 1976. 408 pp. Collection of essays assessing labor force conditions exploiting the wage-earning women.

5734. Bharadwaj, Aruna. "Police Modernization in India: A Study of Women Police in Delhi," INDIAN JOURNAL OF SOCIAL WORK, vol. 37 (April 1976), pp. 39-48.

5735. Bloch, Peter B. and Deborah Anderson. "Policewomen on Patrol: Final Report." Arlington, VA: ERIC Document Reproduction Service, 1974. 76 pp.

5736. Brandeis, Louis Dembitz and Josephine Goldmark. WOMEN IN INDUSTRY: DECISION OF THE U.S. SUPREME COURT IN *CURT MULLER* V. *STATE OF OREGON,* UPHOLDING THE CONSTITUTIONALITY OF THE OREGON TEN-HOUR LAW FOR WOMEN AND BRIEF FOR THE STATE OF OREGON. New York: Arno Press, 1969. 113 pp. Reprint of 1907 edition.

5737. Bujra, Janet M. "Women 'Entrepreneurs' of Early Nairobi," CANADIAN JOURNAL OF AFRICAN STUDIES, vol. 9, no. 2 (1975), pp. 213-234. Interviews with 127 landlords (76 women) revealed that most women had been prostitutes, enabling them to gain economic equality with men.

5738. Cadbury, Edward, M. Ceiles Matheson, and George Shann. WOMEN'S WORK AND WAGES: A PHASE OF LIFE IN AN INDUSTRIAL CITY. New York: Gordon Press, 1976. 187 pp. Reprint of 1906 edition. A complaint of the working conditions in Birmingham and an effort to raise the standard of life.

5739. Davis, Rebecca Harding. LIFE IN THE IRON MILLS. Old Westbury, NY: Feminist Press, 1976. 176 pp. Reprint of 1861 article in ATLANTIC. Commentary on the dehumanizing results of industrialization in Appalachia, with a biographical essay by Tille Olesen.

5740. DeWolfe, Elsie. AFTER ALL. New York: Harper, 1935. 278 pp. Autobiography of the author's struggle for success in the field of interior decorating—she was the first woman to pursue a career in that field.

5741. Donovan, Frances R. THE SALESLADY. New York: Arno Press, 1974. 267 pp. Reprint of 1929 edition.

5742. ———. THE WOMAN WHO WAITS. Boston, MA: R. G. Badger, 1920. 228 pp. Waitress work.

5743. Dublin, Thomas. "Women, Work, and Protest in the Early Lowell Mills: 'The Oppressing Hand of Avarice Would Enslave Us'," LABOR HISTORY, vol. 16, no. 1 (Winter 1975), pp. 99-116. Lowell mill women's opposition to oppressive management labor policies.

5744. Fenn, Margaret P., ed. "Women in Business: A New Look," JOURNAL OF CONTEMPORARY BUSINESS, vol. 5, no. 1 (Winter 1976), pp. 1-76. Special Issue. Contributors include Simon W. Polachek, Jane W. Torrey, Mary T. Matthies, and Eleanor Brantley Schwartz.

5745. Filene, Catherine, ed. CAREERS FOR WOMEN. New York: Arno Press, 1974. 576 pp. Reprint of 1920 edition.

5746. Fogarty, Michael P., Rhona Rapoport, and Robert Rapoport. "Women and Top Jobs: The Next Move." London, England: Research Publications Services, 1972. 93 pp. Working conditions for women in England.

5747. Gregory, Chester W. WOMEN IN DEFENSE WORK DURING WORLD WAR II: AN ANALYSIS OF THE LABOR PROBLEM AND WOMEN'S RIGHTS. Hicksville, NY: Exposition Press, 1974. 243 pp.

5748. Griffin, Barbara. A SUCCESSFUL BUSINESS OF YOUR OWN. Los Angeles, CA: Sherbourne Press, 1974. 222 pp.

5749. Grossman, Allyson Sherman. "Women in the Labor Force: The Early

Years," MONTHLY LABOR REVIEW, vol. 98, no. 11 (Nov. 1975), pp. 3-9. See also Deborah Pisetzner Klein and Beverly Johnson McEaddy.

5750. Hammill, Frances. "Some Unconventional Women Before 1800: Printers, Booksellers, and Collectors," BIBLIO SOCIETY PAPERS, vol. 49 (4th Quarter 1955), pp. 300-314.

5751. Hedges, Anna Charlotte. WAGE WORTH OF SCHOOL TRAINING: AN ANALYTICAL STUDY OF 600 WOMEN-WORKERS IN TEXTILE FACTORIES. New York: AMG Press, 1972. 173 pp. Reprint of 1915 edition.

5752. Hilton, Teri. "Small Business Ideas for Women—And How to get Started." New York: Pilot Books, 1975. 32 pp.

5753. Holcombe, Lee. VICTORIAN LADIES AT WORK: MIDDLE-CLASS WORKING WOMEN IN ENGLAND AND WALES, 1850-1914. Hamden, CT: Shoe String Press, 1973. 253 pp.

5754. Hourwich, Andria T. and Gladys L. Palmer, eds. I AM A WOMAN WORKER: A SCRAPBOOK OF AUTOBIOGRAPHIES. New York: Arno Press, 1974. 152 pp. Personal accounts of women during the early days of the New Deal.

5755. Howe, Louise Kapp. PINK COLLAR WORKERS: INSIDE THE WORLD OF WOMEN'S WORK. New York: G. P. Putnam's Sons, 1976. 301 pp. Women employed as beauticians, keypunch operators, sales clerks, etc.

5756. Hunt, Audrey. MANAGEMENT ATTITUDES AND PRACTICES TOWARDS WOMEN AT WORK: AN EMPLOYMENT SURVEY CARRIED OUT IN 1973 BY THE SOCIAL SECURITY DIVISION OF THE OFFICE OF POPULATION CENSUSES AND SURVEYS ON BEHALF OF THE DEPARTMENT OF EMPLOYMENT. London, England: Her Majesty's Stationery Office, 1975. 221 pp. One of the greatest obstacles to women's advancement and entrance in "men's jobs" is the traditionalist theory—since there have never been women in this job, there shouldn't be any.

5757. Jesperson, Karen, Barbara Fruger, Bioethe Marker, and Toni Liversage. KVINDER PÅ FABRIK [WOMEN IN THE FACTORY]. København: Forlag, Hans Reitzel, 1971. 112 pp. Interviews with women workers on their attitudes toward their work and life-styles.

5758. Jessup, Claudia and Genie Chipps. SUPERGIRLS: THE AUTOBIOGRAPHY OF AN OUTRAGEOUS BUSINESS. New York: Harper & Row, 1972. 182 pp. Supergirls Enterprises, Ltd. began in 1967 as an all-purpose service with emphasis on the unusual, evolving into a creative service specializing in advertising promotions to women.

5759. ———. THE WOMAN'S GUIDE TO STARTING A BUSINESS. New York: Holt, Rinehart & Winston, 1976. 266 pp.

5760. Johnson, Curtiss C. AMERICA'S FIRST LADY BOSS: A WISP OF A GIRL, MACY'S AND ROMANCE. Norwalk, CT: Silvermine Publishers, 1965. 164 pp. Biography of Margaret Swain LaForge.

5761. Kane, Paula and Christopher Chandler. SEX OBJECTS IN THE SKY. Chicago, IL: Follett Publishing, 1974. 160 pp. Another well-deserved dart to industries that package and market women as commodities, namely the airlines.

5762. Katzell, Mildred E. and William C. Byham, eds. "Women in the Work Force: A Confrontation with Change." New York: Behavioral Publications, 1972. 76 pp.

5763. Killian, Ray. WORKING WOMEN: A MALE MANAGER'S VIEW. New York: American Management Association, 1971. 214 pp.

5764. Klein, Deborah Pisetzner. "Women in the Work Force: The Middle Years," MONTHLY LABOR REVIEW, vol. 98, no. 11 (Nov. 1975), pp. 10-16. See also Allyson Sherman Grossman and Beverly Johnson McEaddy.

5765. Lapidus, Gail Warshofsky. "U.S.S.R. Women at Work: Changing Patterns," INDUSTRIAL RELATIONS, vol. 14, no. 2 (May 1975), pp. 178-195.

5766. Lea, Tom. THE KING RANCH. Boston, MA: Little, Brown, 1957. 838 pp. Biography of Henrietta Chamberlain King, who turned a heavily-debted inheritance into a multinational conglomerate of oil wells, racehorse breeding, game preserves, and scientific cattle/beef raising.

5767. Lembeck, Ruth. JOB IDEAS FOR TODAY'S WOMAN. Englewood Cliffs, NJ: Prentice-Hall, 1974. 224 pp.

5768. Lyle, Jerolyn R. and Jane L. Ross. WOMEN IN INDUSTRY: EMPLOYMENT PATTERNS OF WOMEN IN CORPORATE AMERICA. Lexington, MA: D.C. Heath, 1973. 164 pp. Found that the firms with the largest number of employees practice the least occupational discrimination against women, though the proportion of women employed was not considered. Includes annotated bibliography.

5769. Malan, Nancy E. "How 'Ya Gonna Keep 'Em Down: Working Women and World War I," PROLOGUE: THE JOURNAL OF THE NATIONAL ARCHIVES, vol. 5 (Winter 1973). pp. 209-239. Photo essay on women working on farms, in factories, and on railroads.

5770. McCurry, Dan C., ed. CANNERY CAPTIVES: WOMEN WORKERS IN THE PRODUCE PROCESSING INDUSTRY. New York: Arno Press, 1975. 442 pp. Reprint of U.S. Women's Bureau publications: 1926 edition of "Women in the Fruit Growing and Canning Industries in the State of Washington," 1927 edition of "Women's Employment in Vegetable Canneries in Delaware," 1930 edition of "The Employment of Women in the Pineapple Canneries of Hawaii," and 1940 edition of "Application of Labor Legislation to the Fruit and Vegetable Canning and Preserving Industries."

5771. McDaniel, William H. THE HISTORY OF BEECH. Wichita, KA: McCormick-Armstrong, 1971. 366 pp. Olive Ann Beech successfully built Beech Aircraft from a small operation to the multimillion dollar business it now is.

5772. McEaddy, Beverly Johnson. "Women in the Labor Force: The Later Years," MONTHLY LABOR REVIEW, vol. 98, no. 11 (Nov. 1975), pp. 17-24. See also Allyson Sherman Grossman and Deborah Pisetzner Klein.

5773. Maule, Frances. SHE STRIVES TO CONQUER. New York: Funk & Wagnalls, 1937. 301 pp. Analysis of the opportunities and pitfalls of employment in the business world.

5774. Millgardh, Marianne. "Women in 'Male' Occupations," CURRENT SWEDEN, no. 60 (Jan. 1975), pp. 1-4. Report on an experimental program of the Advisory Council to the Prime Minister of Equality Between Men and Women, placing women in traditionally male positions in the manufacturing processes of the local factories.

5775. Newman, Dorothy K., et al. OCCUPATIONAL ATTAINMENT OF ETHNIC GROUPS AND WOMEN IN FIFTEEN INDUSTRIES, 1969-1971. Edison, NJ: Transaction Books, 1977.

5776. Paulsen, Marit. DU, MENNESKE: SKARPT NAERBILLEDE AF EN INDUSTRIARBEJDERSKES LIV [YOU, A PERSON? CLOSEUP OF THE LIFE OF A FEMALE INDUSTRIAL WORKER]. København, Denmark: Fremad, 1973.

5777. Pennington, Patience (Pseud. Mrs. Elizabeth Waties Pringle). A WOMAN RICE PLANTER. New York: Macmillan, 1928. 450 pp. Rice processing in South Carolina and Georgia.

5778. Pinchbeck, Ivy. WOMEN WORKERS AND THE INDUSTRIAL REVOLUTION 1750-1850. Clifton, NJ: Augusta M. Kelley Publishers, 1975. 342 pp. Reprint of 1930 edition. Economic study of the living conditions of working women; employment of women during the agrarian revolution; women in industry and trades, textiles, mines, and metal trades; and craftswomen and business women.

5779. Pinckney, Elise, ed. "The Letterbook of Eliza Lucas Pinckney, 1737-1762." Charlotte, NC: Univ. of North Carolina Press, 1972. 30 pp. Reprint of 1850 edition. She began the growth and export of indigo in North Carolina.

5780. Power, Eileen. "Women Traders in Medieval London," ECONOMIC JOURNAL (London), (June 1916).

5781. Robinson, Harriet Harson. "Early Factory Labor in New England." Boston, MA: Wright & Potter Printing, 1889. 26 pp.

5782. ———. LOOM AND SPINDLE: OR, LIFE AMONG THE EARLY MILL GIRLS. Kailua, HA: Press Pacifica, 1976. 216 pp. Reprint of 1898 edition. The story of the first American factory women.

5783. Scoresby, William. AMERICAN FACTORIES AND THEIR FEMALE OPERATIVES: WITH AN APPEAL ON BEHALF OF THE BRITISH FACTORY POPULATION AND SUGGESTIONS FOR THE IMPROVEMENT OF THEIR CONDITION. New York: Burt Franklin, 1967. 122 pp. Reprint of 1845 edition. Uses Lowell, Massachusetts as an example.

5784. Seifer, Nancy. NOBODY SPEAKS FOR ME: SELF-PORTRAITS OF AMERICAN WORKING-CLASS WOMEN. New York: Simon & Schuster, 1976. 477 pp. The life stories of ten working-class women.

5785. Stollenwerk, Antoinette. "Back to Work, Ladies! A Career Guide for the Mature Woman." New York: Pilot Books, 1967. 55 pp.

5786. Sweet, James A. WOMEN IN THE LABOR FORCE. New York: Seminar Press, 1973. 211 pp.

5787. Symanski, Richard. "Prostitution in Nevada," ASSOCIATION OF AMERICAN GEOGRAPHERS. ANNALS, vol. 64, no. 3 (Sept. 1974), pp. 357-377. Describes the legal, locational, and ecological aspects of brothel prostitution in Nevada.

5788. "A Symposium: Women in the Labor Force," INDUSTRIAL RELATIONS, vol. 7, no. 3 (May 1968), pp. 187-248. Contributors include Margaret S. Gordon, Eli Ginzberg, Gertrude Bancroft McNally, Valerie Kincaid Oppenheimer, and Harold Wilensky.

5789. Twentieth Century Fund Task Force. EXPLOITATION FROM NINE TO FIVE: REPORT. Lexington, MA: Lexington Books, 1975. 201 pp.

5790. U.S. Dept. of Commerce. Bureau of the Census. Office of Minority Business Enterprise. WOMEN-OWNED BUSINESSES 1972. Washington, D.C.: SUDOC, GPO, 1976. 277 pp. Statistical report.

5791. U.S. Dept. of Labor. Employment Standards Administration. Women's Bureau. "Steps in Opening the Skilled Trades to Women." Washington, D.C.: SUDOC, GPO, 1974. 8 pp. Recruiting, training, and employing women in the apprentice-type trades and craft jobs.

5792. U.S. Dept. of Labor. Manpower Administration. Office of Research and Development. A STUDY ON THE DEVELOPMENT OF A NON-STANDARD WORK DAY OR WORK WEEK FOR WOMEN. By Ruth W. Prywes. Washington, D.C.: SUDOC, GPO, 1974. 395 pp.

5793. Van Vorst, Bessie and Marie Van Vorst. THE WOMAN WHO TOILS: BEING THE EXPERIENCES OF TWO LADIES AS FACTORY GIRLS. Los Angeles, CA: Univ. of California, Industrial Relations, 1975. 303 pp. Reprint of 1903 edition.

5794. "Women in Blue-Collar Jobs." New York: The Ford Foundation, 1976. 28 pp. Women in industrial and service jobs.

5795. WOMEN IN INDUSTRY: FROM SEVEN POINTS OF VIEW. London, England, 1908. 217 pp. The opinions of Gertrude M. Tuckwell, Constance Smith, Mary R. MacArthur, Mary Tennant, Nettie Adler, Adelaide M. Anderson, and Clementina Black.

G. Women in the Professions

"Business needs more of the professional spirit. The professional spirit seeks professional integrity, from pride, not from compulsion. The professional spirit detects its own violations and penalizes them."

—Henry Ford

"The woman who climbs to a high post and then wants everybody to know how important she is, is the worst enemy of her own sex."

—Claire Giannini Hoffman

5796. Anderson, Mrs. Eugenie. "Women in the Boardroom: A Woman Director Looks at Corporate Responsibility," COMMERCIAL WEST (Sept. 19, 1973), pp. 20-24. The former ambassador discusses the role of women at the corporate policymaking level.

5797. Ashby, Sir Eric. SCIENTIST IN RUSSIA. New York: Penguin Books, 1947. 252 pp. Describes the extent to which Soviet women have come to occupy extremely significant positions in the areas of science and technology.

5798. Berkman, Ted. THE LADY AND THE LAW: THE REMARKABLE STORY OF FANNY HOLTZMANN. Boston, MA: Little, Brown, 1976. 403 pp. Woman lawyer and influential lobbyist for both the establishment of the United Nations headquarters in New York, and the creation of the state of Israel.

5799. Epstein, Laurily Keir, ed. WOMEN IN THE PROFESSIONS. Lexington, MA: D.C. Heath, 1975. 142 pp. Papers from a conference sponsored by Monticello College and Washington University.

5800. Finifter, Ada. "The Professional Status of Women Political Scientists: Some Current Data," PS, vol. 6, no. 4 (Fall 1973), pp. 406-419. Includes citations to other APSA and regional surveys and reports.

5801. Fox, Mary Virginia. LADY FOR THE DEFENSE: A BIOGRAPHY OF BELVA LOCKWOOD. New York: Harcourt Brace Jovanovich, 1975. 158 pp.

5802. Frooks, Dorothy. LADY LAWYER. New York: Robert Speller & Sons, 1975. 210 pp. Autobiographical.

5803. Gale, George W. "Myra Bradwell: The First Woman Lawyer," AMERICAN BAR ASSOCIATION JOURNAL (Dec. 1953), pp. 1080-1083, 1120-1121. Succeeded in convincing the Illinois State Legislature to pass a law prohibiting discrimination in employment, won passage of an Illinois statute giving married women the right to their own wages, and founded the CHICAGO LEGAL NEWS.

5804. Grossblat, Martha and Bette H. Sikes, eds. "Women Lawyers: Supplementary Data to the 1971 Lawyer Statistical Report." Chicago, IL: American Bar Association, 1973. 91 pp.

5805. Kistiakowsky, Vera. "Women in Engineering, Medicine, and Science." Washington, D.C.: National Research Council, Commission on Human Resources, 1975. 64 pp.

5806. Kundsin, Ruth B., ed. WOMEN AND SUCCESS: THE ANATOMY OF ACHIEVEMENT. New York: William Morrow, 1974. 256 pp. Reprint of ANNALS OF THE ACADEMY OF SCIENCES (1972).

5807. McHugh, Mary. LAW AND THE NEW WOMAN. New York: Praeger Books, 1974. 160 pp. A report on the burgeoning opportunities for women in the legal profession.

5808. Metcalf, Henry C. and L. Urick, eds. DYNAMIC ADMINISTRATION: THE COLLECTED PAPERS OF MARY PARKER FOLLET. New York: Harper & Bros., 1941. Originated organizational decision-making theories, and expounded on the role of executives.

5809. Professional Women's Caucus. "Sixteen Reports on the Status of Professional Women." Pittsburgh, PA: KNOW, Inc., 1970. 74 pp.

5810. Rebiere, A. "Les femmes dans la science." Paris, France: NONY, 1894. 85 pp. Brief biographical sketches.

5811. Ruina, Edith. "Women in Science and Technology: A Report of an MIT (Massachusetts Institute of Technology) Workshop." Cambridge, MA: MIT Press, 1974. 39 pp.

5812. Salembier, Olive and Alfred C. Ingersoll, eds. WOMEN IN ENGINEERING AND MANAGEMENT. New York: Engineering Foundation Conferences, 1972. 138 pp. Proceedings of an Engineering Foundation Conference, New England College, Henniker, New Hampshire, July 16-21, 1972.

5813. Schwartz, Helene E. LAWYERING. New York: Farrar, Strauss, & Giroux, 1976. 308 pp. A partly personal, partly professional memoir by a constitutional lawyer.

5814. Strober, Myra H. "Women Economists: Career Aspirations, Education, and Training," AMERICAN ECONOMIC REVIEW, vol. 65, no. 2 (May 1975), pp. 92-99. Suggests a need for positive career counseling in high schools and more financial aid.

5815. Thomson, Dorothy Lampen. ADAM SMITH'S DAUGHTERS: SIX DISTINGUISHED WOMEN ECONOMISTS FROM THE 18TH CENTURY TO THE PRESENT. Hicksville, NY: Exposition Press, 1973. 140 pp. Jane Haldimand Marcet, Harriet Martineau, Millicent Carroll Fawcett, Rosa Luxemburg, Beatrice Potter Webb, and Joan Robinson.

5816. Walsh, Mary Roth. "DOCTORS WANTED: NO WOMEN NEED APPLY:" SEX BARRIERS IN THE MEDICAL PROFESSION, 1835-1975. New Haven, CT: Yale Univ. Press, 1977.

5817. "Women in Science: A Man's World," IMPACT OF SCIENCE ON SOCIETY (UNESCO), vol. 25, no. 2 (April 1975), pp. 99-170. Special Issue. Contributors include Dolly Ghosh, Lucia Tose, Deborah Shapley, Jacqueline Fellman, International Labour Office, Halina Lewicka, and Jacqueline Juillard.

5818. "Women in Science and Technology: Careers for Today and Tomorrow." Iowa City, IA: American College Testing Program, 1976. 18 pp.

H. Women in the Semiprofessions

"Many minor executives prefer a generous expense account to a raise in salary which would be heavily taxed and more soberly spent. It is they who support the so-called "expense account restaurants," places of exotic decor where patrons lunch in a darkness which is all but complete. They cannot see to read the prices on the menu, but these, in the special circumstances, are irrelevant."
                                                                    —Cyril Northcote Parkinson

5819. Adams, Harriet. "Women in Distribution," DISTRIBUTION WORLDWIDE (Nov. 1974), pp. 35-39. Opportunities for women in the fields of transportation and distribution.

5820. Adams, Jean, Margaret Kimball, and Jeannette Eaton. HEROINES OF THE SKYS. Freeport, NY: Books for Libraries, 1970. 295 pp. Reprint of 1942 edition. Women in aeronautics.

5821. Alexander, Shana. TALKING WOMEN. New York: Delacort, 1976. 352

pp. Collection of the author's publications from LIFE, NEWSWEEK, and McCALLS.
5822. Ambassade de France. Service de Presse et d'Information. WOMEN IN THE FRENCH CIVIL SERVICE. New York: Service de Presse et d'Information, 1974.
5823. Archibald, Kathleen A. "Sizing up the Future of Women in Banking," BANKING, vol. 66, no. 1 (July 1973), pp. 28-30, 64. Providing equal opportunity for women and men in banking.
5824. Auriol, Jacqueline. I LIVE TO FLY. New York: E. P. Dutton, 1970. 197 pp. Autobiography of the French aviator who set many women's records during the 1950's.
5825. Bennett, E. Arnold. "Journalism for Women: A Practical Guide." Saint Clair Shores, MI: Scholarly Press, 1976. 98 pp. Reprint of 1898 edition.
5826. Bird, Caroline. "Women: Opportunity for Management." New York: President's Association, 1973. 37 pp.
5827. Boughner, Genevieve Jackson. WOMEN IN JOURNALISM: A GUIDE TO THE OPPORTUNITIES AND A MANUAL OF THE TECHNIQUE OF WOMEN'S WORK FOR NEWSPAPERS AND MAGAZINES. New York: D. Appleton, 1926. 348 pp.
5828. Brazelton, Ethel M. WRITING AND EDITING FOR WOMEN: A BIRD'S-EYE VIEW OF WIDENING OPPORTUNITIES FOR WOMEN IN NEWSPAPER, MAGAZINE, AND OTHER WRITING WORK. New York: Funk & Wagnalls, 1927. 258 pp.
5829. Buchanan, Estill H. "Women in Management," PERSONNEL MANAGEMENT, vol. 32, no. 5 (Sept.-Oct. 1969), pp. 21-26. Stereotypes of women workers and suggestions for better utilization of the female labor force.
5830. Burrows, Martha G. "A Worldwide View of Management Development Needs." New York: AMACOR, 1976. 21 pp.
5831. Carleton, B. N. "The Status of Women in Accounting," MANAGEMENT ACCOUNTING, vol. 55, no. 3 (Sept. 1973), pp. 59-62.
5832. Cheney, Lynne Vincent. "Mrs. Frank Leslie's Illustrated Newspaper," AMERICAN HERITAGE, vol. 26 (Oct. 1975), pp. 42-48, 90-96. Miriam Follin's shrewd business acumen made her one of America's leading publishers in the nineteenth century. After the death of her third husband, newsman, Frank Leslie, she legally changed her name to Frank Leslie to avoid any dispute about the ownership of the paper.
5833. Cole, Doris. FROM TIPI TO SKYSCRAPER: A HISTORY OF WOMEN IN ARCHITECTURE. New York: Braziller, 1973. 136 pp.
5834. Dickerson, Nancy. AMONG THOSE PRESENT: A REPORTER'S VIEW OF TWENTY-FIVE YEARS IN WASHINGTON. New York: Random House, 1976. 283 pp.
5835. Dunlap, Jan. PERSONAL AND PROFESSIONAL SUCCESS FOR WOMEN. Englewood Cliffs, NJ: Prentice-Hall, 1972. 165 pp.
5836. Earhart, Amelia. THE FUN OF IT: RANDOM RECORDS OF MY OWN FLYING AND OF WOMEN IN AVIATION. Detroit, MI: Gale Research, 1975. 218 pp. Reprint of 1932 edition.
5837. Eaton, Jeannette and Bertha M. Stevens. COMMERCIAL WORK AND

TRAINING FOR GIRLS. New York: Macmillan, 1915. 289 pp.
5838. Elliot, Linda Anne. "Black Women in the Media," in OTHER VOICES: BLACK, CHICANO, AND AMERICAN INDIAN, edited by Sharon Murphy. Dayton, OH: Pflaum/Standard, 1974. Pp. 47-52.
5839. Entrikin, Isabelle Webb. SARA JOSEPHA HALE AND "GODEY'S LADY'S BOOK." Philadelphia, PA: Lancaster Press, 1946. 160 pp.
5840. Fogarty, Michael, A. J. Allen, Isobel Allen, and Patricia Walters. WOMEN IN TOP JOBS: FOUR STUDIES IN ACHIEVEMENT. London, England: George Allen & Unwin, 1971. 328 pp. Four studies in Great Britain: 1. Women in 2 Large Companies; 2. The Woman Director; 3. Women in the BBC; 4. Women in the Administrative Class of the Civil Service.
5841. Frank, Harold H. WOMEN IN THE ORGANIZATION. Philadelphia, PA: Univ. of Pennsylvania Press, 1976.
5842. Gallas, Nesta M., ed. "Symposium on Women in Public Administration," PUBLIC ADMINISTRATION REVIEW, vol. 36, no. 4 (Aug. 1976), pp. 347-389. Contributors include Joan Fiss Bishop, Andrea Stoloff, Debra W. Stewart, Mary M. Lepper, Peggy Newgarten, Nancy R. Hooyman, Judith S. Kaplan, Robert B. Denhardt, Jan Perkins, and Jennifer Dorn Oldfield.
5843. Gelfman, Judith S. WOMEN IN TELEVISION NEWS. New York: Columbia Univ. Press, 1976. 186 pp.
5844. Gerrard, Meg, June Oliver, and Martha Williams, eds. "Women in Management: Proceedings of the conference 'Women and Men—Colleagues in Man—?' May 16-17, 1975." Austin, TX: Univ. of Texas at Austin, School of Social Work, Center for Social Work Research, 1976. 79 pp.
5845. Ginzberg, Eli and Alice M. Yohalem, eds. CORPORATE LIB: WOMEN'S CHALLENGE TO MANAGEMENT. Baltimore, MD: Johns Hopkins Univ. Press, 1973. 153 pp.
5846. Gordon, Francine E. and Myra H. Strober. BRINGING WOMEN INTO MANAGEMENT. New York: McGraw-Hill, 1975. 168 pp. Most notable feature was dealing directly with sex as an issue in management relations.
5847. Guy, Henry A., ed. WOMEN IN THE CARIBBEAN. Port of Spain: Quick Services, 1966. 173 pp. A record of career women in the Caribbean, their backgrounds, services, and achievements.
5848. Hennig, Margaret and Anne Jardin. WOMEN AND MANAGEMENT. Garden City, NY: Doubleday, 1977.
5849. Higginson, Margaret V. and Thomas L. Quick. THE AMBITIOUS WOMAN'S GUIDE TO A SUCCESSFUL CAREER. New York: AMACOM, 1975. 240 pp.
5850. Jacobs, Judith E. and Jean M. Alberti, eds. "Realizing Human Potential: Alternatives for Women," EDUCATIONAL HORIZONS, vol. 53, no. 3 (Spring 1975), pp. 95-143. Special Issue. Contributors include Elaine C. Davis, Martha E. Sloan, Carol S. Shapiro, Rosaria Piomelli, Betsy Ancker-Johnson, Sandi E. Cooper, Helen Diamond, Norma Deitch Feshbach, Mary Ellen Verheyden-Hilliard, and Lorraine Mathies.

5851. Jewell, Donald O., ed. WOMEN AND MANAGEMENT: AN EXPANDING ROLE. Atlanta, GA: Georgia State Univ., 1977. 250 pp. 3-part volume focuses on women's lifestyles and changes in roles and attitudes, statistical data on women in the workforce, and women in management—stereotypes, training, decision-making.

5852. Jewell, Donald O. and Carolyn R. Pollard, eds. "The Changing Face of Management: Women as a Managerial Resource," ATLANTA ECONOMIC REVIEW, vol. 26, no. 2 (March-April 1976), pp. 4-50. Special Issue. Contributors include Sandra Ekberg-Jordan, Donald R. Stacey, Gail McKnight Beckman, Virginia E. Schein, Jayne I. Gackenbach, Marian Burke, Stephen M. Auerbach, Douglas W. Bray, and Holley H. Ulbrich.

5853. Johnson, Diane. "Women in Meteorology: A Small Glimpse at the Large-Scale Pattern," WEATHERWISE, vol. 28, no. 3 (June 1975), pp. 108-113. Overview of the current status of women in the atmospheric sciences.

5854. Kahne, Hilda. "Women in Management: Strategy for Increase." Washington, D.C.: Business and Professional Women's Foundation, 1974. 11 pp. Advancing opportunities for women in management.

5855. Knight, Ruth Adams. STAND BY FOR THE LADIES! THE DISTAFF SIDE OF RADIO. New York: Coward-McCann, 1939. 179 pp.

5856. Krantz, Harry. THE PARTICIPATORY BUREAUCRACY: WOMEN AND MINORITIES IN A MORE REPRESENTATIVE PUBLIC SERVICE. Lexington, MA: Lexington Books, 1976. 244 pp. Women and minorities in the U.S. Civil Service.

5857. Lutz, Alma. "Early American Women Historians," BOSTON PUBLIC LIBRARY QUARTERLY, vol. 8 (1956), pp. 85-99.

5858. Lynch, Edith M. THE EXECUTIVE SUITE—FEMININE STYLE. New York: AMACOM, 1973. 258 pp.

5859. Oldham, Ellen M. "Early Women Printers of America," BOSTON PUBLIC LIBRARY QUARTERLY, vol. 10 (Jan. 1958), pp. 6-26; (April 1958), pp. 78-92; (July 1958), pp. 141-150.

5860. Osipow, Samuel H., ed. EMERGING WOMAN: CAREER ANALYSIS AND OUTLOOKS. Columbus, OH: Charles E. Merrill, 1975.

5861. Place, Irene Magdaline and Alice Armstrong. MANAGEMENT CAREERS FOR WOMEN. Louisville, KY: Vocational Guidance Materials, 1975. 219 pp.

5862. Rogalin, Wilma C. and Arthur R. Pell. WOMEN'S GUIDE TO MANAGEMENT POSITIONS. New York: Simon & Schuster, 1975. 149 pp.

5863. Schilling, Gerhard F. and M. Kathleen Hunt. "Women in Science and Technology: U.S./USSR Comparisons." Santa Monica, CA: The Rand Corp., 1974. 38 pp. Participation of women in all spheres of economic life is greater in the USSR; U.S. is in the process of reassessing policies with regard to the social and economic status of women.

5864. Schuyler, George S. "Madame C. J. Walker, Pioneer Big Businesswoman of America," THE MESSENGER (Aug. 1924), pp. 251-266.

5865. Shuler, Marjorie, Ruth Adams Knight, and Muriel Fuller. LADY EDITOR: CAREERS FOR WOMEN IN PUBLISHING. Norwood, PA: Norwood Editions, 1976. 288 pp. Reprint of 1941 edition.

5866. Sommerkorn, Ingrid, R. Nave-Herz, and Christine Kulke. WOMEN'S CAREERS: EXPERIENCE FROM EAST AND WEST GERMANY. London, England: Political & Economic Planning, 1970. 132 pp.

5867. Splaver, Sarah. NONTRADITIONAL CAREERS FOR WOMEN. New York: Julian Messner, 1973. 224 pp. Lists more than 500 traditionally male occupations offering employment opportunities for women, grouped into ten major classifications. Current addresses for more source materials are included as well as a bibliography.

5868. Stead, Bette Ann. "Women's Contributions to Management Thought," BUSINESS HORIZONS, vol. 17, no. 1 (Feb. 1974), pp. 32-36. Discusses the contributions of Lillian Gilbreth, Mary Parker Follett, Jane Mounton, Joan Woodward, Riva Poor, and Christel Kammerer.

5869. Stewart, Debra W. "Women and the Public Service," PUBLIC ADMINISTRATION REVIEW, vol. 35, no. 6 (Nov.-Dec. 1975), pp. 641-646. Review of recent literature on women employed in the governmental sector.

5870. Strainchamps, Ethel, ed. ROOMS WITH NO VIEW: A WOMAN'S GUIDE TO THE MAN'S WORLD OF THE MEDIA. Compiled by the Media Women's Association. New York: Harper & Row, 1974. 320 pp.

5871. "Up the Ladder, Finally!" BUSINESS WEEK, no. 2408 (Nov. 24, 1975), pp. 58-68. Women in top-level management.

XI. GENERAL REFERENCE WORKS ON WOMEN

A. Bibliographies

"Knowledge is of two kinds: we know a subject ourselves, or we know where we can find information upon it."
—Samuel Johnson

5872. American Personnel and Guidance Association. Sex Equality in Guidance Opportunities Project. "Resources for Counselors, Teachers, and Administrators." Washington, D.C.: SUDOC, GPO, 1975. 11 pp. Includes citations to bibliographic materials available as well as a directory of S.E.G.O. Trainers.

5873. Babcock, Barbara, Anne E. Freedman, Eleanor Holmes Norton, and Susan Deller Ross. "Women and The Law: A Collection of Reading Lists." Pittsburgh, PA: KNOW, Inc., 1971. 31 pp.

5874. Barnard College Women's Center. WOMEN'S WORK AND WOMEN'S STUDIES, 1973-1974. New York: Barnard College, 1976. 370 pp. Interdisciplinary bibliography; thousands of references to published works in humanities and social sciences, including bibliographies and references to research in progress.

5875. ———. WOMEN'S WORK AND WOMEN'S STUDIES, 1972. Edited by Dicki Lou Ellis, Kathleen Graves, Kirsten Grimstad, Dorothy Marks, Fanny Pollack, Jean Thompson, and Mary Wexford. New York: Barnard College, 1974. 350 pp. Bibliography for 1972 plus Addendum for 1971.

5876. Bickner, Mei Liang. WOMEN AT WORK: AN ANNOTATED BIBLIOGRAPHY. Irvine, CA: Univ. of California Press, 1974. 437 pp. More than 600 entries with author, title, category, and key word indexes.

5877. Bickner, Mei Liang and Marlene Shaughnessy. WOMEN AT WORK: AN ANNOTATED BIBLIOGRAPHY, VOLUME II. Los Angeles, CA: Univ. of California, Institute of Industrial Relations, 1976.

5878. Bullough, Vern L. and Barrett W. Elcano. AN ANNOTATED BIBLIOGRAPHY OF PROSTITUTION. New York: Garland Publishing, 1976.

5879. Business and Professional Women's Foundation. Library. "Women and Work in U.S. History." Washington, D.C.: Business and Professional Women's Foundation, 1976. 28 pp. Bibliography.

5880. Buvinic, Mayra, et al. WOMEN AND WORLD DEVELOPMENT: AN ANNOTATED BIBLIOGRAPHY. Washington, D.C.: Overseas Development Council, 1976. 162 pp. Sponsored by the American Association for the Advancement of Science, Office of International Science. Comprehensive annotation of about 400 unpublished and published works. Each subject category is subdivided according to geographic focus.

5881. Cabello-Argandona, Roberto. THE CHICANA: A COMPREHENSIVE BIBLIOGRAPHY. Los Angeles, CA: Univ. of California, Chicano Studies Center, 1975. 308 pp.

5882. Cardinale, Susan. "Special Issues of Serials About Women 1965-1975. Monticello, IL: Council of Planning Librarians, 1976. 41 pp. Exchange Bibliography No. 995. 298 citations.

5883. CATALOGS OF THE SOPHIA SMITH COLLECTION, WOMEN'S HISTORY ARCHIVES, SMITH COLLEGE, NORTHAMPTON, MASSACHUSETTS. Boston, MA: G. K. Hall, 1975. 7 vols. Emphasizes history of women in the United States; also international materials. 24,000 manuscript entries.

5884. Chrisman, Sara B. "Women and American Politics: A Selected Bibliography, 1965-1974." New Brunswick, NJ: Rutgers Univ., Center for the American Woman and Politics, 1974. 64 pp. Guide to information regarding women's participation in American politics: women holding office, women in political parties, women's election campaigns, and public policy issues—ERA, abortion, employment.

5885. Christenson, Susan J., comp. "Women and Drug Use: An Annotated Bibliography," JOURNAL OF PSYCHEDELIC DRUGS, vol. 6, no. 4 (Oct.-Dec. 1974), pp. 371-414. 154 English-language journal articles, unpublished papers, and dissertations, dealing with subjects ranging from women and alcohol to women and drug advertising.

5886. Cismaresco, Françoise. "Education and Training of Women," EDUCATIONAL DOCUMENTATION AND INFORMATION, vol. 49, no. 196 (3rd Quarter 1975), pp. 14-43. Annotated bibliography covering the years 1970-1975.

5887. Dasgupta, Kalpana. WOMEN ON THE INDIAN SCENE: AN ANNOTATED BIBLIOGRAPHY. Columbia, MO: South Asia Books, 1976.

5888. Davis, Audrey B. "Bibliography on Women: With Special Emphasis on Their Roles in Science and Society." New York: Science History Publications, 1974. 50 pp. Compilation of selected titles listed under the appropriate Library of Congress woman-related subject headings.

5889. Davis, Lenwood G. THE BLACK WOMAN IN AMERICAN SOCIETY: A SELECTED ANNOTATED BIBLIOGRAPHY. Boston, MA: G. K. Hall, 1975. 159 pp. 1,186 numbered items, 701 bibliographic citations, plus directory and statistical data.

5890. ———. "Black Women in the Cities 1872-1975: A Bibliography of Published Works on the Life and Achievements of Black Women in Cities of the United States." Monticello, IL: Council of Planning Librarians, 1975. 75 pp. Exchange Bibliographies No. 751-752.

5891. ———. "The Policewoman in American Society: A Preliminary Survey." Monticello, IL: Council of Planning Librarians, 1976. 15 pp. Exchange Bibliography No. 1045. 103 citations divided by articles, books, pamphlets, government documents, and theses and dissertations.

5892. ———. "The Woman in American Society—A Selected Bibliography." Monticello, IL: Council of Planning Librarians, 1975. 99 pp. 2nd edition. Does not include periodical literature.

5893. Dollen, Charles, comp. ABORTION IN CONTEXT: A SELECT BIBLIOGRAPHY. Metuchen, NJ: Scarecrow Press, 1970. 150 pp. More than 1,400 entries in English, includes a "resource index" to trace incomplete citations.

5894. Edwards, Richard and Bruce Gronbeck. "A Partial List of Educational, Instructional, and Documentary Films Treating Women's Roles, Problems, and Communication Strategies." Arlington, VA: ERIC Document Reproduction Service, 1975. 42 pp. 189 films listed.

5895. Eichler, Margrit. "Annotated Selected Bibliography of Bibliographies on Women." Toronto, Ontario: Association of Universities and Colleges of Canada, Commission on the Status of Women, 1973. 17 pp.

5896. Eichler, Margrit, John Marecki, and Jennifer Newton. "Women: A Bibliography of Special Periodical Issues (1960-1975)." Toronto, Ontario: Canadian Newsletter of Research on Women, 1976. 75 pp.

5897. Equal Rights Amendment Project, comp. THE EQUAL RIGHTS AMENDMENT: A BIBLIOGRAPHIC STUDY. Edited by Anita Miller and Hazel Greenburg. Westport, CT: Greenwood Press, 1976.

5898. Felmley, Jenrose, comp. "Working Women: Homemakers and Volunteers: An Annotated Selected Bibliography." Washington, D.C.: Business and Professional Women's Foundation, 1975. 25 pp. A "Review of the Resources" precedes the 82-citation bibliography.

5899. The Feminist Theory Collective. "American Women: Our Lives and Labor: An Annotated Bibliography of Women and Work in the United States, 1900-1975." Eugene, OR: The Feminist Theory Collective, 1976. 36 pp. 71 citations grouped by time periods, using readability and availability as major criteria for selection.

5900. Foreman, JoAnn T. "Women: A Selected Annotated Bibliography on Their Equal Opportunity and Employment." Baton Rouge, LA: Louisiana State Univ., College of Business Administration, Division of Research, 1973. 20 pp.

5901. Freeman, Leah, comp. "The Changing Role of Women: A Selected Bibliography." Sacramento, CA: Sacramento State College Library, 1972. 50 pp.

5902. Froschl, Merle and Jane Williamson. "Feminist Resources for Schools and Colleges." Old Westbury, NY: Feminist Press, 1976. 48 pp. Newly revised edition. More than 500 sources of materials on sexism in education, bibliography and multi-media resources.

5903. Gehr, Marilyn. "Employment Discrimination Against Women: A Selected Annotated Bibliography." Albany, NY: New York State Library, Legislative Reference Library, 1975. 38 pp. See also Ila M. Hallowell.

5904. Goodwater, Leanna. WOMEN IN ANTIQUITY: AN ANNOTATED BIBLIOGRAPHY. Metuchen, NJ: Scarecrow Press, 1975. 175 pp. Materials dealing with women from earliest records to 476 A.D.; also includes modern works about women in antiquity.

5905. Hallowell, Ila M. "Employment Discrimination Against Women: A Selected Annotated Bibliography." Albany, NY: New York State Library, Legislative Reference Library, 1972. 41 pp. See Also Marilyn Gehr.

5906. Harrison, Cynthia Ellen. WOMEN'S MOVEMENT MEDIA: A SOURCE GUIDE. New York: Bowker, 1975. 268 pp. Guide to the information, services, and products available to women in every state and Canada.

5907. Henley, Nancy and Barrie Thorn. SHE SAID/HE SAID: AN ANNOTATED BIBLIOGRAPHY OF SEX DIFFERENCES IN LANGUAGE, SPEECH, AND NON-VERBAL COMMUNICATION. Pittsburgh, PA: KNOW, Inc., 1975. 311 pp.

5908. Hixon, Don L. and Don Hennessee. WOMEN IN MUSIC: A BIBLIOGRAPHY. Metuchen, NJ: Scarecrow Press, 1975. 358 pp. Identifies more than 4,000 women of all periods and countries with a brief biographical entry for each musician.

5909. Israel, Stan, comp. and ed. A BIBLIOGRAPHY ON DIVORCE. New York: Bloch Publishing, 1974. 300 pp. 152 categories with annotations and complete tables of contents; 64 citations without detailed entries, 115 earlier U.S. publications, and 76 international publications on divorce.

5910. Jacobs, Sue-Ellen. WOMEN IN PERSPECTIVE: A GUIDE FOR CROSS-CULTURAL STUDIES. Urbana, IL: Univ. of Illinois Press, 1974. 299 pp. Extensive bibliography.

5911. Key, Mary Ritchie. MALE/FEMALE LANGUAGE WITH A COMPREHENSIVE BIBLIOGRAPHY. Metuchen, NJ: Scarecrow Press, 1975. 200 pp. Discussion of male/female differences in language and communication, with a comprehensive bibliography on male/female linguistic behavior.

5912. Knaster, Meri. WOMEN IN SPANISH AMERICA: AN ANNOTATED BIBLIOGRAPHY FROM PRE-CONQUEST TO CONTEMPORARY TIMES. Boston, MA: G. K. Hall, 1977. 696 pp. Over 2,500 publications in Spanish and English, organized both by subject matter and geographically.

5913. Kohen, Andrew I., Susan C. Breinich, and Patricia Shields. "Women and the Economy: A Bibliography and A Review of the Literature on Sex Differentiation in the Labor Market." Columbus, OH: Ohio State Univ., College of Administrative Science, Center for Human Resource Research, 1975. 88 pp. 500-item bibliography is divided topically: history, labor supply, earnings, occupations, unionism, unemployment attitudes, legal status, domestic aspects, and bibliographies.

5914. Kowalsky, Rosemary. WOMEN AND FILM: A BIBLIOGRAPHY. Metuchen, NJ: Scarecrow Press, 1976. 278 pp.

5915. Kratochvil, Laura and Shauna Shaw, comps. "African Women: A Select Bibliography." Cambridge, England: Cambridge Univ., African Studies Center, 1974. 74 pp.

5916. Krauss, Wilma Rule. "Political Implications of Gender Roles: A Review of the Literature," AMERICAN POLITICAL SCIENCE REVIEW, vol. 68, no. 4 (Dec. 1974), pp. 1706-1723.

5917. Kusnerz, Peggy A. and Ann M. Pollack, comps. "Women: A Select Bibliography." Ann Arbor, MI: Univ. of Michigan, Univ. Extension Services, 1975. 46 pp. Topical arrangement of books, monographs, journals, and newsletters relating to women's studies, feminism, and other perspectives on women, including women's studio films and videotapes. Not annotated.

5918. Lerner, Gerda, comp. "Women's Studies: History of Women in America." Bronxville, NY: The Author, 1974. 40 pp. Bibliography for students and teachers of women's history.

5919. Loyd, Bonnie. "Women and Geography: An Annotated Bibliography and Guide to Sources of Information." Monticello, IL: Council of Planning Librarians, 1976. 18 pp. Exchange Bibliography No. 1159. 108 citations; Part I, references on women in the field of geography, Part II, geographic research on women.

5920. McKenney, Mary. DIVORCE: A SELECTED ANNOTATED BIBLIOGRAPHY. Metuchen, NJ: Scarecrow Press, 1975. 157 pp. 613 items in English on divorce and related areas, basis for inclusion being current or historical significance, or representation of particular viewpoints.

5921. "Michigan Women: Biographies, Autobiographies, and Reminiscences." Lansing, MI: Michigan Dept. of Education, State Library Services, 1975. 7 pp. Over 100 citations to writings on women's experiences from pioneer days to the present.

5922. Moser, Collette and Deborah Johnson. "Rural Women Workers in the 20th Century: An Annotated Bibliography." East Lansing, MI: Michigan State Univ., Center for Rural Manpower and Public Affairs, 1973. 70 pp.

5923. Myers, Carol Fairbanks. WOMEN IN LITERATURE: CRITICISM OF THE SEVENTIES. Metuchen, NJ: Scarecrow Press, 1976. 263 pp. Bibliography of articles, books, and dissertations published between Jan. 1970 and Spring 1975, including selected book reviews, interviews, and biographical studies.

5924. Nicholas, Suzanne. BIBLIOGRAPHY ON WOMEN WORKERS, 1861-1965. Geneva, Switzerland: International Labor Office, 1970. 252 pp. 1,782 items in several languages, cross-indexed by author, subject, and country.

5925. "1975, Año Internacional de la Mujer: Bibliografia (Disponible en las Bibliotecas Benjamin Franklin)." Mexico, D.F.: Biblioteca Benjamin Franklin, 1975. 27 pp. 64 citations to materials in various media on women, annotated in English and Spanish.

5926. Pinto, Patrick R. and Jeanne O. Buchmeier. "Problems and Issues in the Employment of Minority, Disadvantaged, and Female Groups: An Annotated Bibliography." Minneapolis, MN: Univ. of Minnesota, Industrial Relations Center, 1973. 62 pp.

5927. Quebec (Prov.). Conseil du Statut de la Femme. LES QUEBECOISES: GUIDE BIBLIOGRAPHIQUE SUIVI D'UNE FILMOGRAPHIE. Quebec City, Quebec: l'Editeur Officiel de Quebec, 1976. 160 pp. Feminism, history, biography, women in society, legal status, political participation, women at work, and women in religion.

5928. Rosenfelt, Deborah Silverton. "Strong Women: An Annotated Bibliography of Paperbacks for the High School Classroom." Old Westbury, NY: Feminist Press, 1976. 64 pp. More than 100 books organized into sections on novels, short stories, autobiography, biography, anthologies, drama and poetry; and cross-listed by six topics: adolescence, female sexuality, women in the arts and professions, women and political commitment, third world women and working class women.

5929. Rosenzweig, Marianne and Annette Brodsky, eds. "The Psychology of the Female Offender: A Research Bibliography." University, AL: Univ. of Alabama, The Center for Correctional Psychology, 1976. Annotated bibliography on theory research and treatment of juvenile and adult offenders, covering the years 1950-1975.

5930. Rowbotham, Sheila, comp. "Women's Liberation and Revolution." London, England: Falling Wall Press, 1976. 24 pp. Reading list on the relationship between revolutionary politics and feminism; covers women at work, the changing nature of the family, the socialist movement, role of women in revolution, etc.

5931. Roysdan, Christy. "Women in Engineering: A Bibliography on Their Progress and Prospects." Monticello, IL: Council of Planning Librarians, 1975. 22 pp. Exchange Bibliography No. 878. General background information on women and work, conference papers, i.e. Henniker conferences at New England College.

5932. Ruzek, Sherl K. "Women and Health Care: A Bibliography." Evanston, IL: Northwestern Univ., 1975. 76 pp. + Addendum (1976). Documentation of the women's health movement.

5933. Samuels, Victoria. "Nowhere to be Found: A Literature Review and Annotated Bibliography on White Working Class Women." New York: American Jewish Committee Project on Group Life and Ethnic America, 1975. 29 pp. Images of white working class women, especially mass media images.

5934. Schlacter, Gail and Donna Belli. "The Changing Role of Women in America: A Selected Annotated Bibliography of Reference Sources." Monticello, IL: Council of Planning Librarians, 1975. 36 pp. 84 citations of information sources and citation sources, indexed by author and title.

5935. Sharma, Prakash C. "Female Working Role and Economic Development: A Selected Research Bibliography." Monticello, IL: Council of Planning Librarians, 1974. 16 pp. Exchange Bibliography No. 663. 218 citations; books and monographs, articles and papers.

5936. Stakelon, Anne E. and Joel H. Magisos, comps. "Sex Stereotyping and Occupational Aspirations: An Anotated Bibliography." Arlington, VA: ERIC Document Reproduction Service, 1975. 49 pp. 88 citations chosen to assist those persons applying for grants under the Vocational Education Act of 1963.

5937. Steiner-Scott, Elizabeth, comp. NEW JERSEY WOMEN, 1770-1970: A BIBLIOGRAPHY. Cranbury, NJ: Fairleigh-Dickinson Univ. Press, 1977.

5938. Strugnell, Cecile. ADJUSTMENT TO WIDOWHOOD AND SOME RELATED PROBLEMS: A SELECTIVE AND ANNOTATED

BIBLIOGRAPHY. New York: Health Sciences Publishing, 1974. 201 pp. 790 citations to books and articles published before 1972.

5939. Swanwick, Lynne Struthers. "A Checklist of Canadian Federal, Provincial, and Municipal Government Publications of Special Significance for Women." Monticello, IL: Council of Planning Librarians, 1976. 20 pp. Exchange Bibliography No. 1118. 240 citations arranged by governmental unit.

5940. ———. "Women in Canadian Politics and Government: A Bibliography." Monticello, IL: Council of Planning Librarians, 1974. 29 pp. Exchange Bibliography No. 697. 245 citations indexed by subject, lists of organizations and women's newsletters.

5941. Todd, Janet M. MARY WOLLSTONECRAFT: AN ANNOTATED BIBLIOGRAPHY OF HER WORKS AND CRITICISM. New York: Garland Publishing, 1975. 124 pp.

5942. Tominaga, Thomas T. and Wilma Schneidermeyer. IRIS MURDOCH AND MURIEL SPARK: A BIBLIOGRAPHY. Metuchen, NJ: Scarecrow Press, 1976. 237 pp.

5943. United Nations. Secretariat. STATUS OF WOMEN: A SELECT BIBLIOGRAPHY. New York: United Nations, 1975. 121 pp. Prepared by the Dag Hammarskjold Library. 1,180 citations categorized by subject and grouped according to country.

5944. U.S. Air Force Academy. Library. "Women in the Military." Compiled and edited by Betsy Coxe and Florence Klam. Colorado Springs, CO: U.S. Air Force Academy, 1975. 60 pp.

5945. ———. "Women and the American Economy." Compiled by Ottie K. Sutton. Colorado Springs, CO: U.S. Air Force Academy, 1976.

5946. U.S. Council of National Defense. WOMAN IN THE WAR: A BIBLIOGRAPHY. Edited by Marion R. Nims. Washington, D.C.: Zenger Publications, 1976. Reprint of 1918 edition.

5947. U.S. Dept. of Health, Education, and Welfare. National Institute for Mental Health. SEX ROLES: A RESEARCH BIBLIOGRAPHY. By Helen S. Astin. Washington, D.C.: SUDOC, GPO, 1975. 374 pp. Covers literature originating in the United States and abroad, directed toward social and behavioral scientists.

5948. ———. WOMAN AND MENTAL HEALTH: SELECTED ANNOTATED REFERENCES, 1970-1973. Edited by Phyllis E. Cromwell. Washington, D.C.: SUDOC, GPO, 1974. 247 pp.

5949. U.S. Dept. of Labor. Employment Standards Administration. Women's Bureau. "A Guide to Sources of Data on Women and Women Workers for the United States and for Regions, States and Local Areas." Washington, D.C.: SUDOC, GPO, 1972. 15 pp. Identifies publications available from various government agencies.

5950. Waldrip, Louise and Shirley Ann Bauer. A BIBLIOGRAPHY OF THE WORKS OF KATHERINE ANNE PORTER AND A BIBLIOGRAPHY OF THE CRITICISM OF THE WORKS OF KATHERINE ANNE PORTER. Metuchen, NJ: Scarecrow Press, 1969. 219 pp.

5951. Walstedt, Joyce Jennings. "The Psychology of Women: A Partially

Annotated Bibliography." Pittsburgh, PA: KNOW, Inc., 1973. 76 pp.
5952. Ward, Dennis F., comp. "Sex Discrimination in Employment, 1969-1975: A Selective Bibliography, Part I—Cases and Comments." Sacramento, CA: California State Library, 1976. 15 pp. Annotated bibliography of over 150 cases treating U.S. statutory and case law.
5953. ———. "Sex Discrimination in Employment, 1969-1975: Part II—Periodical Articles." Sacramento, CA: California State Library, 1976.
5954. Watermuller, Georgia P. "Careers for College Women: A Bibliography of Vocational Materials." Ann Arbor, MI: Univ. of Michigan, Center for the Continuing Education of Women, 1968. 61 pp.
5955. Whaley, Sara S. and Margrit Eichler. "A Bibliography of Canadian and U.S. Resources on Women." Rush, NY: Women's Studies Abstracts, 1974. 22 pp. About 40 abstracted publications: reference books, bibliographies of books and pamphlets, mimeo bibliographies, and forthcoming bibliographies.
5956. Wheeler, Helen Rippier. "Alice in Wonderland, or Through the Looking Glass: Resources for Implementing Principles of Affirmative Action Employment for Women." Arlington, VA: ERIC Document Reproduction Service, 1975. 14 pp. 64 annotated multi-media references.
5957. ———. WOMANHOOD MEDIA: CURRENT RESOURCES ABOUT WOMEN. Metuchen, NJ: Scarecrow Press, 1972. 335 pp. Annotated bibliography of more than 350 books, and directory of sources for materials relating to the contemporary women's movement. Part I emphasizes the reasons for the resurgence of the movement.
5958. ———. WOMANHOOD MEDIA SUPPLEMENT: ADDITIONAL CURRENT RESOURCES ABOUT WOMEN. Metuchen, NJ: Scarecrow Press, 1975. 489 pp. Supplement to the bibliography and directory sections of WOMANHOOD MEDIA, bringing the listing of available books to 826 and listing more than 1,000 audiovisual materials available.
5959. White, William, Jr., ed. REFERENCE ENCYCLOPEDIA OF WOMEN'S LIBERATION. Philadelphia, PA: North American Publishing, 1972. 194 pp.
5960. Williams, Ora. AMERICAN BLACK WOMEN IN THE ARTS AND SOCIAL SCIENCES: A BIBLIOGRAPHIC SURVEY. Metuchen, NJ: Scarecrow Press, 1973. 161 pp. 2,000 works by and about black women writers, musicians, poets, artists, sculptors, and other contributors to the social sciences and arts. Includes a list of black periodicals and publishing houses.
5961. Women's History Research Center. "Bibliographies on Women: Indexed by Topic." Berkeley, CA: Women's History Research Center, 1974. 200 bibliographies listed covering topics ranging from "Image of Women," to "Scandinavian Women."
5962. Young, Katherine K. and Arvind Sharma. "Images of the Feminine, Mythic, Philosophic and Human, in the Buddhist, Hindu, and Islamic Traditions: A Bibliography." Detroit, MI: New Horizons, 1974. 36 pp.

B. Biographical Dictionaries

"The poor dear dead have been laid out in vain; turned into cash, they are laid out again."
— *Thomas Hood*

"Biography is the personal and home aspect of history."
— *Robert Eldredge Aris Willmott.*

5963. Berkowitz, Tamar, Jean Mangi, and Jan Williamson, eds. WHO'S WHO AND WHERE IN WOMEN'S STUDIES. Old Westbury, NY: Feminist Press, 1974. 256 pp. Directory of college-level women's studies courses and faculty in the United States; includes 4,900 courses listed by instructor, institution, and department.

5964. Cameron, Mabel Ward, ed. and comp. THE BIOGRAPHICAL CYCLOPAEDIA OF AMERICAN WOMEN. Detroit, MI: Gale Research, 1975. 2 vols. Reprint of 1924 edition. Pronounced aristocratic slant to inclusion—usually based on wealth, either born or married into. Often the women actually did perform valuable community service in a volunteer capacity.

5965. Engelbarts, Rudolf. WOMEN IN THE UNITED STATES CONGRESS, 1917-1972: THEIR ACCOMPLISHMENTS, WITH BIBLIOGRAPHIES. Littleton, CO: Libraries Unlimited, 1974. 184 pp. Biographies of the 81 women in the House and Senate, arranged chronologically by year of entry into Congress; provides bibliography of materials by and about each woman as well as general listing.

5966. Evans, Gwynneth, comp. "Women in Federal Politics: A Bio-Bibliography/Les femmes au federal: Une bio-bibliographie." Ottawa, Canada: National Library of Canada, 1975. 81 pp. Sketches of the 41 women who have served in the Canadian Parliament (1920 to the present): 27 House of Commons, 14 senators. Detailed analysis of legislative careers; includes a general bibliography on women in politics.

5967. FAMOUS WISCONSIN WOMEN. Madison, WI: Wisconsin Historical Society, 1974. 6 vols.

5968. Howes, Durward, ed. AMERICAN WOMEN: THE STANDARD BIOGRAPHICAL DICTIONARY OF NOTABLE WOMEN: VOLUME III, 1939-1940. Teaneck, NJ: Zephyrus Press, 1974. 1,083 pp. Only women living at that time are included, over 10,000 women are listed, includes directory of women's organizations, geographical index, and statistical data.

5969. Love, Barbara J., ed. FOREMOST WOMEN IN COMMUNICATION: A BIOGRAPHICAL REFERENCE WORK ON ACCOMPLISHED WOMEN IN BROADCASTING, PUBLISHING, ADVERTISING, PUBLIC RELATIONS, AND ALLIED PROFESSIONS. New York: Bowker, 1970. 788 pp.

5970. Mayer, Gertrude T. WOMEN OF LETTERS. Freeport, NY: Books for

Libraries, 1973. 2 vols. Reprint of 1894 edition.

5971. Modern Language Association. Commission on the Status of Women in the Profession. DICTIONARY OF WOMEN SCHOLARS IN THE MODERN LANGUAGES. New York: Modern Language Association of America, 1973.

5972. Rutgers University. Eagleton Institute. Center for the American Woman and Politics. WOMEN IN PUBLIC OFFICE: A BIOGRAPHICAL DIRECTORY AND STATISTICAL ANALYSIS. New York: Bowker, 1976. 455 pp. The results of a survey of several thousand women currently holding office around the country. The analysis explores the demographic characteristics, family situations, organizational affiliations, political experience, and the implications of the patterns and trends developed.

5973. WOMAN'S WHO'S WHO OF AMERICA: A BIOGRAPHICAL DICTIONARY OF CONTEMPORARY WOMEN OF THE UNITED STATES AND CANADA, 1914-1915. Detroit, MI: Gale Research, 1976. Reprint of 1914 edition.

5974. THE WORLD'S WHO'S WHO OF WOMEN, VOLUME III. Totowa, NJ: Rowman & Littlefield, 1976.

5975. THE WORLD'S WHO'S WHO OF WOMEN, VOLUME II. Totowa, NJ: Rowman & Littlefield, 1974. 1,000 pp

5976. THE WORLD'S WHO'S WHO OF WOMEN, VOLUME I. Totowa, NJ: Rowman & Littlefield, 1973. 976 pp.

C. Directories of Woman's Organizations and Institutes

"In an arch, each single stone, which, if severed from the rest, would be perhaps defenceless, is sufficiently secured by the solidity and entireness of the whole fabric of which it is a part."

—Robert Boyle

5977. American Medical Association. DIRECTORY OF WOMEN PHYSICIANS IN THE UNITED STATES. Chicago, IL: American Medical Association, 1974.

5978. Barrer, Myra E., ed. WOMEN'S ORGANIZATIONS AND LEADERS DIRECTORY: 1975-1976. Washington, D.C.: Today Publications, 1976.

5979. ———. WOMEN'S ORGANIZATIONS AND LEADERS: 1973 DIRECTORY. Washington, D.C.: Today Publications, 1972.

5980. CHICAGO WOMEN'S DIRECTORY: ARTICLES AND LISTINGS. Chicago, IL: Inforwoman, 1974. 225 pp. Text in both English and Spanish. Lists agencies, groups, and literature sources; directory of schools, employment assistance, child care resources, etc., and includes essays on issues affecting women, i.e. welfare and the ERA.

5981. De Noyelles, Dana A. and Joan D. Smith. WOMEN IN CALIFORNIA: A GUIDE TO ORGANIZATIONS AND INFORMATION SOURCES.

Claremont, CA: Center for California Public Affairs, 1976.

5982. DIRECTORY OF WOMEN ATTORNEYS IN THE UNITED STATES. Butler, IN: Ford Associates, 1974. 2 vols. with supplement.

5983. Keene, Josephine Bond. "National Directory of Negro Business and Professional Women." Philadelphia, PA: The Author, 1942. 19 pp.

5984. Vetter, Betty M. and Eleanor L. Babco. PROFESSIONAL WOMEN AND MINORITIES: A MANPOWER RESOURCE SERVICE. Washington, D.C.: Scientific Manpower Commission, 1975. 656 pp. Loose-leaf bound; plans are for semi-annual updating.

5985. Wilson, Christine, Gumecindo Salas, and Linda Carrick. WOMEN AND MINORITY RECRUITMENT: A RESOURCE GUIDE. East Lansing, MI: Michigan State Univ. Office of Women's Programs/Office of Minority Programs, 1974. 251 pp. Women's directories and resources.

5986. Wisconsin. Governor's Commission on the Status of Women. "A Directory for Wisconsin Women's Groups." Madison, WI: Governor's Commission on the Status of Women, 1976.

5987. The Womanpower Project. THE NEW YORK WOMAN'S DIRECTORY. New York: Workman Publishing, 1973. 262 pp. Consumer's guide to women professionals, businesses owned by women, and services provided by women.

5988. Women's History Research Center. "Films By and/or About Women, 1972: Directory of Film-makers and Distributors, Internationally, Past and Present." Berkeley, CA: Women's History Research Center, 1972. 72 pp.

F. Handbooks and Almanacs

"Modern invention has banished the spinning wheel, and the same law of progress makes the woman of today a different woman from her grandmother."
—Susan Brownell Anthony

"Everything that looks to the future elevates human nature; for life is never so low as when occupied with the present."
—Letitia Elizabeth Landon

5989. Abarbanel, Karen and Connie Seigel. WOMEN'S WORK BOOK. New York: Praeger Books, 1975. 320 pp. Practical guide for job-seeking women; placement information, skills determination, etc.

5990. Conroy, Mary. THE RATIONAL WOMAN'S GUIDE TO SELF-DEFENSE: HOW TO AVOID DANGER AND HOW TO FIGHT BACK IF YOU CAN'T. New York: Grosset & Dunlap, 1975. 127 pp.

5991. Edry, Carol Freedman and Ginnie Goulet, eds. THE WOMEN'S YELLOW PAGES: ORIGINAL SOURCEBOOK FOR WOMEN. Boston, MA: Boston Women's Collective, 1973. 159 pp. Good general guide aimed at women with low incomes; organization and agency directory (for Boston), and how-to's on child care, medicine and health, etc.

5992. Gager, Nancy, ed. WOMEN'S RIGHTS ALMANAC, 1974. Bethesda, MD: Elizabeth Cady Stanton Publishing, 1974. 620 pp. State-by-state listing of information concerning demographic statistics, women officials, voting records of congressional members on women's issues, current legislation, and a chronology of women's events in 1973 and the prior 200 years of American and international feminism. Lists 300 major women's organizations, and includes a bibliography of bibliographies.

5993. Grimstad, Kirsten and Susan Rennie, eds. THE NEW WOMAN'S SURVIVAL SOURCEBOOK. New York: Alfred A. Knopf, 1975. 245 pp. Sequel to 1973 edition. Lists materials available and provides a directory.

5994. ———. THE NEW WOMAN'S SURVIVAL SOURCEBOOK. New York: Coward, McCann & Geoghegan, 1973. 223 pp. Catalogs and documents activities aimed at the development of an alternative women's culture.

5995. Loring, Rosalind K. and Herbert Arthur Otto. NEW LIFE OPTIONS: THE WORKING WOMAN'S RESOURCE BOOK. New York: McGraw-Hill, 1976. 487 pp.

5996. Mitchell, Joyce Slayton. I CAN BE ANYTHING: CAREERS AND COLLEGES FOR YOUNG WOMEN. New York: College Entrance Examination Board, 1975. 256 pp. Sketches of 90 occupations, both traditional and nontraditional careers, and statistical information on women.

5997. Paulsen, Kathryn and Ryan A. Kuhn, eds. WOMAN'S ALMANAC: TWELVE HOW-TO HANDBOOKS IN ONE. Philadelphia, PA: J. B. Lippincott, 1976. 640 pp.

5998. The Source Collective. ORGANIZING FOR HEALTH CARE: A TOOL FOR CHANGE. Boston, MA: Beacon Press, 1974. 249 pp. Reference book for community groups, includes directories and bibliographies.

5999. Weisl, Reyna, Jane Fleming, and Mary Janey. WASHINGTON OPPORTUNITIES FOR WOMEN: A GUIDE TO PART-TIME WORK AND STUDY FOR THE EDUCATED WOMAN. New York: Robert B. Luce, 1967. 182 pp.

6000. Women's Action Alliance. HOW TO ORGANIZE A MULTI-SERVICE WOMEN'S CENTER. Washington, D.C.: Women's Action Alliance, 1975.

AUTHOR-ORGANIZATION INDEX

A

Abarbanel, Karen, 5989
Abbott, J. S. C., 5261
Abbott, Lyman, 4533
Abbott, Sidney, 3853
Abrahams, Roger D., 4833
Abramson, Joan, 4462
Abzug, Bella, 4256, 4587, 4597
Academic Collective Bargaining Information
   Service, 4463
Ackerman, Winona B., 4023
Adams, Arvil, 5664
Adams, Harriet, 5819
Adams, Hazard, 5303
Adams, Jean, 5820
Adams, Mrs. Laura Merrihew, 3662
Adams, Margaret, 3807
Addison, Daniel Dulaney, 5166
Addison, Hilda, 5304
Adelstein, Michael E., 4276
Adler, Bill, 4772
Adler, Felix, 3735
Adler, Freda, 4859
Adler, Nancy E., 4128
Adler, Nettie, 5795
Afetinan, A., 4277
African Studies Association Committee on
   Women, 3933
Aggarwal, J. C., 4039
Aguilar, Grace, 5027
Ahern, Dee Dee, 5496
Ahlum, Carol, 3986
Aikman, Lonnelle, 4896
Aird, Eileen, 5305
Aitken, Judith, 3926
Alberti, Jean M., 5850
Albrecht, Margaret, 3663
Alcott, William Andrus, 5102
Aldaba-Lim, Estefania, 4730
Alexander, Rodney, 5626
Alexander, Ruth, 4086
Alexander, Shana, 4382, 5821
Alexandersson, Birgitta, 3664

Allan, Donald A., 4603, 5550
Allen, A. J., 5840
Allen, Ann, 4631
Allen, Gina, 3854
Allen, Isobel, 5840
Allen, Pamela, 4278
Allendorf, Florence, 4897
Allewelt, Millicent, 4629
Alliluyeva, Svetlana (Stalina), 5167
Alloway, Lawrence, 5306
Almquist, Elizabeth M., 3927, 4042
Alpern, David M., 4129
Alta, 5168
Altschul, Susan, 4445
Amali, Ebele, 4733
Ambassade de France. Service de Presse et
   d'Information, 3987, 4630, 5497, 5822
American Association of School
   Administrators, 4464-4466
American Association of University Women,
   4631
American Federation of Teachers, 4467
American Medical Association, 5977
American Mothers Committee. Bicentennial
   Project 1974-1976, 3665
American Personnel and Guidance
   Association. Sex Equality in Guidance
   Opportunities Project, 5872
Amin, F., 4744
Amsden, Alice H., 4446
Amundsen, Kirsten, 4614
Āmūzgār, Habīb-Allāh, 3928
Ancker-Johnson, Betsy, 5850
Anderson, Adelaide M., 5795
Anderson, Deborah, 5735
Anderson, Ellen, 4040
Anderson, Mrs. Eugenie, 5796
Anderson, K., 4511
Anderson, Kitty, 4041
Anderson, Margaret, 4745
Anderson, Margaret, 5444
Andors, Phyllis, 3931, 3974
Andreski, Iris, 5474

Budig, Gene A., 4478
Buechler, Judith-Maria Hess, 5495
Buek, Alexandra, 4469
Bujra, Janet M., 5737
Bullough, Bonnie, 4651
Bullough, Vern L., 3861, 4651, 5878
Bumpass, Larry L., 3628
Bunkle, P., 4045
Bunnell, Rhoda, 4387
Burcart, Janie M., 3604
Burdick, Loraine, 5184
Burke, Judith, 5460
Burke, Marian, 5852
Burke, Toby, 4730
Burkhart, Kathryn W., 4865
Burnap, George Washington, 4823
Burns, Edward, 5185
Burris, Carol, 4409
Burrows, Martha G., 5830
Burstyn, Joan N., 4023, 4046-4047
Burtle, Vasanti, 5440
Business and Professional Women's
    Foundation. Library, 5879
Bussi de Allende, Hortensia, 4256
Bustamente, Dale Hoffman, 4894
Butler, Edgar W., 4704
Butler, Josephine, 5229, 5509
Butler, Pamela, 5433
Butler, Phyllis, 4617
Buvinic, Mayra, 5880
Byer, Curtis O., 3884
Byham, William C., 5762
Bysiewicz, Shirley R., 4409

C

Cabello-Argandona, Roberto, 5881
Cadbury, Edward, 5738
Caffrey, Kate, 4783
Cahill, Susan, 5031
Cahn, Robert, 4596
Cain, Glen G., 4629, 5674
Caine, Lynn, 3813
Calaway, Candy, 5659
Calder-Marshall, Arthur, 4784
California. Commission on the Status of
    Women, 4388
Calloway, Helen, 3959
Cameron, Mabel Ward, 5964
Camp, Kay, 4256
Campbell, Margaret A. See Howell, Dr.
    Mary.

Campion, Nardi Reeder, 5032
Campos de Rozsavolgyi, Paula, 3959
Canada. Dept. of Labour, 5695
Canada. Liberation Support Movement,
    4903
Canadian Council on Social Development,
    3672
Canoy, Reuben B., 4209
Cantor, Donald J., 3746
Cantor, Milton, 4712
Caprio, Frank Samuel, 3862-3863
Carden, Maren Lockwood, 4288
Cardinale, Susan, 5882
Cardozo, Arlene Rossen, 3673
Carey, William A., 5639
Carleton, B. N., 5831
Carlson, Dale, 4499
Carlsson, May Britt, 4447
Carnegie Commission on Higher Education,
    4048, 4476-4477
Caro, Elme Marie, 5319
Carpenter, Edward, 3747
Carr, Shirley, 4447, 4451
Carrick, Linda, 5985
Carrington, Evelyn M., 4950
Carroll, Berenice A., 4289
Carroll, L., 4262
Carron, Christine, 4445
Carson, Dorothy Lee, 4136
Carson, Penelope H., 4977
Carson, William English, 3748
Carter, Dianne K., 5462
Carter, Margaret, 4475
Cary, Meredith, 4049
Case, Barbara, 4911
Casey, Jane Barnes, 5186
Casey, Robert P., 4389
Cassirer, Sidonie, 3991
Castro, Fidel, 4904
Castro de Peñaloza, Dolores, 3955
Catt, Carrie Chapman, 4751
Cavendish, Margaret (Duchess of
    Newcastle), 5033
Center for the Study of Democratic
    Institutions, 4628
Centra, John A., 4050
Cernea, Mihail, 3602
Chacko, V. I., 4209
Chafetz, Janet S., 3864
Challice, Annie E., 5187
Chan, Anita, 4905
Chance, Barbara J., 3604
Chandler, Christopher, 5761

INDEX OF SPECIAL JOURNAL ISSUES/
SECTIONS DEVOTED TO WOMEN

INDEX OF PERSONS NOT CITED AS AUTHORS

A

Adam, 4719
Adams, Abigail, 4350, 5232, 5268
Addams, Jane, 4237, 4257, 4604, 5213
Aeschylus, 5035
Alcott, Louisa May, 5177, 5360, 5374
Anastaise, 5372
Anderson, Marian, 4248
Andreas-Salome, Lou, 5173, 5266, 5287
Anguissola, Sofonisba, 5413
Anthony, Susan B., 4923, 5285
Aphra Behn, 5228
Arnold, Peggy Shippen, 5232
Astor, Alice, 5265
Atherton, Gertrude, 5269
Austin, Jane, 5284, 5348
Ayer, Harriet Hubbard, 5170

B

Bacon, Delia Salter, 4862, 4947
Bailey, Brigadier General Mildred, 4982
Bakunin, Mikhail, 4909
Baringer, Emily, 5137
Barney, Natalie, 5300
Barton, Clara, 5147, 5178, 5285
Beale, Dorothea, 5231
Beech, Olive Ann, 5771
Bell, Gertrude, 5208
Bell, Quentin, 5393
Benedict, Ruth, 5486
Bernard, Kate, 4248, 4604
Bernhardt, Sarah, 5410
Betham, Matilda, 5205
Bethune, Mary McLeod, 5290
Bikkerdyke, Mother Mary Ann, 4975
Bilby, Doll, 4839
Bishop, Isabel, 5306
Black, Shirley Temple, 5184
Blackwell, Elizabeth, 4248, 5146, 5151,
    5161, 5230, 5285
Bland, Edith Nesbit, 5378
Blessington, Lady Marguerite Power Farmer,
    5211
Blixen, Baroness Karen Dinesen, 4899
Bloomer, Amelia, 4234, 5293
Boadicea, Queen, 4978

Bogan, Louise, 5364
Boleyn, Anne, 5005
Bonaparte, (Marie) Josephine de
    Beauharnais, 5022, 5187, 5280
Bonaparte, Napoleon, 5022
Booth, Catherine, 5188
Bordon, Lizzie, 5233
Borgia, Lucrezia, 5233
Bradstreet, Anne, 4953, 5230
Bradwell, Myra, 5803
Braun, Eva, 5225
Bremer, Fredericka, 5316
Breshkovskaya, Catherine, 4508
Brontë, Anne, 4778, 5246, 5282, 5333,
    5345, 5373, 5400
Brontë, Charlotte, 4778, 5208, 5246, 5282,
    5333, 5345, 5361, 5373, 5375, 5400,
    5406
Brontë, Emily Jane, 4778, 5246, 5282,
    5333, 5345, 5348, 5373, 5400
Brooks, Romaine, 5396
Brown, Brockdon, 4562
Brown, Maria Dean Foster, 5181
Buber, Martin, 5266
Burdett-Coutts, Baroness Angela, 5188
Burnett, Frances Hodgson, 5412
Burney, Fanny, 4556, 5348, 5360
Burns, Lucy, 4564
Buss, Miss, 5231
Byron, George Gordon Lord, 5296

C

Caballero, Fernan, 5205
Canuck, Janey. See Murphy, Emily.
Capello, Bianca, 5172
Carpenter, Mary, 4244
Carter, Elizabeth, 4556, 5205
Carter, Pres. Jimmy C., 5539
Cather, Willa, 5402
Catherine of Aragon, 5012
Catherine II, Empress of Russia, 5008, 5019
Cavalleri, Rosa, 4993
Cenci, Beatrice, 5175
Centlivre, Susanna, 5228, 5418
Chao, Empress, 5006
Chaplin, Matilda, 5129
Charles II, 4787

INDEX OF PLACES, SUBJECTS, AND TOPICS

Bill of Rights (Canada), 4443
Biography and Autobiography, 4043, 4052,
    4067, 4073, 4074, 4088, 4090, 4095,
    4108, 4110, 4113, 4124, 4203, 4208,
    4234, 4235, 4237, 4240, 4244, 4245,
    4246-4255, 4257, 4259, 4260, 4286,
    4293, 4298, 4299, 4307, 4312, 4322,
    4334, 4357, 4386, 4534, 4561, 4608,
    4781, 4782, 4785, 4787, 4792, 4796,
    4797-4799, 4801, 4808, 4811, 4815,
    4835, 4837, 4838, 4840, 4846, 4862,
    4884, 4896, 4898-4900, 4907, 4909,
    4912, 4915, 4920, 4922, 4923, 4926,
    4928, 4933, 4940, 4945, 4947, 4949,
    4952, 4954, 4956, 4965, 4967, 4970,
    4975, 4986, 4993, 5001, 5032, 5036,
    5038, 5040, 5041, 5072, 5073, 5082,
    5084, 5087, 5095, 5098, 5112, 5114,
    5120, 5128, 5129, 5134, 5137-5139,
    5143, 5144, 5146, 5147, 5149, 5151,
    5153, 5156, 5159, 5161-5163, 5474,
    5501, 5519, 5606, 5696, 5697, 5754,
    5760, 5766, 5771, 5777, 5784, 5798,
    5813, 5824, 5832, 5836, 5839, 5927,
    5928. See also Contents for other
    appropriate categories.
Birmingham, 5738
Birth Control, 3713. See also Contents I.I.
    Birth Control, Abortion and
    Demography.
Bisexuality, 4329
Black (Negro) Americans, 3687, 3723,
    3803, 3927, 3934, 3941, 4052, 4091,
    4165, 4219, 4235, 4251, 4253, 4322,
    4354, 4355, 4429, 4560, 4570, 4609,
    4622, 4644, 4645, 4671, 4672, 4694,
    4755, 4765, 4772, 4800, 4834, 4915,
    4976, 4983, 5055, 5209, 5216, 5217,
    5290, 5317, 5366, 5481, 5552, 5605,
    5838, 5889, 5890, 5960, 5983
Blacksmiths, 4896
Bloomers, 4234
Blue Collar Wives, 3816
Body Language, 5907
Bohemia. See Czechoslovakia.
Bolivia, 5549
Booksellers, 5750
Boston (Massachusetts), 4548, 5204, 5262,
    5513, 5623, 5991
Brazil, 4615, 5488
Breastfeeding, 3714
Brides, 4958
Brook Farm, 5048. See also Contents IV.

Women in Philosophy and Religion.
Buddhism, 5962
Bulgaria, 3938
Businesswomen, 5501, 5519, 5657, 5864,
    5874, 5983, 5987. See also Contents X.
    F. Women in Business, Industry, and
    Production.

C

California (U.S.), 3790, 3802, 4388,
    4440, 4512, 4883, 4886, 4972,
    5501, 5981
Cambodia. See also Khmer.
Cameroon. See West Cameroon.
Camp Followers, 4981
Canada. See also individual provinces. 3656,
    3672, 3710, 4010, 4094, 4221, 4249,
    4347, 4443, 4445, 4447, 4451, 4452,
    4479, 4549, 4623, 4707, 4745, 4840,
    4960, 5191, 5240, 5511, 5529, 5534,
    5691, 5895, 5896, 5927, 5939, 5940,
    5955, 5966
Canneries, 5770
Capitalism, 4356
Career Women, 3696, 5688, 5690, 5745,
    5860, 5861, 5954, 5996
Caribbean, 3952, 4724, 4752, 4759, 4904,
    4911, 4936, 4937, 4943, 5847
Cartoons, 3603
Castration. See Sterilization, and Contents
    V. Women in Medicine and Health
Catholic (Roman), 3843, 4095, 4188, 4199,
    5175, 5239. See also Churches;
    Convents, Nunneries and Holy Orders;
    and Contents IV. Women in Philosophy
    and Religion.
Celibacy, 4180, 4884. See also Convents,
    Nunneries and Holy Orders.
Central America. See also individual
    countries. 4356
Chastity, 3870. See also Virginity.
Chicago (Illinois), 5708, 5980
Chicanas. See Mexican-Americans.
Childbirth, 5117, 5127, 5152. See also
    Maternity, and Contents V. Women in
    Medicine and Health.
Child Care, 3680, 3704, 3719, 3720, 4300,
    4767, 5443, 5991. See also Contents I.
    B. Family.
Childlessness, 3839. See also Pregnancy,
    Unwanted.

D

Dahomey, 4169
Dancers, 5252, 5269, 5313, 5328, 5362,
    5377, 5407
Day Care. See Child Care, and Contents I. B.
    Family
Delaware, 5770
Delinquency, 4859, 4863, 4868, 4870,
    4872, 4874, 4877, 4886, 4889, 4892,
    5451, 5467, 5929
Democrats (U.S. party), 4575, 4597, 4601
Demographic Studies. 4752, 5500, 5545,
    5571, 5593-5599, 5650. See also
    Contents I.I. Birth Control, Abortion
    and Demography.
Denmark. 3814, 4369, 4713, 4899, 5101,
    5376, 5757, 5776
Dentists, 5501
Dependency, 3608, 3619, 3823, 4390,
    5510, 5672
Depression (economic), 4737, 5508
Detroit (Michigan), 3741, 5670
Diplomats. See U.S. Ambassadors.
Directors, Corporate, 5796, 5840
Discrimination (by women), 3651
Discrimination, 4732, 5050, 5075, 5076,
    5575, 5577, 5602, 5903, 5905, 5952,
    5953. See also Contents II. D.
    Feminism: Equal Rights, and X. B.
    Women and Job Discrimination.
District of Columbia (U.S.), 4536
Divorce, 3676, 4201, 4412, 5909,
    5920. See also Contents I. C. Marriage
    and Divorce, and II. D. 3. Feminism:
    Equal Rights-Marriage and Divorce.
Divorcee, 3666, 3671, 3672, 3695, 3701,
    3718, 3777, 3905
Domestic Service, 3682, 4789, 5553. See
    also Housework, and Contents X. E.
    Women in Domestic Labor.
Dowry, 4379
Drama, 5928. See also Contents VII.
    Women in Literature and the Arts.
Drugs, 4859, 5885
Dual-Career, 3820, 4071, 5690

E

Economic Development, 5514, 5517, 5520,
    5524, 5549, 5550, 5561, 5574, 5576,
    5577, 5620, 5880, 5928, 5935
Economic Role, 3602, 3628, 4638, 5107
Economic Status, 3823, 3830, 3983, 4220,
    4383, 4732, 4737, 4738, 4753, 4905,
    5499, 5507, 5509, 5510, 5536, 5554,
    5562, 5571, 5572, 5600, 5607
Economists, 4446, 5814, 5815
Ecuador (S.A.), 3658
Editors, 4896, 5865, 5839
Edmonton (Alberta, Canada), 4549
Education, 3605, 3612, 3635, 3657, 3659,
    4216, 4513, 4663, 4702, 4706, 4713,
    5031, 5120, 5235, 5509, 5751, 5886.
    See also Contents for other appropriate
    categories.
Egypt. 3632, 3881, 4174, 4808, 4828, 5004
Eire. See Ireland.
Elective Office, 4093. See also Contents II.
    G. 2. Politicians-Elective Office.
Elopement, 3769
Engineers, 5805, 5811, 5812, 5818, 5863,
    5930
Entrepreneurs, 5501, 5737
Episcopal. See also Protestant Episcopal,
    and Contents IV. Women in Philosophy
    and Religion.
Equal Credit Opportunity, 4383, 4399,
    4408, 5618
Equal Educational Opportunity, 4064,
    4079, 4099, 4115, 4117, 4118
Equal Employment Opportunity, 4062,
    4064, 4068, 4079, 4082, 4096, 4099,
    4122, 4418, 5498, 5531, 5577, 5578,
    5580, 5581-5585, 5612, 5641, 5651,
    5653, 5667, 5823, 5845, 5867, 5900,
    5903, 5905, 5952, 5953
Equal Employment Opportunity
    Commission (U.S.), 5664, 5667
Equality, 3638, 4014, 4292, 4310
Equal Pay (Canada), 4451, 4452
Equal Pay (U.S.), 4449, 4460, 5513, 5634,
    5635, 5642, 5651, 5661, 5665
Equal Rights Amendment (U.S. proposed),
    4368, 4388, 4391, 4393, 4398, 4420,
    4429, 4431, 4432, 4437, 4441, 4442,
    5884, 5897, 5980
Ethiopia, 4169
Europe. See also individual countries. 4285,
    4356, 4426, 4713, 4750, 4845, 4939,
    5266, 5640, 5687
European Economic Community, 4713,
    5604

ABOUT THE EDITORS

JoAnn Delores Een *obtained her B.B.A. in Marketing at the University of Wisconsin-Eau Claire in 1976. From Fall 1974 through Spring 1976, Ms. Een served as research assistant and office manager for the Eau Claire office of the Institute of Governmental Affairs, University of Wisconsin–Extension. Through Oct. 1977 she devoted her efforts entirely to the production of this book. Ms. Een is now the Manpower Research Assistant to the Personnel Department of the City of Eugene, Oregon.*

Marie Barovic Rosenberg *majored in law at Stanford University where she received her B.A. in 1944. After marriage and three children, and twenty years in business and industry, she returned to the University of Washington, completing her doctorate in political science in 1973. During her graduate school years she taught full-time for six years at Seattle Central Community College. In 1972 she received a joint appointment as assistant professor in the Institute of Governmental Affairs, University of Wisconsin–Extension (Madison), and in the School of Business, University of Wisconsin–Eau Claire. Dr. Rosenberg married Dr. Robert B. Dishman in 1974. In 1976 she resigned her position in Wisconsin to accept a teaching appointment at New England College, Henniker, New Hampshire as an associate professor of Public Policy and Management. Dr. Rosenberg-Dishman is active in national and regional political science associations and has served in various positions, including the presidency of Women's Caucus for Political Science, and as a member of the executive council of the Federation of Organizations of Professional Women. She has critiqued manuscripts for a number of major publishers, and her own publications are listed in the indexes of both volumes of WOMEN AND SOCIETY.*